Lecture Notes in Computer Science 16626

The series Lecture Notes in Computer Science (LNCS), including its subseries Lecture Notes in Artificial Intelligence (LNAI) and Lecture Notes in Bioinformatics (LNBI), has established itself as a medium for the publication of new developments in computer science and information technology research, teaching, and education.

LNCS enjoys close cooperation with the computer science R & D community, the series counts many renowned academics among its volume editors and paper authors, and collaborates with prestigious societies. Its mission is to serve this international community by providing an invaluable service, mainly focused on the publication of conference and workshop proceedings and postproceedings. LNCS commenced publication in 1973.

Clément Aubert · Luca Roversi
Editors

Reversible Computation

18th International Conference, RC 2026
Turin, Italy, July 9–10, 2026
Proceedings

Springer

Editors
Clément Aubert
Augusta University
Augusta, GA, USA

Luca Roversi
Università di Torino
Turin, Italy

ISSN 0302-9743 ISSN 1611-3349 (electronic)
Lecture Notes in Computer Science
ISBN 978-3-032-30838-2 ISBN 978-3-032-30839-9 (eBook)
https://doi.org/10.1007/978-3-032-30839-9

This Springer imprint is published by the registered company Springer Nature Switzerland AG
The registered company address is: Gewerbestrasse 11, 6330 Cham, Switzerland

Preface

This volume contains the papers presented at RC 2026: the 18th International Conference on Reversible Computation, held on July 9–10, 2026 in Turin.

This year, the conference received 38 submissions from authors in 19 countries. Two papers were desk-rejected, and the 36 remaining received at least three reviews each, with an average of 3.08 each. Reviews provided detailed evaluations as well as constructive comments and recommendations. For this purpose, an intensive single-anonymized review process was conducted. After extensive discussions (nearly 200 comments!), the Program Committee accepted 13 full papers, 3 work-in-progress papers and 1 tool demonstration paper for presentation at the conference and inclusion in this volume, leading to an acceptance rate of about 45%.

The scientific program was enriched by two invited talks. Hannah Earley gave the invited lecture "Reversing the History of Computing," and Prakash Panangaden gave the invited lecture "Quantum Alternation." We are very grateful to the invited speakers for their contributions to the conference and for accepting our invitation.

The resulting proceedings witness the vitality and diversity of the field of reversible computation, with contributions spanning models, formal developments, applications, language development and support for reversible and quantum programs. More than half of the accepted papers further provide concrete implementation, benchmarks or machine-checked proof of their results, leveraging a variety of languages (Erlang, Haskell, Lean, OCaml, Python or Scala) to further ground and provide evidence of the concrete impact of their contributions.

Past editions of this event took place as workshops in York (2009), Bremen (2010), Ghent (2011), Copenhagen (2012), and as conferences in Victoria (2013), Kyoto (2014), Grenoble (2015), Bologna (2016), Kolkata (2017), Leicester (2018), Lausanne (2019), Oslo (2020), Nagoya (2021), Urbino (2022), Giessen (2023), Toruń (2024) and Odense (2025). Their proceedings can easily be accessed through dblp and Springer (since 2011).

We would like to thank all the authors who submitted their work to RC 2026 and hope their research projects will benefit from the interactions and discussions before, during and after the conference. We are also indebted to the members of the Program Committee and to the eleven additional reviewers for their careful evaluations and for their essential role in shaping the scientific program. Their expertise and commitment were fundamental to the quality of the conference and of these proceedings, and we particularly appreciated their help in managing the higher-than-expected number of submissions. We also thank all the participants for contributing to the success of the event.

Support and patronage from the Università di Torino and the Dipartimento di Informatica di Torino are gratefully acknowledged. We would also like to thank Rodolfo Rosini and his company Vaire for their support of RC 2026. Last but not least, Springer, RC's Steering Committee and Organizing Committee as well as RC's Website Chair

(Michael Kirkedal Thomsen) provided guidance and timely feedback when they were most needed.

May 2026

Clément Aubert
Luca Roversi

Organization

Program Committee Chairs

Clément Aubert	Augusta University, USA
Luca Roversi	Università di Torino, Italy

Steering Committee

Robert Glück	Københavns Universitet, Denmark
Ivan Lanese	Università di Bologna, Italy & Inria, France
Łukasz Mikulski	Uniwersytet Mikołaja Kopernika in Toruń, Poland
Irek Ulidowski	University of Leicester, UK & Stanisław Staszic Mining and Metallurgical Academy in Kraków, Poland
Germán Vidal	Universitat Politècnica de València, Spain

Program Committee

Bogdan Aman	Academia Română Filiala Iaşi, Romania
Clément Aubert	Augusta University, USA
Jacques Carette	McMaster University, Canada
Kostia Chardonnet	Inria, France
Kamalika Datta	Universität Bremen, Germany
Alessandra Di Pierro	Università di Verona, Italy
Anna Gogolińska	Uniwersytet Mikołaja Kopernika in Toruń, Poland
Robin Kaarsgaard	Syddansk Universitet, Denmark
Jarkko Kari	Turun yliopisto, Finland
Ivan Lanese	Università di Bologna, Italy & Inria, France
Doriana Medić	Università degli studi di Torino, Italy
Uwe Meyer	Technische Hochschule Mittelhessen, Germany
Torben Ægidius Mogensen	Københavns Universitet, Copenhagen
Alexandru Paler	Aalto-yliopisto, Finland
Mathys Rennela	Unitary Foundation, France
Neil J. Ross	Dalhousie University, Canada
Luca Roversi	Università di Torino, Italy
Amr Sabry	Indiana University Bloomington, USA

Additional Reviewers

Invited Contributions

Reversing the History of Computing

Hannah Earley

Vaire Computing Inc., Sunnyvale, CA, 94086 USA
hannah@vaire.co

Abstract. It is 90 years on from Church and Turing's first publications, changing the world as we know it. Unfortunately, gaps in our knowledge of physics, thermodynamics, and information have baked in inefficiencies alongside these innovations. We are now suffering the consequences. But how can we extirpate them, sustainably and one step at a time, without overhauling the entirety of our technological infrastructure at once? What can we keep? What must we change? What future will this enable? And why now?

Keywords: Reversible Computation · Thermodynamics · Adiabatic Reversible Computing

Quantum Alternation

Prakash Panangaden

McGill University
University of Edinburgh
prakash.panangaden@mcgill.ca

Abstract. The by now standard paradigm for imperative quantum programming languages is based on Selinger's slogan of quantum data and classical control. Crucially conditionals are based on testing Booleans, i.e. classical bits. There have been suggestions that we should "move on" to quantum control constructs where the conditional is based on qubits. The idea is that one should allow an **if ... then ... else ...** construct where the boolean guard could be a qubit which could be in a superposed state of **true** and **false**. Execution would then proceed in a superposed state.

This naive view is based on taking the programming languages aspect of quantum computation more seriously than the physics. A simple example due to Nengkun Yu shows that there is a basic failure of compositionality. My former student Costin Badescu and I showed that these are worse problems: there is no fixed-point semantics based on the traditional notion of superoperators, the constructs are non-compositional and non-monotone.

We did develop a semantics for quantum flowcharts based on the Kraus decomposition of a superoperator. One can give a semantics in terms of superoperators that works well if there are only unitary transformations involved. We then extended this to more general superoperators using the Kraus decomposition, but it is dependent on a choice of basis. We show that if you try to give a semantics in terms of superoperators only, it will fail to be monotone. Details of this work are published in a Quantum Physics and Logic paper from 2015 [BP15].

Keywords: Reversible Computation · Quantum Programming Languages · Quantum Control

Reference

[BP15] Badescu, C., Panangaden, P.: Quantum alternation: prospects and problems. In: Heunen, C., Selinger, P., Vicary, J. (eds.) Proceedings 12th International Workshop on Quantum Physics and Logic, QPL 2015, Oxford, UK, 15–17 July 2015, EPTCS, pp. 33–42 (2015)

Contents

Reversible Programming Languages

Support for Reversible Programming

Models of Reversible and Quantum Computation

Transversal AND in Quantum Codes

Christine Li[1(✉)] and Lia Yeh[2]

[1] Department of Computer Science, Columbia University, New York, USA
cl4315@columbia.edu
[2] Department of Computer Science and Technology, University of Cambridge, Cambridge, UK
ly404@cam.ac.uk

Abstract. The AND gate is not reversible—on qubits. However, it *is* reversible on qutrits, making it a building block for efficient simulation of qubit computation using qutrits. We first observe that there are multiple two-qutrit Clifford+T unitaries that realize the AND gate with T-count 3, and its generalizations to n qubits with T-count $3n-3$. Our main result is the construction of a novel qutrit $[\![6, 2, 2]\!]$ quantum error-correcting code with a transversal implementation of the AND gate. The key insight in our approach is that a symmetric T-depth one circuit decomposition—composed of a CX circuit, T and T dagger gates, followed by the CX circuit in reverse—of a given unitary can be interpreted as a CSS code. We can increase the code distance by augmenting the code circuit with additional stabilizers while preserving the logical gate. This results in a code with a "built-in" transversal implementation of the original unitary, which can be further concatenated to attain a $[\![48, 2, 4]\!]$ code with the same transversal logical gate. Furthermore, we present several protocols for mixed qubit-qutrit codes which we call Qubit Subspace Codes, and for magic state distillation and injection.

Keywords: Quantum computing · Reversible computation · Quantum error correction · Qutrits · Exact circuit synthesis · ZX-calculus

1 Introduction

When computing with bits, the first gates we often learn are AND, OR, and NOT. When computing with qubits, one of the first concepts that we often learn is that the AND gate is not reversible. However, there *is* a reversible quantum AND gate—just not for qubits. We escape this restriction specific to qubits by working with the simplest possible extension—qutrits, i.e. three-level quantum systems instead of two-level.

Qutrits open up promising avenues due to many advantages, including more efficient algorithms, gates, and error-correcting codes. In many existing hardware architectures for quantum computers, qubits are a choice of two-dimensional subspace in what is natively a higher-dimensional setting. In choosing to actively encode and control quantum information in more levels, quantum computing

C. Aubert and L. Roversi (Eds.): RC 2026, LNCS 16626, pp. 3–40, 2026.
https://doi.org/10.1007/978-3-032-30839-9_1

with qudits is an active area of research in both theory and practice. Qudit computation has been experimentally demonstrated on systems such as nuclear magnetic resonance [24], nuclear spins [30], cold atoms [2], Rydberg atoms [78], linear optics [40, 53], integrated photonics [16], trapped ion [39, 65], and superconducting [15, 32], with a recent demonstration of GKP qutrit error correction beyond break-even [10]. Qudit entanglement has demonstrated improved noise robustness compared to qubits [71], and leveraging qutrit states can improve fidelity of qubit operations [5, 11]. As the most well-studied qudit setting, qutrits can efficiently simulate qubit computation by reducing circuit depth or ancilla overhead, as shown for diagonal qubit unitaries [80], logarithmic-depth Toffoli [31], and binary AND gates [17], as well as factoring algorithms [8], probing lattice gauge theories [43, 56], variational quantum algorithms [15, 53], and unitary decomposition [53]. Qutrit operations can also be used to suppress leakage errors to the $|2\rangle$ state [57].

However, there is a gap between the qudit operations realizable on real-world hardware, and those that conceivably satisfy definitions of fault-tolerance; while definitions vary, the main principles are unchanged from what Gottesman laid out in 1997 [35]. A large reason for this is that pairwise two-level operations in a three-level quantum system, while natural to do in experimental implementations, does not embed naturally into qutrit stabilizer theory the way that it does for qubits. Another reason is that the qubit stabilizer fragment does not embed into the qutrit stabilizer fragment. Qutrit computation also offers a promising path to more efficient error-correcting codes, with better thresholds and yield rates in magic state distillation [13]. While prior work has explored various constructions of qutrit, prime-dimensional qudit, and composite-dimensional [37] codes, less attention has been given to finding qutrit codes with specific transversal logical operators, especially ones that are both non-Clifford and entangling. In this work, we take a logical operator-centric approach to code construction by reversing the typical procedure for designing stabilizer codes. Instead of deriving the logical operators from the fixed stabilizer set of a code, we start with a chosen logical operator, constructing the code around it by adding stabilizers. This work constitutes one of few efforts on improving qubit computation framed with respect to qutrit stabilizer computation, and to our knowledge is the first to construct qutrit stabilizer error-correcting codes expressedly to this end.

Our approach to constructing qutrit codes with a binary AND gate logical operation centers on two components. The first is exact circuit synthesis, leveraging the known connection between exact circuit synthesis and error-correcting code constructions [12,14]. The second is the ZX-calculus, by means of which a number of works have investigated new ways to represent and compile for quantum error-correcting codes. However, while more progress has been made on verifying and proving properties of codes and on compiling fault-tolerant circuits, there has been comparatively less use of ZX-calculus to construct specific new codes and protocols.

Combining the motivating ideas of (1) emulating qubit gates using qutrits and (2) constructing a QEC code around a particular logical operator, the central question we set out to answer in this work is:

How can we construct a non-trivial qutrit QEC code with a transversal implementation of a qubit logical gate?

2 Qubit and Qutrit Reversible Computation

For qutrits, the computational basis states are $|0\rangle$, $|1\rangle$, and $|2\rangle$. A normalized qutrit state is $|\psi\rangle = \alpha|0\rangle + \beta|1\rangle + \gamma|2\rangle$, where $\alpha, \beta, \gamma \in \mathbb{C}$ and $|\alpha|^2 + |\beta|^2 + |\gamma|^2 = 1$. More generally, for a d-dimensional qudit with basis states $|k\rangle$, $k \in \mathbb{Z}_d$, the generalized Pauli X and Z operators are $X|k\rangle = |k+1 \bmod d\rangle$ and $Z|k\rangle = \omega^k|k\rangle$, where $\omega = e^{2\pi i/d}$. For qutrits, $\omega = e^{\frac{2\pi i}{3}}$, and $\overline{\omega} := \omega^2 = \omega^{-1}$.

Definition 1 (Qutrit X permutation gates). *For qutrits, there are five non-trivial permutations of the computational basis states (all are Clifford): $X_{01}, X_{02}, X_{12}, X_{+1}, X_{-1}$. X_{+1} is the Pauli X gate for qutrits, and $X_{-1} = X^\dagger = X^2$. X_{01} swaps $|0\rangle$ and $|1\rangle$ while leaving $|2\rangle$ unchanged. X_{02} and X_{12} are defined analogously. Their respective matrices are*

$$X_{+1} = \begin{bmatrix} 0&0&1\\1&0&0\\0&1&0 \end{bmatrix},\ X_{-1} = \begin{bmatrix} 0&1&0\\0&0&1\\1&0&0 \end{bmatrix},\ X_{01} = \begin{bmatrix} 0&1&0\\1&0&0\\0&0&1 \end{bmatrix},\ X_{02} = \begin{bmatrix} 0&0&1\\0&1&0\\1&0&0 \end{bmatrix},\ X_{12} = \begin{bmatrix} 1&0&0\\0&0&1\\0&1&0 \end{bmatrix}$$

Definition 2 (Qutrit X basis states). *The qutrit X basis is $|+\rangle := \frac{1}{\sqrt{3}}(|0\rangle + |1\rangle + |2\rangle)$, $|\omega\rangle := \frac{1}{\sqrt{3}}(|0\rangle + \omega|1\rangle + \overline{\omega}|2\rangle)$, and $|\overline{\omega}\rangle := \frac{1}{\sqrt{3}}(|0\rangle + \overline{\omega}|1\rangle + \omega|2\rangle)$. These are eigenstates of the qutrit Pauli $X = X_{+1}$.*

Definition 3 (Qutrit Hadamard gate). *The qutrit Hadamard gate maps the computational basis to the X basis: $H|0\rangle = |+\rangle$, $H|1\rangle = |\omega\rangle$, $H|2\rangle = |\overline{\omega}\rangle$. Note that unlike for qubits, $H \neq H^\dagger$, but $H^3 = H^\dagger$. $H^2 = X_{12}$ is the dualizer (also known as the antipode) for qutrits, and $H^4 = I$.*

Definition 4 (Qutrit Z phase gate). *For $a, b \in \mathbb{R}$, define the qutrit Z phase gate $Z(a,b) := diag(1, \omega^a, \omega^b)$. Equivalently, $Z(a,b)|0\rangle = |0\rangle$, $Z(a,b)|1\rangle = \omega^a|1\rangle$, and $Z(a,b)|2\rangle = \omega^b|2\rangle$. The Pauli Z gate is $Z(1,2)$.*

Definition 5 (Qutrit X phase gates). *For $a, b \in \mathbb{R}$, define the qutrit X phase gate by conjugating a Z phase by Hadamards: $X(a,b) := HZ(a,b)H^\dagger$. The Pauli X gate is $X(2,1)$ and $X^\dagger = X(1,2)$.*

Definition 6 (Qutrit T gate). *The qutrit T gate is $T := Z(\frac{1}{3}, -\frac{1}{3})$. Equivalently, $T = diag(1, e^{\frac{2\pi i}{9}}, e^{\frac{-2\pi i}{9}})$. As in the qubit case, this qutrit T gate lies in the third level of the Clifford hierarchy.*

For qutrits, there are different notions of control gates. We use the following two in this work:

Definition 7 (Λ-controlled U). *Given a qutrit unitary U, the Λ-controlled U gate (defined in [8]) acts as $|i\rangle|j\rangle \mapsto |i\rangle \otimes (U^i|j\rangle)$, for $i, j \in \{0,1,2\}$. An example of this is the two-qutrit CX gate, defined as $|i,j\rangle \mapsto |i, i+j \pmod 3\rangle$. Unlike the CNOT gate for qubits, the CX gate is not self adjoint, but $(CX)^2 = (CX)^\dagger$.*

Definition 8 ($|0\rangle$-controlled U gate). *Given a qutrit unitary U, the $|0\rangle$-controlled U is defined as $|0\rangle \otimes |\psi\rangle \mapsto |0\rangle \otimes U|\psi\rangle$, $|1\rangle \otimes |\psi\rangle \mapsto |1\rangle \otimes |\psi\rangle$, and $|2\rangle \otimes |\psi\rangle \mapsto |2\rangle \otimes |\psi\rangle$. The $|1\rangle$- and $|2\rangle$-controlled U gates are analogously defined. We can change the control value by conjugating the control qutrit by X or $X^\dagger$.*

The CX gate is Clifford, while the $|0\rangle$(or $|1\rangle$ or $|2\rangle$)-controlled gates are non-Clifford. Similar to the qubit case, the generators of the qutrit Clifford group are H, S, CX. Adding the non-Clifford T gate to the set, we get the Clifford+T gate set, which is universal [20] and admits an exact circuit synthesis algorithm [29].

Like in the qubit case, for any prime qudit dimension, X and Z generate the Pauli group, and the CX, S, and H gates generate the Clifford group. The $|0\rangle$-controlled gate, or equivalently the CCX gate, when added to the H gate, generates the qudit Toffoli+Hadamard gate set [66]. [81] presents a comprehensive coverage of the Clifford+T and Toffoli+Hadamard gate sets for prime-dimensional qudits, and their representations in qudit ZX- and ZH-calculus.

We note that the qubit Clifford+binary AND gate set is approximately universal for quantum computation. This is because Toffoli can be constructed from binary AND and qubit CX, and Toffoli+Hadamard is universal [1].

2.1 Qubit and Qutrit ZX-Calculus

The ZX-calculus is a graphical formalism for quantum computing in which linear maps are represented by diagrams built from basic generators called Z and X spiders, together with structural elements that allow wires to bend and cross [18]. Each diagram has a precise interpretation as a linear map: Sequential composition corresponds to matrix multiplication, parallel composition to tensor product, and the number of inputs and outputs determines whether the diagram represents a state, effect, map, or scalar. The calculus is equipped with rewrite rules that equate diagrams representing the same linear map. The qubit ZX-calculus is *sound*—any derivable equality reflects genuine equality of the underlying maps; *universal* for qubit linear maps—any qubit operation can be expressed as a ZX diagram; and *complete*—for any two equal diagrams, their equality can be proved entirely within the calculus [38].

We do not use the qubit ZX-calculus in this work; we use the qutrit ZX-calculus, first introduced in [64,77]. All its wires represent a qutrit (three-level quantum information carrier) instead of a qubit (two-level). For qubits [4], qutrits [76], and qudits of any odd prime dimension [9,61], the ZX-calculus is complete for the stabilizer or Clifford fragment of quantum computation.

The qutrit ZX-calculus is generated by the five diagrams

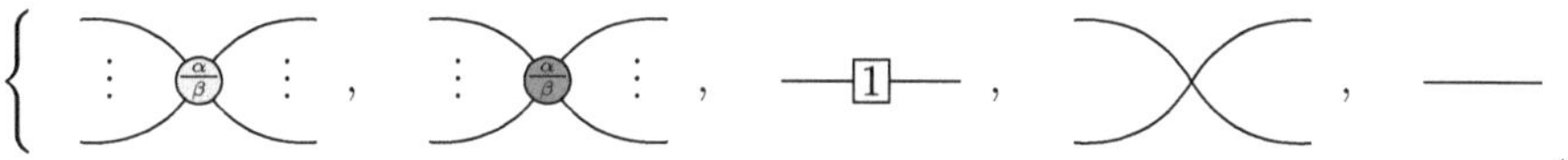
(1)

The interpretations of Z and X spiders as linear maps are

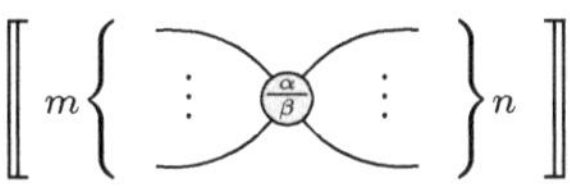
$$:= |0\rangle^{\otimes m}\langle 0|^{\otimes n} + \omega^a |1\rangle^{\otimes m}\langle 1|^{\otimes n} + \omega^b |2\rangle^{\otimes m}\langle 2|^{\otimes n} \quad (2)$$

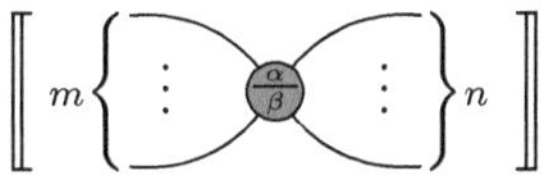
$$:= |+\rangle^{\otimes m}\langle +|^{\otimes n} + \omega^a |\omega\rangle^{\otimes m}\langle \omega|^{\otimes n} + \omega^b |\overline{\omega}\rangle^{\otimes m}\langle \overline{\omega}|^{\otimes n} \quad (3)$$

Note that when $m = n = 1$, the green Z spider corresponds to the Z phase gate $Z(a,b)$ and the X spider corresponds to the X phase gate $X(a,b)$. We use the non-flex-symmetric version of the qutrit ZX-calculus. This means that, unlike the qubit ZX-calculus, it is no longer the case that only connectivity matters. In particular, CX is not equivalent to CX†:

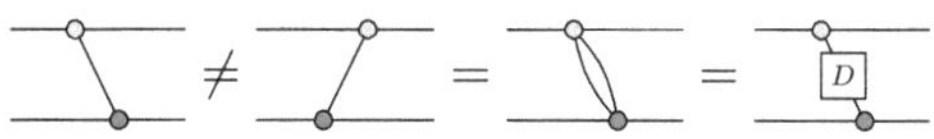
(4)

In this work, we will mostly follow the notation from [74], where H is the yellow box labeled 1 and $H^\dagger$ is the yellow box labeled 2. However, we use the horizontal orientation (left to right), rather than vertical (bottom to top), in keeping with common ZX-calculus usage in quantum error correction and circuit compilation works. We represent the dualizer (antipode), $X_{12} = H^2$, by a white box labeled D. The qutrit ZX-calculus rules are reprinted from [74] in Fig. 1 in Appendix A, which is available in the arXiv version of this work [51].

3 The AND Gate as a Quantum Circuit Primitive

3.1 Emulation: Qubit Computation Using Qutrits

The first difficulty with developing a fault-tolerant theory of emulation is that qubit Cliffords are not a subgroup of qudit Cliffords. As a counterexample to show this: the $\mathrm{diag}(1, -1, 1)$ gate is Clifford-equivalent (by conjugating by Pauli X) to the non-Clifford R gate.

We can also see that restricting a qutrit Clifford gate to its qubit subspace, is not necessarily a qubit Clifford operation. For example, the qutrit Pauli Z gate acts on the qubit subspace as $\mathrm{diag}(1, \omega)$; $\omega = e^{i\frac{2\pi}{3}}$ is not an element of the ring which all qubit Clifford unitary matrices must be over [27].

It is impossible to implement binary AND gate using two qubits. However, it *is* possible to do so using two qu*trits*. By this we mean that we can construct a two-qutrit circuit such that the behavior (i.e., truth table rows) of the first two levels $|0\rangle$ and $|1\rangle$ of the qutrit circuit matches that of the qubit binary AND gate. The behavior of the third level of the qutrit circuit is left unconstrained. The additional space afforded by the third level allows for the binary AND gate to be implemented unitarily. Let us denote that one linear map M_1 emulates another, M_2, by $M_2 \overset{\mathsf{e}}{\hookleftarrow} M_1$.

Lemma 1. *The binary AND gate can be emulated by a two-qutrit Clifford+T unitary with T-count 3.*

Proof. The below Clifford+T two-qutrit unitary emulates the binary AND gate [75, Equation 9]:

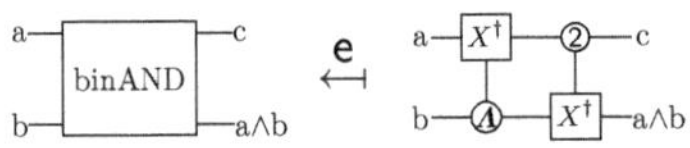

(5)

Its cost is T-count 3 and Clifford CX-count 4. The cost calculation follows from the $|2\rangle$-controlled X_{+1} gate comprising of 3 Clifford CX gates and 3 qutrit T gates [8].

Remark 1. After submission of this manuscript, it was brought to our attention that the above construction is near-identical (up to conjugation by the two-qutrit SWAP gate) to that of [75, Equation 9], which proposed emulation of binary classical reversible computation with ternary classical reversible computation as early as 2011. We thank the author for pointing out their work to us.

Interestingly, it outperforms the Toffoli gate, for which it is known that the optimal cost is 7 qubit T gates in the no-ancilla case [33], 6 qubit Clifford CX gates independent of ancillae count [69], and 5 two-qubit gates [84]. Even when ancillae and operations conditioned on measurement are permitted, the best known qubit Clifford+T decomposition of the Toffoli gate is 4 T gates [42].

A symmetric qutrit circuit which emulates the qutrit binary AND gate is:

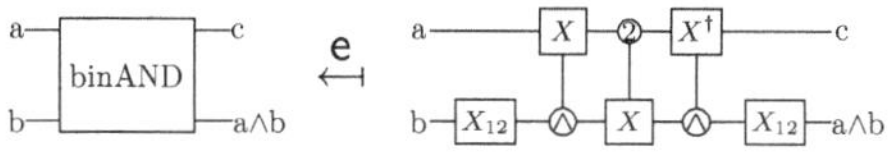

(6)

We can check that both these circuits indeed emulate AND through Table 1.

Table 1. Truth tables for AND emulations of Eqs. (5) (left) and (6) (right).

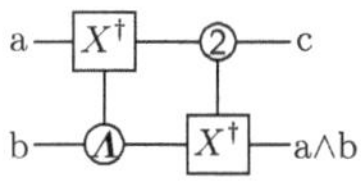

a	b	c	a∧b
0	0	0	0
0	1	2	0
0	2	1	2
1	0	1	0
1	1	0	1
1	2	2	1
2	0	2	2
2	1	1	1
2	2	0	2

a	b	c	a∧b
0	0	0	0
0	1	2	0
0	2	0	2
1	0	1	0
1	1	1	1
1	2	0	1
2	0	1	2
2	1	2	1
2	2	2	2

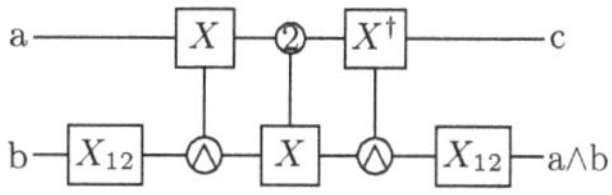

We can change the control value of the $|2\rangle$-controlled X by conjugating by Pauli X gates, and from controlled X to Z by conjugating by Hadamard gates.

Remark 2. Through fixing only the rows and columns corresponding to the binary AND gate (i.e., only rows where the inputs are 0 or 1, and the output column a∧b), the remaining truth table entries shaded in Table 1 are a degree of freedom. We can therefore explore other circuit constructions so long as the AND action is preserved for binary inputs.

By applying the X_{01} gate (which emulates the binary NOT gate) to both inputs and to the AND'd output of Eq. (5), in accordance with DeMorgan's law, the binary OR gate is emulated with the same T-count and Clifford CX-count. This leads us to:

Proposition 1. *All binary classical logic circuits can be emulated through exact synthesis in the qutrit Clifford+T gate set.*

Proof. AND, OR, NOT is a universal gate set for binary classical logic. As NOT can be emulated by a qutrit Clifford, the T-count is upper bounded by 3 times the total number of AND or OR gates.

We present in Table 2 a summary of the most efficient qutrit emulation of each binary or qubit gate that we calculated in Sects. D.1 to D.3 of the appendix [51]. There, we also give constructions for the qubit X, Z, S, CX and CZ gates, and $|+\rangle$ and $|-\rangle$ states, and prove why the qubit H gate cannot be exactly synthesized unitarily in qutrit Clifford+T. In addition to giving the non-Clifford gate count, for near-term applications we give the number of two-qutrit operations

Table 2. T gate, R gate, Clifford CX gate, and 2-qutrit gate counts for emulations of qubit and binary gates, unitarily without ancillae in the Clifford+T+R gate set. For decompositions in the literature given in terms of ternary classical reversible gates, these are computed by substituting the best known decompositions gate-wise, optimizing where possible. The $|+\rangle$, $|0\rangle$, and S gate counts are omitted because they are probabilistic constructions.

Gates	T	R	CX	2Q	Gates	T	R	CX	2Q
AND/OR	3	0	4	1	n-ary AND [17]	$3n-3$	0	$4n-4$	$n-1$
X (i.e. NOT)	0	0	0	0	Z	0	1	0	0
CX [8]	6	0	8	1	CZ [80]	0	3	3	1
CCX [8]	12	0	15	3	CCZ [80]	0	3	5	3
C^nX, linear depth	$6n$	0	$6n+3$	$2n-1$	C^nZ, linear depth	$6n-12$	3	$6n-7$	$2n-1$
C^nX, log depth [17]	$6n$	0	$8n$	$2n-1$	C^nZ, log depth	$6n-12$	3	$8n-5$	$2n-1$

required, as on present-day qubit quantum computers, two-qubit operations are the dominant noise source. We also give the qutrit Clifford CX count where all other operations are single-qutrit Clifford+T gates.

These counts are straightforward, but they show that the asymptotic non-Clifford gate counts of n-ary AND and qubit C^nX in ancilla-free qutrit Clifford+T, outperform the best known constant-ancilla qubit decomposition according to [22]: [45] having T-count $8n-12$. The n-ary AND moreover has lower T-count than the best known $O(n)$ ancilla qubit decompositions [26] having T-count $4n-6$ and T-depth $\lceil \log_2 \frac{n}{3} \rceil + 2$ [58]. More importantly, these qutrit decompositions are unitary, meaning that unlike the best-known qubit decompositions, they do not require feedforward of measurement outcomes to classically control any of their gates. We remark the possibility that similar AND gate-based techniques that halved T-count of multiple-controlled Toffolis and other binary computations in the qubit case [25], could be used to improve the depth of these qutrit constructions by allowing ancillae, for instance by preceding n-ary AND by a depth-1 layer of n CX gates to n ancilla in the $|0\rangle$ state.

Considering evidence that qudit emulation of individual multi-qubit gates in qubit circuits is of limited effectiveness [53], instead of resynthesizing gates in qubit circuits on an individual basis, a more promising approach would be to generalize the above approach for the AND gate, to binary classical reversible functions emulated with ternary classical reversible functions. Explicit constructions exist for any qudit dimension d, of any d-ary classical reversible function $f : \mathbb{Z}_d^n \to \mathbb{Z}_d^n$ on n dits by a circuit of $O(d^n n)$ $|0\rangle$-controlled X gates and $O(n)$ ancillae prepared in the $|0\rangle$ state ([66,85], building on [83]), thus putting the T-count for any odd prime d at $O(d^n n)$. This puts the best known upper and lower bounds at a log factor separation: For any qudit dimension d, there exist d-ary classical reversible functions $f : \mathbb{Z}_d^n \to \mathbb{Z}_d^n$ that require at least $O(nd^n/\log n)$ single-qudit and two-qudit gates to construct, even when allowed $\Omega(n)$ ancillae [66]. More generally, techniques to compress qubit circuits using qudit decompositions [53] or using mixed-dimensional quantum systems by clustering weighted graphs [54] can also be leveraged—from there, the difficult next steps are to decompose into conceivably fault-tolerant gates, or to build error-correcting codes around them as we will next do.

3.2 A T-depth 1 Symmetric Circuit as a $[\![3, 2, 1]\!]$ Qutrit Code

As noted in Remark 2 there are many qutrit circuits that emulate the binary AND gate. From prioritizing those with low T-count, but more importantly, are symmetric and T-depth one, we found:

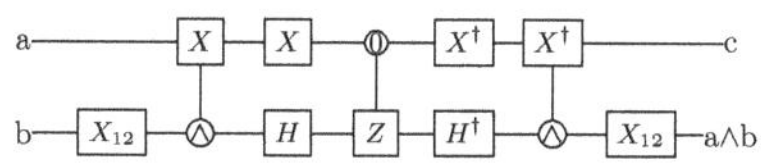

(7)

where we can apply the symmetric T-depth one decomposition of the $|0\rangle$-controlled Z gate from Fig. 7 of [8]. Therefore, the full Clifford+T symmetric T-depth one qutrit circuit decomposition of the qubit binary AND gate is given by

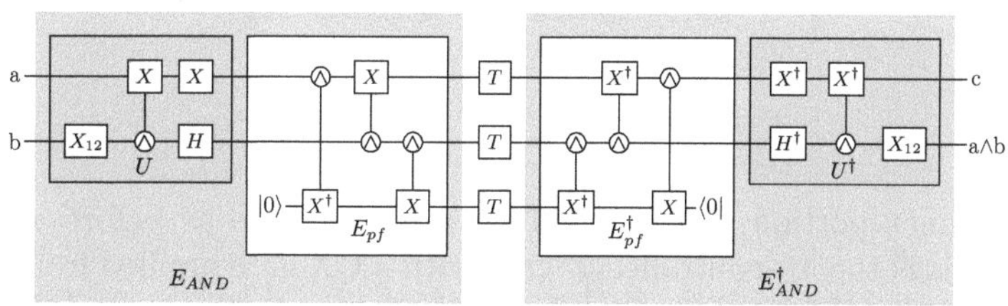

(8)

In the equivalent ZX-diagram, we see that E_{pf} is a phase-free ZX-diagram:

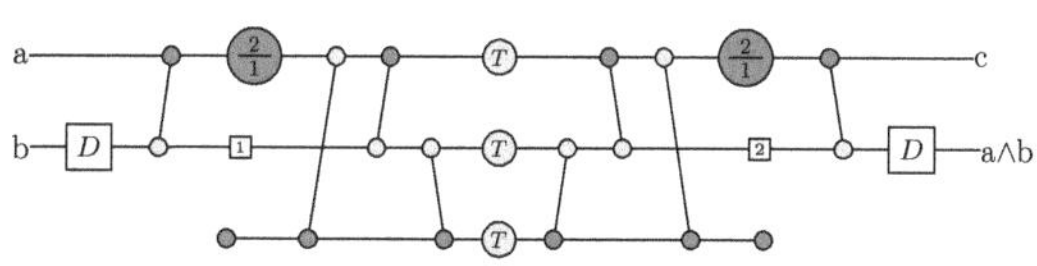

(9)

To see how this forms the encoder (and decoder) of a QEC code, we can use ZX-calculus to transform the first half of circuit into the Generalized Parity Form (GPF). From this we can directly "read off" the Z and X-type logical basis operators and stabilizer generators. Notice that this circuit contains other gates besides CNOTs, which means that the corresponding code is not a CSS code. However, for the purposes of finding the stabilizer generators and logical operators and determining code distance, it is sufficient to focus on just the CSS portion of the circuit, which is composed of the inner CX gates [47]. Therefore, from the CNOT encoder portion, we get the encoder in Z-X (left) and X-Z (right) normal forms [41,47,48]:

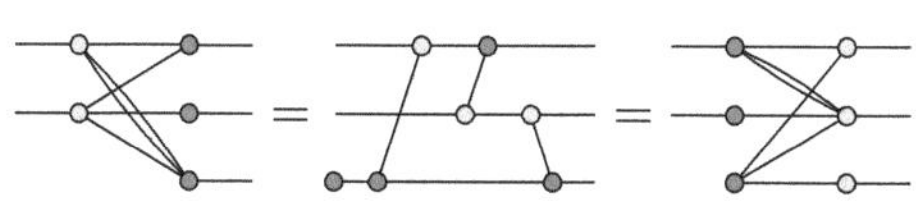

(10)

From the connectivity of the Z-X form of the encoder, the X-type logical operators are $\overline{X}_1 = X_1X_3^2$ and $\overline{X}_2 = X_1X_2X_3$. There are no X-type stabilizers.

From the X-Z form of the encoder, the Z-type logical operators and stabilizer generators are $\overline{Z}_1 = Z_1 Z_2^2$ and $\overline{Z}_2 = Z_2$, and $S_1^Z = Z_1 Z_2 Z_3$. We can observed the code distance is 1, since there is a logical Z-type operator of weight 1.

4 Reconstructing the Code at Higher Distance

To increase the code distance, we would need to add X-type stabilizers, while ensuring that the distance stays the same. We take inspiration from an observation about the qubit $[\![8,3,2]\!]$ code construction from [12], which we deconstruct in the ZX-calculus in Sects. B.1 and B.2 of the appendix, available at [51].

In an attempt to reproduce how to construct the $[\![8,3,2]\!]$ code by adding an X-type stabilizer to all physical qubits of a $[\![7,3,1]\!]$ code with transversal CCZ, we add an X-type stabilizer that checks all qutrits: $S_1^X = X_1 X_2 X_3$. Adding to our earlier encoder, which we conjugate $T^{\otimes 3}$ by, and after applying ZX rewrite rules to "push" the stabilizer outside of the encoder/decoder, we obtain the following symmetric circuit:

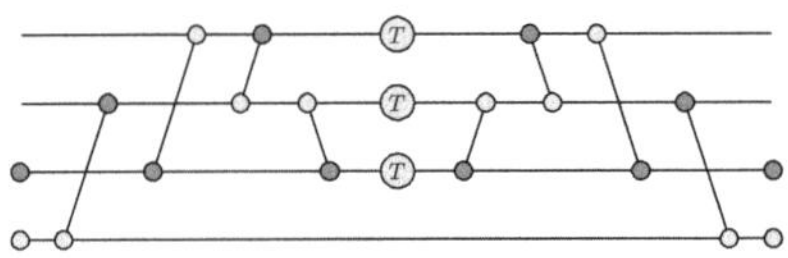

(11)

Since the inner portion of the circuit is still the same as before adding the stabilizer, this is the $|0\rangle$-controlled Z gate with a CX gate applied from an extra ancilla (which is initialized and postselected to $|+\rangle$) to the second data qutrit on either sides. Therefore, the equivalent circuit is

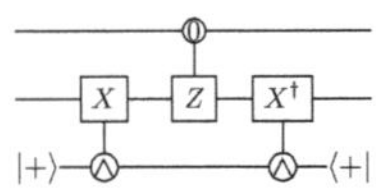

(12)

However, we can see that the logical gate corresponding to this circuit is no longer the same.

4.1 Recovering Logical AND

To figure out how to modify the circuit to preserve the logical binary AND gate, let's first see what is the logical gate implemented by this circuit. Since the ancilla qutrit is in the qutrit $|+\rangle$ state just before the first CX gate, we can consider three cases based on the Z basis state of this superposition. For $|0\rangle$, the CX gates controlled by the ancilla does nothing, so the circuit is the same as simply the $|0\rangle$-controlled Z from the first to the second qutrit. The behavior corresponding to this $|0\rangle$ case of the ancilla can be enforced by adding a second control from the ancilla, as in the leftmost case below.

Ancilla in $|0\rangle$ **Ancilla in $|1\rangle$** **Ancilla in $|2\rangle$**

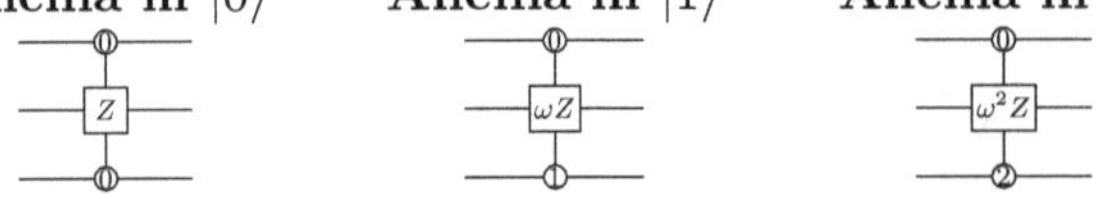

For the $|1\rangle$ case of the ancilla, the CX gates apply a X to the left and $X^\dagger$ to the right of Z on the second qutrit. Observing that $X^\dagger ZX = \omega Z$, this simplifies to the middle case above. Similarly, for the $|2\rangle$ case where two X and $X^\dagger$ gates are applied, since $(X^\dagger)^2 ZX^2 = \omega^2 Z$, we obtain the rightmost case above.

Putting together these three cases, we find that

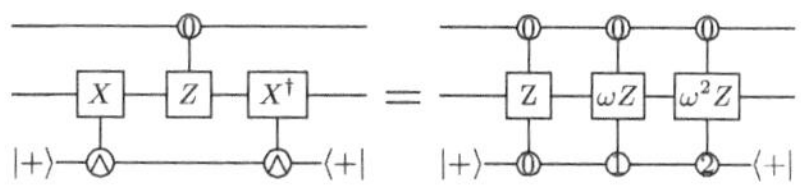

(13)

We can expand out the gates by separating out the Z and the extra phases, then permuting the gates to simplify the circuit:

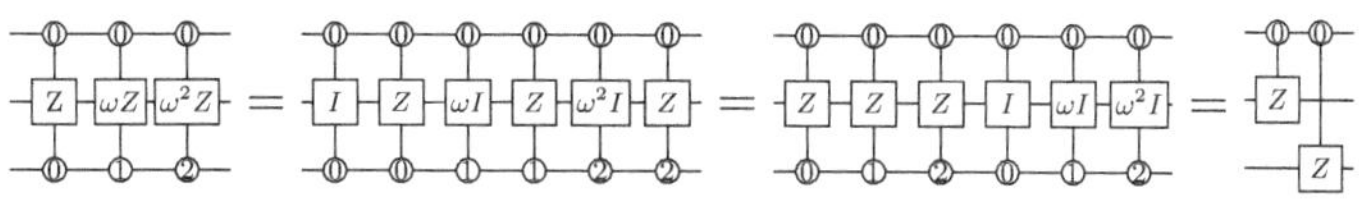

(14)

Moreover, one can check that

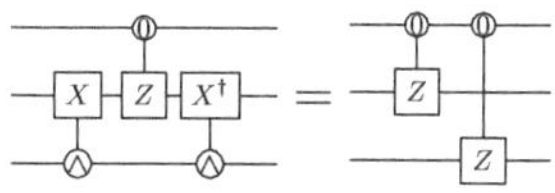

(15)

Putting together Eqs. 14 and 15, we can see that the following steps produce a CX-conjugated circuit which still implements the $|0\rangle$-controlled Z gate (the inner portion of the circuit for AND):

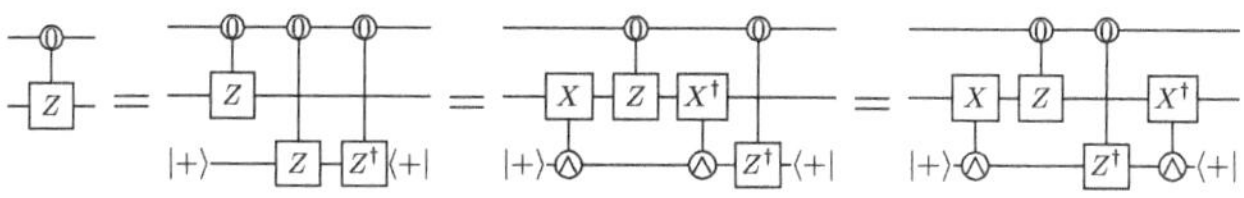

(16)

Thus, the final circuit in Eq. 16 preserves the logical AND gate and has an additional X-type stabilizer. We will now use this to derive the code.

4.2 Deriving the Code as a Symmetric, T-depth One Circuit

In order to determine the corresponding QEC code, our approach is to solve for a symmetric, T-depth one synthesis of the circuit. We can rewrite the circuit in its symmetric form using *phase gadgets*—symmetric multi-qubit interactions native to many hardware architectures [59,60,68] and useful for optimizing quantum circuits [7,19,79].

First, we will find the phase gadgets representation of the $|0\rangle$-controlled Z and $Z^\dagger$ gates. Then, we will find the combined phase gadgets form. From this, we can obtain a T-depth one symmetric form of the circuit.

We begin with the symmetric circuit for $|0\rangle$-controlled from [8]. To rewrite this in phase gadgets form, we will need to use Eq (6) of [80] (which can be derived using spider fusion, bialgebra rule, and dualizing). Therefore,

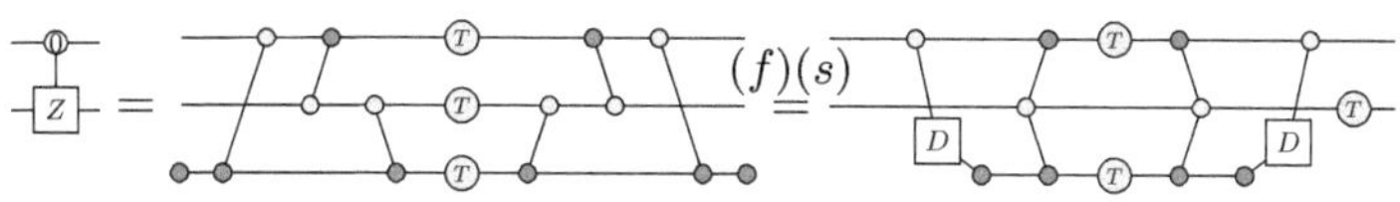

(17)

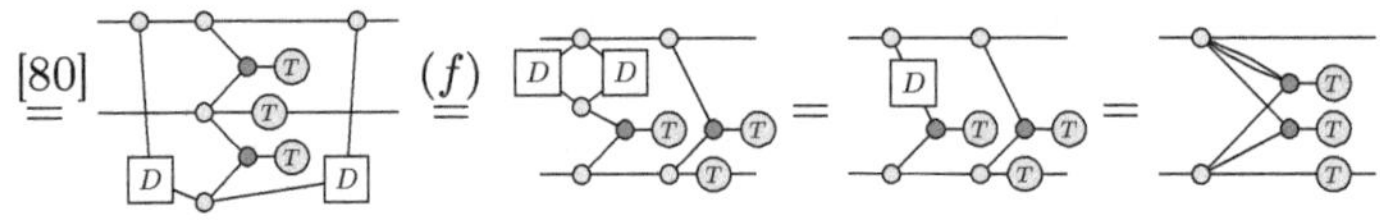

(18)

To find the phase gadget form of its adjoint, $|0\rangle$-controlled $Z^\dagger$, we take the adjoint of the phase gadget diagram that we just found, by taking its horizontal reflection and negating the phases. Applying dualizers to all wires surrounding the red X spiders flips back the direction of the phase gadgets, so we end up with the same diagram for $|0\rangle$-controlled $Z^\dagger$ except with $T^\dagger$ instead of T phases. Therefore, we can replace the $|0\rangle$-controlled Z and $Z^\dagger$ gates with their respective phase gadget representation, then rewrite and apply the rule from [80] to obtain a combined phase gadgets form.

4.3 Finding the Stabilizers and Logical Operators

From the combined phase gadgets diagram, we can obtain a symmetric circuit by reading off the connectivity for each of the phase gadgets' spiders. This is because the above diagram corresponds to phase polynomials based on sum over paths for each of the phase gadgets, which can equivalently be expressed in a symmetric form that computes a parity map on the left then uncomputes on the right, which is also equivalent to a CNOT circuit with phase gates and pre/postselection (see Chap. 7.1 of [48]). Thus, from the combined phase gadget diagram above, we obtain the following symmetric forms:

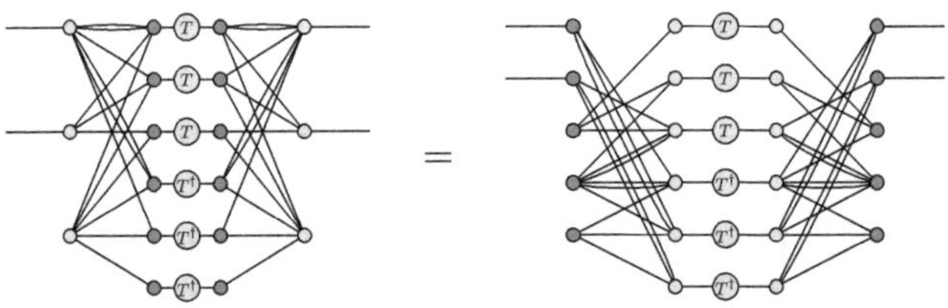

(19)

The left portion of the diagrams represents the encoder maps, and symmetrically, the right portion the decoder map. In the left hand side diagram, the encoder is in the Z-X form [47]. From this, we can read off the X-type stabilizers and logical operators. The diagram on the right hand side is the corresponding X-Z encoder, obtained by applying bialgebra, dual, and fusion rewrite rules. From the X-Z form, we can read off the Z-type stabilizers and logical operators. Thus, for this inner CSS code (which implements the $|0\rangle$-controlled Z), the two equivalent encoder maps, along with the corresponding stabilizer generators and logical operators are:

$$\begin{aligned}\overline{X}_1 &= X_1^2X_2X_4^2X_5\\ \overline{X}_2 &= X_1X_2X_3\\ S_{X1} &= X_1X_2X_3X_4X_5X_6\end{aligned}$$

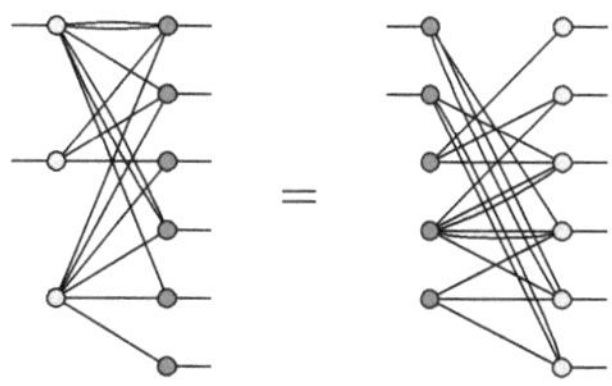

$$\begin{aligned}\overline{Z}_1 &= Z_4Z_5^2\\ \overline{Z}_2 &= Z_3Z_6^2\\ S_{Z1} &= Z_1Z_2Z_3\\ S_{Z2} &= Z_2Z_3^2Z_4^2Z_5\\ S_{Z3} &= Z_4Z_5Z_6\end{aligned} \tag{20}$$

Recall (see Eq. 9) that the overall symmetric T-depth 1 circuit for AND gate consists of outer Clifford gates in addition to the inner CX circuit. The encoders above are for the CSS code corresponding to this inner CX circuit.

By pushing logical X and Z spiders through the full encoder, we obtain the following logical operators for the "overall" code implementing transversal AND:

$$\begin{aligned}\overline{X}_1 &= X_1^2X_2X_4^2X_5 & \overline{Z}_1 &= X_1X_2X_3Z_4Z_5^2\\ \overline{X}_2 &= X_1X_2^2Z_3^2X_4X_5^2Z_6 & \overline{Z}_2 &= X_1X_2X_3\end{aligned} \tag{21}$$

We verify that the code distance is 2 by checking the minimum weight of all possible logical operators (such as by multiplying each logical operator with all possible linear combinations of the stabilizers, for this small code).

We will use E_{pf} to refer to the inner CSS encoder in Eq. 20 (comprised of phase-free "pf" spiders) for the CSS code implementing the $|0\rangle$-controlled Z. We will use E_{AND} to refer to the full encoder (consisting of outer Clifford gates and E_{pf}) for the $[\![6,2,2]\!]$ qutrit code implementing transversal AND.

4.4 Getting to Distance 4 Through Code Concatenation

We remark that our $[\![6,2,2]\!]$ qutrit code with a transversal AND gate (implemented by 3 T and 3 T† gates), can be concatenated as the outer code with the inner $[\![8,1,2]\!]$ qutrit CSS code with transversal T gate from [13]. As both are qutrit CSS codes and the inner CSS code's X and Z logical operators are implemented by physical X's and Z's respectively, the resulting code distance is the product of that of the inner and outer codes[1]: $[\![48,2,4]\!]$, with transversal AND gate implemented by 24 T and 24 T† gates.

5 Qubit Subspace Codes

In this section, we will introduce Qubit Subspace Projection as a logical operation in qutrit codes. In addition, depending on how these results are utilized, these can be viewed from the perspectives of gauge fixing of subsystem codes, and as adding additional stabilizers to construct mixed qubit-qutrit codes which

[1] This is a well-known result [36], deducible by presuming that any logical error can occur if at least d_{outer} logical qubits of the inner CSS code experienced errors, each of which had to have experienced at least d_{inner} physical errors.

we call Qubit Subspace Codes. We begin by deriving for the qutrit setting, the physical action of logical ZX diagrams for CSS codes in Sect. A.1 of the appendix, available at [51].

5.1 Logical Qubit, Physical Qutrits

We describe how to derive a quantum code that encodes a logical qubit ($k = 1$) using $n = 6$ physical qutrits. While we suspect this first Qubit Subspace Code is of more limited use than the one in the next subsection, this also serves as a simpler demonstration of code construction techniques:

Begin with E_{pf}, the encoder for the $[\![6, 2, 2]\!]$ inner qutrit CSS code implementing $|0\rangle$-controlled Z (henceforth denoted ZCZ for short). Fix the bottom logical qutrit to $|0\rangle_L$, apply logical X to the top qutrit (to the left of the encoder), measure the bottom logical qutrit in the X basis, and check if it is $\langle+|_L$ using Steane error correction [72] on a $|0\rangle_L|+\rangle_L$ resource state. This procedure, presented in more detail in Sect. C.4 of the appendix [51], uses gauge fixing to enable a logical operation, by projecting the top logical qutrit into the qubit subspace.

5.2 Qubit Subspace Projection

Now, we will show how to obtain a code with $k = 2$ logical qubits and $n = 6$ physical qutrits that has the same stabilizers as that of E_{AND}, but has two additional stabilizers which project the two logical qutrits into the qubit subspace. The idea is that on the binary-valued inputs and output of the AND gate, physical projective measurements can be made that ensure that the logical qutrit states are in their qubit subspace:

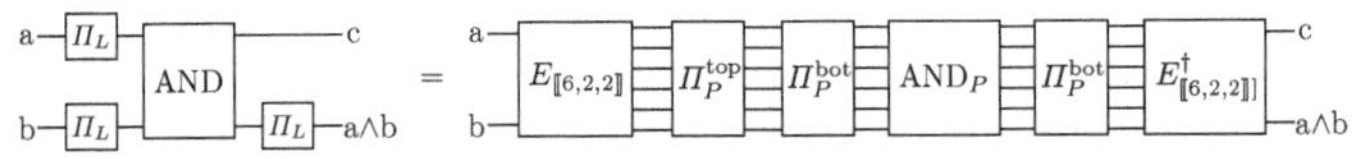

(22)

The following logical circuit implements Π_L, the projection of a qutrit into its $|0\rangle$ and $|1\rangle$ subspace. We call this the qubit subspace projection (SP) gadget. Using the ZH diagram for $\neg|0\rangle$-controlled X from [66], we can derive the ZX diagram for the SP gadget, as shown on the right hand side.

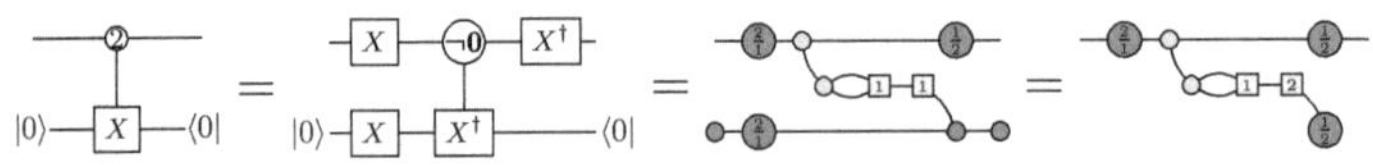

(23)

To find the physical implementation of the SP gadget in the $[\![6, 2, 2]\!]$ code, we can push this diagram through the full Clifford encoder. Below is the derivation for obtaining the physical SP gadget for the second (bottom) logical qutrit[2].

[2] The second logical qutrit is the "answer" qutrit of the AND circuit, mapping to $a \wedge b$. The physical SP gadget for the first (top) logical qutrit can be analogously derived by pushing the logical SP gadget as input to the top wire through the encoder.

This is done by plugging in the SP gadget into the second logical input wire, then applying rewrite rules to push this through the outer Cliffords.

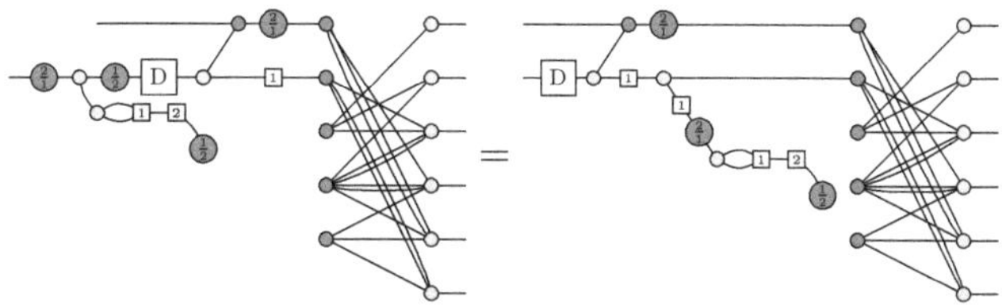

(24)

After using Lemma 2 to push the gadget through the inner CSS encoder E_{pf}, we find the physical implementation of the SP gadget for the second logical qutrit, supported on physical qutrits 3 and 6 as it matches $\overline{Z_2} = Z_3 Z_6^2$ of E_{pf}:

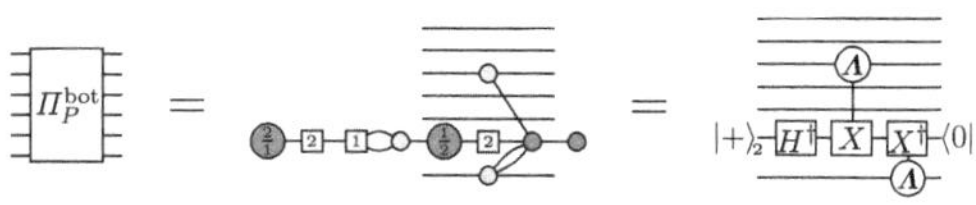

(25)

The right hand side is an equivalent diagram in which the gadget is viewed as a resource state. We observe that the left hand side of the gadget, starting from the $|1\rangle$ input (represented by the red $\frac{2}{1}$ spider) to before the second $H^\dagger$, is a qutrit state prepared as the *qubit* $|+\rangle$, an equal superposition of $|0\rangle$ and $|1\rangle$.

Beyond a static code construction, this technique can be viewed as a form of code switching through subsystem code gauge fixing. This is because we derive the projection operator that uses the qubit $|+\rangle$ state as part of the resource state. When the gauge logical qutrit state is this full gadget state (preparing a qubit $|+\rangle$ followed by $H^\dagger$), it results in a logical qubit. When instead the gauge logical qutrit state is in the qutrit $|+\rangle$ state, there is no Qubit Subspace Projection.

6 Magic State Distillation and Injection

The $|0\rangle$-controlled Z gate is deterministically injectable because it is a diagonal gate in the third level of the Clifford hierarchy, which we prove in Sects. C.1 to C.4 of the appendix [51]:

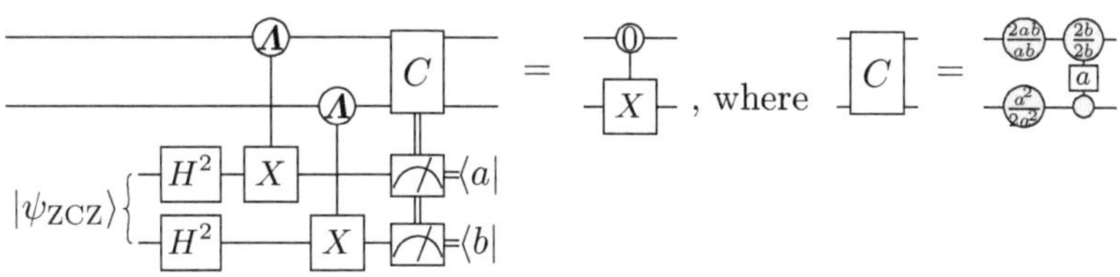

(26)

There we also prove correctness of magic state distillation and deterministic injection of the AND gate for qutrit CSS codes. The injection circuit is:

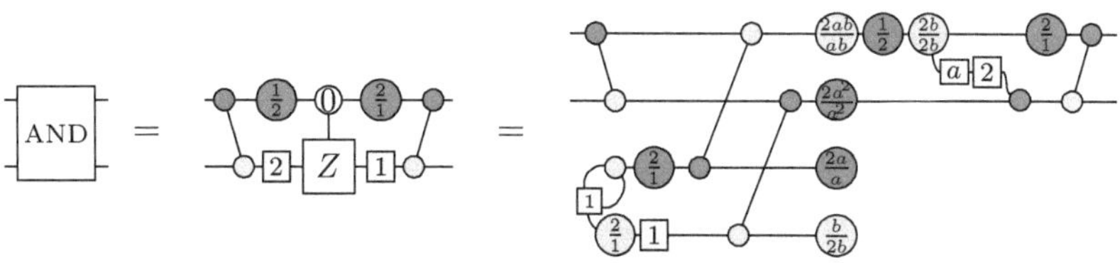

(27)

The correction is a Clifford unitary where all but one gate—the $Z(2b, 2b)$ gate—are Pauli or CX gates, and hence transversally implementable on CSS codes [34].

7 Conclusion

In this work, we demonstrated that moving to qutrit systems enables an efficient unitary realization of the classical binary AND gate within the Clifford+T framework, and we developed explicit low-T-count constructions such as generalizing to multi-input AND. By reinterpreting symmetric compute-phase-uncompute decompositions as encoding and decoding circuits, we showed how to design qutrit stabilizer codes that admit transversal non-Clifford implementations of logical AND, including a $[\![6, 2, 2]\!]$ code and a concatenated extension with increased distance. We further introduced mixed-dimensional subspace constructions and protocols for magic state distillation and deterministic injection compatible with qutrit CSS codes. Together, these results illustrate how higher-dimensional and mixed-dimensional code design can expand the landscape of fault-tolerant logical gates beyond qubit-based constraints, and motivate further investigation of their practical performance and scalability.

A natural question to investigate through in-depth comparative study would be how theorized qutrit codes perform under different noise models and hardware constraints. These could utilize recent software libraries for qudit computation such as [44,55], in order to benchmark via numerical simulation against qubit codes with transversal CCZ gates, such as the $[\![8, 3, 2]\!]$ color code (implemented by physical T and $T^\dagger$ gates) or the $[\![27, 3, 3]\!]$ code of [50] (implemented by a depth-2 physical CCZ circuit).

The other promising direction is to continue pushing the theory of higher-dimensional QEC code constructions. For discovering more codes and dynamic QEC protocols for a fixed qudit dimension, we can leverage normal forms such as for qutrit Clifford circuits [52], for qubit Clifford isometries [46,82] (which we expect admit straightforward generalization to prime-dimensional qudits due to [61,66]), and qutrit Clifford+T circuits [29].

Acknowledgments. Thank you to Nadish de Silva for explaining the approach for efficient multi-qudit gate teleportation described in [70]. We would like to thank Noah Goss, Matt McEwen, Costin Iancu, and Ed Younis for discussions about useful circuit constructions for three-level quantum systems. We would like to thank Sarah Meng Li and Jacky (Jiaxin) Huang for the collaboration on pushing through the encoder and gauge fixing in [41] that greatly informed this work. We would like to thank Aleks Kissinger for discussions on the transversal CCZ of $[\![8, 3, 2]\!]$ code. L.Y. would like to thank the Google PhD Fellowship, and the Tencent Post-Doctoral Research Fellowship at the University of Cambridge, for funding. Much of this work was done while C.L. and L.Y. were at the University of Oxford.

A Qutrit ZX-calculus Rules

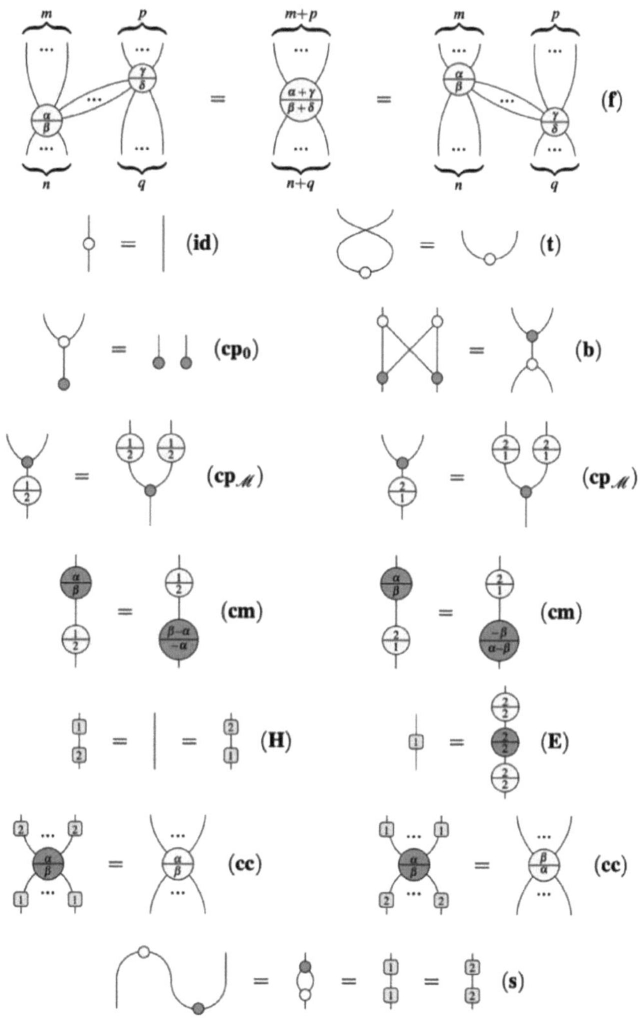

Fig. 1. Rewrite rules for the qutrit ZX-calculus, reprinted from Fig. 1 in [74]

A.1 Pushing Through the Encoder

"Pushing through the encoder" refers to the idea that, for any encoder E for a CSS code (which is a phase-free diagram that is an isometry), any diagram $\mathcal{D}$ on the left of E (which is the logical operator) has a corresponding diagram $\mathcal{D}_P$

on the right of E (which is a physical implementation of $\mathcal{D}$). This was developed for qubit CSS codes in [41]. We generalize this idea to qutrits as follows:

Lemma 2 ("Pushing through the encoder" (PTE) for qutrits). *Let E be the encoder of a qutrit CSS code. For any ZX diagram $\mathcal{D}_L$ on the left of E, it has a corresponding diagram $\mathcal{D}_P$ on the right of E such that $E\mathcal{D}_L = \mathcal{D}_P E$.*

Proof. Similar to the proof for Proposition 3.1 of [41], any Z or X spiders in $\mathcal{D}_L$ on the logical wires that has phases or multiple legs can be unfused so that each logical Z or X spider on the logical qutrit wire has just one external wire. Using strong complementarity with the corresponding choice of diagram of the encoder (for a Z spider, use X-Z normal form, and for X spider, use Z-normal form), one can "push" this supporting leg of the diagram to the right side. For any diagram $\mathcal{D}$ supported on an arbitrary number of logical wires,

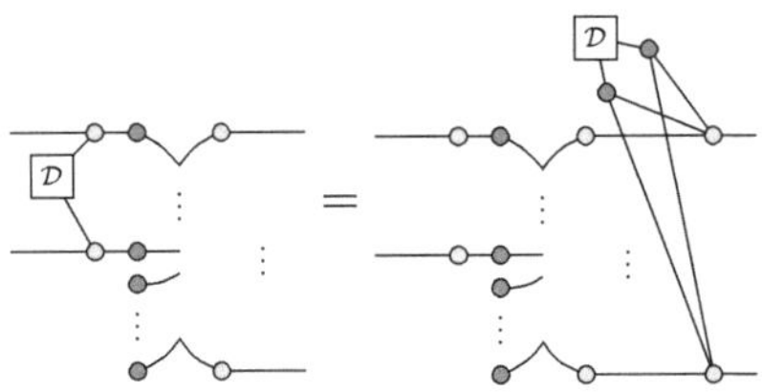

(28)

Note that for qutrits, there may be double wires (which can be represented as a single wire with a "D" dualizer box) in encoders connecting Z and X spiders. The connectivity degree (single or double wires) for each supporting logical qubit to $\mathcal{D}$ is preserved for the corresponding X spider for that logical on the right.

B Deconstruction of the Qubit $[\![8, 3, 2]\!]$ Code

B.1 Circuit Synthesis and ZX-calculus View

Here, we will demonstrate the well-known example of the transversal CCZ gate of the $[\![8, 3, 2]\!]$ code [12] (also called the smallest interesting color code, an instance of transversal CCZ gates described in [49]), in the ZX-calculus.

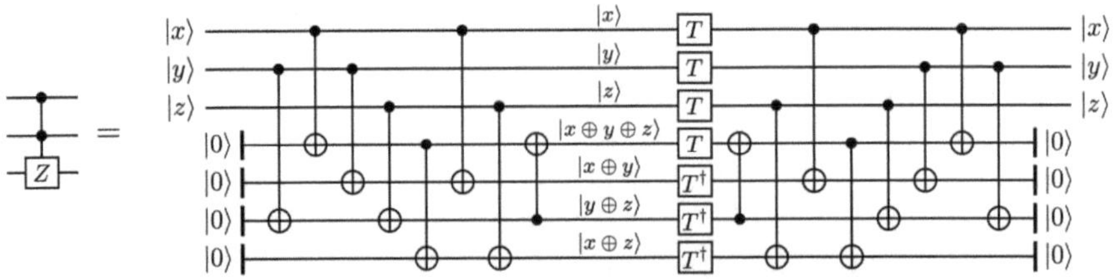

Fig. 2. Figure for a T-depth one decomposition of the qubit CCZ gate, reprinted from [67, Figure 1].

In an observation credited to Campbell [12], the above circuit consists of a CNOT circuit unitary embedding E, a layer of T and $T^\dagger$ gates, and $E^\dagger$. This therefore defines a $[\![7,3,1]\!]$ code. Being distance 1, it has no error-correcting capabilities. To improve the code distance, it suffices to add to the encoder E (whose ZX diagram first appeared in [23]) one physical qubit, and a weight 8 X-type stabilizer generator connected to all 8 physical qubits:

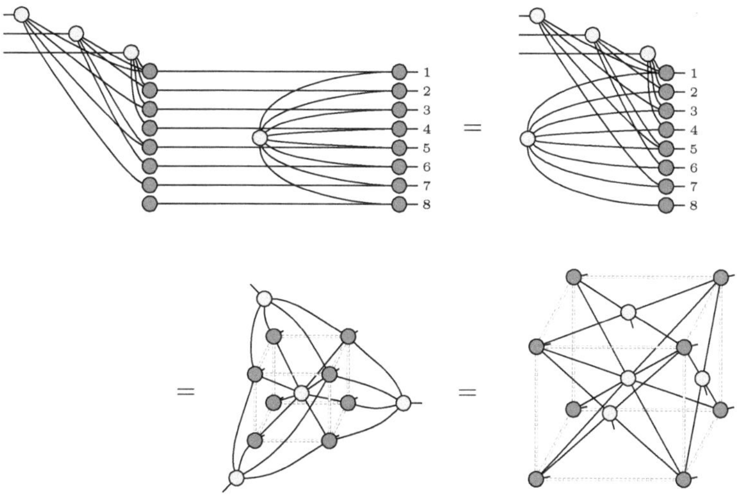

(29)

B.2 Verifying Transversal CCZ Preservation

This construction preserves the transversal CCZ gate, resulting in the $[\![8,3,2]\!]$ code. To show this, we will use the following fact about the phase polynomial representation of the CCZ gate as the map that acts as $|x,y,z\rangle \mapsto (-1)^{x\cdot y\cdot z}|x,y,z\rangle$, where x,y,z are bits denoting computational basis states. As was shown for qutrits in [80], the qubit CCZ gate is identified by the exponent of (-1) being a multiplicative expression $x\cdot y\cdot z$; this can be replaced by an equivalent expression summing over modular addition. For this reason, the qubit CCZ gate is equal to the following spider nest of phase gadgets:

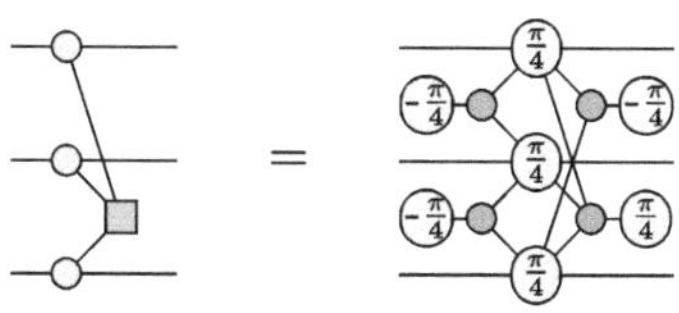

(30)

If instead all phases here are $\pm\frac{\pi}{2}$, then instead of the CCZ gate, this is the identity map on three qubits. More generally, for n qubits, having one of all possible connectivity phase gadgets of 0-n legs, of phases $\pm\frac{\pi}{2^{n-2}}$ where the sign matches the parity of the number of legs, is equal to the n-qubit identity map.

We can substitute the encoder E of the $[\![8,3,2]\!]$ code from [23], to verify that $L = E; P; E^\dagger$ where L is the CCZ gate, and $P = TT^\dagger T^\dagger TT^\dagger TTT^\dagger$.

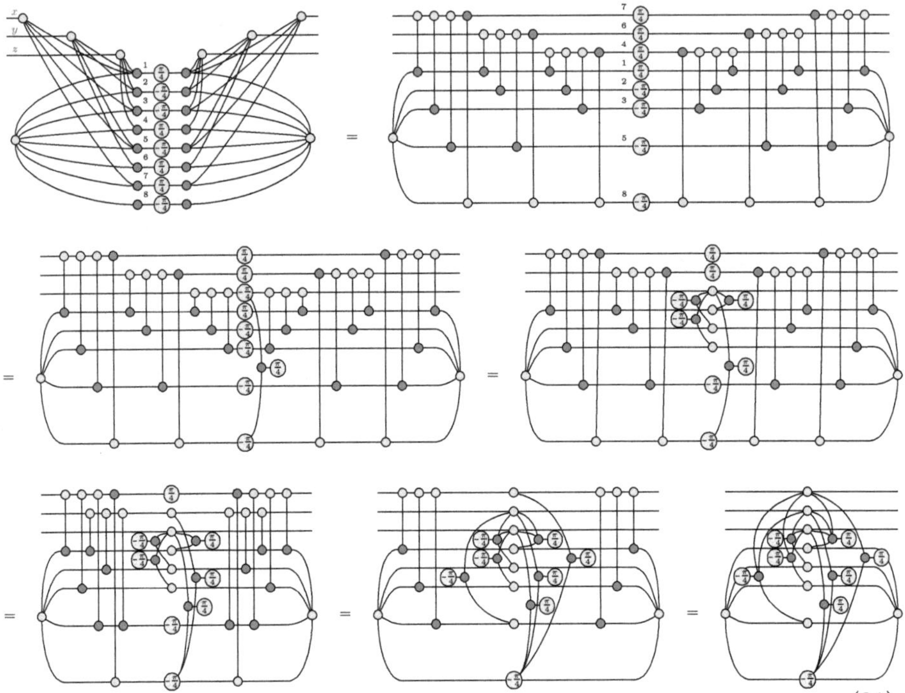

(31)

Continuing from the last step, we now utilize the above observation to recognize that what we have is the spider nest of all 0-4 legged $\mp\frac{\pi}{4}$ phase gadgets, conjugated by all 0-3 legged $\pm\frac{\pi}{4}$ phase gadgets on the upper three qubits. Therefore, we can then apply all 0-4 legged $\mp\frac{\pi}{4}$ phase gadgets, which equals the identity. The end result is precisely the CCZ gate.

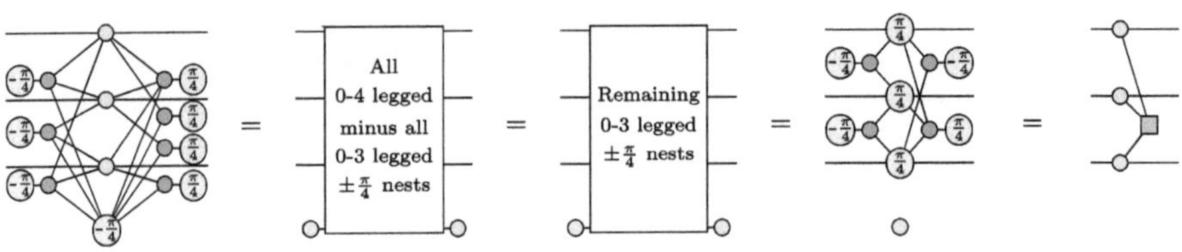

(32)

C Proofs for Magic State Distillation and Injection

C.1 CCZ Magic State Distillation

Here, we give a graphical portrayal of magic state distillation. We have just derived that the logical CCZ gate in the $[\![8,3,2]\!]$ code is physically implemented by 8 T and $T^\dagger$ gates:

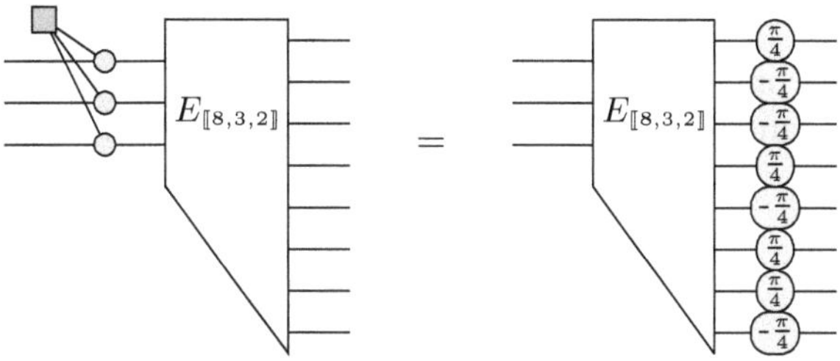

(33)

Taking the conjugate transpose of the above equation and inputting $|+\rangle^{\otimes 8}$, the ideal decoder acts on 8 T and $T^\dagger$ magic states as:

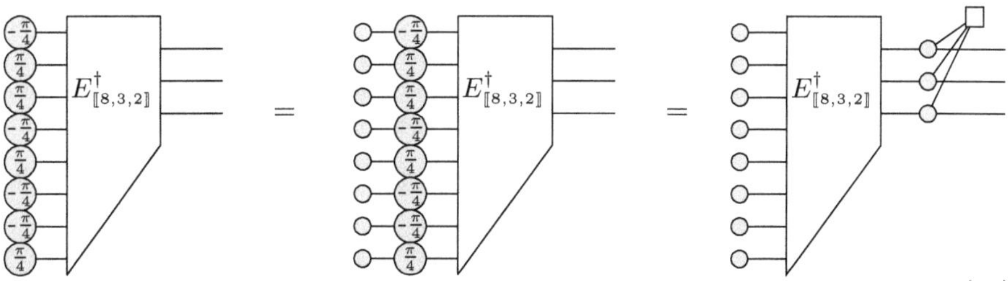

(34)

Substituting in the Z-X GPF of the encoder, the $|+\rangle$ states copy and fuse, leaving just the three-legged H-box.

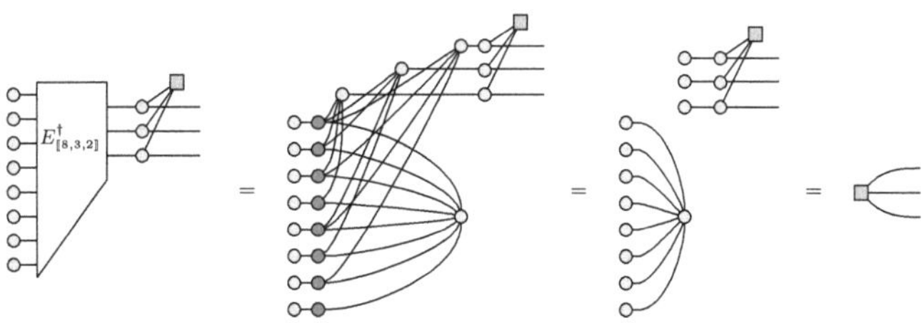

(35)

In other words, the decoding of 8 T and $T^\dagger$ magic states results in a less noisy CCZ magic state.

Were it distilling the $|0\rangle$-controlled Z magic state from the inner CSS code of our qutrit $[\![6,2,2]\!]$ code, the proof steps are identical to the above. Indeed, this proof applies for distilling magic states of any transversal diagonal gate in a CSS code whose X and Z logical operators are realized by physical X's and Z's respectively, i.e. whose encoder is a phase-free isometry in the ZX-calculus.

C.2 CCZ Magic State Injection for Prime-Dimensional Qudits

Proposition 2. *As is the case for qubits, for any odd prime qudit dimension, the Toffoli and CCZ gates are in the third level of the Clifford hierarchy.*

Proof. Noting the ZX diagram interpretations of the Z-basis states:

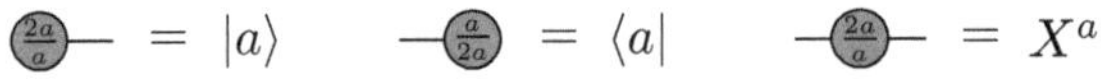

(36)

Pauli Z directly commutes through the CCZ gate because both are diagonal in the Z basis. We can commute Pauli X through the CCZ gate as follows:

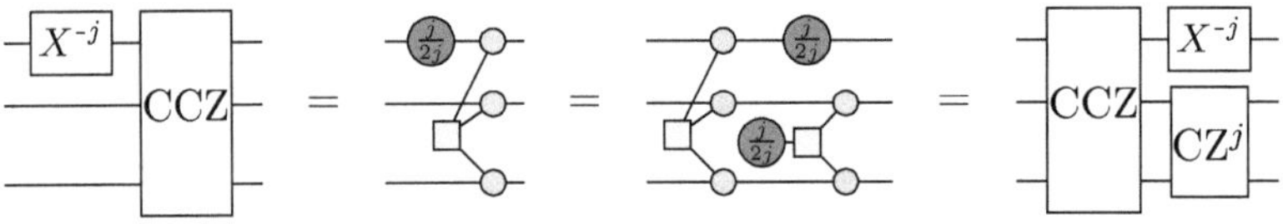

(37)

As it is in the third level of the Clifford hierarchy, the Toffoli and CCZ gates admit magic state injection for any prime qudit dimension. Moreover, both these gates are semi-Clifford [70]:

Definition 9. *A gate G is* semi-Clifford *if it admits a decomposition $G = C_2DC_1$, as a diagonal gate in some level of the Clifford hierarchy D, pre- and post-composed by Clifford gates C_1 and C_2 respectively.*

Therefore, a more efficient (halving the number of ancillae qudits) gate teleportation can be utilized [70]:

Proposition 3. *For any prime qudit dimension, the CCZ gate is deterministically implementable by one round of the below magic state injection protocol, with one copy of the CCZ magic state.*

Proof. The multiqudit case of the teleportation circuit follows from parallelism of the singlequdit case.

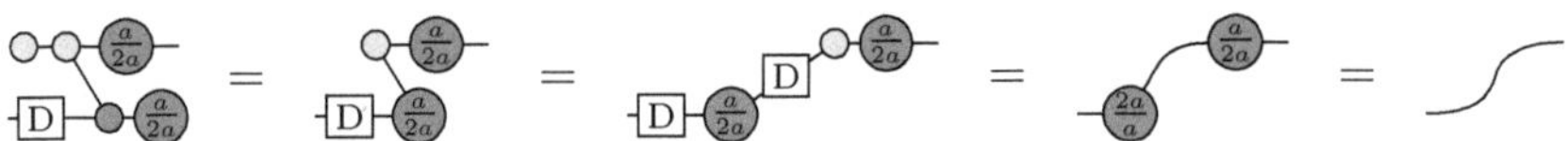

(38)

By commuting the intended gate to teleport (the CCZ gate) through the three-qubit teleportation circuit, we get that the CCZ magic state can be teleported by that circuit, with Pauli X and Clifford CZ gate corrections controlled on the measurement outcomes.

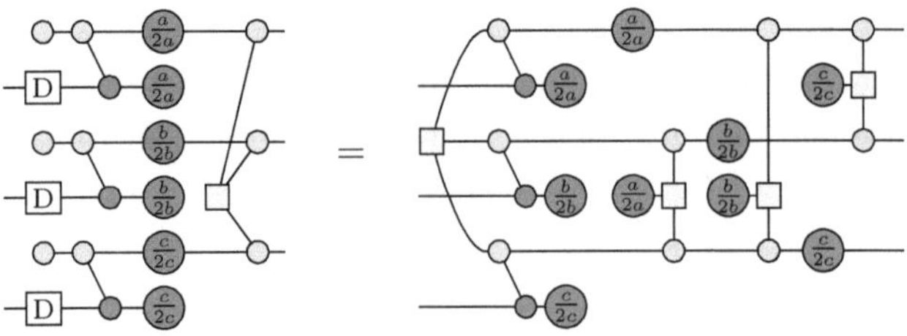

(39)

C.3 $|0\rangle$-Controlled Z Injection

We start by deriving the ZX diagram for the $|0\rangle$-controlled Z gate, by conjugating the $|0\rangle$-controlled $X^\dagger$ from [66, Equation 5]:

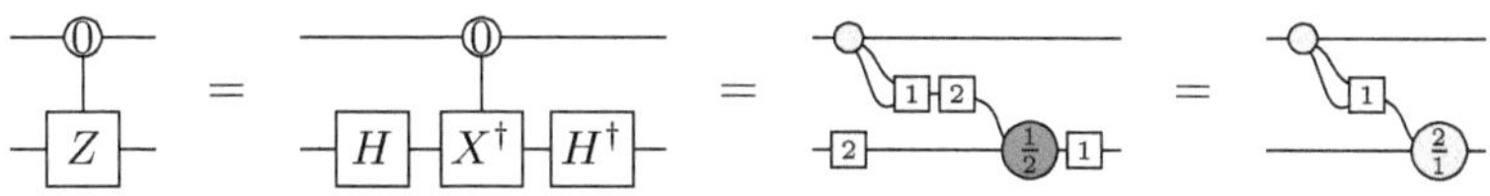

(40)

Its magic state is obtained by inputting $|++\rangle$:

$|ZCZ\rangle =$ 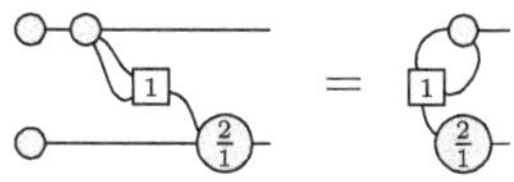

(41)

The standard injection circuit is below. When the measurement outcome is $\langle 00|$, i.e. both a and b are zero, then we have that this circuit implements the $|0\rangle$-controlled Z gate.

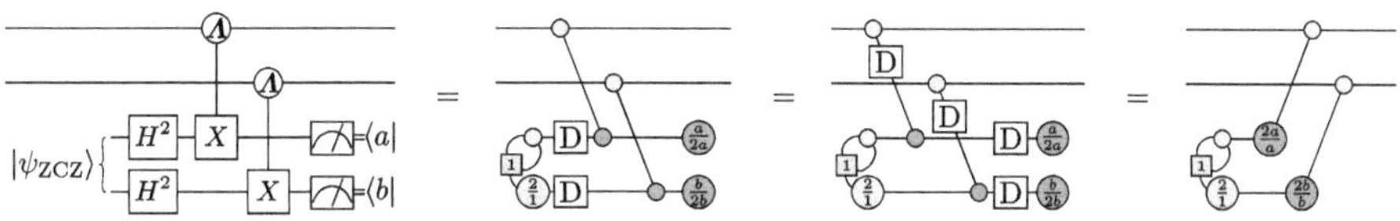

(42)

To see if this can be deterministically injectable, we will need the following lemma:

Lemma 3. *For* $a, b \in \mathbb{Z}$,

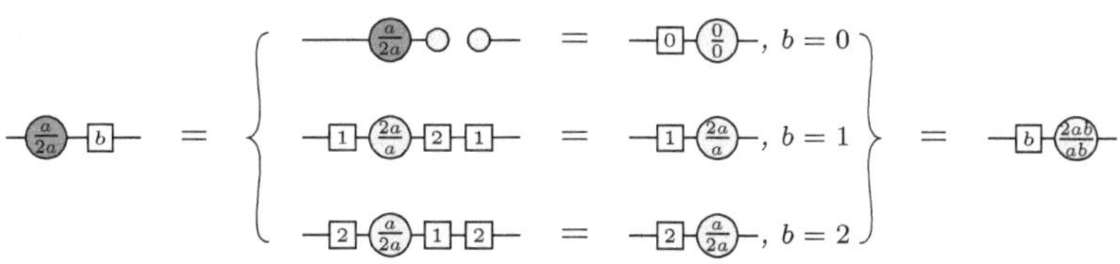

(43)

We can thereafter push both X corrections from measurement through the magic state, to obtain a diagonal Clifford correction.

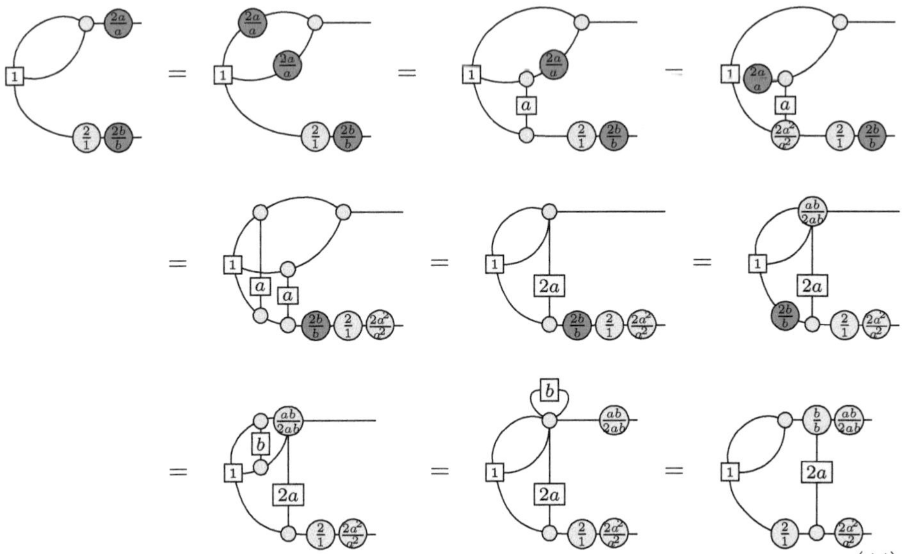

(44)

Pauli Z commutes with the $|0\rangle$-controlled gate because they're both gates diagonal in the Z-basis. Therefore, this proves that the $|0\rangle$-controlled gate is in the third level of the Clifford hierarchy, because pushing through any Pauli operator results in a correction that is Clifford, i.e. in the second level of the Clifford hierarchy.

We can then append to our earlier circuit the inverse of this error term, as a correction parametrized by the measurement outcome.

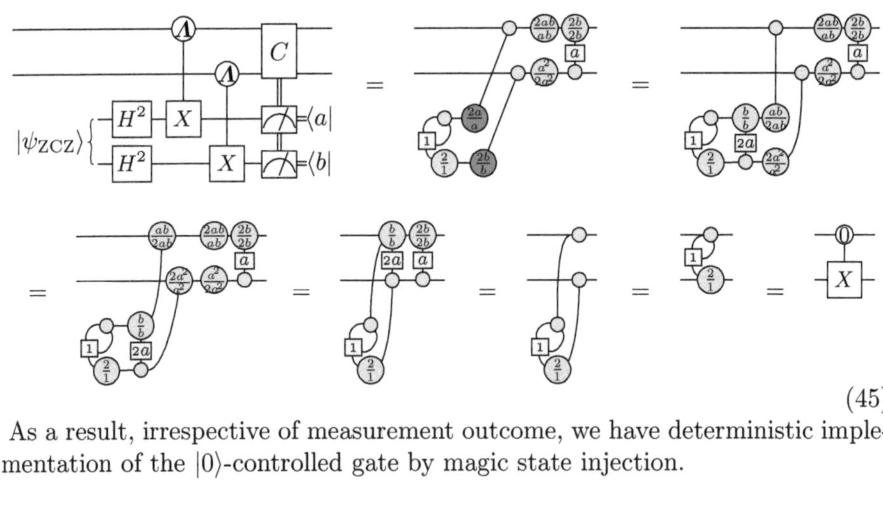

(45)

As a result, irrespective of measurement outcome, we have deterministic implementation of the $|0\rangle$-controlled gate by magic state injection.

C.4 Implementing the AND Gate via Magic State Distillation and Injection

Up to now, we have been working with the simpler setting—injecting diagonal logical gates distilled in a CSS code whose logical X's and Z's are implemented by physical X's and Z's respectively. Our goal is now to distill and inject the AND gate into any qutrit CSS code, so long as you have the capability to do fault-tolerant S gates (for instance, transversal in the code or via subsequent injection). Essentially, we want the protocol to not require the code to have a transversal H gate, i.e. be self-dual.

In the two-qutrit unitary U that fixes our logical operators such that the transversal operation is AND instead of $|0\rangle$-controlled Z, it is the CX gate that causes a problem with injecting the AND magic state directly such that it cannot be corrected as to be deterministic. Instead, as done for $U^\dagger$ below, we push the CX out to be the outermost gate, in order to inject the remaining gates as part of the magic state. As we are injecting into a CSS code, the CX can be executed transversally conjugating the injection.

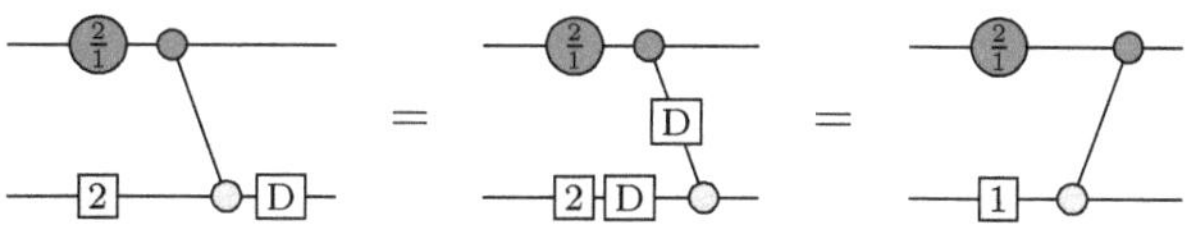

(46)

By decoding 3 T and 3 T† states (which can be recursively distilled) in the code without this CX, we get a magic state for the AND gate up to this CX.

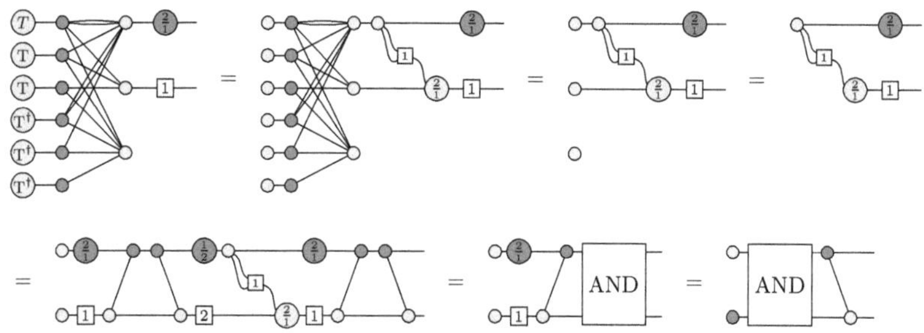

(47)

We can then perform deterministic injection, through proving this as a modification of our earlier protocol in Eq. (45).

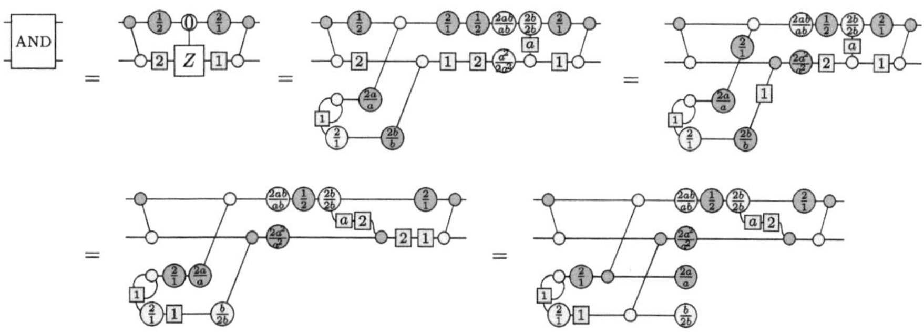

(48)

The resulting correction is a Clifford unitary where all but one gate—the $Z(2b, 2b)$ gate—are Pauli or CX gates, and hence transversally implementable on CSS codes [34]. As a single-qutrit diagonal Clifford unitary, the $Z(2b, 2b)$ gate can be implemented by the standard magic state injection protocol.

The remaining piece of the puzzle, is that the protocol measures two qutrits in two different bases, X and Z. Presume we have access to the $\overline{|0+\rangle}$ logical state in the code as a resource. If there are more than two logical qubits per code block, the resource state should be $\overline{|0+\ldots+\rangle}$ or $\overline{|0\ldots0+\rangle}$, depending on whether you want to measure one logical qubit in the Z or X basis respectively.

Say that we want to measure logical $\overline{\langle a| \otimes I}$, where I is the identity operation on all logical qutrits except the one we want to measure; without loss of generality, let us say we want to measure the first logical qutrit. Observe that the $\overline{|0+\rangle} = E|0+\rangle$ state is representable as a phase-free ZX diagram, where the logical qutrit you want to measure is set to $|0\rangle$ and the rest to $|+\rangle$.

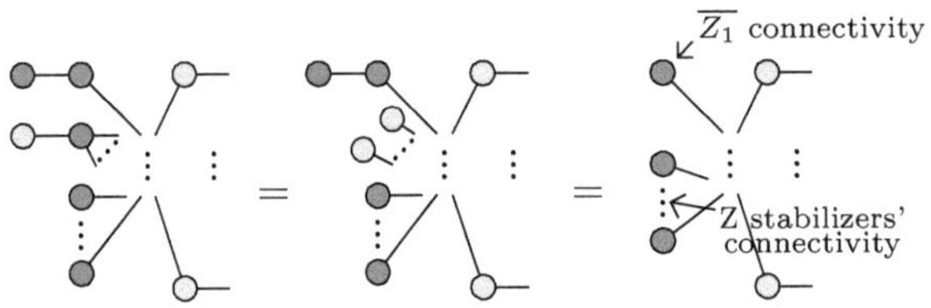

(49)

The resulting ZX diagram is a bipartite graph whose connectivity is that of logical Z_1 and Z stabilizer generators of the code. This correspondence between ZX diagrams of stabilizer codes, stabilizer tableaus, and Tanner graphs is detailed in [82].

Injecting this resource state yields the desired Z-basis measurement of the first logical qutrit.

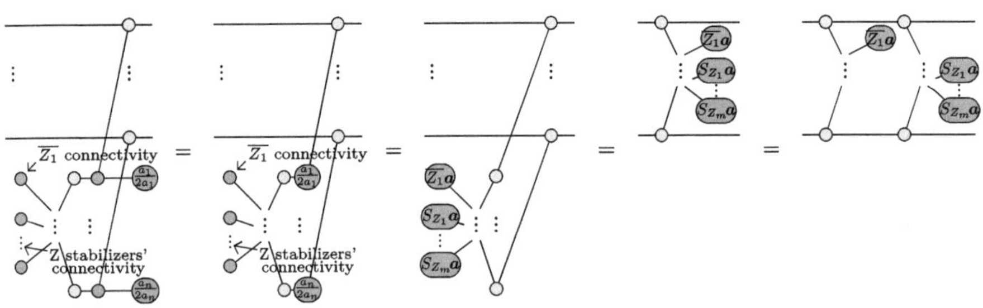

(50)

It additionally performs Steane-style syndrome measurement [73] of the Z checks.

Exchanging the roles of Z and X, and $|0\rangle$ and $|+\rangle$, likewise enables measuring $\overline{I \otimes \langle b|H}$ in addition to Steane-style syndrome measurement of the X checks.

D Gate Counts for Qutrit Emulation of Qubit and Binary Operations

D.1 Emulating the qubit X, Z, S, CX and CZ gates

The qubit Hadamard and CNOT operations cannot be emulated utilizing qutrit Clifford gates [8]. Moreover, we can show that the qubit Hadamard gate cannot be exactly and deterministically emulated using qutrit Clifford+T, despite this being an approximately universal gate set. This follows from normal forms for single-qutrit Clifford+T operators, which impose the necessary but not sufficient condition that the matrix entries belong to the ring $\mathbb{Z}\left[\frac{1}{1-\zeta}\right]$, as independently determined by Prakash, Jain, Kapur, and Seth [63]; and Glaudell, Ross, and Taylor [28]:

Definition 10 ($\mathbb{Z}\left[\frac{1}{1-\zeta}\right]$)**.** *Let $\zeta = e^{i\frac{2\pi}{9}}$. The matrix elements of all single-qutrit Clifford+T unitaries must be elements of the ring*

$$\mathbb{Z}\left[\frac{1}{1-\zeta}\right] = \left\{ \frac{A}{(1-\zeta)^k} \middle| A \in \mathbb{Z}[\zeta], k \in \mathbb{N} \right\} \tag{51}$$

where

$$\mathbb{Z}[\zeta] = \left\{ \sum_{i=0}^{5} a_i(\zeta)^i \middle| \forall i, a_i \in \mathbb{Z} \right\} \tag{52}$$

Because $\frac{1}{\sqrt{2}}$ is not in the ring in Definition 10, it is impossible to exactly and deterministically emulate the qubit Hadamard gate utilizing single-qutrit Clifford+T gates. In general, the qubit Clifford operations do not neatly embed in the qutrit Clifford fragment.

In spite of this, we can still emulate quite a few qubit gates using qutrits. The qubit X gate can be emulated by the qutrit Clifford X_{01} gate. The qubit Z gate can be emulated by Clifford equivalence to the qutrit R gate:

$$\text{qubit } Z \overset{\mathsf{e}}{\hookleftarrow} X_{12}\, \mathrm{R}\, X_{12} \tag{53}$$

Likewise, the qubit S gate can be emulated by Clifford equivalence to the qutrit $\sqrt{R}$ gate:

$$\text{qubit } S \overset{\mathsf{e}}{\hookleftarrow} X_{12}\sqrt{R}X_{12} \tag{54}$$

Extending magic state injection of the R gate [3], despite being nowhere in the Clifford hierarchy, it can be shown that the $\sqrt{R} = \mathrm{diag}(1, 1, i)$ gate admits implementation by a repeat-until-success injection protocol of the $(1, 1, i)^\top$ state, where the probability of success rapidly converges to 1 with the number of rounds.

Lemma 4 ([8])**.** *The qubit CX gate can be emulated by qutrit Clifford+T gates unitarily without ancillae, with T-count 6 and Clifford CX-count 8.*

Proof. For reference, the decomposition by Bocharov, Roetteler, and Svore [8, Proposition 4] is given as a circuit diagram below:

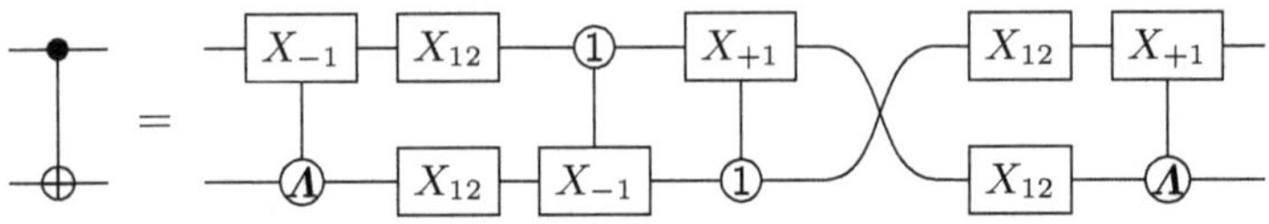

(55)

Like the qubit SWAP gate, the qutrit SWAP gate can be decomposed as three of the same two-qutrit gate applied successively in alternating directions. By optimizing thereafter, the Clifford CX-count can be further reduced to 8.

Lemma 5. *Utilizing one R gate, we can exactly emulate the qubit CZ gate.*

Proof.

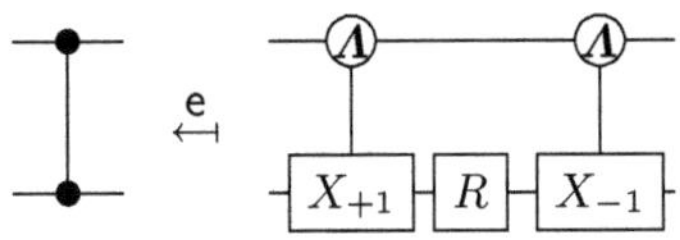

(56)

On qubit input states $|00\rangle$, $|01\rangle$, and $|10\rangle$, the states' sum modulo 3 is 0 or 1, and so no phase factor is applied. When the input state is $|11\rangle$, the states' sum modulo 3 is 2, and so a phase factor of -1 is applied.

This improves on the three R-count decomposition achieved by conjugating the control of the $|2\rangle$-controlled qubit Z gate from [80] by X_{12}.

D.2 The qubit $|+\rangle$ and $|-\rangle$ states

The qubit $|+\rangle$ state is qutrit Clifford equivalent to the Norell state, for which two magic state distillation protocols have been developed by [21,62]. Below, we present a new protocol for synthesizing the qubit $|+\rangle$ state which requires only Clifford+T gates, and computational basis state preparation and measurement. By applying one qutrit Clifford+T gate Clifford equivalent to the R gate before measurement, this protocol can be adapted to synthesize the qubit $|-\rangle$ state, which is Clifford equivalent to the i eigenstate of the qutrit Hadamard gate.

Lemma 6. *The qubit* $|+\rangle = \frac{|0\rangle+|1\rangle}{\sqrt{2}}$ *state can be synthesized with 2/3 probability of success using 3 qutrit T gates and qutrit stabilizer states, gates, and measurements, with one ancilla qutrit.*

Proof. The qutrit Clifford+T circuit below produces the qubit $|+\rangle$ state with 2/3 probability.

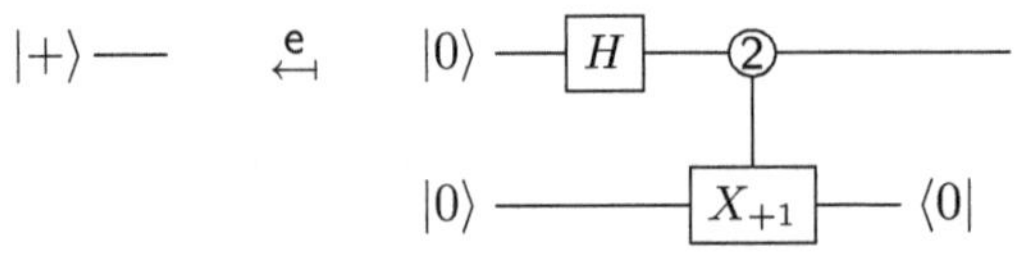

(57)

Before measurement, the state is in uniform superposition of $|00\rangle$, $|10\rangle$, and $|21\rangle$; measuring the bottom qubit to be the $|0\rangle$ state then produces the $\frac{|0\rangle+|1\rangle}{\sqrt{2}}$ state, equal to the qubit $|+\rangle$ state.

Corollary 1. *By application of the* $X_{12}RX_{12} = diag(1, -1, 1)$ *gate before measurement, the qubit* $|-\rangle = \frac{|0\rangle - |1\rangle}{\sqrt{2}}$ *state can be subsequently attained requiring only Clifford+T gates, and computational basis state preparation and measurement, with one ancilla qutrit.*

Corollary 2. *By Clifford equivalence, the above proposition and corollary respectively construct the Norell state* $\frac{|1\rangle + |2\rangle}{\sqrt{2}}$*, and the i eigenstate of the qutrit Hadamard gate* $|H, i\rangle = \frac{|1\rangle - |2\rangle}{2}$.

D.3 Qutrit Clifford+T Emulation of Multiqubit Toffoli and AND Gates

In this subsection, we present qutrit T-counts for ternary classical reversible circuit decompositions of multiple-controlled Toffoli gates, ancilla-free in the qutrit Clifford+T gate set, as presented in Table 2. We note that the gate counts (of either the CCX gate or the $|0\rangle$-controlled X gate, and the qutrit H gate) in the qutrit Toffoli+Hadamard gate set as defined in [29,66] are apparent from the decompositions. We will first present linear depth circuit decompositions, followed by logarithmic depth circuit decompositions—all with linear gate count.

A qubit Toffoli gate can be built from qutrit gates using the decomposition by Gokhale et al. [6,31]:

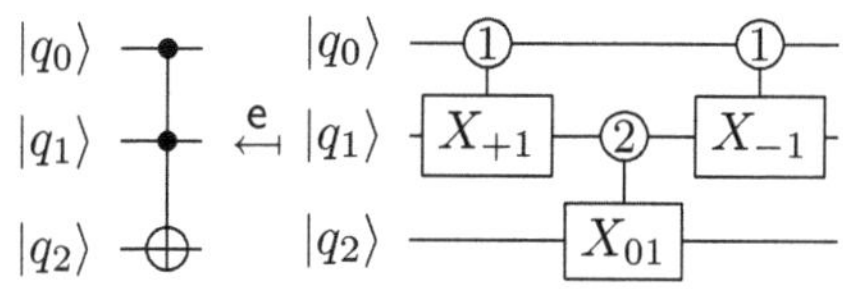

(58)

To exactly emulate the qubit CCX gate, the X gate on the target qutrit must be X_{01}. In their presentation of this gate they simply denoted the gate on the target qutrit as X, referring to any of the five single-qutrit computational basis permutation gates. The action of the gate is irrelevant for the cases where any of the input qutrits are in the $|2\rangle$ state, making it more efficient to use Clifford CX gates to replace the top two controlled gates:

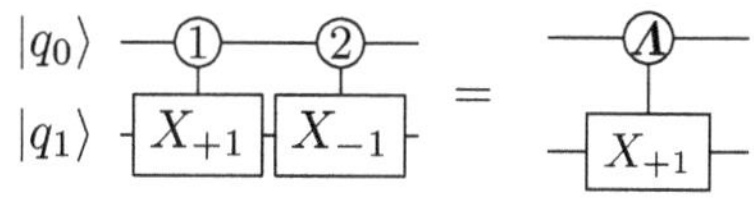

(59)

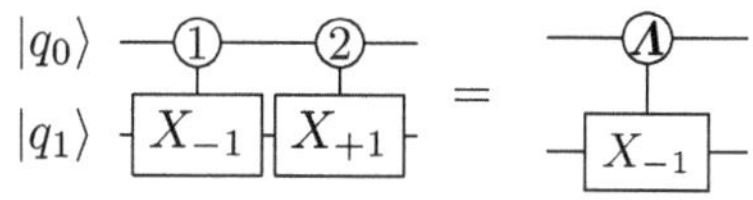

(60)

Without compromising the correctness of the qubit Toffoli gate, the above decomposition in Eq. (58) was modified by Bocharov, Roetteler, and Svore as follows [8, Proposition 6]:

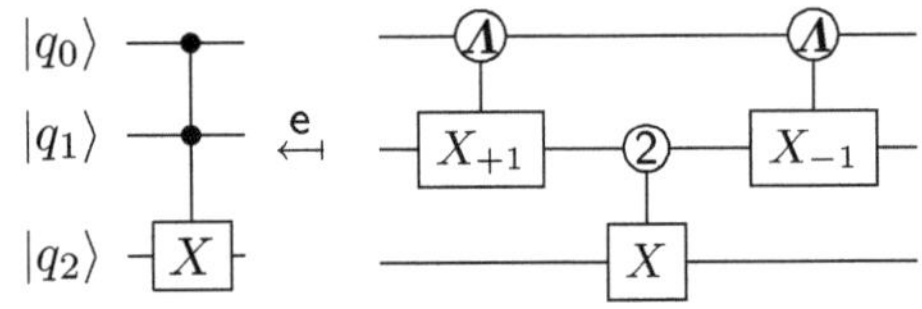

(61)

They concluded that the qubit CCX gate takes 15 T-gates to emulate with qutrit Clifford+T gates, taking the bottom gate to be the $|2\rangle$-controlled X_{01} gate, as the X_{01} gate emulates the qubit X gate. They lower the T-count to 12 by adding one clean ancilla.

We show that the T-count can be 12 without ancillae, by $|2\rangle$-controlling an emulation of the qubit X gate instead of the X_{01} gate.

Proposition 4. *The $|2\rangle$-controlled qubit X gate, which executes the qubit X gate if and only if the control qutrit is in the $|2\rangle$ state, can be emulated fault-tolerantly by a two-qutrit Clifford+T unitary without ancillae, with a T-count of 12.*

Proof. The decomposition is as follows. Recall that each of the 4 $|2\rangle$-controlled $X_{\pm 1}$ gates has a T-count of 3.

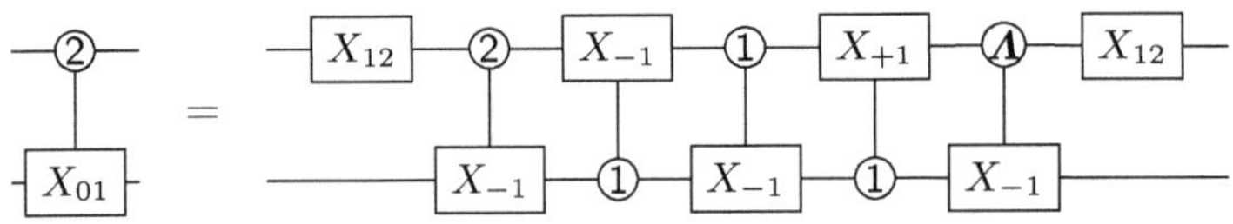

(62)

Corollary 3. *By Eq. (61), the qubit CCX gate can be emulated unitarily without ancillae using Clifford+T gates, with T-count 12.*

For the CCZ gate, from [80, Proposition 5.5]:

Proposition 5. *The qubit CCZ gate can be emulated unitarily without ancillae using Clifford+R gates, with R-count 3 and Clifford CX-count 5.*

Proof. Consider the qubit CCX gate emulation in Eq. (61). If instead the controlled gate on the target is the $|2\rangle$-controlled qubit Z gate in [80, Corollary 5.4], which has R-count 3 and Clifford CX-count 3, the emulated gate is the qubit CCZ gate.

The most straightforward way to generalize this to the qubit multiple-controlled Toffoli is the following linear gate count and linear depth decomposition:

Proposition 6. *The technique of emulating the qubit Toffoli can be generalized to n controls, and for any unitary U which can be $|2\rangle$-controlled.*

Proof.

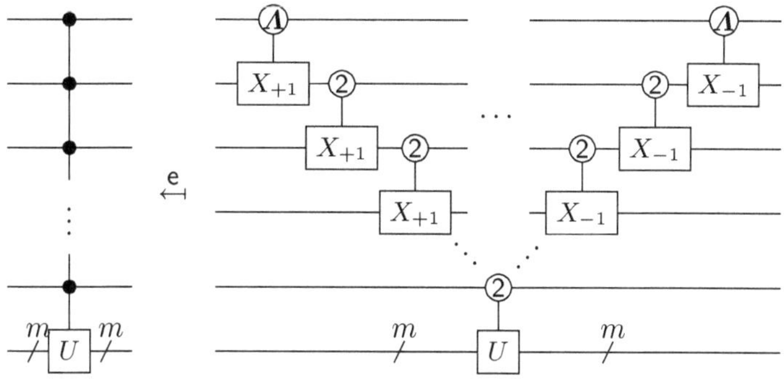

(63)

As each $|2\rangle$-controlled $X_{\pm 1}$ gate is comprised of three qutrit T gates, the T-count is $6(n-2)$ plus the cost of implementing the $|2\rangle$-controlled unitary.

Corollary 4. *As the qubit Toffoli gate $|2\rangle$-controlled qubit X gate can be constructed with T-count 12 according to Proposition 4, the qubit generalized Toffoli with n controls can be unitarily emulated without ancillae using qutrit Clifford+T gates, with T-count of exactly $6n$.*

This is an improvement over [8, Corollary 9], which emulates the qubit CCC-NOT gate (i.e. $n = 3$) with T-count 18 using two clean ancillas, or T-count 21 using one clean ancilla.

In logarithmic depth, qubit multiple-controlled Toffoli gate can be built from qutrit Toffoli gates [6,31]. Gokhale et al. [31] leveraged the $|22\rangle$-controlled gate to construct a qutrit emulation of the qubit Toffoli with n controls, with circuit depth logarithmic in n. We reprint their decomposition in Fig. 3a. They cited the decomposition for the $|22\rangle$-controlled X gates by Di and Wei, in terms of qubit Clifford+T gates pairwise between the three qutrit computational basis states. As far as we know, a protocol to simultaneously error correct for these three gate sets has not been formulated.

Using the decomposition for $|22\rangle$-controlling any qutrit unitary V from [83, Lemma 1] to build $|22\rangle$-controlled X_{12} in 51 T gates, we adapt their decomposition in Fig. 3a to the qutrit Clifford+T gateset. We thereby achieve linear qutrit T-count for the qubit generalized Toffoli gate, whilst retaining the desirable properties of logarithmic circuit depth and no logical ancillae needed (i.e. only using those necessary for magic state injection). We find it to be more efficient in qutrit T-count to modify each of their $|22\rangle$-controlled X_{+1} gates to $|22\rangle$-controlled X_{12} gates, for a constant factor improvement in lowering the T-count. To further decrease the resource requirements, we note that all boundary (either the inputs or outputs are qubits) $|22\rangle$-controlled gates in this decomposition are overconstrained; substituting them with our CCX_{+1} unitary decomposition in Eq. (58) with T-count 3 suffices.

Despite this decomposition being linear in T-count, the coefficient of linearity is quite high, given that our decomposition for the $|22\rangle$-controlled X_{12} gate has T-count 51. It is the first fault-tolerant decomposition for it and we have not

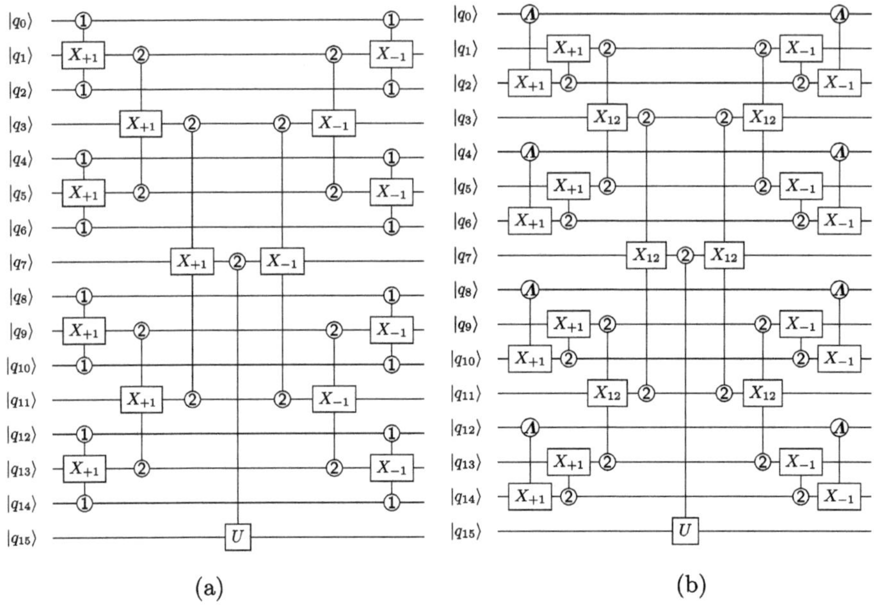

Fig. 3. (a) Qubit Generalized Toffoli gate emulation using intermediate qutrits by Gokhale et al. [31, Figure 5]. (b) We modified the left circuit to optimize T-count, given that we presently have a lower T-count decomposition for the $|22\rangle$-controlled X_{12} gate than the $|22\rangle$-controlled X_{+1} gate.

yet attempted to optimize this, reason being that there is a far more efficient construction using the n-ary AND gate familiar from binary classical computing, implemented on superconducting qutrits in [17], and resynthesized here in qutrit Clifford+T.

Proposition 7. *Consider the n-ary binary AND gate, which returns 1 iff all binary inputs are 1, and 0 otherwise. It can be emulated unitarily by Clifford+T gates without ancillae, in log(n) depth, with T-count* $3n - 3$ *and Clifford CX-count* $4n - 4$.

Proof. This follows from the equivalent well-known construction in classical reversible computation. The idea is to apply the T-count 3 emulation of the binary AND gate from Lemma 1 $n - 1$ times, as a binary tree structure. This generalizes to any positive integer n. The $n = 7$ case is shown below:

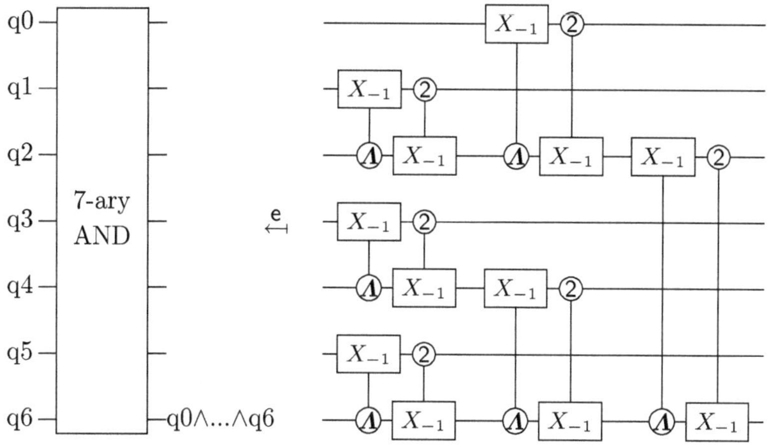

(64)

At first glance, it may seem that with the exception of the AND'd output, the other outputs can be disregarded. However, they are necessary for the gate as a whole to be unitary and thus reversible. At the end of this section, we will demonstrate the usefulness of being able to compute and uncompute the n-ary binary AND gate.

This means that the multiple-controlled qubit Toffoli admits the following decomposition when n-ary AND is available [17], for which we computed the T-count:

Theorem 1. *The qubit C^n X gate can be emulated unitarily without ancillae in qutrit Clifford+T gates in O(log(n)) depth, with T-count exactly* $6n$ *and Clifford CX-count* $8n$.

Proof. First apply the n-ary binary AND gate emulation of Proposition 7 with T-count $3(n-1)$ and Clifford CX-count $4(n-1)$, where the bottommost output wire is the AND'd output. Then, we apply the qubit CX gate emulation of Lemma 4 controlled on the AND'd output, targeting the target of the C^n X gate, with T-count 6 and Clifford CX-count 8. Finally, we uncompute the n-ary binary AND gate by applying its inverse, also with T-count $3(n-1)$ and Clifford CX-count $4(n-1)$.

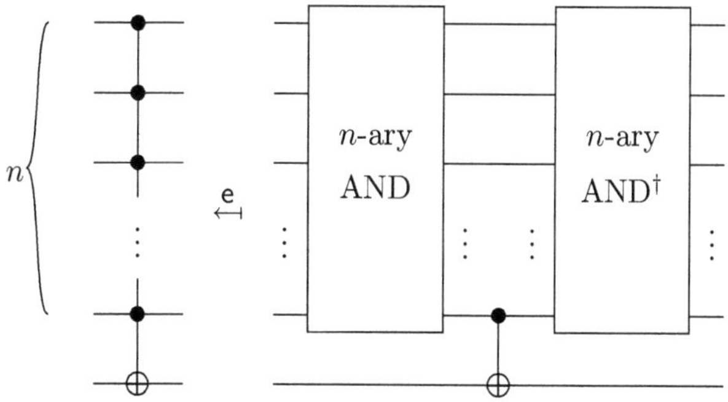

(65)

The T-count totals exactly $6n$ and the Clifford CX-count totals exactly $8n$.

Corollary 5. *This construction can be generalized to gates of the form $C^n\ U$, controlled on $|1\rangle^{\otimes n}$ for qubit inputs, where U is any target unitary acting on m qudits for which a controlled version, for some type of control, can be built.*

References

1. Aharonov, D.: A simple proof that toffoli and hadamard are quantum universal (2003). https://arxiv.org/abs/quant-ph/0301040
2. Anderson, B.E., Sosa-Martinez, H., Riofrío, C.A., Deutsch, I.H., Jessen, P.S.: Accurate and robust unitary transformations of a high-dimensional quantum system. Phys. Rev. Lett. **114**, 240401 (2015). https://doi.org/10.1103/PhysRevLett.114.240401. https://link.aps.org/doi/10.1103/PhysRevLett.114.240401
3. Anwar, H., Campbell, E.T., Browne, D.E.: Qutrit magic state distillation. New J. Phys. **14**(6), 063006 (2012). https://doi.org/10.1088/1367-2630/14/6/063006. https://iopscience.iop.org/article/10.1088/1367-2630/14/6/063006
4. Backens, M.: The zx-calculus is complete for stabilizer quantum mechanics. New J. Phys. **16**(9), 093021 (2014). https://doi.org/10.1088/1367-2630/16/9/093021
5. Bækkegaard, T., Kristensen, L.B., Loft, N.J.S., Andersen, C.K., Petrosyan, D., Zinner, N.T.: Realization of efficient quantum gates with a superconducting qubit-qutrit circuit. Sci. Rep. **9**(1), 13389 (2019). https://doi.org/10.1038/s41598-019-49657-1
6. Baker, J.M., Duckering, C., Gokhale, P., Brown, N.C., Brown, K.R., Chong, F.T.: Improved quantum circuits via intermediate qutrits. ACM Trans. Quantum Comput. **1**(1), 1–25 (2020)
7. de Beaudrap, N., Bian, X., Wang, Q.: Techniques to reduce $\pi/4$-parity-phase circuits, motivated by the ZX calculus. Electron. Proc. Theor. Comput. Sci. **318**, 131–149 (2020). https://doi.org/10.4204/eptcs.318.9
8. Bocharov, A., Roetteler, M., Svore, K.M.: Factoring with qutrits: Shor's algorithm on ternary and metaplectic quantum architectures. Phys. Rev. A **96**(1), 012306 (2017). https://doi.org/10.1103/PhysRevA.96.012306. http://link.aps.org/doi/10.1103/PhysRevA.96.012306
9. Booth, R.I., Carette, T.: Complete zx-calculi for the stabiliser fragment in odd prime dimensions, vol. 241, pp. 24:1–24:15. Schloss Dagstuhl – Leibniz-Zentrum für Informatik (2022). https://doi.org/10.4230/LIPICS.MFCS.2022.24. https://drops.dagstuhl.de/entities/document/10.4230/LIPIcs.MFCS.2022.24
10. Brock, B.L., et al.: Quantum error correction of qudits beyond break-even. Nature **641**(8063), 612–618 (2025). https://doi.org/10.1038/s41586-025-08899-y. https://www.nature.com/articles/s41586-025-08899-y
11. Brown, T., et al.: Trade off-free entanglement stabilization in a superconducting qutrit-qubit system. Nat. Commun. **13**(1), 3994 (2022). https://doi.org/10.1038/s41467-022-31638-0
12. Campbell, E.T.: The smallest interesting colour code (2016). https://earltcampbell.com/2016/09/26/the-smallest-interesting-colour-code/
13. Campbell, E.T., Anwar, H., Browne, D.E.: Magic-state distillation in all prime dimensions using quantum reed-muller codes. Phys. Rev. X **2**(4), 041021 (2012). https://doi.org/10.1103/PhysRevX.2.041021. https://link.aps.org/doi/10.1103/PhysRevX.2.041021

14. Campbell, E.T., Howard, M.: Unified framework for magic state distillation and multiqubit gate synthesis with reduced resource cost. Phys. Rev. A **95**(2) (2017). https://doi.org/10.1103/physreva.95.022316
15. Cao, S., et al.: Emulating two qubits with a four-level transmon qudit for variational quantum algorithms. Quantum Sci. Technol. **9**(3), 035003 (2024). https://doi.org/10.1088/2058-9565/ad37d4
16. Chi, Y., et al.: A programmable qudit-based quantum processor. Nat. Commun. **13**(1), 1166 (2022). https://doi.org/10.1038/s41467-022-28767-x
17. Chu, J., et al.: Scalable algorithm simplification using quantum AND logic. Nat. Phys. **19**(1), 126–131 (2023). https://doi.org/10.1038/s41567-022-01813-7. https://www.nature.com/articles/s41567-022-01813-7
18. Coecke, B., Duncan, R.: Interacting quantum observables: categorical algebra and diagrammatics. New J. Phys. **13**(4), 043016 (2011). https://doi.org/10.1088/1367-2630/13/4/043016
19. Cowtan, A., Dilkes, S., Duncan, R., Simmons, W., Sivarajah, S.: Phase gadget synthesis for shallow circuits. In: Coecke, B., Leifer, M. (eds.) Proceedings 16th International Conference on Quantum Physics and Logic, Chapman University, Orange, CA, USA, 10–14 June 2019. Electronic Proceedings in Theoretical Computer Science, vol. 318, pp. 213–228. Open Publishing Association (2020). https://doi.org/10.4204/EPTCS.318.13
20. Cui, S.X., Wang, Z.: Universal quantum computation with metaplectic anyons. J. Math. Phys. **56**(3), 032202 (2015). https://doi.org/10.1063/1.4914941
21. Dawkins, H., Howard, M.: Qutrit magic state distillation tight in some directions. Phys. Rev. Lett. **115**, 030501 (2015). https://doi.org/10.1103/PhysRevLett.115.030501. https://link.aps.org/doi/10.1103/PhysRevLett.115.030501
22. Dutta, S., Wang, S., Baksi, A., Chattopadhyay, A., Maitra, S.: On exact space-depth trade-offs in multi-controlled toffoli decomposition (2025). https://arxiv.org/abs/2502.01433
23. Garvie, L., Duncan, R.: Verifying the smallest interesting colour code with quantomatic. Electron. Proc. Theor. Comput. Sci. **266**, 147–163 (2018). https://doi.org/10.4204/eptcs.266.10
24. Gedik, Z., et al.: Computational speed-up with a single qudit. Sci. Rep. **5**(1), 14671 (2015). https://doi.org/10.1038/srep14671
25. Gidney, C.: Halving the cost of quantum addition. Quantum **2**, 74 (2018). https://doi.org/10.22331/q-2018-06-18-74
26. Gidney, C., Jones, N.C.: A cccz gate performed with 6 t gates (2021). https://arxiv.org/abs/2106.11513
27. Giles, B., Selinger, P.: Exact synthesis of multiqubit clifford+t circuits. Phys. Rev. A **87**(3) (2013). https://doi.org/10.1103/physreva.87.032332
28. Glaudell, A.N., Ross, N.J., Taylor, J.M.: Canonical forms for single-qutrit clifford+t operators. Ann. Phys. **406**, 54–70 (2019). https://doi.org/10.1016/j.aop.2019.04.001
29. Glaudell, A.N., Ross, N.J., Wetering, J.V.D., Yeh, L.: Exact Synthesis of Multiqutrit Clifford-Cyclotomic Circuits (2024). http://arxiv.org/abs/2405.08136
30. Godfrin, C., et al.: Operating quantum states in single magnetic molecules: implementation of grover's quantum algorithm. Phys. Rev. Lett. **119**, 187702 (2017). https://doi.org/10.1103/PhysRevLett.119.187702. https://link.aps.org/doi/10.1103/PhysRevLett.119.187702
31. Gokhale, P., Baker, J.M., Duckering, C., Brown, N.C., Brown, K.R., Chong, F.T.: Asymptotic improvements to quantum circuits via qutrits. In: Proceedings

of the 46th International Symposium on Computer Architecture, pp. 554–566. ACM, Phoenix Arizona (2019). https://doi.org/10.1145/3307650.3322253. https://dl.acm.org/doi/10.1145/3307650.3322253

32. Goss, N., et al.: High-fidelity qutrit entangling gates for superconducting circuits. Nat. Commun. **13**(1), 7481 (2022). https://doi.org/10.1038/s41467-022-34851-z. https://www.nature.com/articles/s41467-022-34851-z
33. Gosset, D., Kliuchnikov, V., Mosca, M., Russo, V.: An algorithm for the t-count. Quantum Info. Comput. **14**(15–16), 1261–1276 (2014)
34. Gottesman, D.: Stabilizer codes and quantum error correction. Ph.D. thesis, California Institute of Technology (1997). https://doi.org/10.48550/arXiv.quant-ph/9705052
35. Gottesman, D.: Theory of fault-tolerant quantum computation. Phys. Rev. A **57**(1), 127–137 (1998). https://doi.org/10.1103/physreva.57.127
36. Gottesman, D.: 9.1 Concatenated Codes, pp. 141–144. Textbook Manuscript Preprint (2024). http://www.cs.umd.edu/~dgottesm/QECCbook-2024.pdf
37. Gunderman, L.G.: Beyond integral-domain stabilizer codes. Phys. Rev. A **112**, 062430 (2025). https://doi.org/10.1103/4y6f-xx6s. https://link.aps.org/doi/10.1103/4y6f-xx6s
38. Hadzihasanovic, A., Ng, K.F., Wang, Q.: Two complete axiomatisations of pure-state qubit quantum computing. In: Proceedings of the 33rd Annual ACM/IEEE Symposium on Logic in Computer Science, LICS 2018, pp. 502–511. Association for Computing Machinery, New York, NY, USA (2018). https://doi.org/10.1145/3209108.3209128
39. Hrmo, P., et al.: Native qudit entanglement in a trapped ion quantum processor. Nat. Commun. **14**(1), 2242 (2023). https://doi.org/10.1038/s41467-023-37375-2
40. Hu, X.M., Guo, Y., Liu, B.H., Huang, Y.F., Li, C.F., Guo, G.C.: Beating the channel capacity limit for superdense coding with entangled ququarts. Sci. Adv. **4**(7), eaat9304 (2018). https://doi.org/10.1126/sciadv.aat9304. https://www.science.org/doi/abs/10.1126/sciadv.aat9304
41. Huang, J., Li, S.M., Yeh, L., Kissinger, A., Mosca, M., Vasmer, M.: Graphical CSS code transformation using ZX calculus. Electron. Proc. Theor. Comput. Sci. **384**, 1–19 (2023). https://doi.org/10.4204/eptcs.384.1
42. Jones, C.: Low-overhead constructions for the fault-tolerant toffoli gate. Phys. Rev. A **87**, 022328 (2013). https://doi.org/10.1103/PhysRevA.87.022328. https://link.aps.org/doi/10.1103/PhysRevA.87.022328
43. Joshi, R., et al.: Probing hadron scattering in lattice gauge theories on qudit quantum computers (2025). https://arxiv.org/abs/2507.12614
44. Kabir, A., Nguyen, S., Ghosh, S., Kiran, T., Kim, I.H., Huang, Y.: Sdim: a qudit stabilizer simulator (2025). https://arxiv.org/abs/2511.12777
45. Khattar, T., Gidney, C.: Rise of conditionally clean ancillae for efficient quantum circuit constructions. Quantum **9**, 1752 (2025). https://doi.org/10.22331/q-2025-05-21-1752
46. Khesin, A.B., Lu, J.Z., Shor, P.W.: Universal graph representation of stabilizer codes. PRX Quantum **6**, 040325 (2025). https://doi.org/10.1103/1gjs-2rhx. https://link.aps.org/doi/10.1103/1gjs-2rhx
47. Kissinger, A.: Phase-free ZX diagrams are CSS codes (...or how to graphically grok the surface code) (2022). http://arxiv.org/abs/2204.14038
48. Kissinger, A., van de Wetering, J.: Picturing Quantum Software: An Introduction to the ZX-Calculus and Quantum Compilation. Preprint (2024). https://github.com/zxcalc/book/

49. Kubica, A., Yoshida, B., Pastawski, F.: Unfolding the color code. New J. Phys. **17**(8), 083026 (2015)
50. Li, C., Preskill, J., Xu, Q.: Transversal dimension jump for product QLDPC codes (2025). https://arxiv.org/abs/2510.07269
51. Li, C., Yeh, L.: Transversal and in Quantum Codes (2026). https://arxiv.org/abs/2603.04548
52. Li, S.M., Mosca, M., Ross, N.J., van de Wetering, J., Zhao, Y.: A complete and natural rule set for multi-qutrit clifford circuits. Electron. Proc. Theor. Comput. Sci. **426**, 23–78 (2025). https://doi.org/10.4204/eptcs.426.2
53. Lysaght, L., Goubault, T., Sinnott, P., Mansfield, S., Emeriau, P.E.: Quantum circuit compression using qubit logic on qudits (2024). https://arxiv.org/abs/2411.03878
54. Mato, K., Hillmich, S., Wille, R.: Compression of qubit circuits: mapping to mixed-dimensional quantum systems. In: 2023 IEEE International Conference on Quantum Software (QSW), pp. 155–161 (2023). https://doi.org/10.1109/QSW59989.2023.00027
55. Mato, K., Ringbauer, M., Burgholzer, L., Wille, R.: MQT Qudits: a software framework for mixed-dimensional quantum computing (2024). https://arxiv.org/abs/2410.02854
56. Meth, M., et al.: Simulating two-dimensional lattice gauge theories on a qudit quantum computer. Nat. Phys. **21**(4), 570–576 (2025). https://doi.org/10.1038/s41567-025-02797-w
57. Miao, K.C., et al.: Overcoming leakage in quantum error correction. Nat. Phys. **19**(12), 1780–1786 (2023). https://doi.org/10.1038/s41567-023-02226-w. https://www.nature.com/articles/s41567-023-02226-w
58. Nakanishi, K.M., Todo, S.: Systematic construction of multi-controlled pauli gate decompositions with optimal t-count (2024). https://arxiv.org/abs/2410.00910
59. Petit, L., et al.: Design and integration of single-qubit rotations and two-qubit gates in silicon above one kelvin (2022)
60. Pino, J.M., et al.: Demonstration of the trapped-ion quantum CCD computer architecture. Nature **592**(7853), 209–213 (2021). https://doi.org/10.1038/s41586-021-03318-4
61. Poór, B., Booth, R.I., Carette, T., van de Wetering, J., Yeh, L.: The qupit stabiliser zx-travaganza: simplified axioms, normal forms and graph-theoretic simplification. Electron. Proc. Theor. Comput. Sci. **384**, 220–264 (2023). https://doi.org/10.4204/eptcs.384.13
62. Prakash, S.: Magic state distillation with the ternary golay code. Proc. Roy. Soc. A Math. Phys. Eng. Sci. **476**(2241), 20200187 (2020). https://doi.org/10.1098/rspa.2020.0187. https://royalsocietypublishing.org/doi/abs/10.1098/rspa.2020.0187
63. Prakash, S., Jain, A., Kapur, B., Seth, S.: Normal form for single-qutrit clifford+t operators and synthesis of single-qutrit gates. Phys. Rev. A **98**(3) (2018). https://doi.org/10.1103/physreva.98.032304
64. Ranchin, A.: Depicting qudit quantum mechanics and mutually unbiased qudit theories. Electron. Proc. Theor. Comput. Sci. **172**, 68–91 (2014). https://doi.org/10.4204/eptcs.172.6
65. Ringbauer, M., et al.: A universal qudit quantum processor with trapped ions. Nat. Phys. **18**(9), 1053–1057 (2022). https://doi.org/10.1038/s41567-022-01658-0. https://www.nature.com/articles/s41567-022-01658-0
66. Roy, P., van de Wetering, J., Yeh, L.: The qudit zh-calculus: generalised toffoli+hadamard and universality. Electron. Proc. Theor. Comput. Sci. **384**, 142–170 (2023). https://doi.org/10.4204/eptcs.384.9

67. Selinger, P.: Quantum circuits of t-depth one. Phys. Rev. A **87**(4), 042302 (2013). https://doi.org/10.1103/PhysRevA.87.042302
68. Sheldon, S., Magesan, E., Chow, J.M., Gambetta, J.M.: Procedure for systematically tuning up cross-talk in the cross-resonance gate. Phys. Rev. A **93**, 060302 (2016). https://doi.org/10.1103/PhysRevA.93.060302
69. Shende, V.V., Markov, I.L.: On the cnot-cost of toffoli gates. Quantum Info. Comput. **9**(5), 461–486 (2009)
70. de Silva, N.: Efficient quantum gate teleportation in higher dimensions. Proc. Roy. Soc. A Math. Phys. Eng. Sci. **477**(2251) (2021). https://doi.org/10.1098/rspa.2020.0865
71. Srivastav, V., et al.: Quick quantum steering: overcoming loss and noise with qudits. Phys. Rev. X **12**(4) (2022). https://doi.org/10.1103/physrevx.12.041023
72. Steane, A.M.: Active stabilization, quantum computation, and quantum state synthesis. Phys. Rev. Lett. **78**, 2252–2255 (1997). https://doi.org/10.1103/PhysRevLett.78.2252. https://link.aps.org/doi/10.1103/PhysRevLett.78.2252
73. Steane, A.M.: Active stabilization, quantum computation, and quantum state synthesis. Phys. Rev. Lett. **78**(11), 2252–2255 (1997). https://doi.org/10.1103/physrevlett.78.2252
74. Townsend-Teague, A., Meichanetzidis, K.: Simplification Strategies for the Qutrit ZX-Calculus (2022). https://doi.org/10.48550/arXiv.2103.06914
75. Vlasov, A.Y.: Some notes on quantum information theory and emerging computing technologies (2015). https://arxiv.org/abs/1102.2890
76. Wang, Q.: Qutrit ZX-calculus is Complete for Stabilizer Quantum Mechanics (2018). https://doi.org/10.48550/arXiv.1803.00696. http://arxiv.org/abs/1803.00696. arXiv:1803.00696
77. Wang, Q., Bian, X.: Qutrit dichromatic calculus and its universality. Electron. Proc. Theor. Comput. Sci. **172**, 92–101 (2014). https://doi.org/10.4204/eptcs.172.7
78. Weggemans, J.R., et al.: Solving correlation clustering with QAOA and a rydberg qudit system: a full-stack approach. Quantum **6**, 687 (2022). https://doi.org/10.22331/q-2022-04-13-687
79. van de Wetering, J.: Constructing quantum circuits with global gates. New J. Phys. **23**(4), 043015 (2021). https://doi.org/10.1088/1367-2630/abf1b3
80. Wetering, J.v.d., Yeh, L.: Building Qutrit Diagonal Gates from Phase Gadgets (2023). https://doi.org/10.48550/arXiv.2204.13681
81. Yeh, L.: Transdimensional quantum computation: the graphical novel. Ph.D. thesis, University of Oxford (2026)
82. Yeh, L., Huang, J., Kissinger, A., Li, S.M., van de Wetering, J.: A three-way normal form for stabiliser codes across zx diagrams, circuits, and tableaus (2026), in preparation
83. Yeh, L., van de Wetering, J.: Constructing All Qutrit Controlled Clifford+T gates in Clifford+T, pp. 28–50. Springer (2022). https://doi.org/10.1007/978-3-031-09005-9_3
84. Yu, N., Duan, R., Ying, M.: Five two-qubit gates are necessary for implementing the toffoli gate. Phys. Rev. A **88**, 010304 (2013). https://doi.org/10.1103/PhysRevA.88.010304. https://link.aps.org/doi/10.1103/PhysRevA.88.010304
85. Zi, W., Li, Q., Sun, X.: Optimal synthesis of multi-controlled qudit gates. In: 2023 60th ACM/IEEE Design Automation Conference (DAC), pp. 1–6 (2023). https://doi.org/10.1109/DAC56929.2023.10247925

A Reversible Crumbling Abstract Machine for Plotkin's Call-by-Value

Nicolò Pizzo(✉) and Claudio Sacerdoti Coen

Alma Mater Studiorum - Università di Bologna, Bologna, Italy
nicolo.pizzo2@unibo.it

Abstract. Landauer's embeddings enable the reversibility of computations for non-reversible programming languages, augmenting each intermediate state with enough data to reconstruct the previous state. An interesting research question is therefore to try to reduce the space overhead required. In this work we propose a Landauer's embedding for Plotkin's call-by-value calculus (CbV). In order to control the computational complexity of CbV and turn the number of β-steps into a cost model, CbV is typically implemented via reduction machines. We show that one machine, that has not received much attention, exhibits a particularly compact Landauer's embedding, requiring only constant space overhead for each step.

Keywords: lambda-calculus · call-by-value · abstract machines · reversible computation

1 Introduction

The goal of this paper is to equip Plotkin's weak Call-by-Value [20] calculus with a Landauer's embedding [15]. Doing so in a naive way would result in an expensive cost, at each step linear in the size of the term to be reduced, as for each reduction step we need to remember the position of the redex and enough information to recover it from the reduct. For example, to recover $(\lambda x.y)M$ from its reduct y one needs to remember all of M. Moreover, it is well-known [2] that under weak CbV there are families of λ-terms that incur in the phenomenon of size-explosion, where intermediate terms may grow exponentially in the number of steps with respect to the initial term. Therefore nobody implements the λ-calculus naively. Consider for example the term $(\lambda x.xx\dots x)v$ that reduces to $vv\dots v$: the cost of this step entails the cost of copying v as many times as the number of x, and when the size of the argument v is roughly equal to the size of the abstraction, the total cost is quadratic in the size of the term (and the Landauer's embedding would require a linear amount of space to recover the redex).

Partially funded by the INdAM/GNCS project MARQ (CUP_E53C24001950001).

C. Aubert and L. Roversi (Eds.): RC 2026, LNCS 16626, pp. 41–58, 2026.
https://doi.org/10.1007/978-3-032-30839-9_2

All efficient implementations of λ-calculi avoid the size explosion by replacing immediate substitutions with some form of explicit or delayed substitution, eventually collected in larger data structures called environments. With explicit substitutions $(\lambda x.xx\ldots x)v$ reduces in constant time to $(x\ \mathrm{x}\ldots x)\,[x{\leftarrow}v]$ where $[x{\leftarrow}v]$ is sometimes written as `let x = v in t`. It is also obvious that a Landauer's embedding now only needs to record the position of the reduct to fully restore the redex. However, remembering the position of a redex still needs a linear amount of information on the size of the term and one can wonder if it is possible to use only a constant size. Moreover some explicitly substituted occurrences need to trigger the substitution anyway to advance in the computation and thus more ingredients are required.

Abstract Machines. Abstract reduction machines provide for efficient implementations of λ-calculi where all details are taken care. In particular an abstract machine uses explicit substitutions (ES), controls their firing and implements steps to search for the next redex. The most efficient machines for CbV have a complexity that is only bi-linear in the number of reduction steps of the calculus and in the size of the initial term to be evaluated. Among them there is a family of machines that are called Crumbling Abstract Machines (CAM) [3].

In this work we show a new variant of CAM whose complexity is indeed bi-linear and that admits a particularly compact Landauer's embedding, requiring just additional O(1) space for each machine step. We call the resulting machine the Reversible Crumbling Abstract Machine (RCAM).

Crumbling. Equipping λ-calculus with sharing enables a representation of terms where a sharing point can be placed wherever the constructor of a term occurs. This is the same principle used for A-normal forms [11]. For example, the term $(yx)(xy)$ can be represented as $(z_1z_2)\,[z_1{\leftarrow}yx]\,[z_2{\leftarrow}xy]$. The crumbling technique [3] applies this concept hereditarily to completely avoid the immediate nesting of applications: for instance $(x_1(x_2\lambda x_3.x_3))x_4$ is written as $(y_1x_4)\,[y_1{\leftarrow}x_1y_2]\,[y_2{\leftarrow}x_2\lambda x_3.x_3]$. The various variants of crumbling differ in what is still allowed in the terms to be substituted. For example, in some variants $[y_2{\leftarrow}x_2\lambda x_3.x_3]$ is not allowed and must become $[y_2{\leftarrow}x_2y_3]\,[y_3{\leftarrow}\lambda x_3.x_3]$. Not every variant has been exploited in the literature so far: they are introduced and studied when interesting properties of them are noticed, like in [9] where one variant is noticed to be related to Miller's positive λ-calculus [18].

This work builds upon the concept of crumbling abstract machines presented in [3], and aims at showing a new variant of the crumbling for which the Landauer's embedding becomes trivial and economic. We dub the variant the *crumbling* because it is the one that inserts the highest number of explicit substitutions by only allowing as terms to be substituted either λ-abstractions or applications of a variable to another variable. In particular, by ruling out also the case of a variable substituted by another variable, it fully embraces the notion of practical variables [8] by ruling out variables from the set of values where they semantically belong, leading to speed ups in implementations of reduction machines.

This work shows that the finest crumbling is also an interesting variant, as it enables to achieve a Landauer's embedding with a reasonable spatial overhead.

Contributions. The contributions of this work consist in presenting an economic Landauer's embedding for Plotkin's closed CbV by means of a Landauer's embedding for a new reduction machine for the finest crumbling, that we call *Reversible Crumbling Abstract Machine (RCAM).* In addition to showing the reversibility of the machine, we establish the usual properties of crumbling machines, i.e. that the machine implements correctly the calculus and that the computational complexity of a computation made of forward steps only is bilinear in the number of reduction steps of the calculus and the size of the initial term to be reduced.

TERMS	VALUES
$u, t ::= v \mid ut$	$v := x \mid \lambda x.t$
RIGHT V-CONTEXT	REDUCTION RULE
$R ::= \langle\cdot\rangle \mid tR \mid Rv$	$R\langle(\lambda x.t)v\rangle \rightarrow_{\beta_v} R\langle t\{x{\leftarrow}v\}\rangle$

Fig. 1. Plotkin's Closed CbV calculus

2 The Calculus

In this section we first introduce Plotkin's (closed) CbV calculus in its right-to-left variant, describing the basic notions employed by the calculus. We then move on to present the finest crumbling – a variant of the crumbling technique – that is part of the focus of this work.

2.1 Plotkin's Call-by-Value Calculus

In *Plotkin's CbV (λ_{Plot})* terms are defined mutually with values: a term is either a value, or an application of terms; values are either variables or λ-abstractions. In this work we specifically address Plotkin's closed (weak) CbV. In this paper we mainly use the notion of (weak) *right v-context* (see Fig. 1) where holes are outside abstractions and on the right of the hole may only appear values.

Evaluating Terms. Terms are evaluated in weak (i.e. outside abstractions) Call-by-Value: a $\rightarrow_{\beta_v}$ reduction step is triggered by plugging in a context the application of a value to a λ-abstraction, called a *redex.* The reduction step then results in plugging the body of the abstraction where we *immediately substitute* the bound variable with the applied value. The particular shape of right v-contexts forces the rightmost redex to be the first evaluated. To change the evaluation order one would just pick left v-contexts instead and, mutatis mutandis, all the rest of the paper would stand.

An important property of Plotkin's closed CbV is *harmony* that at once characterizes normal forms and rules out stuck computations.

Lemma 1 (Plotkin's CbV harmony). *Let t be a closed term. Then t it is β_v-normal if and only if t is a value.*

Bites	Crumbled Values
$b ::= xy \mid v$	$v ::= \lambda x.\,[*\leftarrow y] \mid \lambda x.E$
Environments	Environment Context
$E ::= \epsilon \mid E\,[x\leftarrow b]$	$C ::= E\,[x\leftarrow \langle\cdot\rangle]$

Reduction Rules

$$E\,[z\leftarrow xy]\,E_v \rightarrow_{m_1} E\,[z\leftarrow b']\,E' E_v \qquad (*)$$

$$E\,[z\leftarrow xy]\,E_v \rightarrow_{m_2} E\,[z\leftarrow E_v(y_1')]\,E_v \qquad (\#)$$

$$\rightarrow_{Cr} = \rightarrow_{m_1} \cup \rightarrow_{m_2}$$

$$(*)\;\; E_v(x)^{\alpha} = \lambda x_1.\,[*\leftarrow b]\,E \qquad ([*\leftarrow b]\,E)\{x_1\leftarrow y\} = [*\leftarrow b']\,E'$$

$$(\#)\;\; E_v(x) = \lambda x_1.\,[*\leftarrow y_1] \qquad [*\leftarrow y_1]\,\{x_1\leftarrow y\} = [*\leftarrow y_1']$$

Fig. 2. Finest crumbled calculus

2.2 The Finest Crumbled Calculus

The idea behind crumbling consists in avoiding the nesting of applications, so that we can write terms such as $(tu)s$ and $t(us)$ as $(xs)\,[x\leftarrow tu]$ and $(tx)\,[x\leftarrow us]$ by using explicit substitutions: this is the most common way for representing the crumbling, and represents the most idiomatic way for representing environment entries. Many forms of crumbling have been presented, from more coarse in [3], to finer ones in [9]. The form we present – that we call *finest crumbling* – is an even finer form of crumbling where an explicit substitution may only appear either as an application of variables or as a λ-abstraction.

We add to this representation another ingredient: the concept of *returning a value* by explicitly assigning it to the special variable $*$ via an explicit substitution. This is reminiscent of Pascal where the return value is the one assigned to the function name in the body of a function. Thanks to $*$ we can get rid of terms altogether and just work with *environments* that are sequences of explicit substitutions. The whole term to be reduced is thus turned into an environment and the same applies to the bodies of abstractions. We present the concept with the following example.

Example 1. Consider the closed term $t := \lambda x.\lambda y.(xx)(yy)$: by using the fresh variables z_1, z_2, the finest crumble representation of the term is

$$[*\leftarrow\lambda x.\,[*\leftarrow\lambda y.\,[*\leftarrow z_1 z_2]\,[z_1\leftarrow xx]\,[z_2\leftarrow yy]]]$$

Note that assignments to $*$ only make sense in the leftmost position of an environment.

By the reduction rules defined in Fig. 2, the crumbling is stable, i.e. a crumble reduces to another crumble. The only tricky point will be given by representing and evaluating the identity and constant functions, i.e. $\lambda x.x$, $\lambda x.y$ as they can only be represented assigning a variable to $*$, which is only allowed in this ad-hoc case since a variable is neither an abstraction nor an application of a variable to a variable.

The original motivation for crumbling is that it trivializes the search for the next redex, as we visit the entries of the environment in a right-to-left order until we find the redex, independently by the particular strategy (right-to-left vs left-to-right) that we want to capture. Consider the following Plotkin term evaluated in a right-to-left order, where v_1, v_2 and v_3 are some values. The colour *blue* indicates the term that is already evaluated, the colour *red* indicates the part of the term that is yet to be evaluated, and the colour *green* indicates the next term to be evaluated.

$$(II)\boxed{(v_1 v_2)}\,v_3$$

The right-to-left crumbled representation of the term would be the following

$$[*\leftarrow z_1 z_2][z_1\leftarrow \underline{I}][z_2\leftarrow z_3 z_4][z_3\leftarrow \underline{I}][z_4\leftarrow z_5 z_6][z_5\leftarrow z_7 z_8]\boxed{z_7\leftarrow \underline{v_1}}\,\boxed{z_8\leftarrow \underline{v_2}}\,\boxed{z_6\leftarrow \underline{v_3}}$$

On the other hand, the same Plotkin term evaluated with a left-to-right strategy would be "coloured" as follows

$$\boxed{(II)}\,(v_1 v_2)v_3$$

whereas its left-to-right crumbled representation would be

$$[*\leftarrow z_1 z_2][z_2\leftarrow z_3 z_4]\,\boxed{z_4\leftarrow \underline{v_3}}\,[z_3\leftarrow z_5 z_6]\,\boxed{z_6\leftarrow \underline{v_2}}\,\boxed{z_5\leftarrow \underline{v_1}}\,[z_1\leftarrow z_7 z_8][z_8\leftarrow \underline{I}][z_7\leftarrow \underline{I}]$$

It is evident then that the strategy adopted to search the next β-redex is induced by the crumbling process, as it is embedded in the ordering of the concatenation of the environment. The net effect is that the reduction machine for crumbled calculi, that we will introduce later, does not need applicative stacks nor dumps or other additional data structures that are required to implement the search for the next redex in the scenario of non crumbled calculi.

Syntax: Crumbled Forms and Environment Contexts. Terms from λ_{Plot} are replaced by crumbles, which take the form of an environment. An environment is defined as a sequence of explicit substitution of bites for variables; a bite is either a crumbled value or an application of two variables.

Definition 1 (Crumble). *A crumble E is an environment where the leftmost explicit substitution is in the form $[*{\leftarrow}b]$, i.e. $E = [*{\leftarrow}b]\, E'$*

We also introduce *environment contexts* for which the plugging operation is defined as $C\langle b\rangle = (\mathrm{E}\,[z{\leftarrow}\langle\cdot\rangle])\langle b\rangle = E\,[z{\leftarrow}b]$. A crumbled value is either the crumbling of an identity or constant function, or the crumbling of an abstraction whose body is a generic term. Note that this distinction is needed for ensuring that every term has a corresponding crumble. For example, $\lambda x.y$ has crumbled form $[*{\leftarrow}\lambda x.\,[*{\leftarrow}y]]$: obviously, this crumble could not be represented with the rule we give for generic abstractions, so we need to explicitly define syntax and rules for these terms.

We postpone the discussion on the evaluation of crumbled forms to Subsect. 2.4 after the presentation of the mutual translations between λ_{Plot}-terms and their corresponding crumbled forms.

2.3 The finest crumbling Translation and Its Inverse

Let Λ and $\underline{\Lambda}$ denote respectively the set of all λ_{Plot}-terms and the set of all finest crumbled forms. We define the crumbling translation $\underline{\cdot} : \Lambda \to \underline{\Lambda}$ in order to translate a term from the λ_{Plot} calculus to its crumbled representation. Together with this translation function we define the *read-back* function $\cdot_{\downarrow} : \underline{\Lambda} \to \Lambda$ that is the inverse function of the crumbling, used to translate a crumble back to its λ_{Plot} representation. The formal definitions of the functions are summarized in Fig. 3. Note that the read-back of an environment context may not always be a context: as a simple example, let $C := [*{\leftarrow}\lambda x.\,[*{\leftarrow}xx]\,[x{\leftarrow}\langle\cdot\rangle]]$ then $C_{\downarrow} = \lambda x.\langle\cdot\rangle\langle\cdot\rangle$ that is not a context. We will however provide some invariants so that all environment contexts we consider will read-back to Plotkin's right v-contexts.

CRUMBLING

$$\underline{xy} = [*{\leftarrow}xy] \qquad \underline{\lambda x.y} = [*{\leftarrow}\lambda x.\,[*{\leftarrow}y]] \qquad \underline{\lambda x.t} = [*{\leftarrow}\lambda x.\underline{t}]$$

$$\begin{aligned}
\underline{uy} &= [*{\leftarrow}xy]\,[x{\leftarrow}b]\,E && \text{with } x \text{ fresh, } \underline{u} = [*{\leftarrow}b]\,E\\
\underline{xu'} &= [*{\leftarrow}xy]\,[y{\leftarrow}b']\,E' && \text{with } y \text{ fresh, } \underline{u'} = [*{\leftarrow}b']\,E'\\
\underline{uu'} &= [*{\leftarrow}xy]\,[x{\leftarrow}b]\,E\,[y{\leftarrow}b']\,E' && \text{with } x,\, y \text{ fresh, } \underline{u} = [*{\leftarrow}b]\,E, \underline{u'} = [*{\leftarrow}b']\,E'
\end{aligned}$$

READ-BACK

$$(xy)_{\downarrow} = xy \qquad (\lambda x.\,[*{\leftarrow}y])_{\downarrow} = \lambda x.y \qquad (\lambda x.E)_{\downarrow} = \lambda x.E_{\downarrow}$$

$$[*{\leftarrow}b]_{\downarrow} = b_{\downarrow} \qquad (E\,[x{\leftarrow}b])_{\downarrow} = E_{\downarrow}\{x{\leftarrow}b_{\downarrow}\}$$

$$[*{\leftarrow}\langle\cdot\rangle]_{\downarrow} = \langle\cdot\rangle \qquad (E\,[z{\leftarrow}\langle\cdot\rangle])_{\downarrow} = E_{\downarrow}\{z{\leftarrow}\langle\cdot\rangle\}$$

Fig. 3. Translation from λ_{Prot}-terms to crumbled forms and back

Size of Terms

$$|x| = 1 \qquad |\lambda x.t| = |t| + 1 \qquad |uu'| = |u| + |u'| + 1$$

Size of bites

$$|\lambda x.\, [* \leftarrow y]| = 2 \qquad |\lambda x.E| = |E| + 1 \qquad |xy| = 2$$

$$\begin{array}{llll} \text{Size of Environments} & |\epsilon| = 0 & |E\,[z \leftarrow b]| & = |E| + |b| \\ \text{Length of Environments} & |\epsilon|_{len} = 0 & |E\,[z \leftarrow b]|_{len} & = |E|_{len} + 1 \end{array}$$

Domains

$$\begin{array}{ll} \mathrm{dom}(\epsilon) & = \emptyset \\ \mathrm{dom}(E\,[x \leftarrow b]) & = \mathrm{dom}(E) \cup \{x\} \end{array}$$

Free Variables

$$\begin{array}{ll} \mathrm{fv}(\epsilon) & = \emptyset \\ \mathrm{fv}(E\,[z \leftarrow \lambda x.E']) & = \mathrm{fv}(E) \backslash \{z\} \cup (\mathrm{fv}(E') \backslash \{x\}) \\ \mathrm{fv}(E\,[z \leftarrow xy]) & = \mathrm{fv}(E) \backslash \{z\} \cup \{x, y\} \\ \mathrm{fv}(E\,[z \leftarrow \lambda x.\, [* \leftarrow y]]) & = \mathrm{fv}(E) \backslash \{z\} \cup (\{y\} \backslash \{x\}) \end{array}$$

Bound Variables

$$\begin{array}{ll} \mathrm{bv}(\epsilon) & = \emptyset \\ \mathrm{bv}(E\,[z \leftarrow \lambda x.E']) & = \mathrm{bv}(E) \cup \{x\} \cup \mathrm{bv}(E') \\ \mathrm{bv}(E\,[z \leftarrow xy]) & = \mathrm{bv}(E) \\ \mathrm{bv}(E\,[z \leftarrow \lambda x.\, [* \leftarrow y]]) & = \mathrm{bv}(E) \cup \{x\} \end{array}$$

Fig. 4. Measures for terms, bites and environments; bound and free variables, domains

Properties of Crumbling. We now define some notions that characterize the properties of crumbling; we will also show that these properties become invariants of the reduction on crumbles.

In the top half of Fig. 4 we define the measures of size for terms and environments, together with the definition of length of an environment, that simply counts the number of entries it contains.

The definitions of free variables and bound variables are extended from λ_{Plot} to environments with the auxiliary notion of *domains*. The formal definitions are shown in the bottom half of Fig. 4.

Definition 2 (Well-named crumbles). *A crumble E is* well-named *if all the variables appearing in* $\mathrm{dom}(E)$ *are pair-wise distinct and* $\mathrm{dom}(E) \cap \mathrm{bv}(E) = \emptyset$ *and if $E = E_1\,[z \leftarrow b]\,E_2$ then $z \notin \mathrm{fv}(b) \cup \mathrm{fv}(E_2)$.*

Lemma 2 (Properties of Crumbling). *For every closed term t:*

1. *Freshness: $\underline{t}$ is well-named.*
2. *Closure: $\underline{t}$ is closed.*
3. *Bodies: each body in $\underline{t}$ is the translation of a term.*
4. *Size: the size $|\underline{t}|$ is linear with respect to the size of the initial term t.*
5. *Contextual decoding: if $\underline{t} = E_1\,[z \leftarrow xy]\,E_2$ then $(E_1\,[z \leftarrow \langle\cdot\rangle])_{\downarrow}$ is a right v-context.*

EXAMPLE

$$[* \leftarrow z_1 z_2]\, [z_1 \leftarrow \lambda x.\, [* \leftarrow x z_3]\, [z_3 \leftarrow x x]]\, [z_2 \leftarrow \lambda y.\, [* \leftarrow y]]$$
$$\to_{m_1} [* \leftarrow z_2 z_4]\, [z_4 \leftarrow z_2 z_2]\, [z_1 \leftarrow \lambda x.\, [* \leftarrow x z_3]\, [z_3 \leftarrow x x]]\, [z_2 \leftarrow \lambda y.\, [* \leftarrow y]]$$
$$\to_{m_2} [* \leftarrow z_2 z_4]\, [z_4 \leftarrow \lambda y.\, [* \leftarrow y]]\, [z_1 \leftarrow \lambda x.\, [* \leftarrow x z_3]\, [z_3 \leftarrow x x]]\, [z_2 \leftarrow \lambda y.\, [* \leftarrow y]]$$
$$\to_{m_2} [* \leftarrow \lambda y.\, [* \leftarrow y]]\, [z_4 \leftarrow \lambda y.\, [* \leftarrow y]]\, [z_1 \leftarrow \lambda x.\, [* \leftarrow x z_3]\, [z_3 \leftarrow x x]]\, [z_2 \leftarrow \lambda y.\, [* \leftarrow y]]$$

Fig. 5. Example of evaluation of the crumbling of the term $(\lambda x.x(xx))\lambda y.y$

2.4 Evaluating Crumbles

The reduction rules for the finest crumbled calculus are also given in Fig. 2. All environment marked E_v in the paper are required to be *v-environment*:

Definition 3 (v-environment). *An environment is a $v-$environment if each entry maps a variable to a value, i.e. is in the form $[x \leftarrow v]$.*

The use of E_v in the rules forces evaluation to proceed in a right-to-left order and therefore the longest v-environment suffix of the environment represents the already fully-evaluated part.

By $E_v(x)^\alpha$ we denote the crumbled value obtained from $E_v(x)$ by α-renaming the variables in the domain of $E_v(x)$ with fresh ones, so that the resulting concatenation of environments is well-named.

The reduction rules are triggered either if the abstraction is an identity/constant function (in which case m_2 is triggered) or if it is a more generic function (in which case m_1 is triggered). The rule m_1 substitutes the β-redex with the bite (on which is performed the immediate substitution $\{x_1 \leftarrow y\}$) returned by the λ-abstraction and concatenates the tail of the environment contained in the body of the abstraction mapped to the variable x. Since the rule m_2 is triggered when the abstraction is an identity or constant function, it substitutes the β-redex with the value mapped to variable of the body on which is performed the immediate substitution $\{x_1 \leftarrow y\}$ and does not need to perform concatenation. Figure 5 shows an example of how evaluation works.

Definition 4 (Reachable Crumble). *A crumble is reachable if it is obtained by a sequence of $\to_{Cr}$-steps starting from the translation $\underline{t}$ of a closed term t.*

Definition 5 (v-crumble). *A v-crumble is a v-environment that is also a crumble, i.e. its in the form $[* \leftarrow v]\, E_v$.*

Lemma 3 (Harmony for finest crumbling). *A reachable crumble E is normal if and only if it is a v-crumble.*

The next Lemma shows that the properties of the finest crumbling shown in Lemma 2 are preserved during the evaluation.

Lemma 4 (Invariants of finest crumbling). *For a reachable crumble E:*

1. *Freshness: E is well-named.*
2. *Closure:* $\mathrm{fv}(E) = \emptyset$.
3. *Bodies: each body occurring in E is a subterm (up to renaming and substitution of variable to variable) of the initial crumble.*
4. *Contextual decoding: if $E = E_1 [z \leftarrow xy] E_2$ then the context $(E_1 [z \leftarrow \langle \cdot \rangle])_\downarrow$ is a right v-context.*

The bodies invariant is often referred to as the *subterm invariant* [3,9] and is mostly used for the complexity analysis, as it forces the size of the terms duplicated along an evaluation to be bound by the size of the initial term, since the size is not affected by α-renaming and variable substitution. Moreover, nobody has ever discovered so far a machine that does not exhibit this invariant but still has a reasonable complexity. In our work we will also exploit the subterm invariant and the contextual decoding invariant to prove that the transitions $\rightarrow_{m_1}, \rightarrow_{m_2}$ project on evaluation steps $\rightarrow_{\beta_v}$ in λ_{Plot}.

In the next section we show that evaluating the crumbles faithfully implements the semantics of λ_{Plot}, i.e. the finest crumbling *implements* λ_{Plot}.

2.5 The Implementation Theorem

In [6] it is proven that, given

- a calculus to be implemented, whose transition relation, made deterministic if necessary via an evaluation strategy, is $\rightarrow$
- an abstract machine M given by a set of states and a transition relation $\rightsquigarrow_M$ that splits into
  - principal transitions $\rightsquigarrow_p$, corresponding to evaluation steps on the calculus;
  - overhead transitions $\rightsquigarrow_o$, that take care of looking for the next redex and have no computational meaning in the calculus
- a decoding $\cdot_\downarrow$ of states of M into terms

M correctly implements $\rightarrow$ via $\cdot_\downarrow$ whenever $(M, \rightarrow, \cdot_\downarrow)$ forms an *implementation system*, i.e. whenever the following conditions hold true:

1. Initialization: there is an encoding $\underline{\cdot}$ of terms such that $\underline{t}_\downarrow = t$.
2. Principal projection: $s \rightsquigarrow_p s'$ implies $s_\downarrow \rightsquigarrow s'_\downarrow$.
3. Overhead transparency: $s \rightsquigarrow_o s'$ implies $s_\downarrow = s'_\downarrow$.
4. Determinism: $\rightsquigarrow_M$ is deterministic.
5. Halt: M final states (to which no transition applies) decode to $\rightarrow$-normal terms.
6. Overhead termination: $\rightsquigarrow_o$ terminates.

As shown in [6], a machine implementation is such that there is a perfect match between the number of steps of the strategy and the number of principal transitions of the execution.

Theorem 1 (Machine Implementation). *If a machine M, a strategy $\rightarrow$ on λ-terms and a decoding $\cdot_\downarrow$ form an implementation system, then:*

1. *Executions to derivations: for any M-execution* $\rho : \underline{t} \rightsquigarrow^*_M s$ *there is a* $\rightarrow$*-derivation* $d : t \rightarrow^* s_\downarrow$.
2. *Derivations to executions: for every* $\rightarrow$*-derivation* $d : t \rightarrow^* u$ *there is an M-execution* $\rho : \underline{t} \rightsquigarrow^*_M s$ *such that* $s_\downarrow = u$.
3. *Principal Matching: in both previous points the number* $|\rho|_p$ *of principal transitions in* ρ *is exactly the length* $|d|$ *of the derivation* d*, i.e.* $|d| = |\rho|_p$.

The finest crumbled calculus is not yet an abstract machine, but the implementation theorem is general enough to apply nevertheless. In particular we can apply the theorem where the states of the machine are the reachable crumbles, the principal transitions are $\rightarrow_{m_1}, \rightarrow_{m_2}$ and the set of overhead transitions is empty, since the discovery of the redex is embedded in the principal transitions.

Theorem 2 (Implementation System). *The finest crumbling, Plotkin's weak CbV evaluation* $\rightarrow_{\beta_v}$ *and the read-back* $(\cdot)_\downarrow$ *form an implementation system.*

Proof. We present just a rough sketch of the proof. For the full proof details see the full paper version [19].

1. Initialization: by induction on the shape of t. It exploits the well-naming property (see Lemma 4.1).
2. Principal projection: by the contextual decoding property (see Lemma 4.4) the read-back of the left hand side of each principal rule is a redex, i.e. the application of a value to an abstraction in a right v-context.
3. Determinism: to show determinism it suffices to show that the two multiplicative steps cannot be triggered simultaneously, but their side conditions are mutually exclusive.
4. Halt: by closure property (see Lemma 4.2), if the crumble is normal then it is a v-crumble that reads-back to a value that is normal in Plotkin's CbV. □

3 The Reversible Crumbling Abstract Machine

The finest crumbled calculus shown in the previous section solves the size-explosion issue with the use of explicit substitutions; however the search of the redex is embedded in the reduction rules, so the cost of each transition is not constant yet.

We present the Reversible Crumbling Abstract Machine (RCAM) that enacts the Landauer's embedding through a history stack, and that presents an explicit transition for searching the next redex. We then show that the complexity of the RCAM is bi-linear in the number of β_v-steps and the size of the initial term, that each transition of the machine is reversible and deterministic, and that the amount of additional space added to the history stack entry by each reduction rule is constant.

3.1 The Machine

The Reversible Crumbling Abstract Machine (RCAM) is easily derived from the finest crumbling calculus by enriching crumbles with an explicit pointer in the machine states that is used to visit the environment entries from right to left until a redex is found. Moreover a history stack is coupled with the crumble under evaluation to allow the reversibility of the transitions. Since the pointer already keeps track of where searching arrived, the entries in the history stack can be very concise: either the information that the pointer was moved, or the bite (of the form xy) that triggered the reduction step. The machine is formally defined in Fig. 6. The state of the machine is represented by three components: the *active environment*, the *evaluated environment* and the *history stack*. The splitting of the environment into active and evaluated corresponds nicely on paper to having a pointer into an environment. Indeed the read-back from machine states to crumbles just concatenates the two, dropping the history. In realistic implementations the pair of active and evaluated environments form a zipper [13] where each cell (explicit substitution) points to the next one that is on the left for the active part and on the right on the evaluated part.

HISTORY STACK

$$\mathcal{H} ::= \epsilon \mid \langle\rangle : \mathcal{H} \mid \langle x, y\rangle : \mathcal{H}$$

STATE

$$S ::= (E, E_v, \mathcal{H})$$

INITIALIZATION

$$\iota(E) = (E, \epsilon, \epsilon)$$

READ-BACK

$$(E, E_v, \mathcal{H})_{\Downarrow} = EE_v$$

TRANSITIONS

ACT. ENV	EV. ENV	HIST		ACT. ENV	EV. ENV	HIST	
$E_1\,[x{\leftarrow}v]$	E_v	H	$\overset{sea^b}{\underset{sea}{\leftrightsquigarrow}}$	E_1	$[x{\leftarrow}v] : E_v$	$\langle\rangle : H$	
$E_1\,[z{\leftarrow}xy]$	E_v	H	$\overset{m_1^b}{\underset{m_1}{\leftrightsquigarrow}}$	$E_1\,[z{\leftarrow}b']\,E'$	E_v	$\langle x, y\rangle : H$	(*)
$E_1\,[z{\leftarrow}xy]$	E_v	H	$\overset{m_2^b}{\underset{m_2}{\leftrightsquigarrow}}$	E_1	$[z{\leftarrow}E_v(y_1')]\,E_v$	$\langle x, y\rangle : H$	(#)

$$(*)\quad E_v(x)^\alpha = \lambda x_1.\,[*{\leftarrow}b]\,E \qquad ([*{\leftarrow}b]\,E)\{x_1{\leftarrow}y\} = [*{\leftarrow}b']\,E'$$

$$(\#)\quad E_v(x) = \lambda x_1.\,[*{\leftarrow}y_1] \qquad [*{\leftarrow}y_1]\,\{x_1{\leftarrow}y\} = [*{\leftarrow}y_1']$$

$$\rightsquigarrow_f = \rightsquigarrow_{m_1} \cup \rightsquigarrow_{m_2} \cup \rightsquigarrow_{sea} \qquad \rightsquigarrow_b = \rightsquigarrow_{m_1^b} \cup \rightsquigarrow_{m_2^b} \cup \rightsquigarrow_{sea^b}$$

$$\rightsquigarrow_{rCr} = \rightsquigarrow_f \cup \rightsquigarrow_b$$

Fig. 6. Reversible Crumbling Abstract Machine

The Transitions. It is easy to see that the forward transitions $\rightsquigarrow_{m_1}, \rightsquigarrow_{m_2}$ are exactly the $\rightarrow_{m_1}, \rightarrow_{m_2}$ transitions of the finest crumbling calculus once read-back is applied and that the $\rightsquigarrow_{sea}$ is the identity up to read-back. In Subsect. 3.2 we will deeply discuss the reversibility of each transition.

Definition 6 (Reachable State). *A state is reachable if it is obtained by a sequence of evaluation steps in $\rightsquigarrow_{rCr}$ starting from the initialization $\iota(E)$ of a closed, well-named crumble E.*

The harmony property extends also to the RCAM. Since all machine rules require the evaluated environment to be a v-environment, proving harmony entails proving that in every reachable state the evaluated environment is always a v-environment. Therefore a concrete implementation of the machine can avoid to check whether the environment is indeed a v-environment.

Lemma 5 (Harmony for the RCAM). *A reachable by forward-only transitions state S is $\rightsquigarrow_f$-normal if and only if it is in the form $S = (\epsilon, E_v, \mathcal{H})$.*

Lemma 6 (Invariants for the RCAM). *Let S be a reachable by forward-only transitions state of the RCAM:*

1. *Freshness: S is well-named.*
2. *Closure: S is closed.*
3. *Rightmost: $S = (E, E_v, \mathcal{H})$ for some environment E, v-environment E_v and history stack $\mathcal{H}$.*

The Implementation Theorem. We prove now that, when restricted to forward transitions only, the RCAM correctly implements the finest crumbled calculus. We exploit once again the implementation theorem, this time also considering overhead transitions.

Lemma 7 (Implementation Theorem for the RCAM). *The RCAM, $\rightarrow_{Cr}$ evaluation and $(\cdot)_{\Downarrow}$ form an implementation system.*

Proof. The proof can be found in [19]. The only non trivial part is overhead termination: we will show in Sect. 3.3 that, when restricted to forward transitions only, the number of $\rightsquigarrow_{sea}$ transitions is bi-linear in the number of principal transitions and the maximal length of an environment in the initial crumble, so the $\rightsquigarrow_{sea}$ transition terminates. □

3.2 Reversing the Transitions

The new (backward) transitions $\rightsquigarrow_{m_1^b}, \rightsquigarrow_{m_2^b}, \rightsquigarrow_{sea^b}$ are the reverse of $\rightsquigarrow_{m_1}, \rightsquigarrow_{m_2}$, $\rightsquigarrow_{sea}$ respectively, and they exploit the history stack. From Fig. 6 we can see that the history stack will guide us in reversing each evaluation step, as we only have two scenarios:

- If the top of the stack is $\langle\rangle$, then the evaluation step was an overhead search transition, so we just need to move the pointer to the next cell on the right.

- If the top of the stack is $\langle x, y\rangle$, since we have saved x on the stack, we know exactly the value $E_v(x)$. From the shape of $E_v(x)$ we also understand if the step to be performed is $\rightsquigarrow_{m_1^b}$ or $\rightsquigarrow_{m_2^b}$. For the case $\rightsquigarrow_{m_1^b}$ only, from $E_v(x)$ we know the length of E', as $|E|_{len} = |E'|_{len}$, and we can remove $|E'|_{len}$ entries from the environment. Then in both cases we turn the substitution for z into $[z\leftarrow xy]$ and, in case of $\rightsquigarrow_{m_2^b}$, shift it back to the active environment.

Size of the History Entries. Note that the amount of information we save on the history stack is reasonably minimal, as we need to distinguish which transition led to the current state of the machine. Consider the following state of the machine where we have removed the history stack component

$$(\epsilon, [*\leftarrow\lambda x.\,[*\leftarrow x]]\,[z_1\leftarrow\lambda x.\,[*\leftarrow x]]\,[z_2\leftarrow\lambda x.\,[*\leftarrow x]])$$

We may reach this state in five different ways:

1. With a transition m_2 reducing the redex $y_1 y_2$, with the 4 possible combinations of $y_1, y_2 \in \{z_1, z_2\}$ i.e. starting from one of the possible states $([*\leftarrow y_1 y_2]\,, [z_1\leftarrow\lambda x.\,[*\leftarrow x]]\,[z_2\leftarrow\lambda x.\,[*\leftarrow x]])$ for $y_1, y_2 \in \{z_1, z_2\}$.
2. With a transition *sea* if the machine still needs to evaluate the last entry, i.e. starting from the state $([*\leftarrow\lambda x.\,[*\leftarrow x]]\,, [z_1\leftarrow\lambda x.\,[*\leftarrow x]]\,[z_2\leftarrow\lambda x.\,[*\leftarrow x]])$.

To distinguish the four scenarios described by the possible combinations of $z_1 z_2$, we need to save on the stack both variables in the bite associated to $*$; moreover, to distinguish the last scenario, we need to save something different on the stack: this is the role of $\langle\rangle$ in Fig. 6. Note that the amount of information we store on the history stack is small enough to be acceptable: the concrete implementation shown in [19] represents an explicit substitution $[x\leftarrow b]$ with a record in the heap that holds b together with a pointer to the previous substitution in the environment. In such an implementation the occurrences of the variable x are just pointers to the memory address of the record, i.e. variables are pointers and thus can be stored in $O(1)$ space. Therefore each history stack entry uses size $O(1)$ as well holding at most two pointers (the two variables).

Properties of Reversible Transitions and Computations. We now identify some properties of the reverse transitions of RCAM. The terminology is taken from [16] and [10] when applicable. Note, however, that since our language is sequential most properties of [16] hold trivially and therefore we skip them.

We define an *execution* $\rho : S_0 \rightsquigarrow^*_{rCr} S$ as a sequence of RCAM transitions that start in the initial state S_0 and end in S. A state S is said to be reachable through an execution ρ if $\rho : S_0 \rightsquigarrow^*_{rCr} S$.

Lemma 8 (Backward determinism). *The transitions $\rightsquigarrow_b$ are deterministic.*

Corollary 1 (Loop). *Let S' be any state of the RCAM, such that $S \rightsquigarrow_f S'$. Then the evaluation step can always be reverted, i.e. $S' \rightsquigarrow_b S$ and vice-versa.*

Corollary 2. *The sequence of a forward transition with a backward one represents the identity, i.e. if* $\rho : S_0 \rightsquigarrow_f S' \rightsquigarrow_b S$ *then* $S_0 = S$.

Lemma 9. *Given an execution* ρ *such that a state* S' *is reachable from an initial state* S_0 *through* ρ*, i.e.* $\rho : S_0 \rightsquigarrow^*_{rCr} S'$*, then* $\exists \rho' : S_0 \rightsquigarrow^*_f S'$.

Theorem 3 (Well-Foundedness). *There is no infinite reverse computation, i.e. we do not have sequences* $(S_i)_{i \in \mathbb{N}}$ *such that* $S_{i+1} \rightsquigarrow_f S_i$ *for all* $i \in \mathbb{N}$.

Theorem 4. *A reachable state* S *is* $\rightsquigarrow_b$*-normal if and only if it is initial.*

3.3 Complexity Analysis

We target now the cost analysis of the machine when restricted to forward rules only, with the aim of expressing the cost as a function of the number of principal transitions only. Of course we rule out backward rules otherwise the machine could perform and undo a search rule an unbounded number of time before doing the next principal rule.

Following [3], the cost analysis starts by bounding the number of search transitions in an execution ρ. Then, after discussing the cost of implementing single transitions, we will compose the two analyses to obtain the total cost, showing that the RCAM is bi-linear in the size of the initial crumble and the number of principal steps. Finally we will show that the cost of each backward transition is identical to that of its forward counterpart.

Number of Search Transitions. For the complexity analysis of the RCAM we will make use of the measure of size defined in Subsect. 2.2. We define the measure of length of a state of the RCAM as the length of its read-back, i.e. $|S|_{len} = |S_{\Downarrow}|_{len}$. Since after a multiplicative step the measure increases by the length of the body we need to concatenate, we also define the function $L(E)$ that bounds the length of the bodies occurring in E.

$$L(E) = \sup \{|E_b|_{len} : E_b \text{ is a body appearing in } E\}$$

The function can be extended to the states of the RCAM simply by using the read-back of the state.

Lemma 10. *Let* E *be a well-named crumble and let* $\rho : \iota(E) \rightsquigarrow^*_f S$ *an execution in the RCAM with* $S = (E_1, E_v, \mathcal{H})$*. Then* $|E_1|_{len} \leq |E|_{len} + |\rho|_p \cdot L(E) - |\rho|_{sea}$.

Corollary 3 (Number of Search transitions). *Let* t *be a closed term. For a normalizing forward steps only* ρ *in the RCAM starting from* $\iota(\underline{t})$*, we have* $|\rho|_{sea} \leq (|\rho|_p + 1) \cdot |t|$.

Cost of Forward Transitions. Since the read-back of a state of the machine returns a crumble, we will address the cost of transitions by talking in terms of crumbles and environments. Updating the history stack has constant cost and so it will not be part of the discussion. Computing $E_v(x)$ as well as appending environments can be implemented in $O(1)$ on a Random Access Machine as shown in [3] and [19].

The cost of each principal forward transition is bound by the size of the crumble in the abstraction that needs to by copied for α-renaming it and applying the variable-to-variable substitution. By the bodies invariant, the abstraction is the α-renaming of an abstraction present in the initial crumble. By Lemma 2.4, the size of the initial crumble is linear in the size of the initial term, therefore the cost of a principal forward transition is linear in the size of the initial term. The cost of $\rightsquigarrow_{sea}$ is clearly $O(1)$.

Cost of the Execution. By combining the analysis from the previous paragraphs, we obtain the following theorem

Theorem 5 (The RCAM is bi-linear). *For any closed, term t and any RCAM execution $\rho : \iota(\underline{t}) \rightsquigarrow_f^* S$, the cost of implementing ρ on a RAM is $O((|\rho|_p + 1) \cdot |t|)$.*

Theorem 6 (Space overhead of Landauer's embedding). *For any closed, term t and any RCAM execution $\rho : \iota(\underline{t}) \rightsquigarrow_f^* S$, the maximum size of the history during the execution ρ on a RAM is $O((|\rho|_p + 1) \cdot |t|)$.*

Proof. The space overhead of the embedding is given by the history, that grows monotonically during any execution, adding an $O(1)$ entry for each principal and search step. □

Cost of Backward Transitions. The costs of the backward transitions are identical to their forward counterpart. For $\rightsquigarrow_{sea^b}$ we just need to shift a substitution in a Zipper: as for $\rightsquigarrow_{sea}$, the operation costs $O(1)$. The case of $\rightsquigarrow_{m_2^b}$ is similar and costs $O(1)$ as well, exactly as $\rightsquigarrow_{m_2}$. For $\rightsquigarrow_{m_1^b}$, we need to remove the $|E'|_{len}$ substitutions that were concatenated during $\rightsquigarrow_{m_1}$: the cost for the single transition is then the same. For $\rightsquigarrow_{m_1^b}$ we could actually achieve a better result if we saved on the history stack also the variable z, as this would make the cost of $\rightsquigarrow_{m_1^b}$ $O(1)$, leading however to a trade-off between space and time.

4 Conclusions and Future Works

To the best of our knowledge we have presented the first Landauer's embedding for Plotkin's (weak, closed) CbV calculus that requires constant history overhead. The key idea was to made reversible a not yet explored variant of Crumbled Abstract Machine, a proven technology to implement call-by-value calculi with the best known asymptotic cost. We firmly believe that our approach scales seamlessly to other constructs like `if-then-else` or pattern matching over algebraic data types following the same pattern. For example, to accommodate boolean and `if-then-else` similarly to [3], one would add the following bites to the grammar: `true` and `false`, that would also be values, and `if x then y else z` where x, y, z are all variables; the only new history stack entry would be $\langle x, y, z\rangle$ to undo `if-then-else` reduction.

We also believe that the technique would scale as well to open call-by-value [5] and to strong call-by-value [7]. The latter could find applications in the implementation of interactive theorem provers where sometimes reduction is used during speculative proof-search, leading to the need for backtracking.

We conjecture the possibility to find cheap Landauer's embedding for some classes of reduction machines used to implement efficiently call-by-name and the much harder call-by-need, especially in the strong setting. However, the details could differ significantly from what is presented in this paper since the machines for call-by-need are more complicated.

Several reversible functional programming languages have been proposed in the literature, like [21]. Unlike the non reversible case, where Plotkin's CbV represents the core of the language, these languages are not extension of Plotkin's CbV. In particular they tend to exhibit a clear distinction between first-order data and reversible functions. Therefore we do not see any direct correlation between our contribution and that part of the literature.

An easy application of our work is to debugging. Indeed reversible debuggers like [1] have been available and appreciated since a long time. They are typically implemented using snapshots of the state that are taken regularly every n computational steps. In order to undo a step, the computation goes back to the last snapshot and it is then replayed from there. If we consider a standard Crumbled Abstract Machine as an implementation of CbV, taking a snapshot requires recording all the active environment, that is subject to future in-place updates, and a pointer to the v-environment, that will not change. The size of the active environment, and thus of each snapshot, would be $O(|\rho|_p + 1)|t_0|$. Therefore the cumulative amount of space required by the snapshots would be quadratic in $|\rho|_p$ and linear in $|t_0|$, while our RCAM only requires bi-linear space.

A reference implementation in OCaml of the RCAM can be found at https://github.com/Lapis-Team/rcam. An explanation is given in [19]. The implementation is meant for the reader to test the machine on some examples of her choice, to better understand the dynamics. Moreover it confirms that, even at low level, the complexity analysis of Subsect. 3.3 is correct.

4.1 Related Works

Other works have been presented on making abstract machines reversible in [14] and [12], with some space overhead. As it is stated in [14], the size of the overhead in [12] is not minimal, and it is clearly not bi-linear. Regarding the machine outlined in [14], we believe that the size of the overhead should be linear in the number of steps, depending on the actual implementation model. However, no complexity analysis is presented to confirm this. In comparison to the RCAM, the SEMCD machine is significantly more complex, having 14 forward transitions an 8-components states, whereas the RCAM only has 3 transitions and 3-components states.

Another less related line of research is given by the Interaction Abstract Machine (IAM) [17] and its derivation [4] that are naturally reversible but implement a trade-off between space and time that is heavily unbalanced versus space. Therefore, they do not attain the best bi-linear time complexity that our machine achieves.

References

1. ocamldebug. https://ocaml.org/manual/5.4/debugger.html
2. Accattoli, B.: Exponentials as substitutions and the cost of cut elimination in linear logic. Log. Methods Comput. Sci. **19**(4) (2023). https://doi.org/10.46298/lmcs-19(4:23)2023
3. Accattoli, B., Condoluci, A., Guerrieri, G., Sacerdoti Coen, C.: Crumbling abstract machines (2019). https://doi.org/10.1145/3354166.3354169
4. Accattoli, B., Dal Lago, U., Vanoni, G.: The machinery of interaction. In: Proceedings of the 22nd International Symposium on Principles and Practice of Declarative Programming, PPDP 2020, pp. 1–15. Association for Computing Machinery, New York, NY, USA (2020). https://doi.org/10.1145/3414080.3414108
5. Accattoli, B., Guerrieri, G.: Open call-by-value. In: Igarashi, A. (ed.) Programming Languages and Systems, pp. 206–226. Springer, Cham (2016). https://doi.org/10.1007/978-3-319-47958-3_12
6. Accattoli, B., Guerrieri, G.: Implementing open call-by-value. In: Dastani, M., Sirjani, M. (eds.) Fundamentals of Software Engineering, pp. 1–19. Springer, Cham (2017). https://doi.org/10.1007/978-3-319-68972-2_1
7. Accattoli, B., Guerrieri, G., Leberle, M.: Strong call-by-value and multi types. In: Ábrahám, E., Dubslaff, C., Tarifa, S.L.T. (eds.) Theoretical Aspects of Computing – ICTAC 2023, pp. 196–215. Springer, Cham (2023). https://doi.org/10.1007/978-3-031-47963-2_13
8. Accattoli, B., Sacerdoti Coen, C.: On the value of variables. In: Kohlenbach, U., Barceló, P., de Queiroz, R. (eds.) Logic, Language, Information, and Computation, pp. 36–50. Springer, Heidelberg (2014). https://doi.org/10.1007/978-3-662-44145-9_3
9. Accattoli, B., Sacerdoti Coen, C., Wu, J.H.: Positive Sharing and Abstract Machines (2025). https://doi.org/10.48550/arXiv.2506.14131
10. Danos, V., Krivine, J.: Reversible communicating systems. In: Gardner, P., Yoshida, N. (eds.) CONCUR 2004 - Concurrency Theory, pp. 292–307. Springer, Heidelberg (2004). https://doi.org/10.1007/978-3-540-28644-8_19
11. Flanagan, C., Sabry, A., Duba, B.F., Felleisen, M.: The essence of compiling with continuations. SIGPLAN Not. **39**(4), 502–514 (2004). https://doi.org/10.1145/989393.989443
12. Huelsbergen, L.: A logically reversible evaluator for the call-by-name lambda calculus. Int. J. Complex Syst. **46** (1996)
13. Huet, G.: The zipper. J. Funct. Program. **7**(5), 549–554 (1997). https://doi.org/10.1017/S0956796897002864

14. Kluge, W.: A reversible SE(M)CD machine. In: Koopman, P., Clack, C. (eds.) Implementation of Functional Languages, pp. 95–113. Springer, Heidelberg (2000). https://doi.org/10.1007/10722298_6
15. Landauer, R.: Irreversibility and heat generation in the computing process. IBM J. Res. Dev. **5**(3), 183–191 (1961). https://doi.org/10.1147/rd.53.0183
16. Lanese, I., Phillips, I., Ulidowski, I.: An axiomatic approach to reversible computation. In: Goubault-Larrecq, J., König, B. (eds.) Foundations of Software Science and Computation Structures, pp. 442–461. Springer, Cham (2020). https://doi.org/10.1007/978-3-030-45231-5_23
17. Mackie, I.: The geometry of interaction machine. In: Proceedings of the 22nd ACM SIGPLAN-SIGACT Symposium on Principles of Programming Languages, pp. 198–208 (1995)
18. Miller, D., Wu, J.H.: A positive perspective on term representation. In: Klin, B., Pimentel, E. (eds.) 31st EACSL Annual Conference on Computer Science Logic (CSL 2023). Leibniz International Proceedings in Informatics (LIPIcs), vol. 252, pp. 3:1–3:21. Schloss Dagstuhl – Leibniz-Zentrum für Informatik, Dagstuhl, Germany (2023). https://doi.org/10.4230/LIPIcs.CSL.2023.3
19. Pizzo, N., Sacerdoti Coen, C.: A reversible crumbling abstract machine for Plotkin's call-by-value (2026). https://arxiv.org/abs/2605.09179
20. Plotkin, G.D.: Call-by-name, call-by-value and the λ-calculus. Theoret. Comput. Sci. **1**(2), 125–159 (1975). https://doi.org/10.1016/0304-3975(75)90017-1
21. Yokoyama, T., Axelsen, H.B., Glück, R.: Towards a reversible functional language. In: De Vos, A., Wille, R. (eds.) Reversible Computation, pp. 14–29. Springer, Heidelberg (2012). https://doi.org/10.1007/978-3-642-29517-1_2

On Weak Bisimilarities in CCSK

Baptiste Vallée[1] and Ivan Lanese[2(✉)]

[1] École Normale Supérieure Paris-Saclay, Gif-sur-Yvette, France
[2] Olas Team, University of Bologna/INRIA, Bologna, Italy
ivan.lanese@gmail.com

Abstract. In the context of CCSK, a reversible extension of CCS, we study different notions of bisimilarity (strong/weak, forward-only/reversible) and highlight their differences and commonalities. In particular, for the weak reversible case, not previously studied in the literature, we propose two variants, dubbed directional and mixed bisimilarity, depending on whether τ actions should be in the same direction (forward/backward) as the action being matched or not. We show, in particular, that mixed bisimilarity is a congruence and completely abstracts away from τ actions.

Keywords: CCS · CCSK · Reversible Computation · Weak Bisimilarity · Behavioral Theory

1 Introduction

Building concurrent systems is challenging due to the complexity of reasoning about numerous possible interleavings, yet concurrency is essential in modern systems like the Internet, cloud computing, and parallel processing. Reversible computing, which allows systems to execute both forwards and backwards, recovering past states, has significant applications in low-energy computing [9], simulation [5], biological modeling [4,19], and program debugging [8,10,13]. Many of these applications involve concurrent systems, leading to the development of reversible extensions of concurrent process calculi such as CCS [7,18] and the π-calculus [6], and even of concurrent programming languages such as Erlang [11] and Go [17].

A main notion in the theory of process calculi is the notion of bisimilarity [20], allowing one to prove two processes equivalent, e.g., to prove an implementation equivalent to a more abstract specification. In particular, bisimilarity requires equivalent processes to be able to match each other actions, and in doing so going to processes which are still equivalent. While strong and weak bisimilarity (weak bisimilarity differs from the strong one as the former abstracts away from internal actions, focusing only on interactions with the context) have been extensively studied in concurrent systems, the literature lacks an analysis of weak bisimilarities in a reversible setting. Our study addresses this gap by investigating

C. Aubert and L. Roversi (Eds.): RC 2026, LNCS 16626, pp. 59–74, 2026.
https://doi.org/10.1007/978-3-032-30839-9_3

the relationships between different notions of bisimilarity (strong/weak, forward-only/reversible) in the context of CCSK [18], a causal-consistent reversible extension of Milner CCS [15]. In particular, in the definition of weak reversible bisimilarity, a main decision is whether auxiliary τ actions (representing internal steps) allowed in the simulation of some action α need to be in the same direction as α or not. The two alternatives lead to different equivalences.

We consider this work as a first step in the exploration of weak bisimilarity in a reversible setting, paving the way for a deeper exploration in the future. We claim as our main contributions the proposal of two notions of weak reversible bisimilarity (mixed bisimilarity in Definition 3.13 and directional bisimilarity in Definition 3.15, both in Sect. 3), the study of the relations between different notions of bisimilarity in CCSK (Sect. 4), and the study of which of these notions are congruences (Sect. 5). In particular, we show that mixed bisimilarity is a congruence (Theorem 5.6) and completely abstracts away from τ actions (Proposition 5.5 and Theorem 5.7). Another surprising result is that extending CCS bisimilarities to CCSK gives equivalences which are not congruences (Proposition 5.2), even when they are congruences in CCS, as in the case of strong bisimilarity.

2 CCSK

In this section we recall the main elements of CCSK, while referring to [18] for further details. We assume an infinite set of *Names* $\mathcal{A}$, ranged over by $a, b, c, \ldots$, and a disjoint infinite set of *Co-names* $\overline{\mathcal{A}}$, ranged over by $\overline{a}, \overline{b}, \overline{c}, \ldots$, where $\overline{*}$ is an operator such that $\overline{\overline{a}} = a$. We call *actions* the elements of $\mathcal{A} \cup \overline{\mathcal{A}} \cup \{\tau\}$ where $\tau \notin \mathcal{A}$ and $\overline{\tau}$ is undefined, ranged over by $\alpha, \beta, \ldots$ Intuitively, names represent input actions, co-names represent output actions, and τ is an internal synchronisation. CCS processes, which we shall also call *standard* processes, are given by:

$$P, Q := 0 \mid\mid \alpha.P \mid\mid P + Q \mid\mid P \,|\, Q \mid\mid (\nu a)P$$

Intuitively, 0 is the inactive process, $\alpha.P$ is a process that performs action α and continues as P, $P + Q$ is nondeterministic choice, $P \,|\, Q$ is parallel composition and restriction $(\nu a)P$ binds name a and the corresponding co-name $\overline{a}$ inside P. A name is *bound* if it is inside the scope of a restriction operator, *free* otherwise. Function $\mathtt{fn}(P)$ computes the set of free names in process P. We set this convention: unary operators bind stronger than binary operators.

CCSK extends CCS with the possibility of executing backwards. In order to remember which input interacted with which output while going forwards, fresh *keys* are created at each forward step, and the same key is used to label an input and the corresponding output during a synchronisation.

We denote the set of keys by $\mathtt{Keys}$, ranged over by $m, n, k, \ldots$. Prefixes, ranged over by π, are of the form $\alpha[m]$ or α. The former denotes that α has already been executed, the latter that it has not.

CCSK processes are given by:

$$P, Q := 0 \mid\mid \pi.P \mid\mid P + Q \mid\mid P \,|\, Q \mid\mid (\nu a)P$$

hence they are like CCS processes but for the fact that prefixes may be labelled with a key. In the following, we may drop trailing 0s.

Definition 2.1 (Context). *A CCSK* context *is a process with a hole, as generated by the grammar below:*

$$C := \bullet \mid\mid \pi.C \mid\mid C + Q \mid\mid P + C \mid\mid C \,|\, Q \mid\mid P \,|\, C \mid\mid (\nu a)C$$

We denote with $C[P]$ the process obtained by replacing $\bullet$ with P inside C.

We use predicate $\texttt{std}(P)$ to mean that P is standard, that is none of its actions has been executed, hence it has no keys. We assume function $\texttt{toStd}(P)$ that takes a CCSK process P and gives back the standard process obtained by removing all keys from P.

We take from [12, Def. 2.1] the notions of free and bound keys.

Definition 2.2 (Free and bound keys). *A key k is* bound *in a process X iff it occurs either twice, attached to complementary prefixes, or once, attached to a τ prefix. A key k is* free *if it occurs once, attached to a non-τ prefix.*

Figure 1 shows the forward rules of CCSK. Backward rules in Fig. 2 are obtained from forward rules by reversing the direction of transitions. Both relations rely on a definition of structural congruence allowing one to α-convert bound keys, applicable only at top level (this condition is needed to ensure that there are no other occurences of n in the context):

$$P \equiv P[n/m] \qquad m \text{ bound in } P, n \notin \texttt{keys}(P)$$

Rule (TOP) allows a prefix to execute. The rule generates a key m. Freshness of m is guaranteed by the side conditions of the other rules (cf. rule (PAR)). Rule (PREFIX) states that an executed prefix does not block execution. The two rules for (CHOICE) and the two for (PAR) allow processes to execute inside a choice or a parallel composition. The side condition of rule (CHOICE) ensures that at most one branch can execute. Rule (SYNCH) allows two complementary actions to synchronise producing a τ. The key of the two actions needs to be the same. Rule (RES) allows an action which does not involve the restricted name to propagate through restriction.

The forward semantics of a CCSK process is the smallest relation $\rightarrow_f$ closed under the rules in Fig. 1. Analogously, its backward semantics is the smallest relation $\rightarrow_r$ closed under the rules in Fig. 2. The semantics is the union of the two relations. From now on, we let ϑ range over $\alpha[m]$ and μ range over $\alpha[m]$ with $\alpha \neq \tau$. Let $x, y, \ldots$ range over the set of directions $\{f, r\}$, for forward and reverse.

As standard in reversible computing (see, e.g., [18] or the notion of coherent process in [7]), all the developments consider only processes reachable from a standard process.

Definition 2.3 (Reachable process). *A process Q is* reachable *iff there exists a standard process P and a finite sequence of transitions from P to Q.*

$$\text{(TOP)}\ \frac{\mathtt{std}(P)}{\alpha.P \xrightarrow{\alpha[m]}_f \alpha[m].P} \qquad \text{(PREFIX)}\ \frac{P \xrightarrow{\beta[n]}_f P'}{\alpha[m].P \xrightarrow{\beta[n]}_f \alpha[m].P'}\ m \neq n$$

$$\text{(CHOICE)}\ \frac{P \xrightarrow{\alpha[m]}_f P' \quad \mathtt{std}(Q)}{P + Q \xrightarrow{\alpha[m]}_f P' + Q} \qquad \frac{Q \xrightarrow{\alpha[m]}_f Q' \quad \mathtt{std}(P)}{P + Q \xrightarrow{\alpha[m]}_f P + Q'}$$

$$\text{(PAR)}\ \frac{P \xrightarrow{\alpha[m]}_f P' \quad m \notin \mathtt{keys}(Q)}{P \mid Q \xrightarrow{\alpha[m]}_f P' \mid Q} \qquad \frac{Q \xrightarrow{\alpha[m]}_f Q' \quad m \notin \mathtt{keys}(P)}{P \mid Q \xrightarrow{\alpha[m]}_f P \mid Q'}$$

$$\text{(SYNCH)}\ \frac{P \xrightarrow{\alpha[m]}_f P' \quad Q \xrightarrow{\overline{\alpha}[m]}_f Q'}{P \mid Q \xrightarrow{\tau[m]}_f P' \mid Q'}\ (\alpha \neq \tau)$$

$$\text{(RES)}\ \frac{P \xrightarrow{\alpha[m]}_f P'}{(\nu a)P \xrightarrow{\alpha[m]}_f (\nu a)P'}\ \alpha \notin \{a, \overline{a}\}$$

$$\text{(EQUIV)}\ \frac{P \equiv Q \quad Q \xrightarrow{\alpha[m]}_f Q' \quad Q' \equiv P'}{P \xrightarrow{\alpha[m]}_f P'}\ \text{applicable only at top level}$$

Fig. 1. Forward SOS rules for CCSK

3 Bisimilarities

In this section we introduce the various notions of bisimilarity we study. We start from CCS bisimilarities, and then move to bisimilarities specific for CCSK. Note that CCS can be seen as a subset of CCSK, considering only standard processes and only forward semantics. Hence, we will extend CCS bisimulations to CCSK by just considering forward transitions of CCSK terms. As a consequence, history becomes inaccessible, hence ideally irrelevant. However, requiring that a transition is matched by a transition with identical label would leak information on which keys are used in the history, as shown by the following example.

Example 3.1. We have $b \xrightarrow{b[n]}_f b[n]$ while no transition with the same label is enabled from $a[n].b$. The second process hence cannot match the transition of the first one in the bisimulation game if equality of labels is required. Hence, keys of forward transitions leak information about which keys are used in the history.

In order to avoid this issue, we will remove keys from the labels. Hence, we define CCS semantics for CCSK processes as follows:

Definition 3.2 (CCS semantics for CCSK processes). *Given a CCSK process P, $P \xrightarrow{\alpha} P'$ iff there is k such that $P \xrightarrow{\alpha[k]}_f P'$.*

We show now that the semantics above, defined on all CCSK processes, is indeed strictly related to the classical semantics of CCS defined in [14, Chapter

$$\text{(BK-TOP)}\ \frac{\mathtt{std}(P)}{\alpha[m].P \xrightarrow{\alpha[m]}_r \alpha.P} \qquad \text{(BK-PREFIX)}\ \frac{P \xrightarrow{\beta[n]}_r P'}{\alpha[m].P \xrightarrow{\beta[n]}_r \alpha[m].P'}\ m \neq n$$

$$\text{(BK-CHOICE)}\ \frac{P \xrightarrow{\alpha[m]}_r P' \quad \mathtt{std}(Q)}{P + Q \xrightarrow{\alpha[m]}_r P' + Q} \qquad \frac{Q \xrightarrow{\alpha[m]}_r Q' \quad \mathtt{std}(P)}{P + Q \xrightarrow{\alpha[m]}_r P + Q'}$$

$$\text{(BK-PAR)}\ \frac{P \xrightarrow{\alpha[m]}_r P' \quad m \notin \mathtt{keys}(Q)}{P \,|\, Q \xrightarrow{\alpha[m]}_r P' \,|\, Q} \qquad \frac{Q \xrightarrow{\alpha[m]}_r Q' \quad m \notin \mathtt{keys}(P)}{P \,|\, Q \xrightarrow{\alpha[m]}_r P \,|\, Q'}$$

$$\text{(BK-SYNCH)}\ \frac{P \xrightarrow{\alpha[m]}_r P' \quad Q \xrightarrow{\overline{\alpha}[m]}_r Q'}{P \,|\, Q \xrightarrow{\tau[m]}_r P' \,|\, Q'}\ (\alpha \neq \tau)$$

$$\text{(BK-RES)}\ \frac{P \xrightarrow{\alpha[m]}_r P'}{(\nu a)P \xrightarrow{\alpha[m]}_r (\nu a)P'}\ \alpha \notin \{a, \overline{a}\}$$

$$\text{(BK-EQUIV)}\ \frac{P \equiv Q \quad Q \xrightarrow{\alpha[m]}_r Q' \quad Q' \equiv P'}{P \xrightarrow{\alpha[m]}_r P'}\ \text{applicable only at top level}$$

Fig. 2. Reverse SOS rules for CCSK

5][1], which we denote as $\rightarrow_{ccs}$. Let $\mathtt{delHist}()$ be the function that extracts the standard part of a process.

Definition 3.3 ($\mathtt{delHist}()$). *The* $\mathtt{delHist}()$ *function is inductively defined as follows:*

$$\begin{aligned}
\mathtt{delHist}(P) &= P \textit{ if } \mathtt{std}(P) \\
\mathtt{delHist}(a[n].P) &= \mathtt{delHist}(P) \\
\mathtt{delHist}(P + Q) &= \mathtt{delHist}(P) \textit{ if } \neg\mathtt{std}(P) \\
\mathtt{delHist}(P + Q) &= \mathtt{delHist}(Q) \textit{ if } \neg\mathtt{std}(Q) \\
\mathtt{delHist}(P \,|\, Q) &= \mathtt{delHist}(P) \,|\, \mathtt{delHist}(Q) \\
\mathtt{delHist}((\nu a)P) &= (\nu a)\mathtt{delHist}(P)
\end{aligned}$$

The following proposition holds.

Proposition 3.4. *Let P, P' be CCSK processes, and Q a CCS process. If $P \xrightarrow{\alpha} P'$ then $\mathtt{delHist}(P) \xrightarrow{\alpha}_{ccs} \mathtt{delHist}(P')$. If $\mathtt{delHist}(P) \xrightarrow{\alpha}_{ccs} Q$ then there exists P' in CCSK such that $P \xrightarrow{\alpha} P'$ and $Q = \mathtt{delHist}(P')$.*

Proof. By rule inspection. □

Bisimilarities for CCS. We start with the classical notion of CCS bisimilarity, extended as mentioned above.

[1] Actually, the semantics in [14, Chapter 5] includes additional operators, as well as value passing. We consider its restriction to the operators we use in CCSK.

Definition 3.5 (Strong Bisimulation). *A symmetric relation $\mathcal{R}$ on CCSK processes is a* strong bisimulation *if whenever $P \mathcal{R} Q$:*

- *if $P \xrightarrow{\alpha} P'$ then there exists Q' such that $Q \xrightarrow{\alpha} Q'$ and $P' \mathcal{R} Q'$.*

Let $\sim$ be the largest strong bisimulation. Two CCSK processes P, Q are strongly bisimilar *if $(P, Q) \in \sim$.*

We give below some examples of strongly bisimilar processes.

Example 3.6 (Strongly Bisimilar CCSK Processes).

1. $a + a \sim a$
2. $a \mid a \sim a.a$
3. $a[m] \sim b[n]$
4. $a \mid b \sim a.b + b.a$

Note that Item 3 shows that strong bisimilarity (like all other CCS bisimilarities) abstracts away from the history. Item 4 is actually an instance of the Expansion Law [15], a cornerstone of the theory of classical CCS bisimilarity, whose general form is as follows:

$$P_1 \mid P_2 = \sum\{\alpha.(P_1' \mid P_2) : P_1 \xrightarrow{\alpha} P_1'\} + \sum\{\alpha.(P_1 \mid P_2') : P_2 \xrightarrow{\alpha} P_2'\} + \sum\{\tau.(P_1' \mid P_2') : P_1 \xrightarrow{\alpha} P_1', P_2 \xrightarrow{\overline{\alpha}} P_2', \alpha \neq \tau\}$$

where $\sum$ is n-ary choice.

It is well-known [18] that the Expansion Law does not hold for reversible calculi, and indeed we can provide a counterexample using strong forward-reverse bisimilarity (cf. Definition 3.11 and Example 3.12).

In order to introduce weaker notions of bisimilarity we need the notation below. Let $\Rightarrow = (\xrightarrow{\tau})^*$ be the reflexive and transitive closure of τ steps.

Definition 3.7 (Weak Bisimulation). *A symmetric relation $\mathcal{R}$ on CCSK processes is a* weak bisimulation *if whenever $P \mathcal{R} Q$:*

- *if $P \xrightarrow{\tau} P'$ then there exists Q' such that $Q \Rightarrow Q'$ and $P' \mathcal{R} Q'$;*
- *if $P \xrightarrow{\alpha} P'$ with $\alpha \neq \tau$ then there exists Q' such that $Q \Rightarrow\xrightarrow{\alpha}\Rightarrow Q'$ and $P' \mathcal{R} Q'$.*

Let $\approx$ be the largest weak bisimulation. Two CCSK processes P, Q are weakly bisimilar *if $(P, Q) \in \approx$.*

Example 3.8 (Weakly Bisimilar CCSK Processes).

1. $\tau.a \approx a$
2. $a + \tau.a \approx a$
3. $a[m] \approx b[n]$
4. $a \mid b \approx a.b + b.a$

We introduce also an intermediate notion, taken from [16], where τ steps need to be matched by at least one τ step.

Definition 3.9 (Semi-Weak Bisimulation). *A symmetric relation $\mathcal{R}$ on CCSK processes is a* semi-weak bisimulation *if whenever $P \mathrel{\mathcal{R}} Q$:*

- *if $P \xrightarrow{\alpha} P'$ then there is Q' such that $Q \Rightarrow\xrightarrow{\alpha}\Rightarrow Q'$ and $P' \mathrel{\mathcal{R}} Q'$.*

Let $\cong$ be the largest semi-weak bisimulation. Two CCSK processes P, Q are semi-weak bisimilar if $(P, Q) \in\cong$.

Example 3.10 (Semi-Weakly Bisimilar Processes).

- $a + a \cong a$
- $a \mid a \cong a.a$
- $a[n] \cong b[m]$
- $a + \tau.a \cong \tau.a$

Bisimilarities for CCSK. The bisimulations below make sense only in reversible calculi, since they consider both forward and backward transitions. We start with the notion of (revised) forward-reverse bisimulation from [12].

Definition 3.11 (Strong Forward-Reverse Bisimulation). *A symmetric relation $\mathcal{R}$ is a* strong forward-reverse bisimulation *(also called FR-bisimulation) if whenever $P \mathrel{\mathcal{R}} Q$:*

- *if $P \xrightarrow{\vartheta}_x P'$ then there is Q' such that $Q \xrightarrow{\vartheta}_x Q'$ and $P' \mathrel{\mathcal{R}} Q'$.*

Let $\sim_{FR}$ be the largest FR-bisimulation. Two CCSK processes P, Q are FR-bisimilar if $(P, Q) \in\sim_{FR}$.

Example 3.12 (FR Bisimilar Processes).

- $a + a \sim_{FR} a$
- $a \mid a \not\sim_{FR} a.a$
- $a \mid b \not\sim_{FR} a.b + b.a$

As expected, instances of the Expansion Law do not hold any more.

We now introduce notations to study the weak bisimulations in CCSK, and to manipulate τ steps easily. Let $\Rightarrow_x = (\xrightarrow{\tau}_x)^*$ the reflexive and transitive closure of τ steps in the direction x. Let mixed τ reachability be $\Rightarrow_m = (\xrightarrow{\tau}_f \cup \xrightarrow{\tau}_r)^*$. This is an equivalence relation. Let $P \overset{\mu}{\Rightarrow}_{m,x} P'$ iff $\exists Q, Q'$ s.t. $(P \Rightarrow_m Q \xrightarrow{\mu}_x Q' \Rightarrow_m P')$.

We now define two variants of weak reversible bisimulation, which differ in whether the τ steps used to match some action μ need to be in the same direction as μ or not.

Definition 3.13 (Weak Mixed Bisimulation). *A symmetric relation $\mathcal{R}$ is a* weak mixed bisimulation *(called mixed bisimulation) if whenever $P \mathrel{\mathcal{R}} Q$:*

1. *if* $P \xrightarrow{\tau}_x P'$ *then there exists* Q' *such that* $Q \Rightarrow_m Q'$ *and* $P' \mathcal{R} Q'$*;*
2. *if* $P \xrightarrow{\mu}_x P'$ *then there exists* Q' *such that* $Q \stackrel{\mu}{\Rightarrow}_{m,x} Q'$ *and* $P' \mathcal{R} Q'$*.*

Let $\approx_m$ *be the largest mixed weak bisimulation. Two CCSK processes* P, Q *are* weakly mixed bisimilar *if* $(P, Q) \in \approx_m$.

Intuitively, weak mixed bisimilarity abstracts away all the τ steps.

Example 3.14 (Mixed Bisimilar Processes).

- $\tau.a \approx_m a$
- $\tau \mid a \approx_m a$
- $\tau + a \approx_m a$
- $\tau[m] + a \approx_m a$

We also introduce a "directional" weak bisimulation, in which the τ steps have to be in the same direction as the action μ. Let $P \stackrel{\mu}{\Rightarrow}_{d,x} P'$ iff $\exists Q, Q'$ s.t. $(P \Rightarrow_x Q \xrightarrow{\mu}_x Q' \Rightarrow_x P')$.

Definition 3.15 (Weak Directional Bisimulation). *A symmetric relation* $\mathcal{R}$ *is a* weak directional bisimulation *(called directional bisimulation) if whenever* $P \mathcal{R} Q$*:*

1. *if* $P \xrightarrow{\tau}_x P'$ *then there exists* Q' *such that* $Q \Rightarrow_x Q'$ *and* $P' \mathcal{R} Q'$*;*
2. *if* $P \xrightarrow{\mu}_x P'$ *then there exists* Q' *such that* $Q \stackrel{\mu}{\Rightarrow}_{d,x} Q'$ *and* $P' \mathcal{R} Q'$*;*

Let $\approx_d$ *be the largest directional bisimulation. Two CCSK processes* P, Q *are directionally bisimilar if* $(P, Q) \in \approx_d$*.*

Example 3.16 (Directionally Bisimilar Processes).

- $\tau.a \approx_d a$
- $\tau \mid a \approx_d a$
- $\tau + a \not\approx_d a$

4 Relations Between Bisimilarities

We now compare the notions of bisimilarity introduced in the previous section. Interestingly, the considered notions give rise to two hierarchies.

Proposition 4.1 (Hierarchies of Bisimilarities).

1. $\sim_{FR} \subset \sim \subset \cong \subset \approx$;
2. $\sim_{FR} \subset \approx_d \subset \begin{cases} \approx_m \\ \approx \end{cases}$.

Proof. Inclusions follow directly from the definitions. The proof of their strictness will actually be deferred to Proposition 4.2, providing witnesses for each of them. □

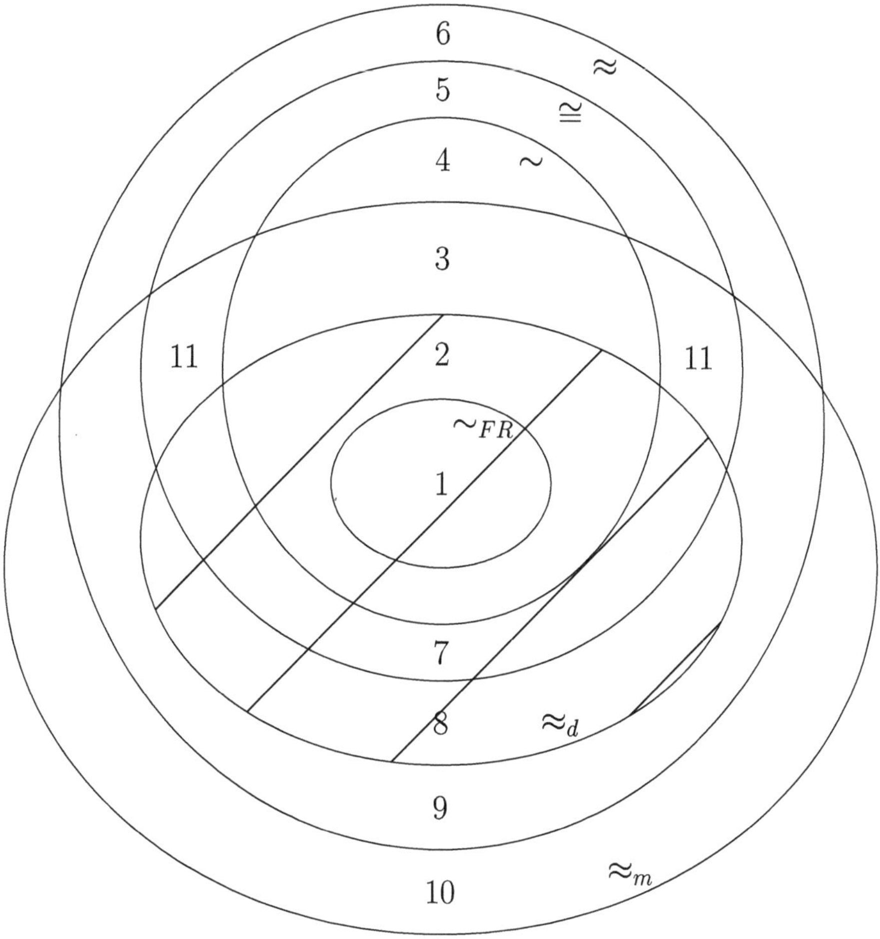

Fig. 3. Hierarchies of bisimilarities

The first hierarchy relates strong forward-reverse bisimilarity to CCS bisimilarities. The second hierarchy instead focuses on reversible bisimilarities. Note that $\approx_d$ is included in both $\approx_m$ and $\approx$ (hence in their intersection). The two hierarchies are graphically represented in Fig. 3. The relations are written just inside the elliptical set they represent. The lines on the set for $\approx_d$ are just a visual help to distinguish the corresponding ellipse.

We now show that there are no other inclusions beyond the ones in Proposition 4.1, and that all the inclusions there are actually strict. Graphically, it means that all the areas in Fig. 3 are not empty. We show this by providing examples of pairs of processes in each of them. Notably, all the examples are made of standard processes, hence none of these notions collapse when restricting the attention to standard processes. In other words, all these notions induce different equivalence relations on CCS processes.

Proposition 4.2 (Hierarchies are Strict on Standard Processes). *All the areas in Fig. 3 are not empty, and each of them contains at least a pair of standard processes.*

Proof. The ones below are witnesses for every area.

1. $\sim_{FR}$: $(a + a, a)$. The two as are indistinguishable.
2. $(\sim \cap \approx_d) \setminus \sim_{FR}$: $(\tau.\tau.(a.b + b.a) + \tau.(a \mid b),\ \tau.\tau.(a \mid b) + \tau.(a.b + b.a))$. We have that $a.b + b.a \sim a \mid b$ is an instance of the expansion law, but the same equivalence is not valid for $\sim_{FR}$. Under $\approx_d$ one can use equal subterms to match the challenge since they can be reached by taking a different number of τ steps.
3. $(\sim \cap \approx_m) \setminus \approx_d$: $(\tau.((a.b+b.a)+(c \mid d))+\tau.((a \mid b)+\tau.(c.d+d.c)),\ \tau.((a \mid b)+\tau.(c \mid d))+\tau.((a.b+b.a)+(c.d+d.c))$. The equivalence holds under $\sim$ thanks to the expansion law. It holds also under $\approx_m$ since the choice of which τ to execute can always be undone to select the desired branch. This is not the case under $\approx_d$ where on the left one can reach a state where the only forward actions enabled are from $c.d + d.c$, while on the right no such state exists (if $c.d + d.c$ is forward enabled, then also $a.b + b.a$ is enabled).
4. $\sim \setminus \approx_m$: $(a \mid b,\ a.b + b.a)$. We use again an instance of the expansion law.
5. $\cong \setminus (\sim \cup \approx_m)$: $(b \mid (a + a.\tau),\ a.(\tau \mid b) + a.b + b.a.\tau)$. This fails under $\approx_m$, since the right hand side has no $a \mid b$ to match the left hand side one. This fails under $\sim$ since on the right if one starts from b, there is no way to avoid a τ, while this can be avoided on the left. This is not an issue under $\cong$ since the a without τ can be matched by executing both a and τ.
6. $\approx \setminus (\cong \cup \approx_m)$: $(a.\tau \mid b,\ a.b + b.a)$. This holds under $\approx$ thanks to the expansion law and since the τ can be abstracted away. Instead, the expansion law fails under $\approx_m$ and the τ needs to be matched by another τ under $\cong$.
7. $(\cong \cap \approx_d) \setminus \sim$: $(a + a.\tau,\ a.\tau)$. This fails under $\sim$ since on the left executing an a leads to a state where no τ can be performed. This is not an issue for $\approx_d$ where the τ can be matched by staying idle. For $\cong$, left a can be matched by executing both a and τ.
8. $\approx_d \setminus \cong$: $(\tau,\ 0)$. This fails under $\cong$ since the τ cannot be matched, instead under $\approx_d$ the τ can be matched by staying idle.
9. $(\approx \cap \approx_m) \setminus (\cong \cup \approx_d)$: $(\tau.((a.b + b.a) + (c \mid d)) + \tau.((a \mid b) + \tau.(c.d + d.c)) + \tau,\ \tau.((a \mid b) + \tau.(c \mid d)) + \tau.((a.b + b.a) + (c.d + d.c)) + \tau.\tau$. This holds under $\approx$ thanks to the expansion law, and since τ and $\tau.\tau$ are weakly bisimilar. However, the latter are not semi-weakly bisimilar, hence $\cong$ fails. Also, this holds under $\approx_m$, since it abstracts away from τ actions. $\approx_d$ fails as well, for the same reason as in item 3.
10. $\approx_m \setminus \approx$: $(a,\ a+\tau)$. This is well-known not to hold under $\approx$. Instead under $\approx_m$ the τ step can be mimicked by staying idle since the a action remains enabled also after the τ, since the τ can be undone to do a.

11. $(\cong \cap \approx_m)\backslash(\sim \cup \approx_d)$: $(\tau.(a.b{+}b.a{+}\tau{+}\tau.\tau){+}(a \mid b), \tau.(a.b{+}b.a{+}(a \mid b){+}\tau.\tau))$. This fails under $\sim$ since $\tau.\tau$ is not matched on the right, since afterwards a third τ would be enabled. This fails under $\approx_d$ since after the first τ we can still go to $(a \mid b)$ on the right, but not on the left. This succeeds under $\approx_m$ since τs are abstracted away, and terms without τs are identical. This succeeds under $\cong$ since τs can always be matched, and thanks to the expansion law. □

If instead of considering only pairs of standard processes we consider only pairs of non-standard processes, then all the areas remain non-empty.

Proposition 4.3. *Each of the areas in Fig. 3 contains at least a pair of non-standard processes.*

Proof. One can take the witnesses from the proof of Proposition 4.2 add a $\tau[n]$ prefix in front of both processes to obtain witnesses made of non-standard processes. □

Finally, if we consider pairs made of a non-standard process and a standard one, then $\sim_{FR}$ becomes empty. The other areas remain non-empty.

Proposition 4.4. *Each of the areas in Fig. 3 contains at least a pair made of a non-standard process and a standard one, but for the area 1, corresponding to* $\sim_{FR}$.

Proof. The area for $\sim_{FR}$ is empty since $\sim_{FR}$ can always distinguish a non-standard process, that can make a backward move, from a standard one, that cannot. For the others, one can take the witnesses from the proof of Proposition 4.2 add a $\tau[n]$ prefix in front of only one of the two components. This preserves all the CCS bisimilarities, which cannot observe the history, as well as the weak CCSK bisimilarities, where the backward $\tau[n]$ can be matched by the other process by staying idle. □

5 Congruence Properties of Bisimilarities

We first discuss whether the considered equivalences are congruences or not, namely in the case of strong CCS bisimilarity whether $P \sim Q \implies C[P] \sim C[Q]$. Note that this implication makes sense only if all the involved processes are well-formed, hence we only consider this case.

Strong bisimilarity is a congruence in CCS [15]. Somehow surprisingly, its extension to CCSK is not a congruence, as shown in the counterexample below.

Example 5.1 ($\sim$ is not a congruence).

$$\tau[n] \sim 0 \;\not\Longrightarrow\; a + \tau[n] \sim a + 0$$

Processes on the left are strongly bisimilar since $\sim$ abstracts away from the history. Processes on the right are not strongly bisimilar since $a + \tau[n]$ cannot execute any forward move, while $a + 0$ can execute a.

The key point here is that forward equivalences abstract away from the history, but adding a choice where the added branch is a non-standard process disables the other branch (which needs to be standard to ensure well-formedness). Thus, the same issue also occurs for the other forward equivalences we consider, namely weak ($\approx$) and semi-weak ($\cong$) bisimilarities, as stated below.

Proposition 5.2 (Forward equivalences are not congruences in CCSK). *None of $\sim$, $\approx$ and $\cong$ are congruences on CCSK terms.*

Proof. Counterexample 5.1 proves the thesis for all the equivalences. □

Note that for $\approx$ the usual problem of CCS that $\tau.a \approx a \not\Rightarrow \tau.a + b \approx a + b$ remains. However, $\cong$ is a congruence in CCS [16], but not in CCSK for the reason above.

Concerning reversible equivalences, $\sim_{FR}$ has been proved to be a congruence in [12, Proposition 4.9]. Instead, for weak directional bisimilarity a problem similar to the one above occurs.

Proposition 5.3 (Weak directional bisimilarity is not a congruence). *$\approx_d$ is not a congruence on CCSK terms.*

Proof. The following counterexample proves the thesis:
$\tau[n] \approx_d 0 \not\Rightarrow a + \tau[n] \approx_d a + 0$ □

This is not the case for weak mixed bisimilarity, which, somehow surprisingly is a congruence. In order to clarify why this is the case, we first show a property of $\approx_m$ which rules out counterexamples as the ones above.

Proposition 5.4. *Assume $P \approx_m Q$ where P is standard. Then $Q \Rightarrow_m Q'$ with Q' standard.*

Proof. Assume towards a contradiction that there is no such Q'. By definition, we have $Q(\xrightarrow{\theta}_r)^*\mathtt{toStd}(Q)$. At least one of the steps is not a τ, otherwise we would have proven the thesis. Let us take the first such action. Then Q can perform a backward non-τ action. However, such an action cannot be matched by P, since P is standard (and executing τ steps only enables backward τ steps, while we need to match a non-τ backward action). □

We also show that indeed weak mixed bisimilarity completely abstracts away from τ steps.

Proposition 5.5 (Weak mixed bisimilarity abstracts away from τ steps).
$P \Rightarrow_m Q$ implies $P \approx_m Q$.

Proof. Thanks to the Loop Lemma (cf. [18, Prop. 5.1]), we also have $Q \Rightarrow_m P$. Hence, any challenge from P can be matched by Q by first reducing to P, and vice versa. □

Note that even if $P \Rightarrow_m Q$ and $P \approx_m Q$ are both equivalence relations, they do not coincide. E.g., $a + a \approx_m a$, but $a + a \not\Rightarrow_m a$.

Theorem 5.6 (Weak mixed bisimilarity is a congruence). *$\approx_m$ is a congruence on CCSK terms.*

Proof. We prove the thesis by induction on the structure of the context, with a case for each operator. Cases for prefix and restriction are trivial. Let us consider choice and parallel composition.

Choice: we have to show that if $P \approx_m Q$ then $P + R \approx_m Q + R$. Note that at most one among P and R can be non-standard due to well-formedness. Assume first both P and R are standard. If the challenge is from P, then Q inside $Q + R$ can match the challenge with the same sequence of moves used in Q alone, all lifted thanks to rule (CHOICE). If R moves, and Q is standard, then the very same moves can be performed in both the cases, again using rule (CHOICE) to lift them. If Q is not standard, thanks to Proposition 5.4 above, we can first reduce Q to $\mathtt{toStd}(Q)$, and then match the moves from R as above. Note that Q and $\mathtt{toStd}(Q)$ are mixed bisimilar thanks to Proposition 5.5, hence the reduction preserves mixed bisimilarity. Assume now P is non-standard. Then only P can move, and transitions can be lifted using rule (CHOICE) since by well-formedness R is standard. Assume now R is non-standard. Analogously to the above, only R can move, in both the cases since P and Q need to be standard due to well-formedness.

Parallel composition: we have to show that if $P \approx_m Q$ then $P \mid R \approx_m Q \mid R$. Assume $P \mid R \xrightarrow{\alpha}_f$. There are three subcases depending on which component contributes to the transition.

Transition from P: Q can match the transition, and the matching computation can be lifted to $Q \mid R$ thanks to rule (PAR).

Transition from R: the same transitions can be done on both the sides, remaining in the relation.

Synchronization: Q can match transitions from P by hypothesis, and transitions from R can be performed on both the sides. This includes the components of the transitions that give rise to the synchronization. Hence we stay in the relation.

The case of backward transitions is analogous.

□

We believe that the notion of mixed bisimilarity is very relevant. Indeed it provides a notion of bisimilarity which completely abstracts away from τ actions, which is coinductive (since it can be formulated as a bisimulation), and which is a congruence. We are not aware of any other notion of bisimilarity which has all these properties.

While leaving a more detailed analysis of this equivalence for future work, we discuss here some relevant axioms enabling to axiomatically reason on this equivalence. Notice that it makes sense to discuss about axioms since mixed bisimilarity is a congruence.

Various correct axioms for $\sim_{FR}$ have been proposed in [12, Theorem 4.10]. While trivially all these axioms are correct also for $\approx_m$, we focus here on axioms which are specific of weak mixed bisimilarity.

The axioms in Fig. 4 hold for weak mixed bisimilarity.

Theorem 5.7. *The axioms in Fig. 4 are correct w.r.t. weak mixed bisimilarity.*

Proof. τ moves can always be matched by the other process by staying idle, while moves from P can be matched by first doing or undoing τ steps as needed. Note that executing τ-steps moves from the top-3 rows to the bottom ones. □

$$
\begin{aligned}
\tau.P &= P && \text{(TAU-PREF-M)}\\
\tau + P &= P && \text{(TAU-CH-M)}\\
\tau \mid P &= P && \text{(TAU-PAR-M)}\\
\tau[n].P &= P && \text{(TAU-PREF-K)}\\
\tau[n] + P &= P && \text{(TAU-CH-K)}\\
\tau[n] \mid P &= P && \text{(TAU-PAR-K)}
\end{aligned}
$$

Fig. 4. CCSK axioms for weak mixed bisimilarity $\approx_m$

The axioms in Fig. 4 are aligned with Proposition 5.5 in showing that mixed bisimilarity completely abstracts away from τ steps.

We remark that as shown in Fig. 3, axioms which hold for weak bisimilarity $\approx$ do not necessarily hold for $\approx_m$. Let us now discuss the well-known Milner τ-laws of weak bisimilarity (collected in Fig. 5). The laws (TAU-CH) and (TAU-SEQ) follow directly from (TAU-PREF-M), and idempotence of $+$ for the former.

Instead (TAU-DUPL-CH) fails, as shown below.

Example 5.8 ((TAU-DUPL-CH) does not hold). Consider the right-hand side challenge:

$$\alpha.(P + \tau.Q) + \alpha.Q \xrightarrow{\alpha[n]}_f \alpha.(P + \tau.Q) + \alpha[n].Q$$

There are two possible answers from the left-hand side, namely:

$$
\begin{aligned}
\alpha.(P + \tau.Q) &\xrightarrow{\alpha[n]}_f \alpha[n].(P + \tau.Q)\\
&\xrightarrow{\alpha[n]}_f \xrightarrow{\tau[m]}_f \alpha[n].(P + \tau[m].Q)
\end{aligned}
$$

(We can also reach the same states after having undone and redone multiple times the τ step.) In both the cases, actions from P are enabled, directly in the first case, and by first undoing $\tau[m]$ in the second case. However, no action from P can be executed in the right-hand side above, since we need to undo one $\alpha[n]$ and do α on the other side.

$$P + \tau.P = \tau.P \qquad \text{(TAU-CH)}$$
$$\alpha.\tau.P = \alpha.P \qquad \text{(TAU-SEQ)}$$
$$\alpha.(P + \tau.Q) = \alpha.(P + \tau.Q) + \alpha.Q \qquad \text{(TAU-DUPL-CH)}$$

Fig. 5. τ laws for weak bisimilarity $\approx$

6 Conclusion and Future Work

In this paper, we contrasted different notions of bisimilarity for CCSK processes, including two definitions of weak bisimilarities not previously discussed in the literature. We also proved that none of these notions are equivalent, not even if we restrict to standard processes only. Notably, weak mixed bisimilarity turns out to be coinductive, to be a congruence, and to completely abstract away from τ-steps, making it a very interesting equivalence.

We hope that these results can be the basis of a more detailed study of bisimilarities in CCSK. We remark that such a deeper understanding may also impact classical concurrency theory, since there are strong relations [1,2] between reversible strong bisimilarities and history-preserving [21] and hereditary history-preserving [3] bisimilarities. Also, weak mixed bisimilarity induces an equivalence on CCS, which is a congruence and abstracts away from τ steps. Notice however that its current definition is not coinductive in CCS, since it relies on CCSK terms.

We present now a few other items for future research. First, we remark that while giving correct axioms for weak mixed bisimilarity, we have not provided a complete axiomatization. This is definitely a relevant item for future work (given the interesting properties of weak mixed bisimilarity) but not easy. Indeed, there are no complete axiomatizations for forward-reverse bisimilarity either, which we expect to be needed as first step before tackling the mixed case.

Another interesting item would be to understand how other bisimilarities, and more in general behavioral equivalences, can be extended from CCS to CCSK. Given that reversibility provides quite a strong observational power (as shown by the relations with history-preserving and hereditary history-preserving bisimilarities), it may be the case that some of them collapse.

References

1. Aubert, C., Cristescu, I.: How reversibility can solve traditional questions: the example of hereditary history-preserving bisimulation. In: Konnov, I., Kovács, L. (eds.) 31st International Conference on Concurrency Theory, CONCUR 2020, Vienna, Austria (Virtual Conference), 1–4 September 2020. LIPIcs, vol. 171, pp. 7:1–7:23. Schloss Dagstuhl - Leibniz-Zentrum für Informatik (2020)
2. Aubert, C., Phillips, I., Ulidowski, I.: Bisimulations and reversibility. In: Mezzina, C.A., Schmitt, A. (eds.) Components Operationally: Reversibility and System Engineering: Essays Dedicated to Jean-Bernard Stefani on the Occasion of His 65th Birthday. Lecture Notes in Computer Science, vol. 16065, pp. 46–67. Springer (2026)

3. Bednarczyk, M.A.: Hereditary history preserving bisimulations or what is the power of the future perfect in program logics. Technical report, Polish Academy of Sciences (1991)
4. Cardelli, L., Laneve, C.: Reversibility in massive concurrent systems. Sci. Ann. Comput. Sci. **21**(2), 175 (2011)
5. Carothers, C.D., Perumalla, K.S., Fujimoto, R.M.: Efficient optimistic parallel simulations using reverse computation. ACM Trans. Model. Comput. Simul. (TOMACS) **9**(3), 224–253 (1999)
6. Cristescu, I., Krivine, J., Varacca, D.: A compositional semantics for the reversible π-calculus. In: 28th Annual ACM/IEEE Symposium on Logic in Computer Science, LICS 2013, New Orleans, LA, USA, 25–28 June 2013, pp. 388–397. IEEE Computer Society (2013)
7. Danos, V., Krivine, J.: Reversible communicating systems. In: International Conference on Concurrency Theory, pp. 292–307. Springer (2004)
8. Engblom, J.: A review of reverse debugging. In: Proceedings of the 2012 System, Software, SoC and Silicon Debug Conference, pp. 1–6. IEEE (2012)
9. Landauer, R.: Irreversibility and heat generation in the computing process. IBM J. Res. Dev. **5**(3), 183–191 (1961)
10. Lanese, I., Nishida, N., Palacios, A., Vidal, G.: CauDEr: a causal-consistent reversible debugger for Erlang. In: Gallagher, J.P., Sulzmann, M. (eds.) FLOPS 2018. LNCS, vol. 10818, pp. 247–263. Springer, Cham (2018). https://doi.org/10.1007/978-3-319-90686-7_16
11. Lanese, I., Nishida, N., Palacios, A., Vidal, G.: A theory of reversibility for Erlang. J. Log. Algebraic Methods Program. **100**, 71–97 (2018)
12. Lanese, I., Phillips, I.: Forward-reverse observational equivalences in CCSK. In: Yamashita, S., Yokoyama, T. (eds.) RC 2021. LNCS, vol. 12805, pp. 126–143. Springer, Cham (2021). https://doi.org/10.1007/978-3-030-79837-6_8
13. McNellis, J., Mola, J., Sykes, K.: Time travel debugging: root causing bugs in commercial scale software. CppCon talk (2017)
14. Milner, R.: A Calculus of Communicating Systems. Lecture Notes in Computer Science, vol. 92. Springer (1980)
15. Milner, R.: Communication and Concurrency. Prentice-Hall, Inc. (1989)
16. Montanari, U., Sassone, V.: CCS dynamic bisimulation is progressing. In: Tarlecki, A. (ed.) Mathematical Foundations of Computer Science 1991, 16th International Symposium, MFCS'91, Kazimierz Dolny, Poland, 9–13 September 1991, Proceedings. Lecture Notes in Computer Science, vol. 520, pp. 346–356. Springer (1991)
17. Oguchi, S., Yuen, S., Yoshida, N.: RevMiGo: reversible channel-based communication in Go language. In: Glück, R., Kaarsgaard, R. (eds.) Reversible Computation - 17th International Conference, RC 2025, Odense, Denmark, 3–4 July 2025, Proceedings. Lecture Notes in Computer Science, vol. 15716, pp. 119–127. Springer (2025)
18. Phillips, I., Ulidowski, I.: Reversing algebraic process calculi. J. Logic Algebraic Program. **73**(1–2), 70–96 (2007)
19. Phillips, I., Ulidowski, I., Yuen, S.: A reversible process calculus and the modelling of the ERK signalling pathway. In: International Workshop on Reversible Computation, pp. 218–232. Springer (2012)
20. Sangiorgi, D.: Introduction to Bisimulation and Coinduction. Cambridge University Press (2012)
21. van Glabbeek, R.J., Goltz, U.: Refinement of actions and equivalence notions for concurrent systems. Acta Informatica **37**(4/5), 229–327 (2001)

Formal Developments in Reversible and Quantum Programs

Exact Quantum State Preparation with the Standard Recursive Block Basis

Giacomo Belli(✉) and Michele Amoretti

Quantum Software Laboratory, Department of Engineering and Architecture, University of Parma, 43124 Parma, Italy
{giacomo.belli,michele.amoretti}@unipr.it
https://www.qslab.unipr.it/

Abstract. Variational approaches to Quantum State Preparation (QSP) allow for low-depth and structured circuit ansatz, at the cost of non-convex optimization landscapes and barren plateaus that severely limit scalability. In contrast, exact synthesis methods typically involve exponential growth in the number of independent parameters, leading to a rapid increase in circuit depth. In this work, it is shown that the algebraic properties of the Standard Recursive Block Basis (SRBB) can partially overcome this delicate trade-off. By exploiting the algebraic structure of the SRBB decomposition and the CNOT-optimized circuit for its diagonal component, an exact parameter-solving procedure for the variational SRBB-based QSP problem is defined by analytically inverting the foundational parametric Lie map. As a consequence, a variationally trained circuit is converted to an exact one without increasing circuit depth or gate count. The resulting framework preserves the expressive power of the variational ansatz, thanks to the completeness of the SRBB, while eliminating optimization-induced limitations, shifting the computational problem entirely to a classical precomputation stage. The new exact QSP algorithm has been implemented via the PennyLane library and tested in HPC simulations (up to 12 qubits) to demonstrate the scalability of the parametric map resulting from the recursive structure of the diagonal component of SRBB. In this new exact framework, circuit design (and hence rotation parameters) is twinned with the Unitary Group Hermitian generators and their properties, opening up new optimization possibilities.

Keywords: Quantum State Preparation · Standard Recursive Block Basis · Uniformly Controlled Gate Synthesis

1 Introduction

In the last decades of quantum computing, the preparation of quantum states has become an increasingly crucial cross-cutting procedure, which is employed as a first stage in many quantum algorithms [17] and is developed on the technological front. Quantum State Preparation (QSP) is the necessary algorithmic primitive

C. Aubert and L. Roversi (Eds.): RC 2026, LNCS 16626, pp. 77–94, 2026.
https://doi.org/10.1007/978-3-032-30839-9_4

for quantum linear system solvers [27], Hamiltonian simulations [7], quantum chemistry [8,13], and quantum machine learning [10,33]. Furthermore, it plays a central role in quantum communication and high-dimensional entanglement distribution [12,23,31] and forms the basis of information encoding in quantum cryptographic protocols [11]. On the technological side, QSP enables high-fidelity state engineering across multiple physical platforms [9,22]. Despite its relevance, efficient QSP algorithms remain an open challenge [15,24–26,40].

The goal of QSP is to construct a unitary operator $U \in U(2^n)$ such that $|\psi\rangle = U|0\rangle^{\otimes n}$, where $|0\rangle^{\otimes n}$ is the conventional n-qubit initial state in the "bra-ket" formalism, and $|\psi\rangle = \sum_{i=0}^{2^n-1} c_i|i\rangle$ represents the desired target state in the computational basis of the quantum system. As usual, the target $|\psi\rangle$ must satisfy the normalization condition $\sum_{i=0}^{2^n-1} |c_i|^2 = 1$ to ensure the probabilistic interpretation of quantum states. The unitary QSP transformation is not always able to describe the entire (Hilbert) state space; this may depend both on its internal operator structure and the method used to decompose and parameterize it. When the discrepancy between the target state and the output state cannot be traced back solely to the precision η of the floating point numerical machine, but rather depends on the algorithm itself (for example, a variational method that is approximate by definition), the QSP is *approximate*. In this case, the effort is to minimize the difference with respect to the target state within $\epsilon > \eta$ errors. Conversely, when the preparation is designed on an algorithm that, by construction, achieves machine precision in a simulated environment, the QSP is said to be exact. In this work, a deterministic map to translate an approximate QSP algorithm into its exact version is defined, showing that when the unitary transformation is decomposed according to precise algebraic structures that guarantee descriptive completeness, it is possible to circumvent the limitations of approximate methods, which become increasingly complex as the size grows, without increasing the circuit costs.

The literature on exact QSP dates back to Grover and Rudolph [14], with a depth upper bound of $\mathcal{O}(n2^n)$ in the special case of integrable probability density functions. Their algorithm already contained structures reminiscent of today's Uniformly Controlled Rotations (UCRs) [29], although the UCR class was only formalized with the 3-stage QSP algorithm of Möttönen et al. [28], with a depth of $\mathcal{O}(2^n)$, $2^{n+2} - 4n - 4$ CNOT, and $2^{n+2} - 5$ rotations. In this model, each UCR layer can be implemented via Gray Code [38], and its parameters can be exactly determined via Binary Search Tree (BST) diagrams, making QSP modular [30]. In 2005, Bergholm et al. [6] systematically analyzed the Uniformly Controlled Gate (UCG or multiplexor) for a general QSP, as a generalization of the UCR class. Their algorithm had an upper bound of $2^{n+1} - 2n - 2$ for the number of CNOT gates, with a depth also of order $\mathcal{O}(2^n)$. In 2011, following the line of research where the UCG class is the key building block for traditional QSP [28,35], Plesch and Brukner [32] focused on minimizing the CNOT count. Subsequently, QSP formalisms were formally incorporated into the systematic synthesis of isometries, thanks to the work of Iten et al. [18]. Their work consolidated the already known link between Gate Synthesis and QSP based on the search for optimal decompositions and the modularity of the UCG class [35].

On the other hand, approximate QSP naturally falls within the framework of Variational Quantum Algorithms (VQAs) and, more generally, Quantum Machine Learning (QML) methodologies. Indeed, it is based on the definition of a parametric circuit ansatz (Variational Quantum Circuit or VQC) and on the classical optimization of parameters concerning a metric criterion (loss function), in order to reproduce the target state. In this sense, approximate QSP inherits its typical limitations of variational approaches, such as local minima, barren plateaus, and performance depending on the optimizer and the training set.

Indeed, as stated in its own definition, the problem of preparing the quantum state is closely connected with the topic of Gate Synthesis [19–21,35,36,39]. Recently, an approach to approximate synthesis introduced a *scalable and recursive* parameterization for any unitary operator by means of the Standard Recursive Block Basis (SRBB), a Hermitian unitary basis for the matrix algebra $M_{2^n}(\mathbb{C})$ [34]. Subsequently, the SRBB-based decomposition procedure was reformulated to facilitate the implementation of unitary evolutions. The corresponding circuits were optimized in terms of CNOT gates, and the variational synthesis algorithm was tested both in simulation and with real quantum computers [5]. Furthermore, the diagonal component of the SRBB was then used in the approximate synthesis of diagonal UCGs within the traditional QSP framework [4], reformulating it in a variational way. The resulting algorithm has depth $\mathcal{O}(2^n)$, and the corresponding VQC should not be considered an ansatz in the traditional sense; in fact, the completeness of SRBB and the role that each basis element has in the circuit design defines, by construction, a circuit capable of describing the entire Hilbert space, where the Lie parameters associated with the generators of the unitary group identify precise rotations depending only on the desired target state. As simulations show, the algorithm has a drastic performance drop at just 5 qubits due to the exponential cardinality of the SRBB, which leads to barren plateau phenomena. In this sense, the SRBB-based variational framework for QSP does not reduce circuit complexity but merely obfuscates an *underlying exact structure* behind a difficult optimization problem. The transition to exact construction based on Lie algebras can remove the problems related to the variational domain and reformulates SRBB-based QSP as a deterministic algebraic synthesis task.

This paper provides the following new contributions: 1) conversion of a variational QSP algorithm based on the Standard Recursive Block Basis (SRBB) into its exact version to overcome training limitations due to barren plateaus, without increasing the gate count or the circuit depth; 2) first use of the SRBB-based decomposition to implement UCGs by means of an exact procedure and a deterministic parametric map; 3) definition of an exact computational framework for traditional QSP in which the circuit design directly depends on the $SU(2^n)$ Lie generators thanks to the SRBB (Lie parameters are precisely rotation angles), which guarantees descriptive completeness; 4) implementation of the new QSP algorithm in PennyLane (available in GitHub [2]) and test via

HPC simulations, up to 12 qubits, with a variety of quantum states, proving the structural scalability of the parametric map.

The remainder of the paper is organized as follows. Section 2 is dedicated to the theoretical framework, which defines the necessary modifications of the traditional QSP scheme as well as the diagonal component of the SRBB. Subsection 2.1 describes in more detail how to use the diagonal component of the algebraic basis to perform *approximate* gate synthesis of diagonal operators and illustrates the corresponding quantum circuits specifically for $n = 2, 3$ qubits. The latter will be useful for understanding the parametric map described in Sect. 3. All details about the classical computation of parameters are illustrated in Sects. 3.1 and 3.2. Section 3.3 focuses on reordering and assigning the entire set of exact parameters (solutions of linear systems) to the rotation gates of the quantum circuit, taking into account the CNOT-optimized recursive structure induced by the SRBB. While Sect. 4 presents the results of HPC simulations, Sect. 5 concludes the paper with a discussion of the main results and future research directions.

2 Theoretical Framework

Quantum State Preparation (QSP) aims to design quantum circuits to prepare any desired n-qubit state $|\psi\rangle = \sum_{i=0}^{2^n-1} c_i|i\rangle$, where $c_i = |c_i|e^{i\phi_i}$ are the complex amplitudes properly normalized according to the l_2-norm, and $\{|i\rangle\}_{i=0}^{2^n-1}$ is the computational basis of the quantum system. The preparation of quantum states can be either exact, when the precision is limited solely by hardware imperfections, or approximate, when the goal is to prepare a state $|\phi\rangle$ which is ϵ-close to a target $|\psi\rangle$ with respect to the chosen metric. The QSP traditional framework [28,35] consists of a ladder structure of Uniformly Controlled Gates (UCGs) [6] on the entire quantum register, as illustrated in Fig. 2a. In this kind of circuit, each qubit k is handled by a UCG that has the task of applying a single qubit unitary on it, conditioned on the basis state of the first $k-1$ qubits. The choice of the target unitary U_k depends on the mathematical structure of the algorithm to be designed. In matrix representation, each UCG is a block-diagonal operator $U_k = \text{diag}(V_1, V_2, ..., V_{2^{k-1}}) \in \mathbb{C}^{2^k \times 2^k}$ and, in the most general setup, each block $V_j = e^{i\alpha_j} R_z(\beta_j) R_y(\gamma_j) R_z(\delta_j)$ belongs to $U(2)$. However, there exist other configurations that allow algebraic reductions; for instance, if the QSP algorithm has a first stage U_{mod} in which only the modulus $|c_i|$ of each component of the target state $|\psi\rangle$ has to be prepared (see Fig. 1), then choosing $SU(2)$ blocks $V_j = R_y(\gamma_j)$ leads to simplifying the overall circuit [1,4]. Actually, this is the case for the present work, and Fig. 2b illustrates the expanded circuit pattern.

Whether or not to use ancillary qubits is a matter of choosing the synthesis technique used to implement the UCG layers. The fundamental paper by Sun et al. [37] on QSP circuit complexity, which determines the *asymptotically* optimal depth-width trade-off bounds, already provides a clear example

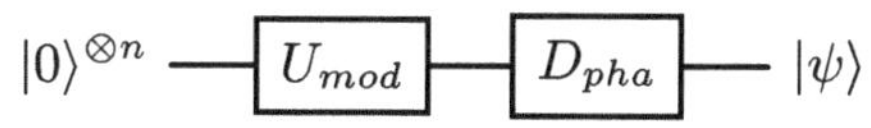

Fig. 1. Decomposition of the QSP circuit into two blocks: U_{mod} prepares each modulus $|c_i|$ of the target state $|\psi\rangle$, while D_{pha} prepares each phase $e^{i\phi_i}$.

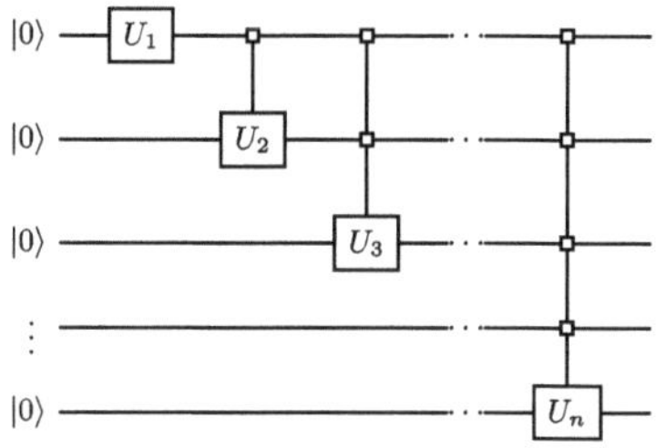

(a) QSP traditional circuit with general Uniformly Controlled Gates (UCGs).

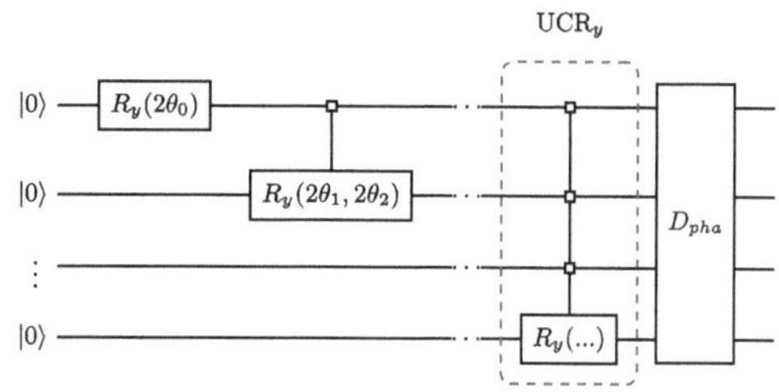

(b) QSP circuit suitable for SRBB insertions. The block U_{mod} is expanded in terms of Uniformly Controlled Rotations (UCR_y).

Fig. 2. QSP framework for SRBB insertions.

of how to gain a depth advantage through parallelization on ancillary registers. However, this paper will not follow that strategy. Indeed, the purpose of this work is not to optimize circuits, but rather to define an *exact* computational framework for traditional QSP that eliminates the bottleneck represented by barren plateaus in previous variational approaches [4] and restores control over the algorithm. It thus solves a structural, not technological, problem where barren plateaus are viewed as an informational and geometric limit. The algorithm proposed in this paper does not require ancillary qubits and uses the *diagonal* component of the Standard Recursive Block Basis (SRBB) [3] to implement each UCG in the gate set[1] $\{R_y, R_z, H, S, CNOT\}$. The SRBB is the hierarchical and recursive construction that defines, for any $n \in \mathbb{N}_+$, the Hermitian unitary basis for the complex matrix algebra[2] $M_{2^n}(\mathbb{C})$. Originally, it was introduced to obtain a recursive parameterization of the Lie group $U(2^n) = \{U \in M_{2^n}(\mathbb{C}) \mid U^\dagger U = \mathbb{I}_{2^n}\}$, enabling the design of scalable Variational Quantum Circuits (VQCs) [34]. A little more formally, SRBB is the basis of the Lie algebra $\mathfrak{u}(2^n)$, which linearly (locally) approximates the group around the identity: while the group $U(2^n)$ describes finite transformations, the algebra $\mathfrak{u}(2^n)$ describes infinitesimal transformations close to the identity [16]. The exponential map $\mathfrak{exp} : (\theta_1, \ldots, \theta_{d^2}) \in \mathbb{R}^{d^2} \longrightarrow \prod_{j=1}^{d^2} \exp\{i\,\theta_j U_j^{(d)}\} \in U(d)$ connects the two instances and generates the entire Lie group. In [5], the SRBB and the related synthesis strategy are described in detail using a formalism oriented toward circuit implementation. The parameterization introduced by the SRBB is important because its elements $U_j^{(d)}$ become the building blocks of a

1 Unless otherwise specified, this work uses the conventions of [37].

2 $M_N(\mathbb{C})$, which is the vector space of all $N \times N$ matrices with complex entries, is endowed with the usual matrix addition and scalar multiplication over $\mathbb{C}$.

(so far) *variational* gate synthesis algorithm capable of approximating any given $U \in SU(2^n)$, according to[3] $U_{approx} \equiv Z(\Theta_Z)\Psi(\Theta_\Psi)\Phi(\Theta_\Phi)$, where $\Theta_Z, \Theta_\Psi, \Theta_\Phi$ collect Lie parameters of each macro-factor. The SRBB component that represents the basis for $\mathfrak{su}(2^n)$ is partitioned into three subsets according to the algebraic properties of its matrix elements $U_j^{(d)}$, and then used to define each macro-factor Z, Ψ, Φ by means of the exponential map $\mathfrak{exp}$. A second aspect that deserves attention is that the exponential map identifies the parameters of the Lie algebra (geometric coordinates in the neighborhood of the group identity) with the variational parameters of the approximating circuit. Therefore, this gate synthesis technique connects quantum evolution operators, quantum circuits, and the geometry of unitary groups in a very natural way.

In the QSP algorithm presented here, the SRBB-based synthesis has been reformulated for an exact approach that only involves the diagonal component of the basis and is applied to each UCG layer. The diagonal Z-factor is defined by the following equation [5]:

$$Z(\Theta_Z) = \prod_{j=2}^{2^n} e^{i\left(\theta_{j^2-1} U_{j^2-1}^{(2^n)}\right)} \tag{1}$$

where $U_{j^2-1}^{(2^n)}$ are all the diagonal SRBB elements related to $\mathfrak{su}(2^n)$ and θ_{j^2-1}, the corresponding Lie parameters. Once the SRBB of order $d = 2^n$ has been constructed following the recursive procedure described in [5, Section 2], Eq. (1) allows us to isolate the elements that contribute to the definition of the Z-factor and its circuit implementation. Section 2.1 shows an example for $n = 2$ qubits. This factor can describe any *diagonal* $SU(2^n)$ operator, thus a diagonal matrix of pure complex phases with a unit determinant. According to the structural reduction of considering UCR$_y$ for the implementation of U_{mod}, as shown in Fig. 2b, the Z-factor can synthesize any uniformly controlled layer if the following change of gate set is considered: $R_y(2\gamma_j) \equiv SH \cdot R_z(2\gamma_j) \cdot HS^\dagger$. The effect of switching to diagonal operators on a level-n UCG is illustrated in Fig. 3a, while Fig. 3b shows an example of a QSP circuit, expanded in the new gate set, where the operators $F_n[R_z]$ are implemented via SRBB. Since D_{pha} is already a diagonal matrix of complex phases, for this block the problem is not the gate set, but rather membership in the SU group, which can be solved with an appropriate global phase collection, as described in Sect. 3.2. This type of circuit has been used for the preparation of quantum states using a *variational* approach based on Quantum Neural Networks (QNNs) [4]. The following sections describe the transition to exact QSP and the deterministic map for circuits designed with SRBB. Keeping the operator decomposition unchanged, the exact algorithm inherits the circuit metrics of the variational approach[4]: depth $D(n) = 6 \cdot 2^n - \frac{n^2+7n}{2} - 3$ and gate count $N_{rot}(n) = 3 \cdot 2^n - n - 3$, $N_{cnot}(n) = 3 \cdot 2^n - 2n - 4$.

---

[3] Only the subset $\{U_j^{(d)} : 1 \leqslant j \leqslant d^2 - 1\}$ forms a basis for $\mathfrak{su}(d)$ when d is even [3].

[4] The proof is referred to [4].

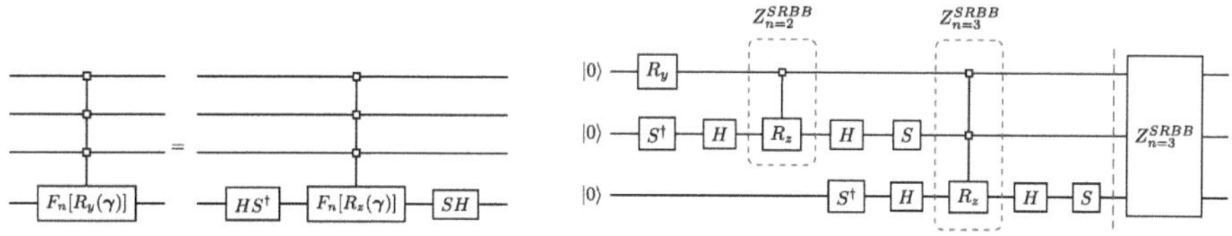

(a) Rewriting UCR$_y$ in terms of diagonal operators $F_n[R_z]$ by means of the new gate set.

(b) Example of QSP circuit for $n = 3$ qubits. For simplicity, the target gate of $F_n[R_z]$ only shows the type of blocks.

Fig. 3. SRBB-based QSP circuit.

$$U_1^{(4)} = \begin{pmatrix} 0&1&0&0\\ 1&0&0&0\\ 0&0&1&0\\ 0&0&0&-1 \end{pmatrix} \quad U_2^{(4)} = \begin{pmatrix} 0&-i&0&0\\ i&0&0&0\\ 0&0&1&0\\ 0&0&0&-1 \end{pmatrix} \quad U_3^{(4)} = \begin{pmatrix} 1&0&0&0\\ 0&-1&0&0\\ 0&0&1&0\\ 0&0&0&-1 \end{pmatrix} \quad U_4^{(4)} = \begin{pmatrix} 1&0&0&0\\ 0&0&1&0\\ 0&1&0&0\\ 0&0&0&-1 \end{pmatrix}$$

$$U_5^{(4)} = \begin{pmatrix} 0&0&1&0\\ 0&1&0&0\\ 1&0&0&0\\ 0&0&0&-1 \end{pmatrix} \quad U_6^{(4)} = \begin{pmatrix} 1&0&0&0\\ 0&0&-i&0\\ 0&i&0&0\\ 0&0&0&-1 \end{pmatrix} \quad U_7^{(4)} = \begin{pmatrix} 0&0&-i&0\\ 0&1&0&0\\ i&0&0&0\\ 0&0&0&-1 \end{pmatrix} \quad U_8^{(4)} = \begin{pmatrix} 1&0&0&0\\ 0&1&0&0\\ 0&0&-1&0\\ 0&0&0&-1 \end{pmatrix}$$

$$U_9^{(4)} = \begin{pmatrix} 1&0&0&0\\ 0&-1&0&0\\ 0&0&0&1\\ 0&0&1&0 \end{pmatrix} \quad U_{10}^{(4)} = \begin{pmatrix} 0&0&0&1\\ 0&-1&0&0\\ 0&0&1&0\\ 1&0&0&0 \end{pmatrix} \quad U_{11}^{(4)} = \begin{pmatrix} 1&0&0&0\\ 0&0&0&1\\ 0&0&-1&0\\ 0&1&0&0 \end{pmatrix} \quad U_{12}^{(4)} = \begin{pmatrix} 1&0&0&0\\ 0&-1&0&0\\ 0&0&0&-i\\ 0&0&i&0 \end{pmatrix}$$

$$U_{13}^{(4)} = \begin{pmatrix} 0&0&0&-i\\ 0&-1&0&0\\ 0&0&1&0\\ i&0&0&0 \end{pmatrix} \quad U_{14}^{(4)} = \begin{pmatrix} 1&0&0&0\\ 0&0&0&-i\\ 0&0&-1&0\\ 0&i&0&0 \end{pmatrix} \quad U_{15}^{(4)} = \begin{pmatrix} 1&0&0&0\\ 0&-1&0&0\\ 0&0&-1&0\\ 0&0&0&1 \end{pmatrix} \quad U_{16}^{(4)} = \begin{pmatrix} 1&0&0&0\\ 0&1&0&0\\ 0&0&1&0\\ 0&0&0&1 \end{pmatrix}$$

Fig. 4. The Standard Recursive Block Basis $\mathcal{U}^{(4)}$.

2.1 Diagonal SRBB Component for $n = 2$ Qubits

The infinitesimal unitary evolution of 2-qubit systems is parameterized according to the basis of the Lie algebra of order $d = 4$, which contains $d^2 = 16$ elements. In [5], it is described how to recursively construct the corresponding SRBB starting from the Pauli basis: Fig. 4 shows its elements $U_j^{(4)}$. Among these, only the elements belonging to the set $\mathcal{J}_Z = \{m^2 - 1,\ 2 \leqslant m \leqslant 4\} = \{3, 8, 15\}$, which are exactly all the diagonal elements of the basis except the last one, contribute to defining the factor $Z(\Theta_Z) = \prod_{j=2}^{4} \exp\{i\,\theta_{j^2-1} U_{j^2-1}^{(4)}\}$. Accordingly, the Z-factor can be written in the following matrix form:

$$Z(\Theta_Z) = \mathrm{diag}(e^{i(\theta_3+\theta_8+\theta_{15})}, e^{i(-\theta_3+\theta_8-\theta_{15})}, e^{i(\theta_3-\theta_8-\theta_{15})}, e^{i(-\theta_3-\theta_8+\theta_{15})}) \quad (2)$$

For consistency with previous papers on SRBB [34], *only* in this section a different convention will be used for rotation operators: $R_z(2\theta) = \mathrm{diag}(e^{i\theta}, e^{-i\theta})$. While for a few qubits it is possible to directly deduce the circuit corresponding to each diagonal element of the basis, as the cardinality increases, one must resort to a diagrammatic rule. By construction, each diagonal element $U_j^{(d)}$ can be represented by means of a Pauli string starting from the binary representation of their position in the set $\mathcal{J}_Z$. Figure 5a illustrates this property, which is useful for building the quantum circuit associated with each diagonal element of the basis. In [5, Appendix B], the case $n = 3$ is treated in detail following the same procedure. The strength of SRBB is precisely the *recursive* construction of the

$\mathfrak{su}(2^n)$ basis, which is reflected in a scalable design of quantum circuits. On the contrary, the weakness lies in the exponential growth of its cardinality, which induces barren plateau issues in native variational approaches. In general, this leads to considering optimization algorithms that reduce depth and parameters in the synthesis scheme defined by SRBB. A first result in this direction was obtained in [5, Section 4], where an algorithm was defined to minimize the number of CNOT gates over the entire synthesis structure and, in particular, over the Z-factor. In this new optimized structure, for $n \geqslant 3$, the diagonal factor is split into two blocks: a first part optimized via Gray Code ordering and a second one that coincides with the Z-circuit of the case $n-1$ (recursive structure). It has been proved that the maximum number of simplifications of CNOT gates is found by ordering the diagonal elements of $\mathcal{J}_Z$ according to the Gray Code matrix of order n. Subsequently, the binary strings ending with 0 represent the Z-factor of the previous case $n-1$, while the remaining ones contribute to the Gray Code ordered-part. As an example of the recursive pattern, Fig. 6 shows the Z-factor circuit for $n = 3$.

Decimal	Binary	String	Matrix	Element
1	01	$\mathbb{I}_2 \otimes \sigma_3$	diag(1,-1,1,-1)	3
2	10	$\sigma_3 \otimes \mathbb{I}_2$	diag(1,1,-1,-1)	8
3	11	$\sigma_3 \otimes \sigma_3$	diag(1,-1,-1,1)	15

(a) Pauli string representation for $\mathcal{J}_Z$ elements.

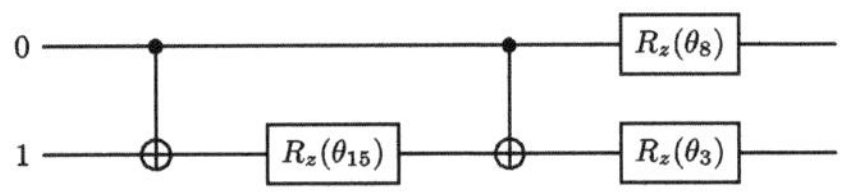

(b) Z-factor circuit for $n = 2$.

Fig. 5. Diagrammatic rule for the Z-factor quantum circuit.

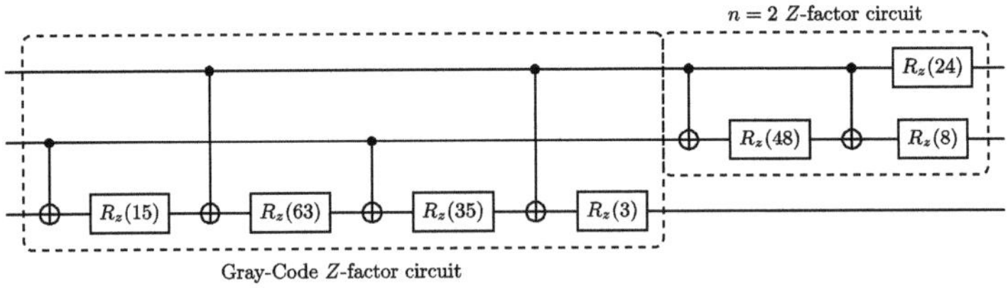

Fig. 6. Z-factor circuit for $n = 3$.

3 Classical Computation of Parameters

The exact version of the SRBB-based QSP algorithm, hereafter denoted as EQSP_{SRBB}, requires a classical precomputation step to determine the circuit parameters. In practice, this involves *recursively* solving a series of n linear systems starting from the knowledge of the complex amplitudes c_i of the desired n-qubit target state $|\psi\rangle$, the only input to the algorithm. Based on the decomposition illustrated in Fig. 1, the real magnitude $|c_i|$ and the complex phase $e^{i\phi_i}$

are extracted from each amplitude c_i, forming, respectively, the 2^n-dimensional vectors $\boldsymbol{v}_{mod}$ and $\boldsymbol{b}_{phase}$: both will be used to determine the vector of known terms for each linear system, as described in the following Sects. 3.1 and 3.2. As explained in Sect. 2, while U_{mod} is decomposed in terms of increasing R_y-block UCGs from level 1 (a single R_y) up to the maximum level n (see Fig. 2b), D_{pha} is the diagonal operator having as its elements the complex phase vector $\boldsymbol{b}_{phase}$. Furthermore, after the gate set change, the R_z-block UCGs are diagonal operators too, allowing each level to be implemented[5] via the SRBB Z-factor (see for example Fig. 3b). Accordingly, the Lie parameters θ_{j^2-1} of each Z-factor, for $2 \leqslant j \leqslant 2^n$, are dependent on the rotation angles γ_i parameterizing each UCR$_z$ with respect to U_{mod}, but they are also dependent on the phase angles ϕ_i of the vector $\boldsymbol{b}_{phase}$ for what concerns D_{pha}. Therefore, the need to solve linear systems to determine the circuit parameters for the Z-circuit insertions derives precisely from the chosen synthesis technique. The matrix representation of the Z-factor, defined by Eq. 1, provides for each level the coefficient matrix of the associated linear system and the vector of solutions is nothing other than the vector of Lie parameters θ_{j^2-1} (which become rotation angles for the Z-circuit, as shown by Fig. 5b). Naturally, each UCG level has its own linear system and therefore its own parametric configuration; and the same is true for D_{pha}. What appears to be a fragmented parametric structure can be unambiguously traced back to the target state $|\psi\rangle$ and exactly determined through a recursive procedure. Indeed, the diagonal component of the SRBB induces a recursive pattern in the coefficient matrix of linear systems, as explained in the following Sect. 3.1.

3.1 UCG Levels for Real Magnitudes

This section focuses on the circuit block U_{mod} responsible for preparing real components $|c_i|$, and on the UCR$_z$ layers (or levels) that, after the gate set change, can be implemented by means of the Z-factor. First of all, it is worth noting that the $k = 1$ level corresponds to a single $R_y(2\gamma_0)$ on the first qubit (see, for example, Fig. 3b). Therefore, the first diagonal UCG is encountered only at the $k = 2$ level: the UCG layers range from $k = 2$ to $k = n$ (the maximum level for a generic n-qubit target state).

For each level $k \geqslant 2$, it is well known that the corresponding UCR$_z$ can be represented by a R_z-block diagonal matrix of size $2^k \times 2^k$. For example, according to the chosen conventions, the level-2 UCR$_z$ corresponds to the following matrix:

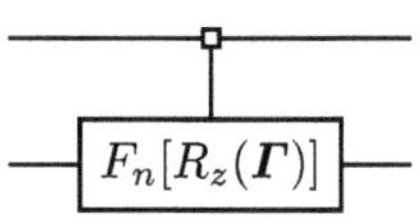

$$\equiv \begin{pmatrix} R_z(2\gamma_1) & 0 \\ 0 & R_z(2\gamma_2) \end{pmatrix} = \begin{pmatrix} e^{-i\gamma_1} & 0 & 0 & 0 \\ 0 & e^{+i\gamma_1} & 0 & 0 \\ 0 & 0 & e^{-i\gamma_2} & 0 \\ 0 & 0 & 0 & e^{+i\gamma_2} \end{pmatrix} \tag{3}$$

[5] While the R_z-blocks guarantee that the UCG levels within U_{mod} belong to $SU(2^n)$, D_{pha} generally belongs to $U(2^n)$, since $\boldsymbol{b}_{phase}$ is an arbitrary vector of complex phases.

From this matrix representation, it is possible to extract the vector of known terms $\boldsymbol{b}_{mod}^{(k)}$ for each level-k linear system: it corresponds to the vector whose elements are the phase angles, taken in the order in which they appear on the UCR$_z$ diagonal. In the example considered above, $\boldsymbol{b}_{mod}^{(2)} := (-\gamma_1, +\gamma_1, -\gamma_2, +\gamma_2)$. This already makes it clear that $\boldsymbol{v}_{mod}$ does not play the role of the vector of known terms for any level k, but rather it is the fundamental input for determining parameters γ_i of the UCR$_z$ in block representation for each level k. In fact, thanks to the well-known Binary Search Tree (BST) diagram, it is possible to find parameters γ_i for each R_z-block from the knowledge of the moduli $|c_i|$ inside $\boldsymbol{v}_{mod}$. This diagram stores the amplitudes $|c_i|$ of the desired state $|\psi\rangle$ in its leaf nodes. Moreover, every internal node stores the square root of the sum of squares of its child nodes, and the root node stores the l_2-norm of the quantum state. A detailed description of this procedure for the circuit structures considered in this work is provided in [4, Section 2.1].

Accordingly, for each level k, a linear system $M_k \boldsymbol{x}_{mod}^{(k)} = \boldsymbol{b}_{mod}^{(k)}$ needs to be resolved, where M_k is the coefficient matrix derived from the Z-factor (1) of level k, and $\boldsymbol{x}_{mod}^{(k)}$ is the solution vector containing the Lie parameters θ_{j^2-1} in increasing order. By definition, the Z-factor induces a block-recursive structure in the coefficient matrix M_k, allowing the linear system to be solved by considering only one of its blocks (and not the entire matrix), which, in turn, coincides with M_{k-1}. To deduce this recursion, levels $k = 2, 3$ are analyzed in succession below. Equation (1), as a product of exponentials of SRBB diagonal elements, indicates that the Z-factor is a diagonal operator of complex phases, in which the parameters of the Lie algebra θ_{j^2-1} appear in various linear combinations with coefficients ± 1. The latter depends on the Pauli string representation (with only $\mathbb{I}_2$ and σ_3) of the diagonal elements $U_{j^2-1}^{(2^n)} \in \mathcal{J}_Z$ (see, for example, Fig. 3b). These strings, in turn, depend on the binary representation of the position of the elements $U_{j^2-1}^{(2^n)}$ in $\mathcal{J}_Z$. In this way, the recursive properties of the binary strings for numbers from 1 to $2^k - 1$ are inherited by the coefficient matrix M_k. By ordering the coefficients of M_k according to $\boldsymbol{x}_{mod}^{(k)}$, and considering only the signs $\pm$ for simplicity, Fig. 7 shows the resulting recursive scheme. The central Lie parameter $\theta_{2^{n-1}}$ in the sequence $\mathcal{J}_Z$, that is, the one identified by the binary string with the first bit 1 and all the others 0 (column highlighted in bold), allows for any level k to isolate 4 blocks, 2 above and 2 below the continuous line, and always corresponds to the Pauli string with the first element σ_3 and all the others $\mathbb{I}_2$. The blocks thus defined coincide with the matrix M_{k-1} of the previous level and with its opposite:

$$M_k = \begin{pmatrix} M_{k-1} & +1 & M_{k-1} \\ M_{k-1} & -1 & -M_{k-1} \end{pmatrix} \tag{4}$$

The block-structure of the matrix M_k suggests a precise decomposition of the solution space for efficient resolution. While the vector $\boldsymbol{x}_{mod}^{(k)}$ can be partitioned into $(\boldsymbol{u}, c, \boldsymbol{v})$, where $\boldsymbol{u}, \boldsymbol{v} \in \mathbb{R}^{2^{k-1}-1}$ and $c \in \mathbb{R}$, the vector $\boldsymbol{b}_{mod}^{(k)}$ can be decomposed into $(\boldsymbol{p}, \boldsymbol{q})$, with $\boldsymbol{p}, \boldsymbol{q} \in \mathbb{R}^{2^{k-1}}$. This leads to two vector equations,

$$\begin{cases} M_{k-1}\boldsymbol{u} + c\mathbb{I} + M_{k-1}\boldsymbol{v} = \boldsymbol{p} \\ M_{k-1}\boldsymbol{u} - c\mathbb{I} - M_{k-1}\boldsymbol{v} = \boldsymbol{q} \end{cases} \tag{5}$$

where $\mathbb{I}$ indicates the vector of dimension 2^{k-1} with all components $+1$. By adding the two equations, $\boldsymbol{u}$ can be easily obtained from the structure of the previous level, while by subtracting, the role of the constant component c is pointed out in relation to the chosen decomposition:

$$\begin{cases} M_{k-1}\boldsymbol{u} = \frac{\boldsymbol{p}+\boldsymbol{q}}{2} \\ c\mathbb{I} + M_{k-1}\boldsymbol{v} = \frac{\boldsymbol{p}-\boldsymbol{q}}{2} \end{cases} \tag{6}$$

Basically, the chosen decomposition exploits the structural property of M_{k-1}, namely, all its columns have a zero sum: $\mathbb{I}^T M_{k-1} = 0$, which means that the image of M_{k-1} is orthogonal to the constant vector $\mathbb{I}$. It is therefore possible to obtain c by projecting onto $\mathbb{I}$,

$$\mathbb{I}^T(c\mathbb{I} + M_{k-1}\boldsymbol{v}) = \mathbb{I}^T \frac{\boldsymbol{p}-\boldsymbol{q}}{2} \quad \rightarrow \quad c = \frac{1}{2^{k-1}} \sum_i \frac{p_i - q_i}{2} \tag{7}$$

and then subtracting the constant part to recursively obtain $M_{k-1}\boldsymbol{v} = \frac{\boldsymbol{p}-\boldsymbol{q}}{2} - c\mathbb{I}$. From a geometric point of view, c is the projection of $\boldsymbol{b}_{mod}^{(k)}$ onto the constant direction $\mathbb{I}$, which is orthogonal to the image of M_{k-1} (orthogonal decomposition of the space). Therefore, since M_{k-1} exists only in the 0-sum subspace, the constant component needs to be removed to solve recursively.

θ_3	θ_8	θ_{15}
+	+	+
−	+	−
+	−	−
−	−	+

(a) M_2.

θ_3	θ_8	θ_{15}	θ_{24}	θ_{35}	θ_{48}	θ_{63}
+	+	+	+	+	+	+
−	+	−	+	−	+	−
+	−	−	+	+	−	−
−	−	+	+	−	−	+
+	+	+	−	−	−	−
−	+	−	−	+	−	+
+	−	−	−	−	+	+
−	−	+	−	+	+	−

(b) M_3.

Fig. 7. Recursive pattern in the coefficient matrix M_k: M_2 corresponds to the top-left block of M_3, i.e., the block above the solid line and to the left of the bold column. It also coincides with the bottom-left and top-right blocks, while the bottom-right block is precisely $-M_2$.

3.2 Diagonal Z-Factor for Complex Phases

This section focuses on the diagonal operator D_{pha} responsible for preparing each complex phase $e^{i\phi_i}$, and on the Z-factor of level n (maximum level) used to implement it (see, for example, Fig. 3b). Similar to Eq. 3, for arbitrary 2-qubit target states, the matrix to be implemented would be of the following type:

$$D_{pha} = \begin{pmatrix} e^{i\phi_1} & 0 & 0 & 0 \\ 0 & e^{i\phi_2} & 0 & 0 \\ 0 & 0 & e^{i\phi_3} & 0 \\ 0 & 0 & 0 & e^{i\phi_4} \end{pmatrix} \qquad \text{with} \qquad \boldsymbol{b}^{(2)}_{phase} := \begin{pmatrix} \phi_1 \\ \phi_2 \\ \phi_3 \\ \phi_4 \end{pmatrix} \tag{8}$$

which, in general, is an arbitrary $U(4)$ matrix with determinant $e^{i(\phi_1+\phi_2+\phi_3+\phi_4)} \neq 1$. As a consequence, D_{pha} is not representable by the $SU(4)$ traceless generators that construct the Z-factor of Eq. 1. This property is true for any n: without a proper choice of the global phase ϕ_{global} to be removed, the maximum-level system $M_n \boldsymbol{x}^{(n)}_{phase} = \boldsymbol{b}^{(n)}_{phase}$ is not solvable. In other words, the elements $U^{(2^n)}_{j^2-1} \in \mathcal{J}_Z$ can only generate $SU(2^n)$ operators, but not the $U(1)$ global phase. Once the global phase is removed to restrict the parameterization within $SU(2^n)$, the coefficient matrix M_n shows the same structure as discussed for U_{mod} in Sect. 3.1: $\boldsymbol{x}^{(n)}_{phase}$ sorts the Lie parameters θ_{j^2-1} in increasing order, and $\boldsymbol{b}^{(n)}_{phase}$ collects the shifted phase angles $\tilde{\phi}_i$. In the following, we discuss the solvability condition for the linear system that determines the Z-circuit parameters associated with the block D_{pha}.

As pointed out in Sect. 3.1, the left kernel of M_n is generated by the constant vector $\mathbb{I}$, with dimension 2^n and all components $+1$; in formulas, $\mathbb{I}^T M_n = 0$. This immediately implies:

$$\mathbb{I}^T \boldsymbol{b}^{(n)}_{phase} = 0 \qquad \longleftrightarrow \qquad \sum_{j=0}^{2^n-1} b^{(n)}_{phase,j} = 0 \tag{9}$$

which corresponds to the phase configuration needed to achieve a unit determinant and parameterizes $SU(2^n)$. From a practical point of view, the resolvability condition identifies the global phase ϕ_{global} to be removed along with the average of the phases (symmetric choice):

$$\phi_{global} = \frac{1}{2^n} \sum_j \phi_j \tag{10}$$

and the new shifted phases $\tilde{\phi}_j = \phi_j - \phi_{global}$ are centered by construction, $\sum_j \tilde{\phi}_j = 0$.

3.3 Mapping to the Quantum Circuit

For both $\boldsymbol{x}^{(n)}_{phase}$ and $\boldsymbol{x}^{(k)}_{mod}$, where k ranges from 2 to n, the $2^n - 1$ parameters θ_{j^2-1} with $2 \leqslant j \leqslant 2^n$, which constitute the solutions of each of the n linear systems, are ordered from smallest to largest by the construction of the coefficient matrix M_k. As an example, the order of the solution vector for $n = 2, 3$ is shown in Fig. 7. However, as shown by the respective circuits in Figs. 5b and 6, the order in which these parameters enter the circuit is not trivial, especially in light of the recursive scheme of the optimized Z-factor [5, Section 4]. Consequently, it is precisely the Gray Code matrix sorting on which the optimized structure is based that provides the mapping mechanism. After constructing the Gray Code matrix of order n, the elements associated with the strings ending in 1, taken starting from the second and in cyclic order, define the sequence of parameters of the Gray Code-sorted part. The remaining elements make up the part equivalent to the Z-factor of the case $n-1$, and the corresponding binary string is obtained by adding 0 to the binary strings of the case $n-1$. This implies that the parameter associated with the strings ending in 0 of the case n occupies the same position as the parameter associated with the same string minus the last bit of the case $n-1$. Table 1 and Fig. 6 show the parametric mapping in the example case $n = 3$.

Table 1. Parameter mapping rule for $n = 3$.

(a) Binary sorting of $\mathcal{J}_Z^{(3)}$.

Decimal	Binary	Element
1	001	3
2	010	8
3	011	15
4	100	24
5	101	35
6	110	48
7	111	63

(b) Cyclic Gray Code matrices up to $n = 3$.

$n = 1$	$n = 2$		Element	$n = 3$			Element
				0	0	0	-
				0	**0**	**1**	$\mathbf{U_3}$
	0	0	-	**0**	**1**	**1**	$\mathbf{U_{15}}$
0	0	1	U_3	0	1	0	U_8
1	1	1	U_{15}	1	1	0	U_{48}
	1	0	U_8	**1**	**1**	**1**	$\mathbf{U_{63}}$
				1	**0**	**1**	$\mathbf{U_{35}}$
				1	0	0	U_{24}

4 HPC Simulations

Algorithm EQSP_{SRBB} has been implemented with the PennyLane library and is available on GitHub [2]. Its performance has been tested on a Linux machine equipped with an AMD EPYC 7282 CPU and 256 GB of RAM, according to six different metrics: fidelity and trace distance as precision metrics; depth, total number of gates, number of CNOT gates, and number of rotations (R_y, R_z) as circuit metrics. Furthermore, for each type of test, the classical computation time of the exact circuit parameters was indicated. Tables 2, 3, and 4 show, respectively, the preparation of specific quantum states of up to 4 qubits, both dense and sparse random states of up to 6 qubits, and dense random states of up to 12 qubits. Table 2 clearly shows that for real component states (Bell Φ_+, Bell Ψ_+, GHZ, W, Dicke), the total circuit reduces to just U_{mod}, leading to depth reductions. For all configurations of Tables 3 and 4, averaged over 20 random complex states, the fidelity reaches machine precision $\langle F \rangle = 1 - \mathcal{O}(10^{-16} \div 10^{-15})$, with variances in the range $10^{-32} \div 10^{-29}$. The corresponding trace distances are of order 10^{-8}, fully consistent with the relation $D = \sqrt{1-F}$ valid for pure quantum states and with floating-point round-off effects. Instead, the classical preprocessing time exhibits a structured step-like scaling with the number of qubits; this behavior is consistent with the recursive and level-based structure of the algorithm and indicates predictable growth. The results in Tables 2, 3 and 4 can be directly compared with the prior variational QSP approach based on algebraically structured QNNs [4], whose main results are summarized in Table 5. The comparison clearly shows that, for the same circuit costs (same SRBB-based decomposition and therefore same circuit), the translation into an exact paradigm eliminates the issues related to non-convex optimization, while ensuring expressiveness, accuracy, modularity, and an algorithm/circuit algebraically structured on Lie generators.

Table 2. Preparation of well-known quantum states with EQSP_{SRBB}.

Simulation results for specific quantum states								
n	Target State	Fidelity	Trace Distance	Depth	Total Gates	CNOT	R_y, R_z	Time Classical (s)
2	Bell Φ_+	$1 - 3 \times 10^{-16}$	1.49×10^{-8}	8	10	2	4	6.33×10^{-4}
	Bell Φ_-	$1.00 + \mathcal{O}(10^{-16})$	$0.00 + \mathcal{O}(10^{-16})$	12	15	4	7	7.02×10^{-4}
	Bell Ψ_+	$1 - 3 \times 10^{-16}$	1.49×10^{-8}	8	10	2	4	6.88×10^{-4}
	Bell Ψ_-	$1.00 + \mathcal{O}(10^{-16})$	$0.00 + \mathcal{O}(10^{-16})$	12	15	4	7	7.29×10^{-4}
3	GHZ	$1 - 9 \times 10^{-16}$	2.98×10^{-8}	19	27	8	11	1.08×10^{-3}
	W	$1 - 2 \times 10^{-15}$	3.33×10^{-8}					1.10×10^{-3}
	Dicke	$1 - 2 \times 10^{-15}$	3.65×10^{-8}					1.18×10^{-3}
4	GHZ	$1 - 2 \times 10^{-15}$	3.65×10^{-8}	45	60	22	26	2.19×10^{-3}
	W	$1 - 2 \times 10^{-15}$	4.21×10^{-8}					2.14×10^{-3}
	Dicke	$1 - 2 \times 10^{-15}$	4.21×10^{-8}					2.12×10^{-3}

5 Conclusions and Future Work

This work proposes an exact QSP algorithm designed on the $\mathfrak{su}(2^n)$ diagonal component of the SRBB. It implies a recursive circuit structure composed of increasing UCR_z layers, which have been implemented exactly for the first time via the Z-factor of the SRBB. The transition to the gate set $\{R_y, R_z, H, S, CNOT\}$ is mandatory to utilize only the diagonal component of the Hermitian and unitary basis for the complex matrix algebra $M_{2^n}(\mathbb{C})$. This type of decomposition has already been used for QSP, but in a purely variational context susceptible to local minima and barren plateaus, even at a small system size [4]. The difficulties in exploring the non-convex optimization surface as the system size increases are not a technological limitation, but rather a geometric one; consequently, the obstacle to the variational approach when dealing with SRBB is not the non-existence of the circuit, but rather the method

Table 3. Preparation of random quantum states with $EQSP_{SRBB}$.

Simulation results for a sample of 20 random states with complex amplitudes								
n	Type of State	Avg Fidelity $\sigma^2 \in [10^{-32}, 10^{-30}]$	Avg Trace Distance $\sigma^2 \in [10^{-17}, 10^{-16}]$	Depth	Total Gates	CNOT	R_y, R_z	Avg Time Classical (s)
2	dense	$1 - 3 \times 10^{-16}$	2.05×10^{-8}	12	15	4	7	6.30×10^{-4}
	sparse	$1 - 2 \times 10^{-16}$	1.37×10^{-8}					6.29×10^{-4}
3	dense	$1 - 7 \times 10^{-16}$	2.59×10^{-8}	30	40	14	18	1.05×10^{-3}
	sparse	$1 - 6 \times 10^{-16}$	2.45×10^{-8}					1.00×10^{-3}
4	dense	$1 - 2 \times 10^{-15}$	3.44×10^{-8}	71	89	36	41	1.70×10^{-3}
	sparse	$1 - 2 \times 10^{-15}$	3.40×10^{-8}					1.61×10^{-3}
5	dense	$1 - 2 \times 10^{-15}$	3.59×10^{-8}	159	186	82	88	3.14×10^{-3}
	sparse	$1 - 2 \times 10^{-15}$	3.74×10^{-8}					3.08×10^{-3}
6	dense	$1 - 2 \times 10^{-15}$	4.06×10^{-8}	342	379	176	183	5.82×10^{-3}
	sparse	$1 - 2 \times 10^{-15}$	4.07×10^{-8}					5.75×10^{-3}

Table 4. Preparation of random dense quantum states with $EQSP_{SRBB}$.

Simulation results for a sample of 20 random states with complex amplitudes								
n	Type of State	Avg Fidelity $\sigma^2 \in [10^{-31}, 10^{-29}]$	Avg Trace Distance $\sigma^2 \in [10^{-17}, 10^{-15}]$	Depth	Total Gates	CNOT	R_y, R_z	Avg Time Classical (s)
7	dense	$1 - 2 \times 10^{-15}$	4.17×10^{-8}	716	764	366	374	1.16×10^{-2}
8	dense	$1 - 3 \times 10^{-15}$	4.84×10^{-8}	1473	1533	748	757	2.50×10^{-2}
9	dense	$1 - 3 \times 10^{-15}$	4.74×10^{-8}	2997	3070	1514	1524	4.79×10^{-2}
10	dense	$1 - 3 \times 10^{-15}$	5.01×10^{-8}	6056	6143	3048	3059	9.28×10^{-2}
11	dense	$1 - 6 \times 10^{-15}$	6.48×10^{-8}	12186	12288	6118	6130	1.64×10^{-1}
12	dense	$1 - 3 \times 10^{-15}$	4.66×10^{-8}	24459	24577	12260	12273	2.75×10^{-1}

used to search for it. The landscape associated with the loss function has then been replaced with the geometry of the Lie group $SU(2^n)$, whose generators are mapped into circuit elements according to a recursive scheme. The circuit parameters (rotation angles) are directly associated with the Lie parameters by construction and are derived exactly by solving a series of linear systems. The solvability of these systems, and the resulting scalability of the analytic parametric map, are discussed together with the assignment of solutions: it is precisely the recursive structure of the CNOT-optimized Z-circuit that assigns the solutions to the rotation gates in the correct order. The work is not aimed at scalable execution on today's hardware but rather at removing limitations related to variational approaches and building exact evolutions via SRBB, which are prerequisites for future modular optimizations, fault-tolerant synthesis, and efficient compilation. This result eliminates a conceptual bottleneck for SRBB, which has so far been used only in a variational way, and restores control over a type of algorithm naturally connected to Lie algebras. This algebraic control of the new exact framework opens a second line of future development: the proposed algorithm can be thought of as a "conceptual laboratory" where exact unitary computation is a controlled reversible composition plus phase terms.

Table 5. Quantum State Preparation with the SRBB-based QNN.

Simulation results for a sample of 50 random states, including uniform superpositions					
n	Time with Adam	Error with Adam + Fidelity loss	Error with Adam + Trace distance loss	Time with Nelder-Mead	Error with Nelder-Mead + Frobenius loss
2	~ 9 m	$\sim 10^{-15}$	$\sim 10^{-3}$	~ 2 s	$\sim 10^{-15}$
3	~ 16 m	$\sim 10^{-13}$	$\sim 10^{-3}$	~ 30 s	$\sim 10^{-15}$
4	~ 33 m	$\sim 10^{-13}$	$\sim 10^{-3}$	~ 9 m	$\sim 10^{-10}$
5	~ 1 h	$\sim 10^{-7}$	$\sim 10^{-3}$	-	-
6	~ 2 h	$\sim 10^{-3}$	$\sim 10^{-3}$	-	-
7	~ 5 h	$\sim 10^{-3}$	$\sim 10^{-3}$	-	-
8	~ 11 h	$\sim 10^{-3}$	$\sim 10^{-3}$	-	-

One can attempt to describe the quantum (reversible) computational step in a semi-classical way through the formalism of Graphical Linear Algebra, a priori of the choice of coordinates and representative bases. This classical limit of the computational step would not be understood in the sense $\hbar \rightarrow 0$, but in the semantic and informational meaning.

Acknowledgments. The authors acknowledge financial support from the European Union - NextGenerationEU, PNRR MUR project PE0000023-NQSTI. This research benefits from the High Performance Computing facility of the University of Parma, Italy (HPC.unipr.it).

Disclosure of Interests. The authors have no competing interests.

References

1. Belli, G., Amoretti, M.: Algebraic reduction to improve an optimally bounded quantum state preparation algorithm. arXiv preprint arxiv:2602.06535 (2026)
2. Belli, G., Amoretti, M.: Exact Quantum State Preparation with the SRBB (EQSP-SRBB) (2026). https://github.com/qslab-unipr/eqsp-srbb
3. Belli, G., Mordacci, M., Amoretti, M.: A scalable quantum neural network for approximate unitary synthesis. In: 2024 IEEE International Conference on Quantum Computing and Engineering (QCE), vol. 2, pp. 49–54. IEEE (2024)
4. Belli, G., Mordacci, M., Amoretti, M.: SRBB-based quantum state preparation. In: Proceedings of the 22nd ACM International Conference on Computing Frontiers, pp. 172–175 (2025)
5. Belli, G., Mordacci, M., Amoretti, M.: A novel single-layer quantum neural network for approximate SRBB-based unitary synthesis. Quantum **10**, 2034 (2026)
6. Bergholm, V., Vartiainen, J.J., Möttönen, M., Salomaa, M.M.: Quantum circuits with uniformly controlled one-qubit gates. Phys. Rev. A-Atomic Mol. Opt. Phys. **71**(5), 052330 (2005)
7. Berry, D.W., et al.: Improved techniques for preparing eigenstates of fermionic hamiltonians. NPJ Quantum Inf. **4**(1), 22 (2018)

8. Berry, D.W., et al.: Rapid initial-state preparation for the quantum simulation of strongly correlated molecules. PRX Quantum **6**(2), 020327 (2025)
9. Blatt, R., Roos, C.F.: Quantum simulations with trapped ions. Nat. Phys. **8**(4), 277–284 (2012)
10. Caro, M.C., Gil-Fuster, E., Meyer, J.J., Eisert, J., Sweke, R.: Encoding-dependent generalization bounds for parametrized quantum circuits. Quantum **5**, 582 (2021)
11. Cerf, N.J., Bourennane, M., Karlsson, A., Gisin, N.: Security of quantum key distribution using D-level systems. Phys. Rev. Lett. **88**(12), 127902 (2002)
12. Erhard, M., Krenn, M., Zeilinger, A.: Advances in high-dimensional quantum entanglement. Nat. Rev. Phys. **2**(7), 365–381 (2020)
13. Fomichev, S., et al.: Initial state preparation for quantum chemistry on quantum computers. PRX Quantum **5**(4), 040339 (2024)
14. Grover, L., Rudolph, T.: Creating superpositions that correspond to efficiently integrable probability distributions. arXiv preprint quant-ph/0208112 (2002)
15. Gui, K., Dalzell, A.M., Achille, A., Suchara, M., Chong, F.T.: Spacetime-efficient low-depth quantum state preparation with applications. Quantum **8**, 1257 (2024)
16. Hall, B.C.: Lie groups, lie algebras, and representations. In: Quantum Theory for Mathematicians, pp. 333–366. Springer (2013)
17. Iaconis, J., Johri, S., Zhu, E.Y.: Quantum state preparation of normal distributions using matrix product states. NPJ Quantum Inf. **10**(1), 15 (2024)
18. Iten, R., Colbeck, R., Kukuljan, I., Home, J., Christandl, M.: Quantum circuits for isometries. Phys. Rev. A **93**(3), 032318 (2016)
19. Jiang, J., Sun, X., Teng, S.H., Wu, B., Wu, K., Zhang, J.: Optimal space-depth trade-off of CNOT circuits in quantum logic synthesis. In: Proceedings of the Fourteenth Annual ACM-SIAM Symposium on Discrete Algorithms, pp. 213–229. SIAM (2020)
20. Kliuchnikov, V., Bocharov, A., Roetteler, M., Yard, J.: A framework for approximating qubit unitaries. arXiv preprint arXiv:1510.03888 (2015)
21. Kliuchnikov, V., Maslov, D., Mosca, M.: Fast and efficient exact synthesis of single qubit unitaries generated by clifford and t gates. arXiv preprint arXiv:1206.5236 (2012)
22. Kokail, C., et al.: Self-verifying variational quantum simulation of lattice models. Nature **569**(7756), 355–360 (2019)
23. Krenn, M., Huber, M., Fickler, R., Lapkiewicz, R., Ramelow, S., Zeilinger, A.: Generation and confirmation of a (100× 100)-dimensional entangled quantum system. Proc. Natl. Acad. Sci. **111**(17), 6243–6247 (2014)
24. Lee, S., et al.: Evaluating the evidence for exponential quantum advantage in ground-state quantum chemistry. Nat. Commun. **14**(1), 1952 (2023)
25. Malz, D., Styliaris, G., Wei, Z.Y., Cirac, J.I.: Preparation of matrix product states with log-depth quantum circuits. Phys. Rev. Lett. **132**(4), 040404 (2024)
26. Mao, R., Tian, G., Sun, X.: Toward optimal circuit size for sparse quantum state preparation. Phys. Rev. A **110**(3), 032439 (2024)
27. Morales, M.E., et al.: Quantum linear system solvers: a survey of algorithms and applications. arXiv preprint arXiv:2411.02522 (2024)
28. Mottonen, M., Vartiainen, J., Bergholm, V., Salomaa, M.: Transformation of quantum states using uniformly controlled rotations. Quantum Inf. Comput. **5**(6), 467–473 (2005)
29. Möttönen, M., Vartiainen, J.J.: Decompositions of general quantum gates. Trends Quantum Comput. Res. 149 (2006)
30. Möttönen, M., Vartiainen, J.J., Bergholm, V., Salomaa, M.M.: Quantum circuits for general multiqubit gates. Phys. Rev. Lett. **93**(13), 130502 (2004)

31. Muralidharan, S., Li, L., Kim, J., Lütkenhaus, N., Lukin, M.D., Jiang, L.: Optimal architectures for long distance quantum communication. Sci. Rep. **6**(1), 20463 (2016)
32. Plesch, M., Brukner, Č: Quantum-state preparation with universal gate decompositions. Phys. Rev. A-Atomic Mol. Opt. Phys. **83**(3), 032302 (2011)
33. Rath, M., Date, H.: Quantum data encoding: a comparative analysis of classical-to-quantum mapping techniques and their impact on machine learning accuracy. EPJ Quantum Technol. **11**(1), 72 (2024)
34. Sarkar, R.S., Adhikari, B.: Scalable quantum circuits for n-qubit unitary matrices. In: 2023 IEEE International Conference on Quantum Computing and Engineering (QCE), vol. 1, pp. 1078–1088. IEEE (2023)
35. Shende, V.V., Bullock, S.S., Markov, I.L.: Synthesis of quantum logic circuits. In: Proceedings of the 2005 Asia and South Pacific Design Automation Conference, pp. 272–275 (2005)
36. Shende, V.V., Markov, I.L., Bullock, S.S.: Minimal universal two-qubit controlled-not-based circuits. Phys. Rev. A-Atomic Mol. Opt. Phys. **69**(6), 062321 (2004)
37. Sun, X., Tian, G., Yang, S., Yuan, P., Zhang, S.: Asymptotically optimal circuit depth for quantum state preparation and general unitary synthesis. IEEE Trans. Comput. Aided Des. Integr. Circuits Syst. **42**(10), 3301–3314 (2023)
38. Vartiainen, J.J., Möttönen, M., Salomaa, M.M.: Efficient decomposition of quantum gates. Phys. Rev. Lett. **92**(17), 177902 (2004)
39. Vatan, F., Williams, C.: Optimal quantum circuits for general two-qubit gates. Phys. Rev. A-Atomic Mol. Opt. Phys. **69**(3), 032315 (2004)
40. Ward, N.J., Kassal, I., Aspuru-Guzik, A.: Preparation of many-body states for quantum simulation. J. Chem. Phys. **130**(19) (2009)

A Lean Mechanization of Reversible Occurrence Nets

Daniel Dávalos[1] and Hernán Melgratti[1,2](✉)

[1] Facultad de Ciencias Exactas y Naturales, Instituto de Ciencias de la Computación (ICC), Universidad de Buenos Aires, Buenos Aires, Argentina
davalos@uba.ar, hmelgra@dc.uba.ar
[2] CONICET, Buenos Aires, Argentina

Abstract. Petri nets constitute a foundational model of concurrency, which makes their reversible counterparts particularly relevant. Reversible Petri nets have been used to investigate the relationships between different models of concurrency, such as process calculi and event structures. In this paper, we address the problem of mechanizing the theory of reversible Petri nets with causally consistent reversibility. Specifically, we present a full mechanization of reversible Occurrence Petri nets in the Lean proof assistant. We formally verify that this model satisfies causal-dependent reversibility by mechanizing the so-called parabolic lemma.

Keywords: Reversibility · Concurrency · Proof mechanization

1 Introduction

Over the past decades, significant research has been devoted to equipping computational models with reversible semantics [1,15]. As a foundational model for concurrency, Petri nets have been the subject of numerous extensions aimed at incorporating reversible behaviours [12–14,20,21].

Previous efforts to mechanize reversible models have focused primarily on sequential computation. In the imperative setting, [19] employs the Matita proof assistant to establish a full abstraction result between the operational and denotational semantics of a C-like reversible language, while [18] introduces S-CORE in Coq, certifying its operational semantics as a system of total bijections. Developments in functional and algebraic models include [9], which uses Lean to formalize Reversible Primitive Permutations (RPP) and verify their equivalence to primitive recursive functions. Also, [6] uses Agda to mechanize an iterative calculus capable of handling dynamic data structures. Despite these advances, the formalization of concurrent models remains limited. The only existing mechanization of a reversible concurrent model is $CCSK^p$ in [4]. Our work extends

This work has been partially supported by the MSCA SE project QCOMICAL (Grant Agreement ID: 101182520).

C. Aubert and L. Roversi (Eds.): RC 2026, LNCS 16626, pp. 95–111, 2026.
https://doi.org/10.1007/978-3-032-30839-9_5

this landscape by providing the first mechanization of reversible Petri nets. To carry out this mechanization, we selected Lean as the proof assistant. Lean [16] is an interactive theorem prover based on dependent type theory with inductive types [3]. Our work makes the following contributions:

- The first mechanization of Petri nets in Lean, including their operational semantics; the notion of occurrence nets and a proof that they are safe.
- The mechanization of reversible Petri nets and reversible occurrence nets.
- A complete mechanized proof of the fundamental reversibility properties: cancellation, the loop lemma, backtracking, and the parabolic lemma.

Notably, our formalization clarifies a critical theoretical requirement: the proof of the parabolic lemma relies on the **safety** of reversible occurrence nets to justify the swapping of transitions. This condition, essential for the correctness of the mechanized proof, was not made explicit in the original presentation [14].

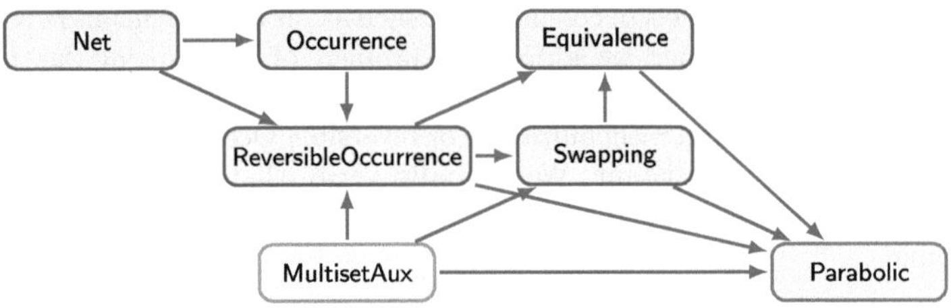

Fig. 1. Organizational structure of the library's files and their dependencies.

The resulting formalization[1] comprises seven modules totaling over 2,000 lines of code and builds upon Mathlib4. The architectural dependencies and the specific role of each file are illustrated in Fig. 1 and summarized below:

- `Net` (Sect. 2): Formalizes standard Petri nets and their operational semantics in terms of firing sequences.
- `Occurrence` (Setion 3): Focuses on the construction of occurrence nets and their properties, specifically 1-safety and basic structural constraints.
- `ReversibleOccurrence` (Sect. 4): Extends nets with reversing transitions, establishing the cancellation property, and formalizes reversible occurrence nets by verifying that both backtracking and the loop lemma hold.
- `Swapping` (Sect. 5): Establishes properties regarding the swapping of concurrent transitions.
- `Equivalence` (Sect. 5): Formalizes an equivalence relation over firing sequences underlying the statement of the parabolic lemma.
- `Parabolic` (Sect. 5): Provides the mechanization and formal proofs of the parabolic lemma.
- `MultisetAux`: Supplies auxiliary definitions and lemmas on multisets utilized throughout the library.

[1] https://github.com/DanielDavalos93/reversible-occ-nets.

2 Nets

We present the Lean formalization of Place/Transition nets, detailing their syntax, semantics, and examples. We begin by introducing some preliminary concepts on multisets. Let S be a set, a *multiset* over S is a function $m : S \to \mathbb{N}$, where $m(s)$ denotes the number of times that the element s occurs in S, called *multiplicity*. We denote by $\mathbb{N}^S$ the set of all multisets over S. For $m \in \mathbb{N}^S$, we define its *cardinality* as $|m| = \sum_{s \in S} m(s)$. We write $\emptyset$ for the empty multiset, i.e., $|\emptyset| = 0$. For $s \in S$, we write s for the singleton multiset consisting of s, i.e., the multiset m with $m(s) = 1$ and $m(x) = 0$ for all $x \neq s$. Let $m_1, m_2 \in \mathbb{N}^S$ be two multisets. The standard operations on multisets are defined pointwise for $s \in S$: addition as $(m_1+m_2)(s) := m_1(s)+m_2(s)$, subtraction as $(m_1-m_2)(s) := \max\{m_1(s) - m_2(s), 0\}$, intersection as $(m_1 \cap m_2)(s) := \min\{m_1(s), m_2(s)\}$, and the subset relation $(m_1 \leq m_2)$ as $\exists m, m_1 + m = m_2$. In our implementation of nets, we use the type `Multiset S` provided by the Mathlib project on Lean, which represents multisets of elements of type S.

Definition 1 (Net and Marked Net). *A* net *N is a tuple $N = (\alpha, \beta, {}^\bullet\_, \_^\bullet)$, where α is a nonempty set of places, β is the set of transitions, and ${}^\bullet\_, \_^\bullet : \beta \to \mathbb{N}^\alpha$ assign source and target to each transition. We consider only nets in which every transition both consumes and produces, i.e., ${}^\bullet\mathsf{t} \neq \emptyset$ and $\mathsf{t}^\bullet \neq \emptyset$ for all $\mathsf{t} \in \beta$. A* marking *m of a net N is a multiset of places, i.e., $m \in \mathbb{N}^\alpha$. A* marked net *is a pair (N, m_0) where N is a net and m_0 is a marking of N.*

Our definition in Lean is in Listing 1, where a net is a structure `Net` (line 1), which is parameterized on the set of places α and the set of transitions β. The components `pre` and `post` implement the preset and postset functions, and `cons_prod` is a proof that every transition is both consuming and producing, i.e., each preset and postset is non-empty (lines 2–4). A marked net is defined (lines 6–7) using Lean's inheritance mechanism (`extends`), making it essentially a net together with an additional multiset m_0 representing the marking.

```
1 structure Net (α : Type) (β : Type) where
2   pre       : β → Multiset α
3   post      : β → Multiset α
4   cons_prod : (∀ t, pre t ≠ ∅ ∧ post t ≠ ∅)
5
6 structure MarkedNet α β extends Net α βwhere
7   m₀ : Multiset α
```

Listing 1. Definitions of nets and marked nets.

Example 1. Consider the net $N_1 = (\mathsf{Pl}, \mathsf{Tr}, {}^\bullet\_, \_^\bullet)$, where Pl is $\{\mathsf{a}, \mathsf{b}, \mathsf{c}, \mathsf{d}, \mathsf{e}\}$, Tr is $\{\mathsf{t}_1, \mathsf{t}_2\}$, and the pre- and postset functions are as follows: ${}^\bullet t_1 = \{\mathsf{a}, \mathsf{b}\}$ and ${}^\bullet t_2 = \{\mathsf{b}, \mathsf{c}\}$, $t_1^\bullet = \{\mathsf{d}\}$ and $t_2^\bullet = \{\mathsf{e}\}$. The net N_1 is depicted in Fig. 2: places are represented as circles, transitions as rectangles, and arcs connect each transition with the places in its pre- and postsets. The marked net $M_1 = (N_1, m_0)$, composed by N_1 and the marking $m_0 = \mathsf{a} + \mathsf{b} + \mathsf{c}$, is illustrated in Fig. 2b. While places represent resources, each occurrence of a place in a marking represents an instance of that resource. Such instances are called **tokens**. Hence, for a marking

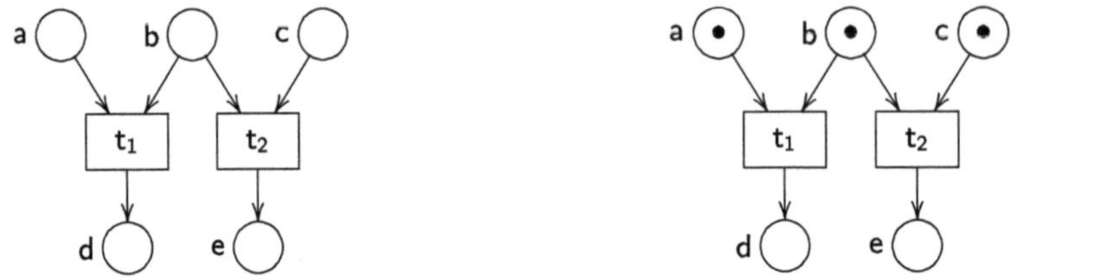

(a) Net N_1 (b) Marked net $M_1 = (N_1, \mathsf{a} + \mathsf{b} + \mathsf{c})$

Fig. 2. A simple example of net and their corresponding marked net.

m and a place p, the value $m(p)$ denotes the number of tokens in p. Graphically, tokens are represented as bullets inside their corresponding places.

```
8 inductive Pl | a | b | c | d | e deriving DecidableEq
9 inductive Tr | t₁ | t₂
10 open Pl Tr
11
12 def pre : Tr → Multiset Pl
13   | t₁ => {a,b}
14   | t₂ => {b,c}
15
16 def post : Tr → Multiset Pl
17   | t₁ => {d}
18   | t₂ => {e}
19
20 def cons_prod : ∀ t : Tr, pre ≠ ∅  ∧ post ≠ ∅ := by
21   intro t
22   cases h: t; all_goals {unfold pre post; simp_all}
23
24 def N₁ : Net Pl Tr := ⟨pre, post, cons_prod⟩
25
26 def M₁ : MarkedNet Pl Tr := ⟨N₁, {a,b,c}⟩
```

Listing 2. Definition of N_1 and M_1.

The definitions of N_1 and M_1 in Lean are in Listing 2. The inductive types `Pl` and `Tr` (lines 8–9) represent the sets of places and transitions, respectively. The functions `pre` (lines 12–14) and `post` (lines 16–18), which are defined by cases, map each transition to the corresponding set of places. Finally, `cons_prod` consists of a proof that every transition is both consuming and producing (lines 20–22), obtained by case analysis on transitions and applying the definitions of `pre` and `post`. `N₁` (line 24) and `M₁` (line 26) are structures of type `Net Pl Tr` and `MarkedNet Pl Tr`, respectively, using the elements previously introduced. □

The pre- and postsets of a place p are ${}^\bullet p = \{t \mid p \in t^\bullet\}$ and $p^\bullet = \{t \mid p \in {}^\bullet t\}$. Their Lean definitions, along with those for transitions, appear in Listing 3 (lines 27–31). Lines 33–36 introduce the shorthand $\bullet\{\!\!\{N\}\!\!\}x$ and $x \bullet \{\!\!\{N\}\!\!\}$ for unified pre- and postset syntax. The *minimal* elements of a net are those with an empty preset; as all transitions are consuming, these are necessarily places. This is defined in line 38.

```
27 def presetₚ  (N : Net α β) (p : α) : Set β :=  {t | p ∈ N.post t}
28 def postsetₚ (N : Net α β) (p : α) : Set β :=  {t | p ∈ N.pre t}
29
```

```
def preset_t  (N : Net α β) (t : β) : Multiset α :=  N.pre t
def postset_t (N : Net α β) (t : β) : Multiset α :=  N.post t

notation:max "•⦃" N "⦄ " p:max => preset_p ↑N p
notation:max p:max "•⦃" N "⦄"  => postset_p ↑N p
notation:max "•⦃" N "⦄ " t:max => preset_t ↑N t
notation:max t:max "•⦃" N "⦄"  => postset_t ↑N t

def minimal (N : Net α β) : Set α := {p | •⦃N⦄ p = ∅ }
```

Listing 3. Pre- and postset for places and transitions.

2.1 Operational Semantics

The Lean operational semantics follow [2], defining *firing* of single *enabled* transition, and then *firing sequences* for their successive execution.

Definition 2 (Enabled transition). *Let N be a net. A transition* t *is* enabled *at a marking m, denoted $m[\![\mathtt{t}]\!]_{\{\!\{N\}\!\}}$, if ${}^\bullet\mathtt{t} \leq m$.*

A transition is *enabled* if the marking contains its preset, i.e., as many tokens as those required by the transition's preset. The Lean definition (Listing 4, lines 39–40) uses the multiset order ≤. Line 42 introduces the notation `m⟦t⟧⦃N⦄`.

```
39 def is_enabled (N : Net α β) (m : Multiset α) (t : β) : Prop :=
40   •⦃N⦄ t ≤m
41
42 notation:50  m:51 "⟦" t:51 "⟧⦃" N "⦄" => is_enabled ↑N m t
```

Listing 4. Enabled transition.

The *firing semantics* defines the transition $m \xrightarrow{t} m'$ where an enabled transition t *consumes* its preset ${}^\bullet t$ and *produces* its postset $t^\bullet$.

Definition 3 (Firing and firing sequence). *The* firing *of a transition t enabled at m is denoted $m[\![t\rangle_{\{\!\{N\}\!\}}m'$, where $m' = m - {}^\bullet t + t^\bullet$. For a (possibly empty) sequence $s = t_1; \ldots; t_n$, the* firing sequence *$m[\![s\rangle\!\rangle_{\{\!\{N\}\!\}}m'$ is defined by the chain:*

$$m[\![\mathtt{t}_1\rangle_{\{\!\{N\}\!\}}m_1 \wedge m_1[\![\mathtt{t}_2\rangle_{\{\!\{N\}\!\}}m_2 \wedge \cdots \wedge m_{n-1}[\![\mathtt{t}_n\rangle_{\{\!\{N\}\!\}}m'$$

The Lean implementation of Definition 3 is shown in Listing 5. Lines 43–45 define the marking reached after firing a transition t from m, where the empty parameter _ ensures t is enabled. We include the `[DecidableEq α]` constraint because Lean's multiset operations require decidable equality on places to remain constructive. Finally, lines 47–49 define the firing relation $m[\![t\rangle_{\{\!\{N\}\!\}}m'$, which holds if firing t at m results in m'.

```
43 def marking_after_firing [DecidableEq α] (N : Net α β) (m : Multiset α)
44     (_: m⟦t⟧⦃N⦄) : Multiset α:=
45   m - •⦃N⦄ t + t•⦃N⦄
46
47 def is_firing [DecidableEq α] (N : Net α β) (m : Multiset α)
48     (h : m ⟦t⟧⦃N⦄) (m' : Multiset α) : Prop :=
49   marking_after_firing N m h = m'
50
```

```
51 notation:50 m:50 "⟦" h:51 "⟩{{" N "}}" q:51 => is_firing ↑N m h q
52
53 inductive firing_sequence : Net α β → Multiset α → List β →
54   Multiset α →Prop
55   | empty m :
56       firing_sequence _ m [] m
57   | step {N : Net α β} {t : β} {ts : List β} {m m' m'' : Multiset α}
58       (et : m ⟦t⟧{{N}})
59       (f : m ⟦et⟩{{N}}m')
60       (fs : firing_sequence N m' ts m'') :
61       firing_sequence N m (t :: ts) m''
62
63 notation:50  m:50 "⟦" h:50 "⟫{{" N "}}" q:51 => is_firing_sequence ↑N m h q
```

Listing 5. Firing and firing sequence.

We formalize firing sequences in Lean via the inductive type `firing_sequence` (Listing 5), which relates a net N, an initial marking m, a list of transitions, and a final marking m''. The definition consists of two constructors: `empty` (line 55–56) represents the base case where an empty sequence leaves the marking unchanged; and `step` (lines 57–61) recursively builds a firing sequence for the list of transitions `t :: ts`. A step requires a proof that t is enabled at m (`et`), a proof that its firing produces an intermediate marking m' (`f`), and a proof of the existence of a firing sequence for the remainder `ts` from m' to m'' (`fs`).

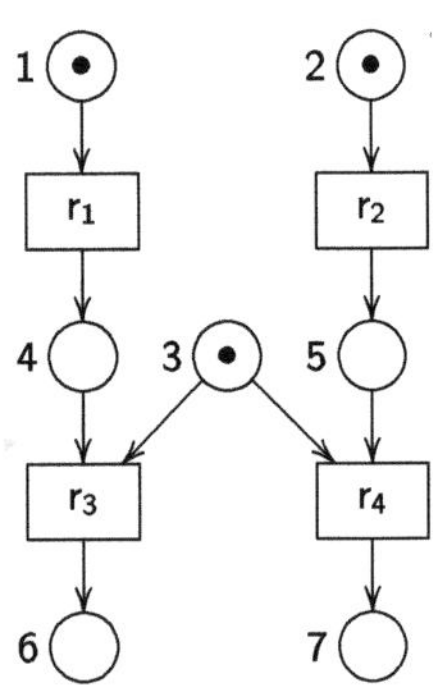

Fig. 3. $(N_2, 1+2+3)$

```
/-- Net N₂ previously defined in
     Nets.lean
-/
example : {1,2,3} ⟦[r₁,r₂,r₃]⟫{{N₂}} {5,6}
     := by
  unfold is_firing_sequence
  have et₁ : {1,2,3} ⟦r₁⟧{{N₂}} := ...
  have fir₁ : {1,2,3} ⟦et₁⟩{{N₂}} {4,2,3}
     := ...
  have et₂ : {4,2,3} ⟦r₂⟧{{N₂}} := ...
  have fir₂ : {4,2,3} ⟦et₂⟩{{N₂}} {4,5,3}
     := ...
  have et₃ : {4,5,3} ⟦r₃⟧{{N₂}} := ...
  have fir₃ : {4,5,3} ⟦et₃⟩{{N₂}} {5,6} :=
     ...
  apply firing_sequence.step et₁ fir₁ <|
        firing_sequence.step et₂ fir₂ <|
        firing_sequence.step et₃ fir₃ <|
        firing_sequence.empty {5,6}
```

Listing 6. An example of the firing sequence for the net N_2, from $1 + 2 + 3$ to $5 + 6$ throughout the transitions r_1, r_2 and r_3 (in this order). In this code we present the proof of this firing sequence.

Example 2. Consider the net N_2 (Fig. 3), defined analogously to N_1 in Example 1. We formalize the firing sequence from $m = 1 + 2 + 3$ to $m' = 5 + 6$ via $s = [r_1, r_2, r_3]$ as shown in Listing 6 (where `...` stands for elided code). The proof proceeds by establishing that each r_i is enabled at its respective marking m_{i-1} as auxiliary hypothesis introduced by tactic have (lines 68, 70 and 72), where $m_0 = 1+2+3$, $m_1 = 4+2+3$, $m_2 = 4+5+6$ and $m_3 = 5+6$. These enablings are verified by unfolding definitions and simplifying the multiset expressions. Subsequently, we prove that each transition r_i fires from m_{i-1} to m_i (lines 69, 71 and 73). Finally, the proof is concluded by repeatedly applying the `step` constructor of the `firing_sequence` type. □

We conclude by recalling the notion of reachable marking and 1-safe nets.

Definition 4 (Reachable markings and safe nets). *The set of* reachable markings *of a net N starting from m_0, denoted by reach(N, m_0), is the set of all markings obtainable through some firing sequence, i.e., $\{m' \mid \exists s,\ m_0\ [\![s\rangle\!\rangle_{\{\!\{N\}\!\}}\ m'\}$. A marked net is* 1-safe *(or simply, safe) if every reachable marking is a set, i.e., $m \in$ reach(N, m_0) implies $m \in 2^\alpha$.*

The Lean implementation in Listing 7 characterizes reachability via the auxiliary `is_reachable` predicate (lines 78–79). Accordingly, the reachability set of a marked net (N, m_0) is defined as the collection of all markings reachable from m_0 (lines 81–82). To formalize the property of 1-safety, we utilize the `Nodup` predicate (lines 86–87), which ensures that every reachable marking is a set, i.e., it contains no duplicate elements.

```
78 def is_reachable (N : Net α β) (m m': Multiset α) : Prop :=
79   ∃ fs : List β, firing_sequence N m fs m'
80
81 def reachable (M : MarkedNet α β) : Set (Multiset α) :=
82   {m' | is_reachable M.toNet M.m₀ m'}
83
84 notation:50 N:51 "⇝" m:51  =>  m ∈ reachable ↑N
85
86 def safe [DecidableEq α] (M : MarkedNet α β) : Prop :=
87   ∀ m, M ⇝ m → Nodup m
```

Listing 7. Reachable marking definition.

3 Occurrence Nets

Occurrence nets provide a causal semantics for Petri nets by modeling all possible execution histories as an acyclic structure [17]. The structure of an occurrence net induces a partial order over transitions, explicitly capturing their *causal dependencies*. Furthermore, it distinguishes between *conflicts*, i.e., events that cannot coexist in the same execution, and *concurrent* events, which are causally independent and not in conflict. We start by introducing the main ingredients in the definition of occurrence nets.

Definition 5 (Causal Dependency). *Let N be a net. The* immediate dependency relation $<_{\{\!\{N\}\!\}} \subseteq (\alpha \cup \beta) \times (\alpha \cup \beta)$ *is defined by*

$$<_{\{\!\{N\}\!\}} := \{(x, y) \mid (y \in \beta \wedge x \in {}^\bullet y) \vee (x \in \beta \wedge y \in x^\bullet)\} \quad (1)$$

We denote the transitive closure of $\lessdot_{\{\!\{N\}\!\}}$ *as the* causal relation $\prec_{\{\!\{N\}\!\}}$, *and its reflexive-transitive closure as the* causal preorder $\preceq_{\{\!\{N\}\!\}}$. *A net is* acyclic *if its causal relation is irreflexive, i.e., there is no* $x \in \alpha \cup \beta$ *such that* $x \prec_{\{\!\{N\}\!\}} x$.

Intuitively, y causally depends on x if y consumes tokens from place x, or if x produces tokens in place y. The Lean implementation of immediate dependency and causal preorder is presented in Listing 8. Immediate dependency (lines 1–4) is defined via *pattern matching* over the disjoint union $\alpha \oplus \beta$, using the canonical embeddings `inl` and `inr` for places and transitions, respectively. This encoding directly formalizes Definition 5 by specifying dependencies between adjacent elements (lines 2–3) while mapping all other combinations to false (line 4). The transitive and reflexive-transitive closures are subsequently derived using the Lean `TransGen` and `ReflTransGen` types. The acyclicity property is straightforwardly defined in lines 18–19.

```
1 def immediate (N: Net α β) : (α ⊕ β) → (α ⊕ β) →Prop
2   | inl p, inr t   =>   p ∈ •{{N}}t
3   | inr t, inl p   =>   p ∈ t •{{N}}
4   | _, _           =>   false
5
6 notation:200 l:201 " < {{" N "}} " r:202 => immediate ↑N l r
7
8 def causal (N : Net α β) : (α ⊕ β) → (α ⊕ β) → Prop :=
9   TransGen (immediate N)
10
11 notation:200 l:201 " ≺ {{" N "}} " r:202 => causal ↑N l r
12
13 def preorder (N : Net α β) : (α ⊕ β) → (α ⊕ β) → Prop :=
14   ReflTransGen (immediate N)
15
16 notation:200 l:201 " ≼ {{" N "}} " r:202 => preorder ↑N l r
17
18 def acyclic (N : Net α β) : Prop :=
19   ∀ x : α ⊕ β, ¬(x ≺ {{N}} x)
```

Listing 8. Immediate dependency, causal preorder, and acyclicity.

Definition 6 (Conflict). *Two distinct transitions* t_1, t_2 *are in* immediate conflict *if they share a common pre-place, i.e.,* ${}^\bullet t_1 \cap {}^\bullet t_2 \neq \emptyset$, *denoted by* $t_1 \#_{0\{\!\{N\}\!\}} t_2$. *The* conflict relation $\#_{\{\!\{N\}\!\}}$ *is then defined over* $x, y \in \alpha \cup \beta$ *if there exist transitions* t_1, t_2 *such that* $t_1 \preceq_{\{\!\{N\}\!\}} x$, $t_2 \preceq_{\{\!\{N\}\!\}} y$, *and* $t_1 \#_{0\{\!\{N\}\!\}} t_2$.

The Lean implementation of immediate conflict and conflict relations is shown in Listing 9. Both predicates are direct formalizations of Definition 6, utilizing the `Disjoint` predicate to assert that two presets are disjoint. The corresponding notations are introduced in lines 23 and 28.

Definition 7 (Backward conflict). *A place* s *has a* backward conflict *if it is produced by two distinct transitions:* $\exists t_1, t_2, (t_1 \neq t_2) \wedge (s \in t_1^\bullet) \wedge (s \in t_2^\bullet)$.

```
20 def immediate_conflict (N : Net α β) (t t' : β) : Prop :=
21   t ≠ t' ∧ ¬(Disjoint (•{{N}} t) (•{{N}} t'))
22
23 notation:50 l:50 " #0{{" N "}} " r:51 => immediate_conflict ↑N l r
24
25 def conflict (N : Net α β) (x y : α ⊕ β) : Prop :=
```

```
  ∃ t t' : β, (inr t ⪯{N} x) ∧ (inr t' ⪯{N} y) ∧ (t #₀{N} t')

notation:50 l:50 " #{" N "} " r:51 => conflict ↑N l r

def backward_conflict (N : Net α β) (a : α) : Prop :=
  ∃ t t' : β, t ≠ t' ∧ inr t ≺{N} inl a ∧ inr t' ≺{N} inl a
```

Listing 9. Conflict and backward conflict.

Two distinct elements $x, y \in \alpha \cup \beta$ are *concurrent*, denoted $x\ co_{\{\!\{N\}\!\}}\ y$, if they are neither causally dependent ($x \not\preceq_{\{\!\{N\}\!\}} y$ and $y \not\preceq_{\{\!\{N\}\!\}} x$) nor in conflict ($\neg(x \#_{\{\!\{N\}\!\}} y)$). A multiset X consists of *concurrent places* if it has no duplicates and every pair of distinct places is concurrent. The formalization (Listing 10) implements the definition of concurrent elements in lines 32–33 and characterizes the set of concurrent places in lines 37–38.

```
32 def concurrent (N : Net α β) (x y : α ⊕ β) : Prop :=
33   x ≠ y ∧ ¬(x ⪯{N} y) ∧ ¬(y ⪯{N} x) ∧ ¬(x #{N} y)
34
35 notation:200 l:200 "co{" N "} " r:201 => concurrent ↑N l r
36
37 def Concurrent (N : Net α β) (m : Multiset α) : Prop :=
38   Nodup m ∧ (∀ {x y : α}, x ∈ m → y ∈ m → x ≠ y → inl x co{N} inl y)
```

Listing 10. Concurrency.

Occurrence nets admit different formulation. We recall the definition given in [11].

Definition 8 (Occurrence net). *A marked net (N, m_0) is an occurrence net if it satisfies the following statements:*

1. *N is acyclic;*
2. *there is no self-conflict, i.e., $\neg(\mathtt{t}\#_{\{\!\{N\}\!\}}\mathtt{t})$ for all transition* t*;*
3. *there is no backward conflict;*
4. *N is 1-safe, i.e., marking is a set;*
5. *the initial marking is the set of initial places, i.e., m_0 is minimal.*

Our formalization in Lean takes a slight detour for the sake of simplicity and convenience when proving the main result of this paper. Instead of requiring the net to be 1-safe as in condition (4), we impose an alternative constraint: the preset and postset of every transition must be a set. We later show that this alternative formulation implies that the net is indeed safe.

The Lean definition is given in Listing 11. We split our implementation into two parts: the constraints on the structure of the net (Lines 39–44) and then, we add the conditions on the initial marking (Lines 46–49). Lines 40–42 correspond to conditions (1)–(3) of Definition 8. Lines 43–44 reflect our alternative to condition (4): it ensures that no transition has duplicate tokens in its pre- or postset.

Lines 46–49 define a marked occurrence net, requiring that the net satisfies the structural conditions (via `is_occurrence`) and that the marking itself is a set of minimal places. We note that our implementation is weaker than condition (5) of Definition 8, as it does not enforce that every initial place is marked.

This limitation arises because sets in Lean are potentially infinite and cannot be directly converted into multisets. However, we emphasize that this does not affect the reversibility results presented in the paper.

```
structure is_occurrence (N : Net α β) : Prop where
  acyclicity : acyclic N
  no_self_conflict : (∀ t : β, ¬ (N : inr t #⦃N⦄ inr t))
  no_backward_conflict : (∀ a : α, ¬backward_conflict N a)
  set_preset : (∀ t : β, Nodup (•⦃N⦄ t))
  set_postset : (∀ t : β, Nodup (t •⦃N⦄))

structure is_marked_occurrence (M : MarkedNet α β) : Prop where
  occurrence :  is_occurrence M.toNet
  initial_set : Nodup M.m₀
  initial_minimal : ∀ {x}, x ∈ M.m₀  → x ∈ minimal M.toNet
```

Listing 11. Definition of an occurrence net.

We conclude this section by noting that our Lean definition of marked occurrence nets (Listing 11) implies that it is *safe*, by a theorem namely `occ_net_safe`.

As for occurrence nets, we have shown that marked reversible occurrence nets are 1-safe (theorem `reversible_occ_net_safe`).

4 Reversible Occurrence Nets

A *reversible occurrence net* is essentially a net in which transitions are classified as either *forward* or *backward* and its executions are causally consistent [11,22]. Forward transitions correspond to the standard transitions of a net, governing the normal flow of execution, whereas backward transitions are intended to undo the effect of firing their corresponding forward transitions. While various formulations of reversible nets exist [12–14,20,21], we follow the presentation in [14], where every forward transition is uniquely reversible. This differs from selective models where only a subset of transitions may be undone [13]. We adopt an explicit naming convention where $\overleftrightarrow{t}$ denotes the reversal of t, in contrast to abstract approaches that partition transitions into forward and backward subsets and leave the functional correspondence implicit [11].

Definition 9. *A* reversible occurrence net *is a net* $N = (\alpha, \beta \uplus \{\overleftrightarrow{t} \mid t \in \beta\}, {}^\bullet\_, \_^\bullet)$ *defined by the following conditions:*

1. $(\alpha, \beta, ({}^\bullet\_)_{|\beta}, (\_^\bullet)_{|\beta})$ *is an occurrence net, where* $f_{|\beta}$ *denotes the restriction of the function* f *to the domain* β.
2. *For every* $t \in \beta$, ${}^\bullet t = (\overleftrightarrow{t})^\bullet$ *and* $t^\bullet = {}^\bullet(\overleftrightarrow{t})$.

A reversible occurrence net is an occurrence net (Condition 1) augmented with a set of reversing transitions $\{\overleftrightarrow{t} \mid t \in \beta\}$. Each $\overleftrightarrow{t}$ undoes its forward counterpart t by swapping its preset and postset: ${}^\bullet(\overleftrightarrow{t}) = t^\bullet$ and $(\overleftrightarrow{t})^\bullet = {}^\bullet t$ (Condition 2).

Example 3. Figure 4 depicts the reversible occurrence net R_1, obtained as the reversible extension of the occurrence net M_1 shown in Fig. 2b. The net R_1 preserves the places of M_1 and augments its set of transitions with two additional backward transitions, $\overleftarrow{t_1}$ and $\overleftarrow{t_2}$. Restricting R_1 to its forward transitions yields exactly M_1, which is an occurrence net. Furthermore, the pre- and postsets of the backward transitions satisfy condition 2 of Definition 9. □

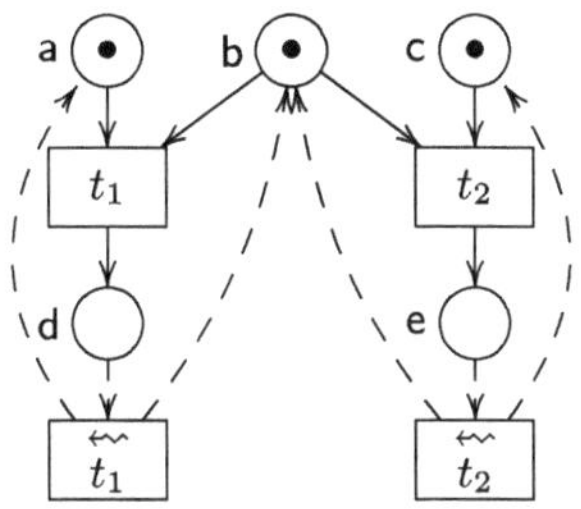

Fig. 4. Reversible net R_1.

```
1 inductive TransitionType
2 | fwd : TransitionType
3 | bwd : TransitionType
4 abbrev Transition (β : Type) :=
5     β×TransitionType
```

Listing 12. Transition types.

We adopt a concrete representation of the disjoint union $\beta \uplus \{\overleftarrow{t} \mid t \in \beta\}$ as a Cartesian product. In this representation, each transition is a pair consisting of a name and a direction: the first component records the transition's name, while the second component specifies its direction. Forward and backward transitions with the same name correspond to one another under this mapping. To this end, we introduce the inductive type `TransitionType` for indicating the direction of a transition as shown in Listing 12 (lines 1–3). Then, the set $\beta \uplus \{\overleftarrow{t} \mid t \in \beta\}$ is abbreviated as `Transition` β (line 5). The pair $\langle t, \mathsf{fwd}\rangle$ represents a forward transition t, while $\langle t, \mathsf{bwd}\rangle$ is its reversing counterpart. To manage these, we introduce the `isFwd` and `isBwd` predicates (Listing 13, lines 6 and 8). We further define the `reverse` function (lines 18–19), which maps a transition to its opposite direction, and the `inverse` predicate (line 34), denoted $t \leftharpoondown\rightharpoonup t'$, which holds if two transitions are reversals of each other. We prove the `inverse` relation is *irreflexive*, *symmetric*, and satisfies *unicity* (one reverse per transition), and induces a *coinvolution*.

Our implementation of reversible occurrence nets is shown in Listing 13. We introduce `Reversible` nets (lines 38–39) as an extension of `Net`. A reversible net with transition names β corresponds to a net with transitions `Transition` β (i.e., backward and forward). The property `welldef` ensures that reversing transitions correctly reverse their corresponding forward transitions (line 39): the pre- and postset of reversing transitions are swapped. Our formulation slightly deviates from Listing 9 by applying the condition to both transition directions and verifying only the correspondence between a transition's preset and its reverse's postset. However, we prove the converse holds for forward transitions; specifically, lemmas `mem_pre_of_mem_pre` and `mem_post_of_mem_post` ensure the second condition of Definition 9 is satisfied.

```
def isFwd (t : Transition β) : Prop := t.snd = fwd

def isBwd (t : Transition β) : Prop := t.snd = bwd

prefix:50 "▷" => isFwd
prefix:50 "◁" => isBwd

def opposite (tt : TransitionType) : TransitionType :=
  match tt with
  | fwd  => bwd
  | bwd  => fwd

def reverse (t : Transition β) : Transition β:=
  (t.fst, opposite (t.snd))

prefix:300 "↼ " => reverse

def all_forward : (l : List (Transition β)) →Prop
  | []        =>  true
  | (h :: t) => ▷h ∧ all_forward t

def all_backward : (l : List (Transition β)) →Prop
  | []        =>  true
  | (h :: t) => ◁h ∧ all_backward t

prefix:50 "▷▷" => all_forward
prefix:50 "◁◁" => all_backward

def inverse (t t' : Transition β) : Prop := t = ↼t'

notation:300 l:300 "↼⇀" r:301 => inverse l r

structure Reversible α β extends Net α (Transition β) where
  welldef (t t' : Transition β) : t ↼⇀ t' → •⦃toNet⦄t = t'•⦃toNet⦄

structure ReversibleOccurrence α β extends Reversible α βwhere
  isOccurrence : is_occurrence (fwd_subnet toNet)

structure MarkedReversibleOccurrence α β extends Reversible α βwhere
  m₀ : Multiset α
  isFwdMarkedOccurrence : is_marked_occurrence ⟨fwd_subnet toNet, m₀⟩

def markedRO_to_RO (MO : MarkedReversibleOccurrence α β) :
    ReversibleOccurrence α β:=
  ⟨MO.toReversible, MO.isFwdMarkedOccurrence.occurrence⟩
```

Listing 13. Reverse transitions and reversible nets.

Reversible occurrence nets (`ReversibleOccurrence`) extend `Reversible` by requiring their forward subnet (`fwd_subnet`) to be an occurrence net (listing 13), as defined by `is_occurrence` in listing 11. Likewise, `MarkedReversibleOccurrence` extends `Reversible` with an initial marking.

4.1 Properties of Reversible Occurrence Nets

We use our formalization to prove (i) *structural properties* of reversible occurrence nets, and (ii) *reversibility properties* that ensure the correct definition of a reversible computational model. The main structural properties are: `forward_disjoint_postset` stating that distinct forward transitions have disjoint postsets; `backward_disjoint_preset` stating that distinct backward transitions have disjoint presets; and `neq_fwd_disjoint_bwd_preset` stating that the presets of the reversing transitions corresponding to two different forward transitions are disjoint.

The last two properties identify pairs of transitions that are not in immediate conflict and, therefore, can be fired concurrently if enabled at the same marking. They are crucial for proving the next set of properties concerning the correct definition of a reversible model (Listing 14). Specifically:

- `cancelation` lemma: If t and t' are reverses (`i`), firing t from m to m' (`f`) followed by t' (`h'`) reproduces the original marking m.
- `loop` lemma: Every computation step is undoable. Transition t fires from m to m' if and only if its reverse t' fires from m' back to m.
- `backtracking` lemma: A generalization of the loop lemma, establishing by induction on the sequence s that any firing sequence can be undone.

```
lemma cancelation (i : t ⇜⇝ t') {e : m ⟦t⟧⦃R⦄} (f : m ⟦e⟩⦃R.toNet⦄ m')
    (h' : m' ⟦t'⟧⦃R⦄) : m' ⟦h'⟩⦃R.toNet⦄m

lemma loop (i : t ⇜⇝ t') : (∃ e : m ⟦t⟧⦃RO⦄, m ⟦e⟩⦃RO.toNet⦄ m') ↔
    (∃ e : m' ⟦t'⟧⦃RO⦄, m' ⟦e⟩⦃RO.toNet⦄ m)

lemma backtracking : (∃ s, m ⟦s⟫⦃RO.toNet⦄ m') → (∃ s, m' ⟦s⟫⦃RO.toNet⦄
    m)
```

Listing 14. Reversible properties.

5 On Causal Reversibility

This section presents the formalization of the *parabolic* lemma, which states that any firing sequence reduces to a sequence of backward steps followed by forward steps. We omit an explicit proof for the admissibility of causally equivalent computations. Instead, we inherit this property directly from Petri net theory specifically, non-sequential semantics [2,5], where independent concurrent transitions can be reordered without altering the markings, as established, e.g., in Mazurkiewicz trace theory [10].

The statement of the lemma requires a formal notion of *equivalent firing sequences*, which is the smallest congruence[2] $\asymp_{\{\!\{N\}\!\}}$ on transition sequences closed under the following rules: (i) $t; t' \asymp_{\{\!\{N\}\!\}} t'; t$ if $t\ co_{\{\!\{N\}\!\}}\ t'$, (ii) $t;\ \overleftrightarrow{t} \asymp_{\{\!\{N\}\!\}} \varepsilon$, and (iii) $\overleftrightarrow{t}\,; t \asymp_{\{\!\{N\}\!\}} \varepsilon$. Rule (i) permits the swapping of concurrent transitions, while rules (ii) and (iii) enable the cancellation of successive, mutually reversing transitions. We formalize this relation in Lean as the inductive type shown in Listing 15 (lines 2–15), where congruence closure constructors are omitted for brevity.

---

[2] A relation $\sim$ over sequences is a **congruence** if it is an equivalence relation closed by concatenation, i.e., $s_1 \sim s_2$ and $s_3 \sim s_4$ implies $s_1; s_3 \sim s_2; s_4$ for all s_1, s_2, s_3 and s_4.

```
1 /-- Equivalence.lean -/
2 inductive TrEq [DecidableEq α] (R : Reversible α β) :
3     List (Transition β) → List (Transition β) →Prop
4 | swap : (t t' : Transition β) →
5   Disjoint (t•⦃R⦄) (•⦃R⦄ t') →
6   Disjoint (t'•⦃R⦄) (•⦃R⦄ t) →
7   TrEq R [t, t'] [t', t]
8 | cancₗ : (t t' : Transition β) →
9   t ⇌ t' →
10  TrEq R [t, t'] []
11 | cancᵣ : (t t' : Transition β) →
12  t ⇌ t' →
13  TrEq R [] [t, t']
14 ...
15 notation:50 s₁:51 "≍ ⦃" R "⦄ " s₂:51 => TrEq R s₁ s₂
16
17 def TrEq_refl (s : List (Transition β)) : s ≍ ⦃R⦄ s := ...
18
19 def TrEq_symm (h : s₁ ≍ ⦃R⦄ s₂) : s₂ ≍ ⦃R⦄ s₁ := ...
20
21 def TrEq_trans (h : s₁ ≍ ⦃R⦄ s₂) (h' : s₂ ≍ ⦃R⦄ s₃) : s₁ ≍ ⦃R⦄ s₃ := ...
22
23 lemma TrEq_congruence (h : s₁ ≍ ⦃R⦄ s₂) (h' : s₃ ≍ ⦃R⦄ s₄) :
24     (s₁ ++ s₃) ≍ ⦃R⦄ (s₂ ++ s₄) := ...
```

Listing 15. Trace pre-equivalence and trace equivalence.

We prove that TrEq is indeed an equivalence relation, i.e., it is reflexive, symmetric, and transitive (lines 17–21 in Listing 15). We show that it is a congruence (lines 23–24).

Remark 1. We note that, although the paper defines the first case using the relation *co* (following [14]), the Lean constructor swap instead requires transitions to have disjoint presets. Here, *co* does not refer to concurrency in occurrence nets (Listing 10), since reversible occurrence nets are cyclic and thus not occurrence nets. We therefore adopt the standard Petri-net notion of concurrent enablement. As suggested first by [5] and formalized in [2], two transitions t and t' are concurrently enabled at a marking m if ${}^\bullet t + {}^\bullet t' \leq m$ ([2], Def. 3.18). Moreover, in Petri nets, concurrency identifies with independence for 1-safe nets; [2] (Th. 3.19) proves this via non-sequential processes. Since our reversible occurrence nets are 1-safe (Theorem reversible_occ_net_safe), any two concurrent transitions necessarily have disjoint presets. Standardly, concurrent (i.e., independent) transitions in Petri nets can fire in any order, which corresponds to the square lemma, which can be proved rather straightforwardly in our framework (Listing 16). Note that it applies to general nets, and hence to reversible nets.

```
/-- Nets.lean -/
lemma square (N : Net α β)
    {e₁ : m ⟦t₁⟧⦃N⦄} {e₂ : m ⟦t₂⟧⦃N⦄} (_ : m ⟦e₁⟩⦃N⦄ m1) (_ : m ⟦e₂⟩⦃N⦄ m2)
    (d : Disjoint (•⦃N⦄ t₁) (•⦃N⦄ t₂)) :
      ∃ (e1 : m1 ⟦t₂⟧⦃N⦄), ∃ (e2 : m2 ⟦t₁⟧⦃N⦄),
      ∃ m', (m1 ⟦e1⟩⦃N⦄ m' ∧ m2 ⟦e2⟩⦃N⦄ m') := by ...
```

Listing 16. Square lemma.

Lemma 1 (Parabolic lemma). *Let R be a reversible occurrence net, m a reachable marking, and $m[\![\omega\rangle\!\rangle_{\{\!\{R\}\!\}}m'$ a firing sequence. Then there exist two sequences of transitions, ω' and ω'', such that ω' consists only of backward transitions, ω'' consists only of forward transitions, $\omega \asymp_{\{\!\{R\}\!\}} \omega';\omega''$, and $m[\![\omega';\omega''\rangle\!\rangle_{\{\!\{R\}\!\}}m'$.*

Note the requirement that m be reachable, i.e., a valid state. This is crucial, since arbitrary markings may simultaneously enable causally dependent or conflicting transitions. Moreover, reachability ensures that markings are 1-safe, a property used in the proof to infer which pairs of transitions are independent—rather than assuming independence externally, it is derived from the net structure.

The Lean definition and proof outline of the parabolic lemma is in Listing 17. To avoid repetitions, we introduce the predicate `parabolic_decomp` (lines 4–5). It states that a transition sequence ω in a reversible occurrence net decomposes into two sequences, ω' and ω'', satisfying Lemma 1.

```
1 /-- Parabolic.lean -/
2 variable {RO : ReversibleOccurrence α β}
3
4 def parabolic_decomp (s s' s'' : List (Transition β)) (m m' : Multiset α)
    :=
5   ⪡s' ∧ ⪢s'' ∧ m ⟦s' ++ s''⟫⦃RO⦄ m' ∧ s ≍ ⦃RO.toReversible⦄ (s' ++ s'')
6
7 theorem parabolic (MO : MarkedReversibleOccurrence α β)
8     (rr : ⟨MO.toNet, MO.m₀⟩ ⇝ m) (fs : m ⟦s⟫⦃MO⦄ m') :
9     ∃ s' s'', parabolic_decomp (RO := marked_RO_to_RO MO) s s' s'' m m'
10   induction fs with
11   | @empty m =>
12     exists [], []; simp_all [parabolic_decomp, all_backward, all_forward]
13     exact ⟨.empty m, TrEq_refl []⟩
14   | @step t fs' m m₁ _ et f _ IH =>
15     ...
16     by_cases h : isBwd t
17     · ... /-- Case h : ◁t -/
18     · ... /-- Case h : ¬◁t -/
```

Listing 17. Parabolic lemma.

The proof proceeds by induction on the firing sequence `fs`. The base case is trivial, taking empty sequences and applying reflexivity. For the inductive step, we use auxiliary lemmas to handle the transition `t`. If `t` is backward, a lemma extends the parabolic decomposition from `fs` to `t :: fs`. The forward case is analogous but more involved, requiring a similar decomposition strategy. The proof of this case relies on a *swapping lemma* (stated below), which allows a forward transition to commute with a sequence of backward transitions, provided that none of the latter reverses the forward transition. This argument requires the sequence to be a valid firing sequence from a reachable marking, so to ensure that the sequence is a valid firing sequence. Crucially, the **1-safety** of reachable markings in reversible occurrence nets ensures that any backward transition that does not reverse the given forward transition is independent (i.e., concurrent) with it; consequently, the two can be swapped.

```
/-- Swapping.lean -/
def no_rev_in_list (t : Transition β) (ls : List (Transition β)) :=
  ∀ t' ∈ ls, ¬(t ⇜⇝ t')

infix:50 " ∉ʳ " => no_rev_in_list

lemma swapping [DecidableEq α] (MO : MarkedReversibleOccurrence α β)
    (rr : ⟨MO.toNet, MO.m₀⟩ ⤳ m)
    (bw : ◁◁ s) (ft : ▷t) (nrev : t ∉ʳ s)
    (fs : m ⟦t :: s⟫⦃MO⦄ m') :  m ⟦s ++ [t]⟫⦃MO⦄ m' := ...
```

Listing 18. Swapping lemma.

6 Conclusion and Future Works

This work presents the first formalization of Petri nets in Lean, providing a foundation for advanced models of concurrency and reversibility. We mechanize key results, including the backtracking and parabolic lemmas, enabling formal verification of system behaviors and supporting further research. Our formalisation follows the proof strategy sketched in [14]. While we do not explicitly invoke the square lemma to prove the parabolic lemma, several auxiliary results exploit the fact that firing concurrent transitions in a marking commutes. Alternatively, one could leverage the framework of [8], where the parabolic lemma is derived from three primitive axioms: the Square Property, Backward Transitions are Independent, and Well-Foundedness. Whether this axiomatic approach simplifies the formal mechanization in Lean is left for future work.

Our formalization sets the stage for future extensions, including colored Petri nets and probabilistic models [7]. Ultimately, our goal is to develop a unified theory of probabilistic, concurrent, and reversible Petri nets, paving the way toward a reversible and concurrent model of quantum computing.

References

1. Aman, B., et al.: Foundations of reversible computation. In: Ulidowski, I., Lanese, I., Schultz, U.P., Ferreira, C. (eds.) Reversible Computation: Extending Horizons of Computing - Selected Results of the COST Action IC1405. Lecture Notes in Computer Science, vol. 12070, pp. 1–40. Springer (2020)
2. Best, E., Devillers, R.: Sequential and concurrent behaviour in petri net theory. Theoret. Comput. Sci. **55**(1), 87–136 (1987)
3. Carneiro, M.: The type theory of Lean (2019). Lean3
4. Cecilia, G.: A formalization of the reversible concurrent calculus $CCSK^P$ in Beluga. In: Aubert, C., Giusto, C.D., Fowler, S., Pun, V.K.I. (eds.) Proceedings 18th Interaction and Concurrency Experience, ICE 2025, Lille, France, 20th June 2025, pp. 55–72. EPTCS (2025). https://doi.org/10.4204/EPTCS.425.5
5. Goltz, U., Reisig, W.: The non-sequential behaviour of Petri nets. Inf. Control **57**(2–3), 125–147 (1983)
6. Kaarsgaard, R., Veltri, N.: En garde! Unguarded iteration for reversible computation in the delay monad. In: International Conference on Mathematics of Program Construction, pp. 366–384. Springer (2019)

7. Katoen, J., Peled, D.: Taming confusion for modeling and implementing probabilistic concurrent systems. In: Programming Languages and Systems. Lecture Notes in Computer Science, vol. 7792 (2013)
8. Lanese, I., Phillips, I., Ulidowski, I.: An axiomatic theory for reversible computation. ACM Trans. Comput. Log. **25**(2), 11:1–11:40 (2024). https://doi.org/10.1145/3648474
9. Maletto, G., Roversi, L.: Certifying expressive power and algorithms of reversible primitive permutations with Lean. J. Log. Algebraic Methods Program. **136**, 100923 (2024)
10. Mazurkiewicz, A.: Introduction to trace theory. In: The Book of Traces, pp. 3–41 (1995)
11. Melgratti, H.C., Mezzina, C.A., Phillips, I., Pinna, G.M., Ulidowski, I.: Reversible occurrence nets and causal reversible prime event structures. In: Lanese, I., Rawski, M. (eds.) Reversible Computation - 12th International Conference, RC 2020, Oslo, Norway, 9–10 July 2020, Proceedings. Lecture Notes in Computer Science, vol. 12227, pp. 35–53. Springer (2020)
12. Melgratti, H.C., Mezzina, C.A., Pinna, G.M.: A reversible perspective on petri nets and event structures. ACM Trans. Comput. Log. **25**(4), 1–38 (2024)
13. Melgratti, H.C., Mezzina, C.A., Pinna, G.M.: A truly concurrent semantics for reversible CCS. Log. Methods Comput. Sci. **20**(4) (2024)
14. Melgratti, H.C., Mezzina, C.A., Ulidowski, I.: Reversing place transition nets. Log. Methods Comput. Sci. **16**(4) (2020)
15. Mezzina, C.A., et al.: Software and reversible systems: a survey of recent activities. In: Ulidowski, I., Lanese, I., Schultz, U.P., Ferreira, C. (eds.) Reversible Computation: Extending Horizons of Computing - Selected Results of the COST Action IC1405. Lecture Notes in Computer Science, vol. 12070, pp. 41–59. Springer (2020)
16. Moura, L.d., Ullrich, S.: The Lean 4 theorem prover and programming language. In: Automated Deduction – CADE 28: 28th International Conference on Automated Deduction, Virtual Event, 12–15 July 2021, Proceedings, pp. 625–635. Springer, Heidelberg (2021)
17. Nielsen, M., Plotkin, G., Winskel, G.: Petri nets, event structures and domains, part I. Theor. Comput. Sci. **13**(1), 85–108 (1981)
18. Palazzo, M., Roversi, L.: Reversible computation with stacks and reversible management of failures. arXiv preprint arXiv:2501.05259 (2025)
19. Paolini, L.L., Piccolo, M., Roversi, L.: A certified study of a reversible programming language. Leibniz Int. Proc. Inform. **69**, 1–21 (2018)
20. Philippou, A., Psara, K.: A collective interpretation semantics for reversing Petri nets. Theor. Comput. Sci. **924**, 148–170 (2022)
21. Philippou, A., Psara, K.: Reversible computation in nets with bonds. J. Log. Algebraic Methods Program. **124**, 100718 (2022)
22. Vassor, M., Stefani, J.B.: Checkpoint/rollback vs causally-consistent reversibility. In: Kari, J., Ulidowski, I. (eds.) Reversible Computation - 10th International Conference, RC 2018. Lecture Notes in Computer Science, vol. 11106, pp. 286–303. Springer (2018)

Discrete Semantics for Reversible Transistor Network Verification

Hannah Blyton[1,2] and Hugh Potter[1(✉)]

[1] Vaire Computing, Ames, USA
{hannah.blyton,hugh}@vaire.co
[2] University of Birmingham, Birmingham B15 2TT, UK

Abstract. Verification and simulation are critical components of the semiconductor design process. For challenging design components, the use of machine-checkable formal proofs offers a high level of confidence in correct function. In this work, our primary contribution is a formal adiabatic transition relation on discrete transistor network states, described in text and encoded in the Lean 4 language for machine-checked theorem proving. As a test case for this formal verification approach, we present a discrete adiabatic simulation algorithm motivated by the transition relation. We provide detailed proofs in both text and Lean 4 that our algorithmic approach generates the unique successor state as constrained by the transition relation, or reports that no adiabatic successor state exists.

Keywords: reversible · transistor simulation · formal verification · theorem proving

1 Introduction

Adiabatic reversible circuit switching offers the opportunity to escape the tyranny of Landauer's law [10] and extend compute energy scaling without theoretical limit.

In pursuit of realizing these gains, and guided by the lessons of conventional electronics manufacture, we expect to encounter substantial challenges in circuit simulation and verification. These areas are critically important in conventional semiconductor fabrication because of the extreme cost and complexity of design and manufacturing. One prominent subfield is formal verification via machine-checked theorem proving, wherein designers produce a symbolic mathematical proof of design correctness in a format that a computer program can understand and automatically verify. This approach is sometimes labor-intensive, but it can provide confidence that a verified component functions correctly across all input sequences and relevant internal states. It has been widely used and explored in the semiconductor industry.

This paper seeks to apply machine-checked theorem proving to the domain of adiabatic circuits. Our primary contribution is the Discrete Semantics for

C. Aubert and L. Roversi (Eds.): RC 2026, LNCS 16626, pp. 112–129, 2026.
https://doi.org/10.1007/978-3-032-30839-9_6

Reversible Transistor Networks (DSRT), an adiabatic transition relation on transistor network states. We target a discrete-value, discrete-time setting, where we define binary-valued signals and track them at discrete, regular time intervals. The requirements for adiabatic switching are well-known [2]. For this paper, we adopt the switching discipline described in [5] as our physical starting point: avoid diode conduction, turn transistors on only when their endpoints already agree, and turn them off only when current has an alternate low-impedance path. We restate these assumptions in Sect. 2, and formalize them in Sect. 3. DSRT provides a formal criterion for whether a pair of consecutive states (A, B) obeys the switching constraints underlying reversible adiabatic operation. We present definitions and proofs both in a text-based format and using the popular Lean 4 theorem prover [12].

As a test case and demonstration of our framework, we present DSRT-sim, a discrete adiabatic simulation algorithm motivated by DSRT. We will show in Lemma 3 that if a valid successor state as constrained by the DSRT transition relation exists, then it is unique. Given a circuit state and external stimuli, DSRT-sim calculates this unique successor state, or reports that it does not exist.

DSRT-sim leverages the adiabaticity constraint to simplify analysis. In a conventional circuit, a switching event in one transistor can change the voltage on the gate of another transistor, causing the first switching event to cascade into another, which may cascade again, and so on. This complicates analysis, requiring simulators to resolve cyclic cascades via special, dedicated approaches [3]. In an adiabatically-switched circuit, however, a transistor cannot allow current between source and drain while its gate changes from on to off or vice versa, so state changes cannot cascade. This allows DSRT-sim to calculate transitions via flood-fill operations and adiabaticity checks, avoiding cyclic cascade handling.

Because of its relative simplicity, this algorithm is a promising target for formalization. We describe this algorithm and use DSRT to rigorously prove the soundness and completeness of our algorithmic approach, and the uniqueness of its output. As with the DSRT transition relation, we provide both plain-english proofs and formal machine-checkable proofs in Lean 4. Our Lean 4 formalization captures and verifies the denotational specification of DSRT-sim, but a full one-to-one mapping from our implementations to Lean 4 is beyond the scope of this work. For example, we describe flood-fill as a transitive closure instead of as the result of a sequence of operations.

From our anecdotal experience, the approach underlying DSRT-sim appears to be familiar to some researchers in the adiabatic computing space. We are unaware, however, of any related formalization or publication of the exact DSRT-sim approach.

Since the acceptance of this work, we have been made aware of a related adiabatic simulation algorithm [11,13,14]. Like DSRT-sim, this algorithm relies on flood-fill from externally-driven nodes. Unlike DSRT-sim, however, this algorithm tracks voltages as continuous floating-point quantities, and performs a sequence of subtick simulation steps per user-facing tick, defaulting to 100 subticks. As discussed in Sect. 4, the central insight of the DSRT-sim algorithm is that with adiabatic switching, we can use gate connectivities from the current simulation state when flood-filling to calculate the next state. The authors of [11,13,14] also use current-state connectivity, but with their subtick approach a theoretical justification for this choice is less necessary, and we are not aware of any published theoretical exploration of their algorithm.

1.1 Related Work

Machine-checked theorem-proving is well-studied and widely used in the context of semiconductor hardware verification [6–8]. Prominent applications include floating-point verification [15] and general instruction set architecture validation [1]. We are not aware, however, of any published efforts to formalize adiabatic transistor switching rules or apply machine-checked theorem proving to reversible hardware.

For simulation, transistor-level SPICE approaches provide physical fidelity, but their high computational cost makes exhaustive checking prohibitively difficult for larger designs [17]. For this reason, digital simulators are popular for runtime rule checking. Verilog is a widely used hardware description language for digital simulation [9]. Though it is primarily used at the register transfer level, Verilog supports switch-level simulation as well. Another option for transistor simulation is IRSIM [4,16], a dedicated switch-level circuit simulator introduced in the mid-1980s and widely used thereafter.

A close conceptual neighbor to DSRT-sim is symbolic trajectory evaluation (STE), a model-checking approach that symbolically compresses state spaces to address combinatorial explosion [18,22]. STE is a more general tool than DSRT-sim; it is capable of reasoning about entire classes of stimuli simultaneously, and can model many kinds of temporal assertions. The relationship between STE and the unique nature of reversible computation is an interesting question that we shall leave for future work.

The primary advantages of DSRT-sim in the context of this paper are its simplicity and close relation to adiabatic switching, which make it a natural target for verification with DSRT.

1.2 AI Disclosure

We used LLM-based tools to collaboratively assist in code creation for this work, both for the DSRT-sim implementations and the Lean proofs. We also used these tools to generate some of the LaTeX code for figures and algorithms.

2 Adiabatic Switching Rules

A metal-oxide-silicon (MOS) field-effect transistor is a semiconductor device that allows an external voltage on a gate node to control the electrical connection between the source and drain nodes. The complementary MOS (CMOS) semiconductor technology pairs n-channel MOS (NMOS) transistors with p-channel MOS (PMOS) transistors to construct robust logic circuits. Real MOS transistor behavior is complex, but we can understand it here as a binary approximation: for NMOS transistors, source and drain are electrically connected when the gate node is high, and disconnected when the gate is low, and for PMOS, source and drain are connected when the gate node is low, and disconnected when the gate is high.

An NMOS transistor cannot properly connect its source and drain when the voltages on both are high, and likewise for PMOS when source and drain are low. As a consequence, attempting to drive a node high using an NMOS transistor or low using a PMOS transistor will produce a *weak* voltage that is not fully high or low. In Sect. 3, we will model this with the distinction between regular and strong connectivity.

The switching discipline required to construct and operate CMOS circuits adiabatically is well-understood [2,5]. For this paper, we use the following switching rules from Frank et al. [5] as the physical motivation for DSRT.

1. Avoid the use of diodes.
2. Avoid turning a transistor on when its source and drain are at different voltages (no sparks).
3. Avoid turning a transistor off when current is passing through it, unless there is an alternate low-impedance path (no squelches).
4. Allow voltages to change only via slow, linear ramps.

The DSRT state description contains no diodes, guaranteeing rule 1 by construction. We model voltage as either low or high at each regular tick boundary and assume linear interpolation in between, so every voltage transition from low to high or high to low is a linear ramp with a duration of one tick. This suffices to encode rule 4 for nodes under external control; we will argue in Sect. 3 that linear interpolation is physically reasonable for internal nodes as well, as internal nodes only change when they have an electrical path to external nodes.

We encode rules 2 and 3 via the *ADB* (adiabaticity) and *PTC* (path-to-charge) relations in Sect. 3. See Fig. 1 for a conventional CMOS inverter setup that produces a spark and violates *ADB*, and see Fig. 2 for a similar example system with a squelch.

3 Formal Adiabatic Transition Relation

3.1 Assumptions

We make two assumptions when defining our transition relation.

First, we assume that any accessible external loads are capacitive. That is, we exclude situations where the adiabatic logic circuit is used to drive a DC current through a load. This means that current always corresponds to a change in voltage, allowing us to track the state of the system with node voltages alone.

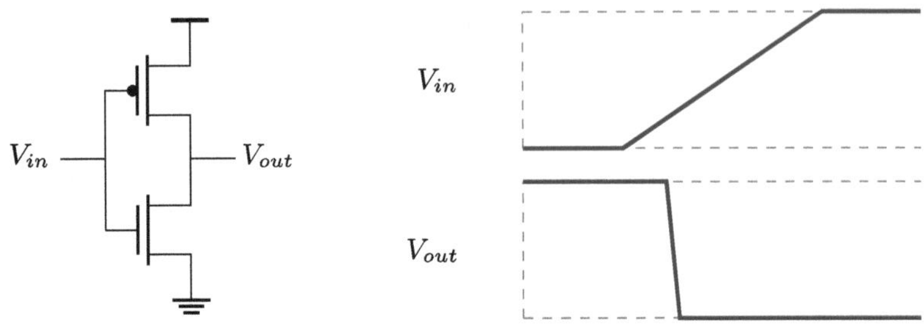

Fig. 1. A conventional CMOS inverter with the input starting low and transitioning high. The upper transistor is a PMOS transistor and the lower transistor is NMOS. When the input node rises high enough to turn on the NMOS transistor, that creates a connection between the output node, which is still high, and ground. The output node rapidly discharges to ground, dissipating energy in a sparking event. In the language of Sect. 3, this is an *ADB* violation, because both transistor gate nodes change, and neither transistor has source-drain agreement. If the output node is driven only by the transistor pair, as in a conventional inverter, it is also a Sect. 3 *PTC* violation. We could produce an *ADB* violation that is not also a *PTC* violation by externally driving the output in a high-to-low ramp.

We illustrate our second assumption in Fig. 2, which shows an output node driven to ramp up, with one driver disconnecting and the other connecting as the output rises. The exact physical outcome in this situation depends on the characteristics of the transistors. In this work, we have adopted a conservative approach and assumed that handoffs like this are non-adiabatic because of a potential time gap between driver connections. We encode this assumption in *PTC*, defined below.

3.2 Definitions and Terminology

A *net* is a tuple (*nodes*, *transistors*). Each transistor specifies source, gate, and drain nodes, and whether it is NMOS or PMOS. All transistor nodes must be in the net nodes set.

A *powered* node is a node that is driven high or low by some external voltage stimulus. A *state* is a pair (*values*, *powered*). Here *values* is a total function from nodes to electrical values, and *powered* is a total function from nodes to external drive settings, indicating whether each node is driven to 0, driven to 1, or not externally driven. Node values range over four electrical values: 0, 1, *L*, and *H*. The weak values *L* and *H* describe nodes that are weakly driven, as for example with a node driven high through an NMOS device. During execution, the DSRT-sim algorithm described in Sect. 4 additionally uses an internal `unknown` placeholder for nodes whose next-state value has not yet been determined.

A *tick* is the shortest discrete unit of time in which we allow state to change. We can encode a simulation history by providing one state at every tick; note that this encodes node values at the instant of each tick boundary.

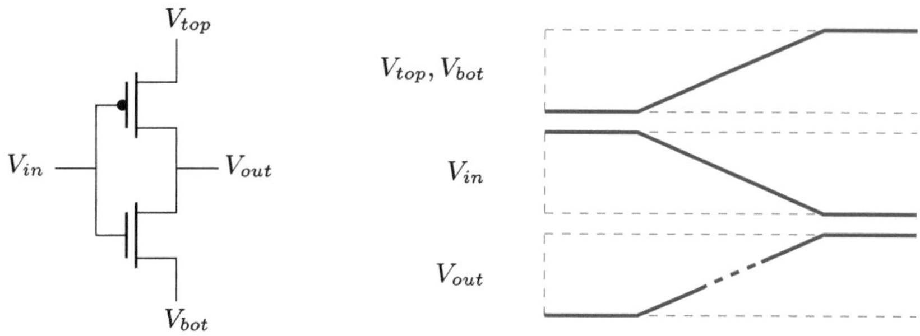

Fig. 2. Here we have rewired the conventional CMOS inverter from Fig. 1 to demonstrate a squelch with no spark. We connect the top and bottom nodes to an external rising ramp voltage, and leave the output without an external connection to drive it. The exact physical outcome here depends on transistor characteristics. If we approximate the output as a linear interpolation, however, it matches the top and bottom nodes throughout the transition. In that case there is no spark, and, in the language of Sect. 3, no *ADB* violation. The changing transistor connectivities hand off the output connection from the top node to the bottom node as the output ramps up. There may be a squelch, however, if the NMOS transistor begins to disconnect at a high enough voltage that the PMOS has not yet fully turned on. In DSRT, we count this as a non-adiabatic transition, and a violation of *PTC* as described in Sect. 3.

The source and drain nodes of an NMOS transistor are *directly A-connected* if the gate is high in state A, and *directly strongly A-connected* if the gate is high and source and drain are both low in state A. For a PMOS transistor, the source and drain nodes are directly A-connected if the gate is low in state A, and directly strongly A-connected if the gate is low and source and drain are both high in state A.

Any two nodes u and v are *A-connected* if and only if there is a path from u to v through source-drain pairs that are directly A-connected, and likewise for strong connectivity. Two nodes are *AB-connected* if they are *both* A-connected and B-connected, and likewise for direct and strong connectivity. For consistency, every node is taken to be A-connected and strongly A-connected to itself in every state A.

3.3 Transition Relation

We first specify three predicates on individual states. We assume these to be true of all input states and require our simulation algorithm to respect them for all output states.

- $CON(B)$: Every pair of nodes that is B-connected has the same value in B.
- $STAT(B)$: Every node in B is strongly B-connected to a B-powered node.
- $CLEAN(B)$: Every node in B has value either 0 or 1.

CON is an obvious consequence of electrical connectivity across low-impedance paths. In the simulation algorithm, if we encounter a situation where two nodes with different values are connected, we will halt the simulation and report it as a short.

We enforce staticity via $STAT$ to eliminate potential nonadiabaticity from floating nodes as discussed in [5], and the $CLEAN$ constraint prohibits weakly driven nodes in the input or output states. For simplicity, we treat $CLEAN$ and $STAT$ as required of the input and output states. Those requirements are not load-bearing in the proofs or algorithms, however, and it is possible to remove them in a straightforward way.

We also impose adiabaticity constraints on pairs (A, B) of consecutive states. That is, if (A, B) is a consecutive state pair that obeys the DSRT relation, we require the following relations to hold.

- $ADB(A, B)$ (adiabaticity): If the gate node of a transistor changes between A and B, the source and drain must have the same value as each other in A, and must have the same value as each other in B.
- $PTC(A, B)$ (path-to-charge): If a node changes from one timestep to the next, it must be strongly AB-connected to an A-powered node, and strongly AB-connected to a B powered node.

Note that ADB and PTC are symmetric.

We propose that these rules imply the adiabatic switching rules discussed in Sect. 1. By construction, our formalism automatically excludes diodes and requires slow, linear ramps for nodes under external control. Since PTC requires nodes to be strongly AB-connected to externally-powered nodes whenever they change from state A to following state B, internal nodes must also transition via slow, linear ramps.

If a transistor turns on when its source and drain are at different voltages, producing a non-adiabatic spark event, that is an ADB violation. Now, suppose a transistor turns off when current is passing through it, with no alternate low-impedance path, producing a non-adiabatic squelch event. This current cannot be driving an external DC load because we have assumed that all external loads are capacitive. If it is passing both out of a driven node and into a driven node, then those nodes must be connected and at different voltages, which is a CON violation. If it is passing between a driven node and a gate node, then the gate node must be changing value; since there is no alternate low-impedance path, this is a PTC violation.

4 Simulation Algorithm

In this section we describe the DSRT-sim algorithm. Our goal is to describe a procedure with the following specification. Given a state A and a powering function $powered_B$ as described in Sect. 3, our procedure must produce the unique state B with powered nodes $powered_B$ such that the consecutive state pair (A, B) satisfies the DSRT transition relation, or report that no such B exists.

4.1 Overview

To motivate DSRT-sim, we introduce two auxiliary relations on consecutive state pair (A, B) that follow from the reversibility criteria in Sect. 3.

- $DDC(A, B)$ (disconnected don't change): If a node v is not strongly A-connected to a node that is powered in B, then v has the same value in A and B.
- $CAP(A, B)$ (connected are powered): If a node v is A-connected to a node p_v that is powered in B, strongly or not, then v and p_v have the same value in B.

We will show in Sect. 5 that if $CON(B)$ holds, then

$$ADB(A, B) \wedge PTC(A, B) \implies DDC(A, B) \wedge CAP(A, B). \quad (1)$$

These constraints are useful because they constrain node values in B in terms of A-connectivity and $powered_B$, which we can calculate or retrieve from DSRT-sim inputs. To generate B, we iterate over B-powered nodes; for each B-powered node, we use flood-fill to set all A-connected nodes to the same value, per CAP. As we fill in connected nodes, we report a short if we encounter a node connected to a different node with conflicting value. If the flood-fill misses any nodes, we set those nodes to their value in A, per DDC. In this way, DSRT-sim computes a candidate next state implied by CAP and DDC.

Note that we must be cautious about the direction of the implications in Eq. 1. It would be convenient to also show that ADB and PTC follow from CON, DDC and CAP, reversing the direction of the rightmost implication, but unfortunately it is possible to construct counterexamples, omitted here for brevity but formalized in Lean as exists_con_ddc_cap_not_adb and exists_con_ddc_cap_not_ptc. We must therefore explicitly check ADB and PTC after the flood-fill and unknown handling. We check $STAT$ and $CLEAN$ at this time as well.

In other words, we can conceptualize DSRT-sim as a two-phase algorithm. First, we generate the unique candidate next state that satisfies DDC and CAP. Second, we validate that this candidate state satisfies all remaining requirements of the transition relation. DSRT-sim is a simulation algorithm, but the validation stage allows it to report when no satisfying next state is possible, as we require in the specification above.

4.2 Algorithm

We separate the algorithm as described in the previous subsection. In the main simulation step, described in Algorithm 1, we perform the initial flood fill and set any remaining unknowns by repeatedly popping a node `near` from the worklist `open` and traversing each transistor connected to `near` to its other endpoint `far`. This constructs the candidate next state. We then explicitly check $STAT$, $CLEAN$, ADB, and PTC.

Algorithm 2 describes the *STAT* and *CLEAN* checks. To check *STAT*, we perform another flood-fill from nodes powered in B through transistors strongly on in B, and report an error if the flood fill misses any nodes. To check *CLEAN*, we iterate through all nodes and verify that all nodes have strong values 0 or 1.

Algorithm 3 describes the *ADB* check, and Algorithm 4 describes the *PTC* check. To check *ADB*, we iterate over transistors and check the *ADB* condition. To check *PTC*, we flood-fill from nodes powered in A, and then from nodes powered in B, in both cases only exploring across transistors that are strongly on in both A and B. We then iterate over all nodes, and if any node changed from A to B but did not show up in both flood fills, we report a *PTC* error for it.

Algorithm 5, provided for reference, describes utility functions used to describe transistor on-conditions and weak signal handling.

DSRT-sim is composed of a constant number of flood fills and iterations over nodes; its runtime is $O(n + t)$, where n is node count and t is transistor count, or $O(t)$ if we assume every node is attached to a transistor. We provide implementations of DSRT-sim in Python [20] and Rust [21].

5 Proofs

5.1 Reversibility and *CON* Imply *DDC* and *CAP*

We first show that *DDC* and *CAP* follow from *ADB* and *PTC*, as claimed in Eq. 1.

Lemma 1. *Let A and B be states defined on the same transistor net, and assume $CON(B)$. Then*

$$ADB(A, B) \wedge PTC(A, B) \implies DDC(A, B) \wedge CAP(A, B). \tag{2}$$

Proof. Let A and B be defined as above, and assume that they obey *CON*, *ADB*, and *PTC* as described above.

First, *DDC* is an obvious consequence of *PTC*. Let u be a node that is not strongly A-connected to a node powered in B. Then u cannot be strongly AB-connected to a node powered in B, and by the contrapositive of *PTC*, it cannot change from A to B.

Now we will show *CAP*. Let v be a node that is A-connected to a node p_v that is powered in B. Let $[v_0, v_1, \ldots, v_{n-1}]$ be the sequence of nodes along the connection between p_v and v in A, so that $p_v = v_0$ and $v = v_{n-1}$. We will show by induction that $B(v_i) = B(v_0)$ for $0 \leq i < n$. The base case is clear. For the inductive step, we will show that if $B(v_i) = B(v)$, then $B(v_{i+1}) = B(v)$. Let t_i be the transistor connecting v_i and v_{i+1}. There are two cases.

- If t_i is on in B, then *CON* gives us $B(v_{i+1}) = B(v_i) = B(v)$.
- If t_i is off in B, then it has changed from on in A to off in B, and *ADB* gives us, as in the first case, $B(v_{i+1}) = B(v_i) = B(v)$.

Therefore $B(v) = B(v_{n-1}) = B(v_0) = B(p_v)$.

Algorithm 1. Simulate transition from state A to state B

```
                          ▷ Initialize: set powered nodes, mark rest unknown
open ← ∅;   changed ← ∅
for each node v do
    if v is powered in B then
        B(v) ← powered value of v
        add v to open
    else
        B(v) ← unknown

                ▷ Flood-fill from powered nodes using A-connectivity (CAP)
while open ≠ ∅ do
    remove some node near from open
    for each transistor T with endpoint near and other endpoint far do
        if T is off in A then continue
        drive ← PASS(type(T), B(near))
        if B(far) = unknown then
            B(far) ← drive
            add far to open and to changed
        else if LOGIC(B(far)) ≠ LOGIC(drive) then
            error: short circuit at far
        else
            B(far) ← STRONGER(B(far), drive)

                            ▷ Set unknowns to previous value (DDC)
for each node v with B(v) = unknown do
    B(v) ← A(v)

                                                        ▷ Validation
CheckStaticAndClean( )
CheckADB( )
CheckPTC( )
```

5.2 Reversibility and *CAP* Imply *CON*

We now show that with *ADB* and *PTC*, *CAP* implies *CON*. This will enable a convenient proof that our update function preserves *CON*.

Lemma 2. *Let A and B be states defined on the same transistor net, and let u and v be two nodes that are B-connected. Then*

$$CON(A) \wedge ADB(A,B) \wedge PTC(A,B) \wedge DDC(A,B) \wedge CAP(A,B) \implies CON(B). \tag{3}$$

Proof. We first show that directly B-connected node pairs have the same value. Let u and v be a directly B-connected node pair; we will show $B(u) = B(v)$. There are three cases.

Algorithm 2. CheckStaticAndClean()

```
                  ▷ Verify every node is B-connected to a B-powered node (STAT)
open ← ∅;   count ← 0
for each node v powered in B do
    mark v;   add v to open
while open ≠ ∅ do
    remove some node near from open
    count ← count + 1
    for each transistor T adjacent to near with other endpoint far do
        if T is off in B then continue
        if far is unmarked then
            mark far;   add far to open
if count ≠ |nodes| then
    error: static violation

                  ▷ Verify every node has a strong value (CLEAN)
for each node v do
    if B(v) ∈ {H, L} then
        error: clean violation at v
```

Algorithm 3. CheckADB()

```
for each transistor T with endpoints u, v and gate g do
    if A(g) ≠ B(g) then
        if A(u) ≠ A(v) or B(u) ≠ B(v) then
            error: ADB violation at T
```

Algorithm 4. CheckPTC()

```
function FloodMark(seed set S)
    open ← S
    for each node v ∈ S do mark v
    while open ≠ ∅ do
        remove some node near from open
        for each transistor T adjacent to near with other endpoint far do
            if T is off in A or B then continue
            if far is unmarked then
                mark far;   add far to open

FloodMark(nodes powered in A)
FloodMark(nodes powered in B)

                  ▷ Any changed node must be marked twice (PTC)
for each node v with A(v) ≠ B(v) do
    if v is not marked twice then
        error: PTC violation at v
```

Algorithm 5. Reference: PASS, LOGIC, and STRONGER

```
function PASS(type, value)
    if type = NMOS then
        if value = 1 then return H
        else return value
    else                                        ▷ PMOS
        if value = 0 then return L
        else return value

function LOGIC(value)
    if value ∈ {0, L} then return low
    else return high

function STRONGER(x, y)
    if x = y then return x
    if (x, y) = (1, H) or (x, y) = (H, 1) then return 1
    if (x, y) = (0, L) or (x, y) = (L, 0) then return 0
```

- Suppose u and v are directly A-connected, and neither u nor v is A-connected to a B-powered node. Then $B(u) = A(u) = A(v) = B(v)$ per $DDC(A, B)$ and $CON(A)$.
- Suppose u and v are directly A-connected, and without loss of generality u is A-connected to a B-powered node p_u. Then, since v is A-connected to u, it is also A-connected to p_u, and we have $B(u) = B(p_u) = B(v)$ via CAP.
- Suppose u and v are not directly A-connected. Let g be the gate node of the transistor that connects them in B. Since g must have changed from A to B, we have $B(u) = B(v)$ by ADB.

Since all directly B-connected nodes have the same value, the transitivity of connection gives us that all B-connected nodes have the same value as well, and $CON(B)$ holds.

5.3 Forward and Backward Determinism

We now show that the DSRT transition relation is forward-deterministic: that is, for every state A and powering function $powered_B$, there is at most one state B matching $powered_B$ and satisfying the relation. This is reassuring for our algorithm, and will prove useful for our correctness proofs below.

Lemma 3 (Forward Determinism). *Let A, B, and C be states defined on the same transistor net, and let B and C have the same set of powered nodes, driven to the same values. Assume $CON(A)$, $CON(B)$, and $CON(C)$. Then*

$$ADB(A, B) \wedge ADB(A, C) \wedge PTC(A, B) \wedge PTC(A, C) \implies B = C. \qquad (4)$$

Proof. Let A, B, and C be defined as above, and assume that they obey CON, ADB, and PTC as described above. Then (A, B) and (A, C) must both obey DDC and CAP, per Lemma 1. Let v be a node. There are two cases.

- If v is A-disconnected from all nodes powered in B and C, then $C(V) = A(V) = B(V)$, using DDC.
- If v is A-connected to a node p_v powered in B and C, then $C(v) = C(p_v) = B(p_v) = B(v)$, using CAP.

Therefore $B = C$.

Because ADB and PTC are symmetric, we can use Lemma 3 to show backward determinism as well. We do not require a proof of backward determinism to show the correctness of DSRT-sim. We will take the opportunity, however, to confirm that transitions obeying the DSRT relation are backward deterministic, as we would expect from an adiabatic transition relation.

Lemma 4 (Backward Determinism). *Let A, B, and C be states defined on the same transistor net, and let B and C have the same set of powered nodes, driven to the same values. Assume $CON(A)$, $CON(B)$, and $CON(C)$. Then*

$$ADB(B, A) \wedge ADB(C, A) \wedge PTC(B, A) \wedge PTC(C, A) \implies B = C. \quad (5)$$

Proof. First, note that ADB and PTC are symmetric.

Now let A, B, and C be defined as above, and assume that they obey CON, ADB, and PTC as described above. Then we also have $ADB(A, B)$, $ADB(A, C)$, $PTC(A, B)$, $PTC(A, C)$, and can immediately conclude that $B = C$ via Lemma 3.

5.4 Algorithm Correctness

We are now in a position to show the correctness of DSRT-sim. We will first show soundness: if our algorithm does not output an error, its output satisfies CON, ADB, PTC, $STAT$, and $CLEAN$. We will then show completeness: if our algorithm does output an error, then those conditions are impossible to simultaneously satisfy. That is, we show both that DSRT-sim constructs a compliant next state when one is found, and that no compliant next state exists when an error is reported.

Lemma 5 (Soundness). *Let A and B be states defined on the same net. Assume $CON(A)$, and let B be the output of DSRT-sim applied to A, with no errors reported. Then $CON(B)$, $ADB(A, B)$, $PTC(A, B)$, $STAT(B)$, and $CLEAN(B)$ all hold.*

Proof. Our algorithm explicitly checks $ADB(A, B)$, $PTC(A, B)$, $STAT(B)$, and $CLEAN(B)$, and produces an error if any is not satisfied. We have assumed there are no errors, so these conditions must hold. We can therefore conclude $DDC(A, B)$ and $CAP(A, B)$ via Lemma 1, and then $CON(B)$ via Lemma 2.

We must prove an auxiliary lemma before showing that all reported errors are justified.

Lemma 6. *If the algorithm completes the first flood fill with no errors, then, after setting unkowns to their values in A, the current state of B satisfies $DDC(A, B)$ and $CAP(A, B)$.*

Proof. Let A and B be as defined above. We first show $DDC(A, B)$. Consider a node that is A-disconnected from every node powered in B. Then the first flood-fill cannot reach it, and it remains unknown until it is set to its value in A during unknown handling.

We now show $CAP(A, B)$. Consider a node v that is A-connected to a node p_v powered in B. There are two cases.

- If the flood-fill from p_v sets v to its final value in B, then $B(v) = B(p_v)$.
- Suppose the flood-fill from p_v does not set v to its final value. Let $[v_0, \ldots, v_{n-1}]$ be the nodes A-connecting p_v to v, so that $p_v = v_0$ and $v = v_{n-1}$. We will show by induction that $B(v_i) = B(v_0)$ for $0 \leq i < n$. The base case is clear. For the inductive step, we will show that if $B(v_i) = B(v)$, then $B(v_{i+1}) = B(v)$. There are two cases.
  - If v_i and v_{i+1} receive their final values in B from the same flood fill, then $B(v_{i+1}) = B(v_i)$.
  - Suppose that v_i and v_{i+1} do not receive their final values in B from the same flood fill. Without loss of generality, suppose that v_i receives its final value first. Then the flood fill that set the final value for v_{i+1} explores v_i when v_i has its final value. If this final value differed from v_{i+1}'s final value, then the algorithm would report a short circuit. Since we have assumed the algorithm completes the first flood fill with no errors, a short circuit is impossible; therefore $B(v_{i+1}) = B(v_i)$.

  We can therefore conclude that $B(v) = B(v_{n-1}) = B(v_0) = B(p_v)$.

We are now in a position to show that all reported errors are justified.

Lemma 7 (Completeness). *Let A be a state satisfying $CON(A)$, and let $powered_B$ be a set of powered nodes and their values. If the algorithm produces an error when applied to A and the nodes in $powered_B$, then there is no state B with powered nodes $powered_B$ that satisfies $ADB(A, B), PTC(A, B), CON(B), STAT(B)$, and $CLEAN(B)$.*

Proof. Let A and $powered_B$ be an error-producing combination as described above. There are two cases.

- If the algorithm reports a short-circuit error, then during the first flood-fill it must have attempted to drive a node v to a logical value that conflicted with that node's previous value. Then v must be connected to two B-powered nodes with different values in B, making CAP impossible to satisfy.
- If the algorithm reports an ADB, PTC, $STAT$, or $CLEAN$ error, then it must have completed the first flood-fill and the unknown assignment without encountering an error. Therefore, by Lemma 6, we have $DDC(A, B)$ and $CAP(A, B)$. By Lemma 3, B is the only output state that could satisfy DDC and CAP, and therefore the only output state that could satisfy ADB, PTC, and CON. Since it does not simultaneously satisfy ADB, PTC, $STAT$, and $CLEAN$, there can be no output state that does so.

Therefore if the algorithm outputs any error, a satisfying output state is impossible.

We may now finally claim that DSRT-sim is sound and complete with respect to the DSRT transition relation.

Theorem 1 (Soundness and Completeness). *Let A be a state satisfying $CON(A)$ and let $powered_B$ be a powering function. DSRT-sim is sound: if DSRT-sim produces a state B when applied to A and $powered_B$, then (A, B) obeys the DSRT transition relation. DSRT-sim is complete: if DSRT-sim produces an error, then no such satisfying state B exists.*

5.5 Lean Formalization

We have formalized DSRT and our DSRT-sim correctness proof in Lean 4, a popular dependently-typed programming language and proof assistant [12]. Our Lean proofs are available online [19].

Basic.lean defines the underlying objects used throughout the development: the four-valued signal domain, transistor and network structures, circuit states, and transistor pass tables. It also gives the inductive notion of connectivity used in the later constraints and proofs: two nodes are connected when there is an active path between them through the network.

Constraints.lean defines the state predicates CON, ADB, PTC, STAT, CLEAN, CAP, and DDC. It also proves reverse_uniqueness for Lemma 4.

Algorithm.lean does not implement an executable simulator. Instead, it defines the result type SimResult and the relation SimStepRelation, which characterizes when a given result is a correct description of one DSRT-sim timestep. The error constructors (`shortCircuit`, `staticError`, `adbError`, `ptcError`) and the success constructor (`ok`) correspond to the possible outcomes of Algorithm 1. This relation therefore specifies what the simulator is allowed to return, rather than directly modeling flood-fill execution or defining a function that computes the next state.

Correctness.lean then proves the headline results from those definitions: soundness ok_sound, completeness complete, uniqueness, and representative per-error impossibility theorems such as adb_no_valid and ptc_no_valid.

We prove the following.

- Soundness: an `ok` result yields a valid next state.
- Completeness: if a valid next state exists, the relation admits an `ok` result for it.
- Uniqueness: any two valid next states for the same input state are pointwise identical.
- Per-error impossibility: each error result certifies that no compliant next state exists.

6 Conclusion

We have created the DSRT transition relation, a discrete adiabatic transition relation on transistor network states, and described it both in text format and using the Lean 4 theorem prover. We have described DSRT-sim, a transistor-level simulation algorithm that leverages the constraints of reversible computing to avoid complex cascade management, and verified both in text format and in Lean 4 that it respects the DSRT transition relation.

6.1 Future Work

We expect that it would be straightforward to extend both DSRT and DSRT-sim in several ways.

It would be interesting to extend our approach to handle adiabatic logic systems with more voltage levels, like SCRL [23]. It would also be profitable to do a thorough analysis of the *PTC* condition in the context of driver handoffs and refine it to flexibly handle different transistor characteristics.

Also, we expect that in the future, as researchers explore and develop reversible computing technologies, many applications will combine adiabatic and nonadiabatic components. It would be advantageous to investigate how to conveniently interface DSRT and DSRT-sim with conventional circuits.

Finally, we hope to see DSRT applied to a wide variety of interesting reversible tools and circuits in the future.

Acknowledgments. We thank Mike Frank for useful discussions and advice. We also wish to thank the reviewers, and in particular Reviewer 1, for their thoughtful and detailed comments.

Disclosure of Interests. This work was supported in part by Vaire computing, where both authors are employed. The authors have no other relevant interests to declare.

References

1. Armstrong, A., et al.: Isa semantics for ARMv8-A, RISC-V, and CHERI-MIPS. Proc. ACM Program. Lang. **3**(POPL) (2019). https://doi.org/10.1145/3290384
2. Athas, W., Svensson, L., Koller, J., Tzartzanis, N., Ying-Chin Chou, E.: Low-power digital systems based on adiabatic-switching principles. IEEE Trans. Very Large Scale Integr. (VLSI) Syst. **2**(4), 398–407 (1994). https://doi.org/10.1109/92.335009
3. Bryant, R.E.: A switch-level model and simulator for MOS digital systems. IEEE Trans. Comput. **C-33**(2), 160–177 (1984). https://doi.org/10.1109/TC.1984.1676408
4. Edwards, R.T.: IRSIM: Switch-level simulator for digital circuits. https://github.com/RTimothyEdwards/irsim, open Circuit Design, http://opencircuitdesign.com/irsim

5. Frank, M.P., Brocato, R.W., Tierney, B.D., Missert, N.A., Hsia, A.H.: Reversible computing with fast, fully static, fully adiabatic CMOS. In: 2020 International Conference on Rebooting Computing (ICRC), pp. 1–8. IEEE Computer Society, Los Alamitos, CA, USA (2020). https://doi.org/10.1109/ICRC2020.2020.00014
6. Goel, S., Slobodova, A., Sumners, R., Swords, S.: Balancing automation and control for formal verification of microprocessors. In: Silva, A., Leino, K.R.M. (eds.) CAV 2021. LNCS, vol. 12759, pp. 26–45. Springer, Cham (2021). https://doi.org/10.1007/978-3-030-81685-8_2
7. Harrison, J.: Formal verification at intel. In: 18th Annual IEEE Symposium of Logic in Computer Science, 2003 Proceedings, pp. 45–54 (2003). https://doi.org/10.1109/LICS.2003.1210044
8. Hunt, Warren A., J., Kaufmann, M., Moore, J.S., Slobodova, A.: Industrial hardware and software verification with ACL2. Philos. Trans. Roy. Soc. A Math. Phys. Eng. Sci. **375**(2104), 20150399 (2017). https://doi.org/10.1098/rsta.2015.0399
9. IEEE: IEEE std 1800-2023: IEEE standard for SystemVerilog—unified hardware design, specification, and verification language. Technical report, IEEE (2024). https://doi.org/10.1109/IEEESTD.2024.10458102
10. Landauer, R.: Irreversibility and heat generation in the computing process. IBM J. Res. Dev. **5**(3), 183–191 (1961). https://doi.org/10.1147/rd.53.0183
11. Miao, D.: Simulation of minimum heat-generating circuits. Undergraduate honors project, Computer and Information Science and Engineering, University of Florida (2004), B.S. Computer Engineering, Summa cum laude, Spring 2004. Not publicly available
12. Moura, L., Ullrich, S.: The lean 4 theorem prover and programming language. In: Platzer, A., Sutcliffe, G. (eds.) CADE 2021. LNCS (LNAI), vol. 12699, pp. 625–635. Springer, Cham (2021). https://doi.org/10.1007/978-3-030-79876-5_37
13. Pollack, P.: Adiabatic circuit simulator. Undergraduate honors project, Computer and Information Science and Engineering, University of Florida (2004), B.S. Computer Engineering, Highest Honors, Spring 2004. Not publicly available
14. Pollack, P., Miao, D.: Adiabatic circuit simulator. Presentation, Computer and Information Science and Engineering, University of Florida (2004), spring 2004. Not publicly available
15. Russinoff, D.: Formal Verification of Floating-Point Hardware Design: A Mathematical Approach. Springer, Cham (2022). https://doi.org/10.1007/978-3-030-87181-9
16. Salz, A., Horowitz, M.: IRSIM: an incremental MOS switch-level simulator. In: 26th ACM/IEEE Design Automation Conference, pp. 173–178 (1989). https://doi.org/10.1145/74382.74412, ISSN: 0738-100X
17. van Santen, V.M., Diep, F.L.F., Henkel, J., Amrouch, H.: Massively parallel circuit setup in GPU-SPICE. IEEE Trans. Comput. **72**(8), 2127–2138 (2023). https://doi.org/10.1109/TC.2020.3032343
18. Seger, C.J.H., Bryant, R.E.: Formal verification by symbolic evaluation of partially-ordered trajectories. Formal Methods Syst. Des. **6**(2), 147–189 (1995). https://doi.org/10.1007/BF01383966
19. Vaire Computing: DSRT Lean formalization (2026). https://github.com/vaire-hannahb/dsrt-lean
20. Vaire Computing: DSRT Python implementation (2026). https://github.com/vaire-hannahb/dsrt-python
21. Vaire Computing: DSRT Rust implementation (2026). https://github.com/vaire-hannahb/dsrt-rust

22. Yang, J., Seger, C.J.: Introduction to generalized symbolic trajectory evaluation. In: Proceedings 2001 IEEE International Conference on Computer Design: VLSI in Computers and Processors. ICCD 2001, pp. 360–365 (2001). https://doi.org/10.1109/ICCD.2001.955052. ISSN: 1063-6404
23. Younis, S.G.: Asymptotically zero energy computing using split-level charge recovery logic. Ph.D. thesis, Massachusetts Institute of Technology (1994). http://hdl.handle.net/1721.1/11620

Applications of Reversible and Quantum Computations

A Proposed Research Platform for Fully Adiabatic, Reversible, and Superscalar (FARS) Microarchitectures

Byron Gregg[1,2] and Christof Teuscher[1(✉)]

[1] Portland State University, Portland, OR, USA
{greggbyr,teuscher}@pdx.edu
[2] Vaire Computing, Portland, OR, USA
byron@vaire.co
https://www.vaire.co

Abstract. Energy constraints increasingly dominate modern processor and high-performance computing system design. Contemporary superscalar and out-of-order (OoO) processors achieve performance through mechanisms that rely on destructive state transitions, including register overwrites, speculative flushing, and memory updates. Reversible computation provides a theoretical pathway toward reducing energy dissipation associated with information destruction, yet prior work has largely remained confined to circuit-level implementations and isolated architectural prototypes. This work explores a framework for Fully Adiabatic, Reversible, and Superscalar (FARS) microarchitectures that reinterpret modern performance-oriented processor structures under reversible execution constraints. We are working to complete a microarchitectural research platform that we are developing to investigate how key high-performance mechanisms can be reformulated to preserve invertibility. As a concrete artifact, we have implemented and evaluated reversible branch predictors, demonstrating that complex speculative microarchitectural structures can be expressed as bijective state transitions. This provides quantitative insight into the storage and coordination overheads required for reversible scheduling mechanisms and establishes a foundation for extending reversibility to additional superscalar structures. This work-in-progress identifies architectural gaps to be filled and presents an example of an implemented reversible microarchitectural component as a step toward thermodynamically aware high-performance processor design.

Keywords: Fully Adiabatic Reversible and SuperScalar · FARS · Reversible Computing · Adiabatic Computing · Reversible Core · Adiabatic Core · Reversible Architectures · Adiabatic Architectures · Adiabatic and Reversible CMOS · ARC

C. Aubert and L. Roversi (Eds.): RC 2026, LNCS 16626, pp. 133–140, 2026.
https://doi.org/10.1007/978-3-032-30839-9_7

1 Background and Motivation

The physical limits of computation are thermodynamically grounded. Landauer demonstrated that logically irreversible operations incur a minimum energy cost proportional to temperature and the number of erased states [9]. While transistor density continued scaling for decades, the breakdown of Dennard scaling halted voltage reduction and led to increasing power density [4,5]. Modern performance growth shifted toward increasingly complex microarchitectural mechanisms such as superscalar issue, out-of-order scheduling, and speculation.

These mechanisms sustain throughput but rely fundamentally on overwriting state, discarding speculative results, and irreversibly updating memory. In contrast, reversible computation, formalized by Bennett [3], enables computation via bijective state transitions without mandatory information destruction. Subsequent work by Fredkin and Toffoli established reversible logic elements suitable for hardware realization [7,11].

Architectural realizations of reversible computation have been comparatively limited. Vieri's Pendulum demonstrated a reversible ISA implemented in CMOS [12,13], while additional work explored reversible instruction semantics and numerical kernels [2,6]. However, these efforts did not integrate modern high-performance mechanisms such as superscalar issue, dynamic scheduling, and speculative execution.

This work investigates how contemporary microarchitectural structures can be reformulated under reversible execution constraints. Rather than abandoning performance-oriented design, we explore whether key coordination mechanisms can be restructured to preserve invertibility.

At present, the completed portion of this research consists primarily of reversible formulations and implementations of branch prediction mechanisms within an out-of-order simulation environment [8]. These predictors demonstrate that speculative microarchitectural structures can be reformulated as bijective state transitions while preserving prediction functionality. The broader FARS framework proposed in this work extends these concepts toward reversible formulations of register renaming, speculative rollback, and memory coordination. These remaining components are currently architectural proposals and active areas of investigation rather than completed implementations.

2 FARS Architectural Framework

The Fully Adiabatic, Reversible, and Superscalar (FARS) framework reinterprets modern high-performance processor structures under reversibility constraints. The framework operates at the architectural level and assumes only that the underlying substrate supports energy-recovering operation.

2.1 Reversible Execution Model

FARS treats instructions as bijective transformations over architectural state. Conventional processors overwrite registers and discard intermediate values.

Reversible execution instead requires retaining sufficient information to reconstruct prior states.

Execution proceeds through structured state transitions that support both forward progress and controlled inversion. Temporary values and scheduling context are expected to remain available until safely uncomputed. Pipeline structures therefore coordinate reversible state evolution rather than propagating and discarding transient artifacts.

2.2 Superscalar and Out-of-Order Coordination

Superscalar issue and dynamic scheduling remain central to performance but would need to be reformulated to preserve invertibility. Register renaming may require becoming a reversible mapping rather than a destructive reassignment. This presents a particularly challenging design point. Conventional rename tables overwrite architectural-to-physical mappings. A reversible mechanism must encode transitions bijectively or retain prior mappings, introducing storage and coordination overhead proportional to rename events.

Speculative execution must also support inversion. Rather than flushing speculative state on misprediction, execution history would have to be unwound through controlled reversal. These adaptations preserve throughput mechanisms while preventing irreversible state loss.

Both of these remain ongoing areas of research, while reversible speculative execution components such as branch prediction have already been implemented and evaluated in prior work [8].

2.3 Memory Implications

Memory presents a primary challenge because conventional writes overwrite prior values. Reversible memory interaction requires retaining sufficient state to enable inversion. Cache replacement and hierarchy transfers must avoid destructive updates or encode overwritten state explicitly.

While a complete reversible memory hierarchy also remains future work, individual stateful structures can be reformulated under reversibility constraints, as demonstrated in the example artifact shown in the next section.

3 Concrete Artifact and Superscalar Integration Path

To ground the FARS framework in a concrete microarchitectural component, we reference our previously completed work on reversible formulations for branch prediction [8]. The contribution of the present work is not a new branch predictor itself, but the proposal and architectural framing for extending reversibility across broader superscalar coordination mechanisms including register renaming, speculative rollback, and memory interaction. For example, the reversible TAGE branch predictor (REV-TAGE), as seen in Fig. 1, has its complete REV-TAGE update policy also shown in Algorithm 1. Predictors such as this will be included within the finished research platform.

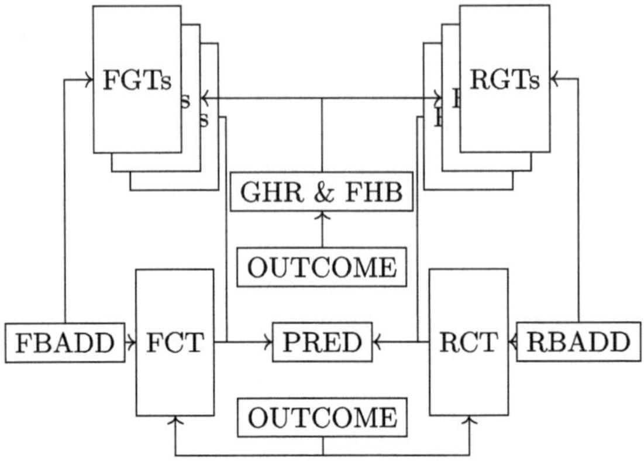

Fig. 1. Reversible TAGE (REV-TAGE) predictor implementation.

In Fig. 1 The Forward Counter Table (FCT) and Reverse Counter Table (RCT) are indexed by the Forward Branch Address (FBADD) and Reverse Branch Address (RBADD), respectively. The Forward and Reverse Geometric Tables (FGT/RGT) are indexed with partial tags hashed from the global history (GHR) and the FBADD or RBADD. Since the history is required for the geometric tables, a Future History Buffer (FHB) is needed to track the future outcomes for later updates. During each prediction, the geometric table with the longest history that has a tag match determines the direction. During updates, both tables are indexed and the counters are updated based on the branch outcome (taken = +1; not-taken = -1), the geometric tables for the given flow mode (FWD or REV) are updated based on the update scheme and the opposite set of tables will stall updates until the future history is computed and the address is shifted off the FHB. Arrows pointing right denote the flow of data in forward mode and arrows pointing left denote the flow in reverse mode. Arrows pointing up or down happen in all modes during update or prediction.

Algorithm 1. REV-TAGE update policy

```
update FCT/FGTs                                  ▷ F=R in REV mode
FHB_R_Outcome_In = outcome;                      ▷ R=F in REV mode
FHB_R_Valid_In = 1;
FHB_R_Addr_In = BADDR;
if FHB_R_Valid_Out then
    Future_Addr = FHB_R_Addr_Out;
    Future_Outcome = FHB_R_Outcome_Out;
    update RCT/RGTs
end if
update GHR
```

Modern superscalar out-of-order processors rely heavily on dynamic branch prediction to sustain instruction-level parallelism. TAGE predictors [10] maintain multiple tagged history tables indexed by global branch history and update them speculatively upon branch resolution. Conventional implementations overwrite predictor entries and discard speculative updates during misprediction recovery.

We reformulated TAGE updates as bijective state transitions. Twin predictor tables retain sufficient information to perform speculation during reverse execution but do so more accurately with maintained history buffers and tables. Future work will investigate recovering logged predictor states during rollback via inversion rather than flush-and-recompute mechanisms, further improving branch prediction energy efficiency.

Our previous work [8] implemented multiple reversible branch predictors with the Simplescalar [1] out-of-order simulator. This served as an effective environment for evaluating early proof-of-concept reversible predictor implementations within an OoO system and showed that such predictors can be integrated into simulated modern superscalar out-of-order execution environments.

However, we would like to extend this work to cover the more modern RISC-V ISA [14]. In particular, we have identified the Berkeley BOOM V3 RISC-V core [15] as it is a superscalar, out-of-order core that uses a TAGE predictor, making it a natural target for future integration of our previously completed work. Integration with BOOM remains incomplete. However, its architectural structure, as seen in Fig. 2, provides a realistic superscalar baseline for evaluating reversible coordination mechanisms.

4 Discussion and Research Direction

The reversible TAGE predictor illustrates that complex stateful speculative structures can be expressed through bijective transitions without sacrificing predictive functionality. However, extending reversibility across the full superscalar pipeline introduces additional challenges.

Register renaming, reorder buffers, speculative issue queues, and memory hierarchies require structured retention or encoding of overwritten state.

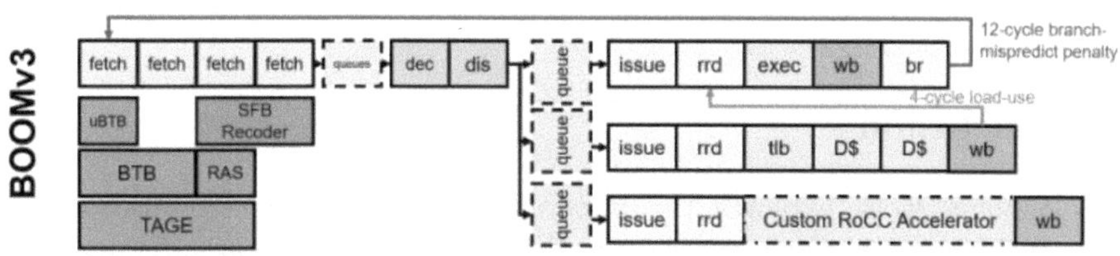

Fig. 2. Berkeley Out-of-Order Machine (BOOM) v3 Architecture [15]. This core was identified as a good candidate for our proposed research platform due to its ease of integration with previous branch predictor work.

These mechanisms introduce storage overhead, logging complexity, and potential latency penalties that would have to be characterized relative to conventional designs.

Future work will extend RISC-V toward a realizable FARS platform utilizing the Berkeley BOOM V3 core as a superscalar out-of-order baseline. This integration will enable quantitative study of:

- Reversible register renaming mechanisms and mapping storage overhead,
- Invertible commit and rollback latency compared to conventional pipeline flush,
- Interaction between reversible branch prediction and speculative execution depth,
- Memory hierarchy implications under non-destructive update constraints.

The objective is architectural validation of whether reversible coordination can coexist with modern throughput-oriented execution while approaching thermodynamic limits. The current status of these tasks can be seen visually in Fig. 3.

Several architectural risks remain open research questions. Reversible coordination mechanisms may introduce increased storage overhead due to retained speculative state and reversible mapping information. Additional buffering and history retention structures may also increase wiring complexity and latency relative to conventional implementations. Furthermore, rollback through inversion may introduce longer recovery paths compared to conventional flush-and-restart mechanisms. Quantifying these tradeoffs remains an important direction for future investigation.

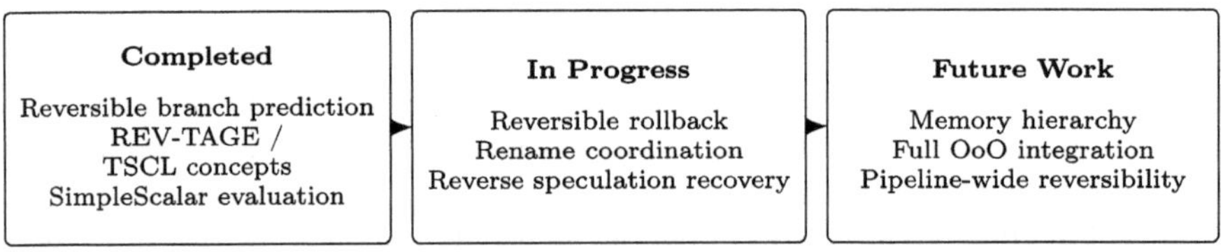

Fig. 3. Current maturity of the FARS research platform.

5 Conclusion

This ongoing work explores the integration of reversible computation with modern superscalar microarchitecture. While prior reversible architectures have focused on logic or ISA design, contemporary processors depend on mechanisms that assume irreversible state transitions.

The FARS framework's goal is to outline how superscalar coordination structures can be reformulated under reversibility constraints. The finished platform will include existing implementations of our reversible branch predictors, demonstrating that speculative microarchitectural mechanisms can be expressed as bijective state transitions.

This work-in-progress will establish an architectural foundation for investigating whether reversible execution can contribute meaningfully to future energy-constrained computing systems.

Disclosure of Interests. The authors have no competing interests to declare that are relevant to the content of this article.

AI Disclaimer. The authors used ChatGPT 5.2 to improve spelling, grammar, clarity, and readability during manuscript preparation. After using this tool, the authors carefully reviewed and edited the text and take full responsibility for the final content.

References

1. Austin, T., Burger, D., Franklin, M., Breach, S., Skadron, K.: The SimpleScalar Architectural Research Tool Set, Version 2.0 (1998). https://pages.cs.wisc.edu/~mscalar/simplescalar.html
2. Axelsen, H.B., Glück, R., Yokoyama, T.: Reversible machine code and its abstract processor architecture. In: Diekert, V., Volkov, M.V., Voronkov, A. (eds.) CSR 2007. LNCS, vol. 4649, pp. 56–69. Springer, Heidelberg (2007). https://doi.org/10.1007/978-3-540-74510-5_9
3. Bennett, C.H.: Logical reversibility of computation. IBM J. Res. Dev. **17**(6), 525–532 (1973)
4. Bohr, M.: The new era of scaling in an SoC world. In: IEEE International Solid-State Circuits Conference-Digest of Technical Papers, pp. 23–28. IEEE (2009)
5. Dennard, R., et al.: Design of ion-implanted MOSFET's with very small physical dimensions. IEEE J. Solid-State Circuits **9**(5), 256–268 (1974). https://doi.org/10.1109/JSSC.1974.1050511
6. Dwarka, V.: Towards energy-efficient scientific computing: reversible numerical linear algebra kernels in floating-point arithmetic. Sustain. Comput. Inform. Syst. **49**, 101261 (2026). https://doi.org/10.1016/j.suscom.2025.101261
7. Fredkin, E.F., Toffoli, T.: Design principles for achieving high-performance submicron digital technologies. In: Collision-based Computing, pp. 27–46. Springer, Salmon Tower Building, New York, New York, USA (2002)
8. Gregg, B., Teuscher, C.: General Principles for Implementing Branch Prediction in Fully Adiabatic, Reversible, and SuperScalar (FARS) Processors (2025). https://doi.org/10.21203/rs.3.rs-7825116/v1. Research Square
9. Landauer, R.: Irreversibility and heat generation in the computing process. IBM J. Res. Dev. **5**(3), 183–191 (1961)
10. Seznec, A., Michaud, P.: A case for (partially) tagged geometric history length branch prediction. J. Instr. Level Parallelism **8**, 23 (2006)
11. Toffoli, T.: Computation and construction universality of reversible cellular automata. J. Comput. Syst. Sci. **15**(2), 213–231 (1977)
12. Vieri, C.J.: Pendulum-A Reversible Computer Architecture, Massachusetts Institute of Technology, Department of Electrical Engineering and Computer Science (1995). Master's thesis

13. Vieri, C.J.: Reversible Computer Engineering and Architecture, Massachusetts Institute of Technology, Department of Electrical Engineering and Computer Science (1999). Ph.D. thesis
14. Waterman, A., Lee, Y., Patterson, D.A., Asanovic, K.: The RISC-V Instruction Set Manual. EECS Department, UC Berkeley, Technical Report UCB/EECS-2011-62, vol. 116(2011), pp. 1–32 (2011)
15. Zhao, J., Korpan, B., Gonzalez, A., Asanovic, K.: SonicBOOM: The 3rd Generation Berkeley Out-of-Order Machine. Fourth Workshop on Computer Architecture Research with RISC-V (2020)

Reversible Deep Learning for ^{13}C NMR in Chemoinformatics: On Structures and Spectra

Stefan Kuhn[1,2](✉), Vandana Dwarka[3], Przemysław Grenda[4], and Eero Vainikko[1]

[1] Department of Computer Science, Tartu University, Tartu, Estonia
{stefan.kuhn,eero.vainikko}@ut.ee
[2] De Montfort University, Leicester, UK
[3] Department of Industrial and Applied Mathematics, Delft University of Technology, Delft, The Netherlands
v.n.s.r.dwarka@tudelft.nl
[4] Faculty of Pharmacy, Charles University, Hradec Králové, Czech Republic
grendap@faf.cuni.cz

Abstract. We introduce a reversible deep learning model for ^{13}C Nuclear Magnetic Resonance (NMR) spectroscopy that uses a single conditional invertible neural network for both directions between molecular structures and spectra. The network is built from i-RevNet style bijective blocks, so the forward map and its inverse are available by construction. We train the model to predict a 128-bit binned spectrum code from a graph-based structure encoding, while the remaining latent dimensions capture residual variability. At inference time, we invert the same trained network to generate structure candidates from a spectrum code, which explicitly represents the one-to-many nature of spectrum-to-structure inference. On a filtered subset, the model is numerically invertible on trained examples, achieves spectrum-code prediction above chance, and produces coarse but meaningful structural signals when inverted on validation spectra. These results demonstrate that invertible architectures can unify spectrum prediction and uncertainty-aware candidate generation within one end-to-end model.

Keywords: NMR · structure elucidation · NMR prediction · spectrum prediction · reversible deep learning · invertible neural networks · conditional invertible neural networks · i-RevNet

1 Introduction

Chemistry largely deals with invisible units of matter, referred to as molecules. Since they are invisible, they have always been imagined as stylized images, e.g. as in Fig. 1 a) and c). For the same reason, physical chemistry has devised methods to create visible measurements, representing the same molecules, e.g. nuclear magnetic resonance (NMR) spectra, as shown in b). In order to avoid

C. Aubert and L. Roversi (Eds.): RC 2026, LNCS 16626, pp. 141–148, 2026.
https://doi.org/10.1007/978-3-032-30839-9_8

the complex field of the exact meaning of those representations we deal, for the purpose of this paper, with "atom and bond" models of molecules as in b) and with NMR spectra consisting of a list of peaks respectively their positions.

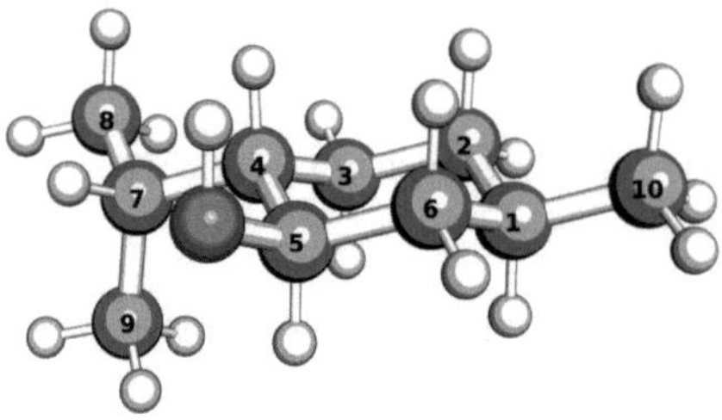

(a) A three dimensional representation (generated with PyMOL[11]).

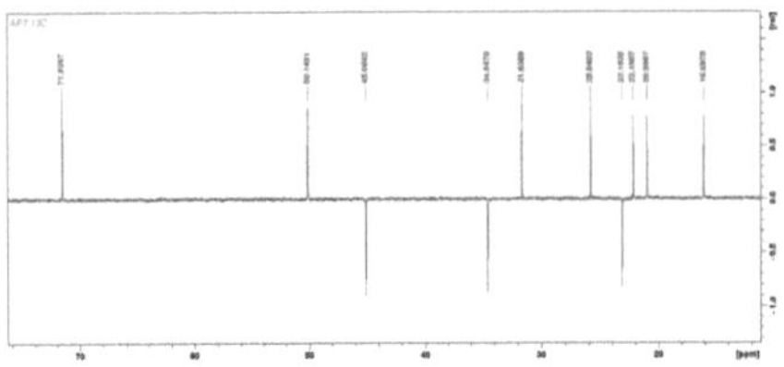

(b) A ^{13}C spectrum of (-)-Menthol, measured at 150 MHz in CDCl3 [2].

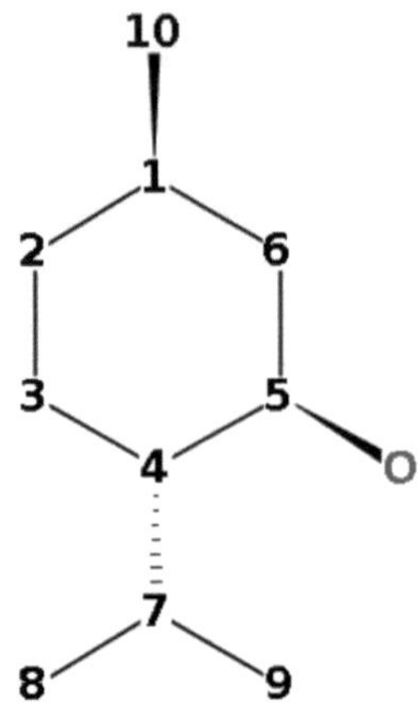

(c) A representation as a 2D graph (generated by nmrshiftdb.org).

Fig. 1. a) c) Representations of the structure, b) A spectrum of (-)-Menthol.

Most importantly, there is an inverse, in principle deterministic, connection between the two: The spectrum is determined by the structure [3,7] and the structure can be inferred from the spectrum. The second task is more complicated [13]. Very recently, there have been attempts to train a neural network to do this task directly without optimization, e.g. [4].

Considering this, the molecule-^{13}C spectrum relationship is an ideal candidate for applications of invertible neural networks. We have very information-rich structures on both sides, the information is different, but there is a strict relationship between them. So there is a reversible, invertible connection between molecular structures and NMR spectra that preserves forward consistency while explicitly modeling inverse ambiguity. That relationship has been shown as learnable in both directions. Therefore, in this paper, we present the first invertible neural network, which delivers an approximation of spectrum simulation in one direction and of structure elucidation in the other direction. To our knowledge, this is the first end-to-end invertible neural network to jointly model molecular property simulation such as ^{13}C NMR spectrum simulation and structure elucidation in the literature. By combining invertible architectures with conditional and latent-variable formulations, our model offers a principled alternative to purely discriminative or autoencoder-based approaches for spectrum-structure inference. We refer the reader to [8] for more background.

With respect to terminology, we use the term *invertible neural network* here for a network which gives a bijective mapping between two information spaces. The term *reversible neural network* is used in the literature for networks where the neurons have reversible functions, but where the network is not necessarily reversible as a whole. The purpose of those networks is mainly to enable memory savings by avoiding the need to save values in the nodes during training.

2 Results and Discussion

When training the model, we noticed that good results are achieved with a small number of training rounds. Figure 2 shows that neither the loss nor the F1 value for Y_{latent} improve beyond six epochs. We therefore have chosen five epochs for training for all subsequent evaluations. The increasing validation loss beyond epoch 5 whilst the training loss still improves suggests that overfitting occurs. Considering the small number of epochs, this could indicate that the amount of available data may be insufficient. We therefore select five epochs as an early-stopping point. Due to the limited size of the dataset and the rapid onset of overfitting, we restrict our evaluation to repeated training/validation splits (80%/20%). As a consequence, all reported performance metrics should be interpreted as validation performance rather than unbiased test estimates.

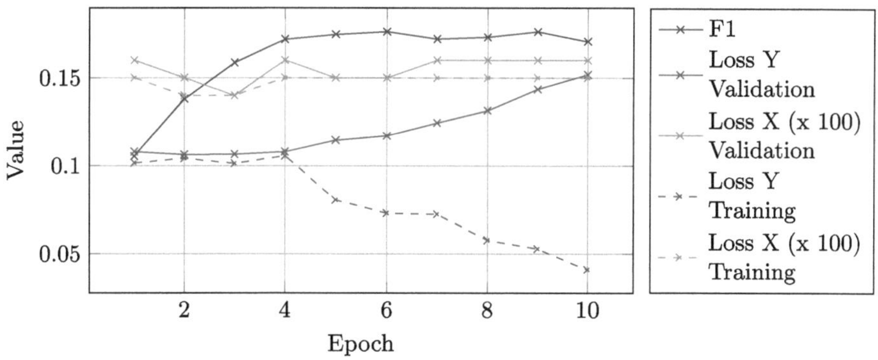

Fig. 2. F1 and loss values during training. For exact values, see Table 1 in [8].

For evaluating the performance of the model, a number of metrics are used. It should be noted that the absolute performance of the model is not as good as that of specialized and highly optimized models. This is currently acceptable, since the invertible nature of the model is a novel concept.

2.1 The Network Can Predict Spectra

The model predicts spectra as a sequence of 128 0 s and 1 s. A typical measure for the correctness of such a task is the F1-value, calculated on Y_{latent}. Running our model 10 times with different, random train/validation splits gives F1 values between 0.1548 and 0.1839, with a mean of 0.1695. For comparison, using the same bit representation and the network from [10], the F1 value is 0.92. Clearly, the result from our INN is not a very good result as such, but it shows that the model learns what it is intended to learn. Given the high sparsity of the output vectors (on average 6.43% 1 s per spectrum), a random predictor with the same probability of 1 s and 0 s achieves an expected F1 of about 0.0643, indicating that the obtained values are substantially above chance. In our context, the number and relative positions of 1 s are more important than exact matches at all positions. A typical example would be a prediction of 76, 77, 78, 79, 80, 82, 83, 84 for a real spectrum of 13, 77, 79, 80, 86, 88. Here, three out of six peaks are correctly predicted. More examples are shown in Table 2 in [8].

2.2 The Network is Invertible for Trained Values

For an invertible network, as a minimum requirement, it should be possible to reconstruct the input from any output in the training set. In our case, this is the possibility to reconstruct the input from the complete output of Y_{latent} and Z_{free}. In theory, this should be perfect. In practice, rounding errors in the network give rise to negligible numerical errors. In our case, the maximum error values observed during ten runs are in the range from 0.00009 to 0.00015 and the mean is between 0.00005 and 0.00007. These numbers indicate perfect reconstruction, as expected from an invertible model.

2.3 Z_{free} Primarily Captures Residual Variation

Since all meaningful content on the output side of the network is in Y_{latent}, we want Z_{free} to be independent from Y_{latent} and to be well-behaved. Table 1 shows that this is supported by the actual values. While the mean of Z_{free} is close to zero, its standard deviation is substantially below one, indicating that the learned distribution is more concentrated than the ideal standard normal. This suggests that the regularization of Z_{free} is only partially effective.

Table 1. Real and ideal values for Z_{free} statistics.

Metric per Sample	Over validation set			
	Real		Ideal	
	Mean	Std	Mean	Std
Z_{free} mean	0.0858	0.0334	0	small
Z_{free} std	0.5861	0.0795	1	small

2.4 The Data Manifold is Well Structured

We study how stable the inverse mapping is when we change the free latent part Z_{free} while keeping the spectrum code Y_{latent} fixed. We calculated two variants, because Z_{free} can be taken either from the forward pass of a real sample or from the learned prior. Details of the calculuation and results as a table can be found in [8].

The conditional deviation increases approximately linearly for small ϵ, indicating local sensitivity to perturbations in Z_{free}. Importantly, the relative deviation does not grow beyond $\epsilon = 0.1$, suggesting that the inverse map remains locally stable over the tested perturbation range. To look beyond the random sample, we have calculated the conditional variation at fixed Y_{latent} across a given set of Z_{free} samples, where Z_{free} comes from the learned prior. Here, we get a mean conditional variation of 3.4648 and a standard deviation of 0.8280. This indicates that changes in Z_{free} lead to meaningful variation in the reconstructed input even when Y_{latent} is fixed. This behavior is consistent with the intended role of Z_{free} as a carrier of residual variation beyond the spectrum code.

2.5 Generated X Values Are Meaningful

Finally, we can show that the X values, representing structures, generated by inverting the network from spectra from the validation set, which were not used during training, combined with a random Z_{free}, are meaningful. It should be clear that the results can hardly be an exact result, since for this, a very specific arrangement of only a few 1 s in the matrices is required. During training, there is nothing that really enforces those arrangements. We have also seen that Y_{latent} (our actual result) is not as independent from Z_{free} as it could be, meaning the random selection of Z_{free} still has an influence on the result of the inversion.

Because of this, we have two tests here, which are rather coarse, but still show that the model has learned something about even those cases. First, we have calculated the correlation coefficient between the number of 1 s in the real inputs and the reconstructed ones. For ten rounds, the mean correlation coefficient was 0.1863, with a minimum of 0.0971 and a maximum of 0.2284. Second, we have calculated the correlation between the number of 1 s in the fourth array of the input for each molecule, which contains the aromatic bonds. Because aromatic atoms are typically represented in the NMR spectrum by high shift values, a particularly strong connection could be expected here. The correlation coefficient was 0.1775 (min=0.09563, max=0.2073) for ten runs.

While these correlations are weak, they are consistently positive across runs and exceed a purely random result, which would have correlation 0, indicating that the model preserves coarse structural information. It clearly shows that the inversion in this case only works very roughly. Still, the network is invertible for some cases and keeps some connection between input and output even in other, more difficult cases.

3 Methods

3.1 Data

The data used in this work are from nmrshiftdb2 [9,12]. We have selected all structures which contain only carbon and hydrogen atoms, which have up to 17 carbon atoms, and for which a one-dimensional ^{13}C spectrum exists. There were 1567 such structures. Those structures and their assigned spectra have been encoded into sequences of 0 s and 1 s, both simplified compared to the original data. We encode the structure into four matrices of size 16x16, and a spectrum as a one-dimensional array of 1024 bits. Details of the encoding are found in [8].

3.2 The Network Architecture

The invertible neural network we have been using is based on the i-RevNet architecture [5,6], but differs in how invertibility is maintained at the output stage. It should be noted that the architecture presented by Jacobsen *et al.* is not fully invertible, in particular, the final classification step in the bijective network is not invertible. The RevNet block used as the main component, however, is fully invertible. Using this block, we construct a conditional invertible neural network (cINN, [1]) which is fully invertible.

At the core of our network (Fig. 3) is a block which increases the number of channels by a factor of four and halves the x and y dimensions of the input layer. This block follows the implementation in i-RevNet. In this way, a multi-dimensional input can be transformed to a one-dimensional output in a provably fully invertible fashion. In our case, the input is structured as a 4x16x16 array, where 4 is the initial number of channels. Each of the matrices holds a 1 for a bond, and a 0 otherwise. The first matrix has single bonds, the second double bonds, and the third triple bonds. The fourth matrix indicates if a bond is an aromatic bond. This is in addi-

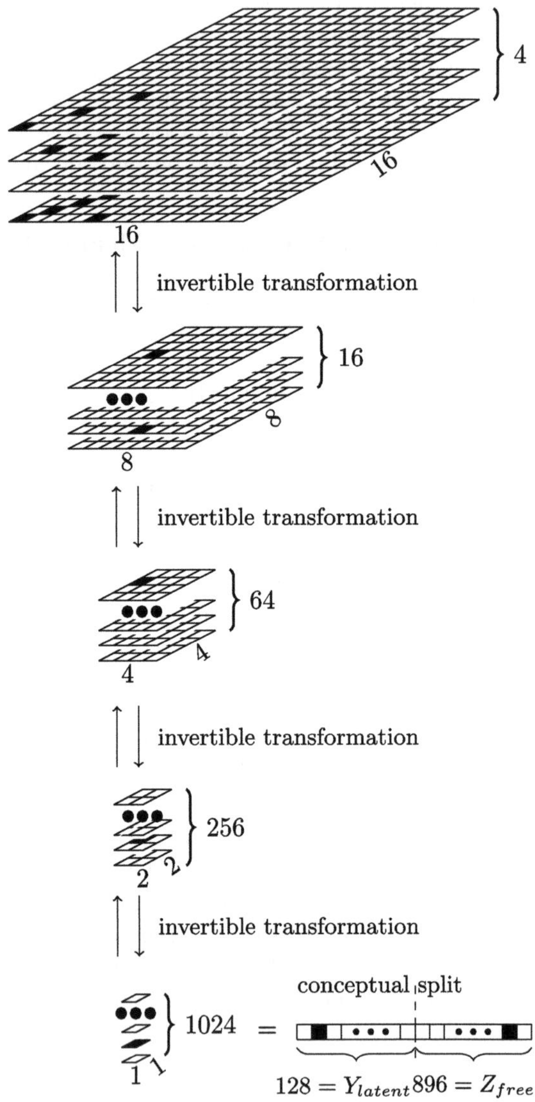

Fig. 3. The network consists of a sequence of invertible iRevNet blocks, which progressively transform the four input matrices into a 1D vector. The final latent space is conceptually partitioned into 128 bits representing a spectrum (Y_{latent}) and 896 unconstrained bits (Z_{free}). Black dots indicate layers or cells omitted for visual clarity. The black boxes indicate 1 values, where in the first layer a benzene molecule, with three single and three double bonds forming a ring, and all bonds marked as aromatic. 1 s in further layers are put in for illustration.

tion to the other matrices, so an aromatic ring is recoded as a number of single and double bonds with an aromatic property recorded in addition. Since atoms cannot bond to themselves, a 16x16 matrix can hold the information for the complete molecule. We do not include the symmetric bonds, so a part of the matrices is always empty, which means set to 0. The network produces an output of 1024 channels with a 1x1 matrix for each. In practice, this is a 1024-bit vector.

Whilst at first sight this would mean that a direct prediction of the 1024-bit spectrum representation could be attempted, a reversible neural network cannot necessarily predict in both directions what is possible from the architecture. The important measure is entropy, and doing a rough entropy estimate for our input gives an entropy of 76 bits. We therefore have divided the output into 128 bits (to keep with the 2^x sizes) for the actual spectral features (referred to as Y_{latent}) and 1024-128=896 bits which absorb the remaining variation (referred to as Z_{free}). It should be noted that this is conceptual split we make on the result, the network still learns the full 1024 bits (but it is incentivized to get Y_{latent} right by the loss function). For mapping from the 1024-bit spectrum to the 128-bit compression, a mapping in which four bits are combined into one bit by applying an OR function is used. This ensures that no information is lost and is equivalent to doing a coarser binning. Our model will only work on the 128-bit spectra. This is a limitation which stems from the requirement of an invertible network to have similarly sized information spaces on both sides.

The loss function is composed of four factors: For measuring the accuracy of the prediction, we have implemented a distance-aware Binary Cross-Entropy (BCE) loss function operating on Y_{latent}. It is composed of several elements (see [8] for details), ensuring reasonably good results in both directions.

4 Conclusion

We have presented a conditional invertible neural network, based on i-RevNet blocks, that is able to predict spectra from structures in one direction and elucidate structures from spectra in the other direction without explicit training for that. In order to maintain entropy on both sides of our network, we divide the output into useful information of 128 bits and leave the rest as residual noise. We demonstrate that the network can predict spectra and that it is invertible for the training examples. Furthermore, we demonstrate that the output outside of the 128 bits is mainly noise and that the data manifold is well structured. Finally, we have also shown that when used in reverse with unknown examples, the network still produces some chemically meaningful results. Future work is outlined in [8].

Data Availability Statement. The code for the invertible neural network is available from github at https://github.com/stefhk3/RevMolSpec.

AI declaration. A Large Languge Model (LLM) was used to analyse the i-RevNet code and to isolate functions for the code at https://github.com/stefhk3/RevMolSpec. No part of the paper was written by the LLM.

References

1. Ardizzone, L., et al.: Conditional invertible neural networks for diverse image-to-image translation (2021). arXiv:2105.02104 arXiv preprint
2. Berger, S., Sicker, D.: Classics in Spectroscopy: Isolation and Structure Elucidation of Natural Products. Wiley-VCH, Weinheim, Germany (2009)
3. Das, S., Merz Jr., K.M.: Exploring the frontiers of computational NMR: methods, applications, and challenges. Chem. Rev. **125**(19), 9256–9295. https://doi.org/10.1021/acs.chemrev.5c00259
4. Hu, F., et al.: Pushing the limits of one-dimensional NMR spectroscopy for automated structure elucidation using artificial intelligence (2025). arXiv:2512.18531 arXiv preprint
5. Jacobsen, J., Smeulders, A.W.M., Oyallon, E.: i-RevNet: Deep Invertible Networks. CoRR **abs/1802.07088** (2018). http://arxiv.org/abs/1802.07088
6. Jacobsen, J.H., Smeulders, A.W., Oyallon, E.: i-RevNet: deep invertible networks. In: International Conference on Learning Representations (2018). https://openreview.net/forum?id=HJsjkMb0Z
7. Jonas, E., Kuhn, S., Schlörer, N.: Prediction of chemical shift in NMR: a review. Magn. Reson. Chem. **60**(11), 1021–1031. https://doi.org/10.1002/mrc.5234
8. Kuhn, S., Dwarka, V., Grenda, P.K., Vainikko, E.: Reversible deep learning for 13c NMR in chemoinformatics: on structures and spectra (2026). https://arxiv.org/abs/2602.03875
9. Kuhn, S., Schlörer, N.E.: Facilitating quality control for spectra assignments of small organic molecules: nmrshiftdb2 – a free in-house NMR database with integrated LIMS for academic service laboratories. Magn. Reson. Chem. **53**(8), 582–589 (2015). https://doi.org/10.1002/mrc.4263
10. Rull, H., Fischer, M., Kuhn, S.: NMR shift prediction from small data quantities. J. Cheminformatics **15**(1), 114 (2023). https://doi.org/10.1186/s13321-023-00785-x
11. Schrödinger, LLC: The PyMOL molecular graphics system, version 3.1.0 (2025). http://www.pymol.org
12. Steinbeck, C., Kuhn, S.: NMRShiftDB - compound identification and structure elucidation support through a free community-built web database. Phytochemistry **65**(19), 2711–7 (2004). https://doi.org/10.1016/j.phytochem.2004.08.027
13. Wenk, M., Nuzillard, J.M., Steinbeck, C.: Sherlock—a free and open-source system for the computer-assisted structure elucidation of organic compounds from NMR data. Molecules **28**(3) (2023). https://doi.org/10.3390/molecules28031448

Toward Quantum Circuit Execution Success Estimation via Graph Neural Network-Based Prediction

Antonio Tudisco[1], Deborah Volpe[2(✉)], Mariagrazia Graziano[1], and Giovanna Turvani[1]

[1] Politecnico di Torino, Turin, Italy
{antonio.tudisco,mariagrazia.graziano,giovanna.turvani}@polito.it
[2] Istituto Nazionale di Geofisica e Vulcanologia, Rome, Italy
deborah.volpe@ingv.it

Abstract. Quantum computing has attracted meaningful interest in recent years due to rapid advancements in applications such as optimization, cryptography, and machine learning. However, the successful implementation of quantum algorithms on real quantum hardware requires selecting the most suitable device via detailed performance evaluation, which is both time- and cost-intensive. This article proposes an automated framework to estimate the Probability of Success per Trial (PST) of executing quantum circuits on specific quantum devices. The approach involves constructing a dataset involving more than 4000 quantum circuits from the MQT Bench set. These circuits are then converted into Directed Acyclic Graph (DAG) representations, and Graph Neural Network (GNN)-based models are trained to predict the optimal associated PST for a target device, avoiding a brute-force exploration based on compiling and executing the quantum circuit, varying the compilation setting. The trained models have achieved good accuracy in estimating the PST value, guaranteeing a Root Mean Squared Error (RMSE) lower than 0.1 for all three target devices considered, significantly reducing the time and cost required for estimating the metric and proving the effectiveness of the proposed methodology.

Keywords: Machine Learning · Predictive models · Quantum Hardware · Compilation · Quantum circuit · Software Stack

1 Introduction

Quantum computing has gained significant attention in recent years, driven by rapid advancements across several applications such as quantum optimization [1,2], cryptography [3], and machine learning [1,4]. Typically, ideal simulators are used for evaluating quantum computer potential for these applications, without accounting for the noise and limitations of current quantum devices. However, executing them on real quantum hardware needs careful device selection based

C. Aubert and L. Roversi (Eds.): RC 2026, LNCS 16626, pp. 149–163, 2026.
https://doi.org/10.1007/978-3-032-30839-9_9

on comprehensive evaluations considering various performance metrics. Traditionally, these metrics are evaluated via brute-force methods involving circuit compilation across multiple backends with varying optimization levels. However, nowadays the end-to-end execution flow, including compilation, mapping, and noise-aware simulation, typically takes from a few minutes to over an hour per circuit. Therefore, sweeping multiple optimization levels and backends quickly scales to tens to hundreds of core-hours. Moreover, running experiments on real hardware is also financially costly. A more efficient alternative involves the use of predictive models to estimate performance metrics, reducing time and cost and enabling early evaluation of an algorithm compatibility with the current maturity of the hardware. Nevertheless, current models reported in the literature frequently exhibit limited generalization and suboptimal accuracy, indicating that there is still substantial room for improvement.

Our work tries to address this challenge by developing a predictive model based on Graph Neural Networks (GNNs) to estimate the optimal Probability of Success per Trial (PST) [5], i.e. probability of obtaining the correct outcome, directly from a high-level circuit representation. The PST metric intuitively reflects the probability that a quantum circuit, when executed on a given device, will produce a correct result in a single run, accounting for hardware noise and compilation quality.

This work represents a first step toward an automated tool capable of analyzing a quantum circuit and, based on selected performance metrics, recommending the most suitable hardware without the need to compile the circuit on each device.

The main contributions of this work are the following:

- **GNN-based PST prediction from high-level circuits:** we propose a GNN model to estimate the PST directly from high-level quantum circuit representations.
- **Avoiding brute-force compilation:** the model predicts optimal PST without the need of compiling circuits across multiple backends or optimization levels, allowing faster and computationally less expensive hardware selection.
- **DAG representation of quantum circuits in the dataset:** we create a dataset of over 4000 MQT Bench circuits, represented as DAGs with structured node features for effective model training.
- **Cross-backend within IBM fake devices generalization:** the model is trained and tested on three different IBM Fake devices, achieving consistent performance with RMSE < 0.1.
- **Performance analysis as a function of the circuit properties:** we analyze the prediction accuracy with respect to circuit type, depth, and qubit count, identifying underrepresented cases.
- **Adaptable prediction framework:** the pipeline supports automatic inference and can be adapted to other devices or performance metrics.

The rest of the article is organized as follows: Sect. 2 presents motivations and general idea behind the work, Sect. 3 reports the related works in the state of the art, Sect. 4 shows the effective implementation of the prediction, Sect. 5 reports the obtained results and in Sect. 6 we draw conclusions.

2 Motivation and General Idea

Estimating the quality of the execution of quantum circuit on real hardware typically requires full compilation and simulation across multiple backends, with different optimization levels. This process is computationally expensive and becomes rapidly unfeasible as the circuit size grows. Currently, existing predictive models are often based on device-specific mappings and fail to generalize across platforms or optimization configurations.

In this work, we show that the achievable Probability of PST, a metric closely correlated with circuit fidelity under noise and compilation constraints, can be estimated without explicitly compiling and executing the circuit on a target device.

We focus on PST since, differently from low-level hardware metrics such as gate fidelities or readout error rates, it provides an application-oriented measure of performance that jointly captures the effects of hardware noise, circuit structure, and compilation. While metrics such as average gate error or circuit depth offer useful but partial insights, they do not directly reflect the probability that a quantum algorithm produces a correct outcome when executed on real hardware. PST inherently accounts for both intrinsic device imperfections and the transformations introduced during the compilation and transpilation procedure, including qubit mapping, routing, and optimization passes. As a result, it provides a holistic view of execution quality that is directly relevant to both end users and algorithm designers. Moreover, being agnostic to the specific internal sources of error, PST enables fair comparisons across different devices and compilation strategies. From a practical standpoint, PST is particularly useful during early-stage decision-making, when users must select a target backend or optimization level before incurring the high cost of full compilation and execution. In this sense, PST bridges the gap between abstract hardware characterization metrics and task-level performance indicators, enabling informed decisions upstream in the quantum software stack.

Our approach relies on a predictor that captures the key structural properties of quantum circuits that influence their execution performance. By leveraging GNNs operating directly on the circuit's Directed Acyclic Graph (DAG) representation, we estimate the maximum achievable PST directly from the high-level circuit description. In this framework, feature extraction is learned implicitly by the model, eliminating the need for manual feature engineering.

To prove the validity of the proposed approach, we analyze a dataset of over 4000 quantum circuits from the MQT Bench tool [6], whose qubits count ranges from 2 to 10, varying the Qiskit optimization level available in the Qiskit [7] compiler, which influences the execution performance of the circuit (Fig. 1). We then train a GNN on DAG representations of the circuits, learning a mapping from circuit structure to optimal PST values for multiple IBM hardware targets.

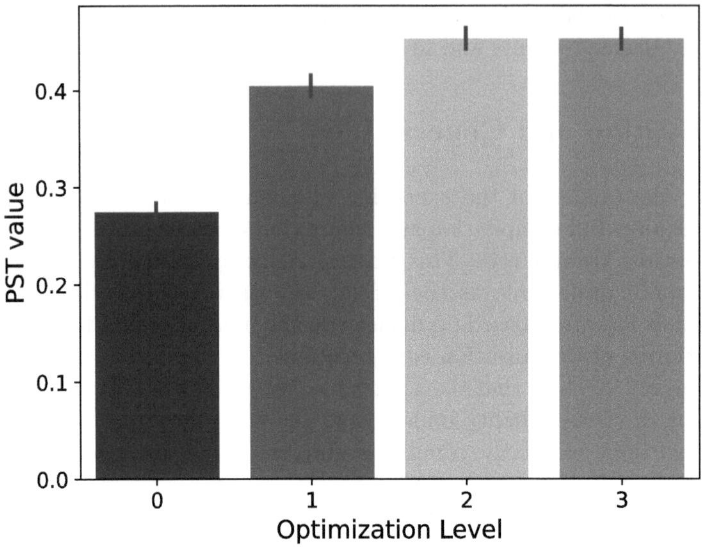

Fig. 1. Average values of the PST obtained from quantum circuit composing the dataset on the IBM FakeGeneva varying the optimization level.

The trained model exhibits strong accuracy (RMSE < 0.1) across different circuit sizes and topologies, showing promising generalization capabilities across the considered IBM fake backends.

This approach represents a conceptual advancement: rather than handling the hardware and compiler stack as a black box, we extract predictive insight directly from the circuit's structure. Differently prior work, which typically focuses on post-mapping circuits or assumes fixed architectures, our method enables pre-deployment performance analysis, supporting early-stage hardware selection and reducing compilation overhead. Theoretical advantages include model portability, compiler-independence, and a decoupling between circuit generation and device-specific simulation, all of which open the way to scalable, architecture-agnostic benchmarking strategies for quantum software.

3 Related Works

In recent years, supporting and automating the selection of optimal backends for quantum circuit execution has become an active area of research. As a result, several preliminary studies and tools have been proposed to assist in the backend selection process [8,9] and in performance estimation. To the best of our knowledge, the most relevant works in the second category include the following:

- Wang et al. [10] employ a Graph Transformer model to predict PST for quantum circuits after they have been mapped onto a specific hardware architecture, including device characteristics (such as T_1/T_2 times, gate errors, and

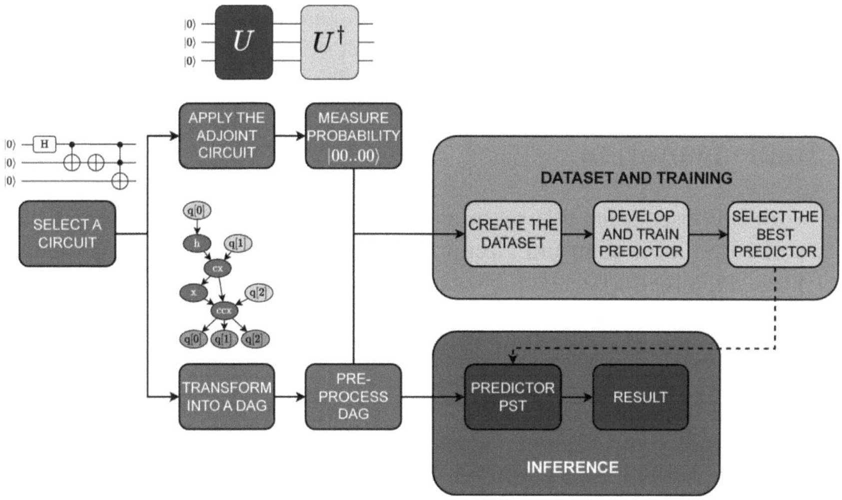

Fig. 2. Workflow for implementation of the proposed PST estimator and for its exploitation from the user perspective.

readout errors) into the node embeddings. On the other hand, our model operates directly on the high-level (unmapped) circuit description and predicts the optimal PST without requiring any information about the target device or its mapping. This allows early-stage performance estimation and hardware selection without the need to compile the circuit for each candidate backend.

- He et al. [11], where the performance of the Variational Quantum Eigensolver are predicted by employing a GNN-based model. In this case, they present a model trained to predict the lowest expectation value of the problem Hamiltonian once the gate parameters of the variational circuit have been optimized. On the other hand, our work estimates the PST, a more general performance metric, and the validity of our predictor has been proved across a wider range of applications.
- Vadali et al. [12] employ a 3D Convolutional Neural Network to estimate circuit fidelity, using a dataset composed of fixed-depth quantum circuits. On the other hand, our approach is not constrained by circuit depth or qubit count. The model remains valid across a wider range of circuit configurations and can be further extended to larger problem instances simply by expanding the training dataset.
- Hothem et al. [13]propose a transfer learning approach using ResNet50 to predict circuit performance. Their method is constrained to circuits with fixed depth and limited to 1–5 qubits. Each circuit is encoded as a matrix of dimensions $n \times d \times h$, where n is the number of qubits, d the depth, and h stores the information about which gate is performed on each qubit in each layer. As in previous works, the circuits are already mapped onto specific target devices,

meaning the analysis does not support pre-compilation performance estimation and so cannot guide hardware selection or early optimization decisions.

4 Implementation

This work proposes a flexible methodology for developing a predictor for estimating the PST of a quantum circuit, handling as input a technology-agnostic description, on a target backend. For this article, we considered as target backend the IBM FakeBrisbane [14], the IBM FakeGeneva [15] and IBM FakeMontreal [16], which are three superconducting devices characterized by 127 qubits the first and 27 the other two, respectively.

First of all, a proper dataset has to be created. In this article, we select all circuit with qubit count ranging between 2 to 10[1] from the MQT Bench [6]. The target variable is the PST, computed by executing the quantum circuit followed immediately by its adjoint circuit and measuring the ground state, as shown in Fig. 3. Therefore, the PST, which ranges from 0 to 1, for a noiseless device is 1 for each input circuit. In order to avoid that the compiler eliminates all the quantum gates present in the circuit, a barrier operation is placed at the end of the quantum circuit U. In this research, we specifically evaluated the PST using IBM's FakeBrisbane, FakeGeneva, and FakeMontreal simulators, which model the behavior of IBM's actual quantum devices.

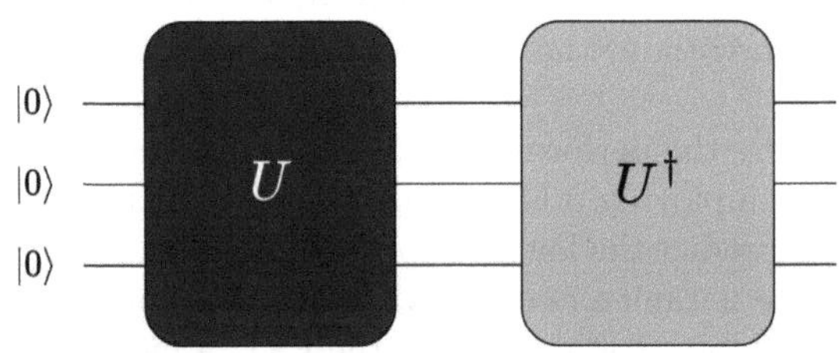

Fig. 3. Schematic diagram of the method used to evaluate PST, beginning with an arbitrary quantum circuit U.

Afterwards, each circuit of the dataset is represented as in DAG form, where the nodes indicate the quantum operations applied and are characterized by a 41-dimensional feature vector. The first 35 elements employ a one-hot encoding scheme to represent the type of quantum gate operation applied. The subsequent three elements specify the target qubit and two possible control qubits. These indices are normalized by the total number of qubits in the circuit (with a value of −1 indicating the absence of control qubits). The last three features are

[1] The qubit count of circuits composing the dataset was limited for limiting the labelling time, which requires compilation and simulation of the circuits whose complexity increase exponentially with the number of qubits.

Table 1. Results related to the best GNN models, reporting the number of output channels and heads of the GAT layer, the number of GCN layers in ResNet configuration, the Hidden Layers of the final FFNN and the results in terms of Mean Loss in Training and Test employing the K fold approach, the R^2 and root mean squared error (RMSE) after re-training the model.

Dataset	Heads	Out Ch GAT	Num GCN	Hidden Layers FFNN	Final $f(x)$	Mean Loss Train	Mean Loss Test	R^2	RMSE
Brisbane	64	4	3	(1024, 1024, 1024)	elu	0.0056	0.0068	0.96	0.075
Geneva	32	8	3	(1024, 1024, 1024)	elu	0.0076	0.0101	0.94	0.086
Montreal	32	8	3	(1024, 1024, 512)	elu	0.0060	0.0074	0.95	0.079

associated with the angle parameters of the quantum gates. Then, we identified the best-performing GNN model through a grid search over different hyperparameters, such as the dimension of the feed-forward neural network and the size of the vector output from the Graph Attention layer. This model provides the most accurate prediction of the PST value from a quantum-technology-agnostic quantum circuit.

To estimate the PST of a new circuit, the user has just to provide the quantum circuit. This circuit is converted into DAG form, preprocessed, and passed through the trained model to obtain the predicted PST.

A graphical representation of the presented steps are reported in Fig. 2.

4.1 Dataset

The dataset includes quantum circuits from the MQT Bench [6]. For practical reasons, we focused on circuits with a qubit count ranging from 2 to 10, as compilation and simulation times grow exponentially with circuit size. Each circuit of the dataset is represented as a DAG, where the nodes represents the quantum operations applied and are characterized by a 41-dimensional feature vector. The first 35 elements employ a one-hot encoding scheme to represent the type of quantum gate operation applied. The subsequent three elements specify the target qubit and two possible control qubits. These indices are normalized by the total number of qubits in the circuit (with a value of -1 indicating the absence of control qubits). The last three features are associated with the angle parameters of the quantum gates.

4.2 Model

The models considered are GNN characterized by 1 Graph Attention Layer (GAT) [17] followed by one, two or three Graph Convolutional Layers (GCL) [18] in residual configuration [19]. Then, there is a final Neural Network with three hidden layers whose hyper-parameters, such as the number of unit and the activation function adopted, has been opportunely fine-tuned. In particular, the space of possible number of units for each layer is chosen moving by power of 2 from 16 to 1024, while the final activation function can be the *sigmoid* or the

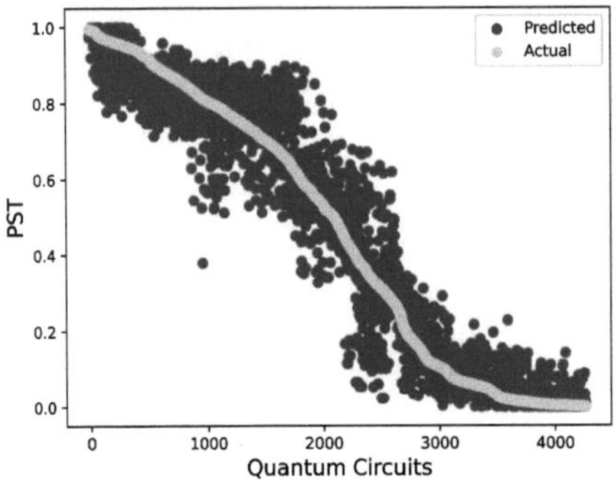

(a) IBM FakeBrisbane

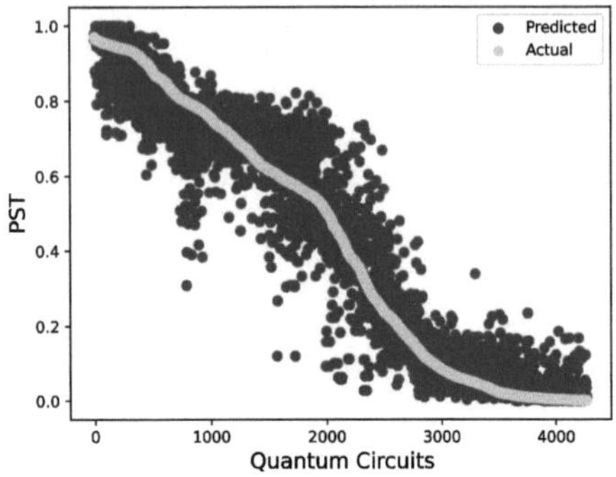

(b) IBM FakeGeneva

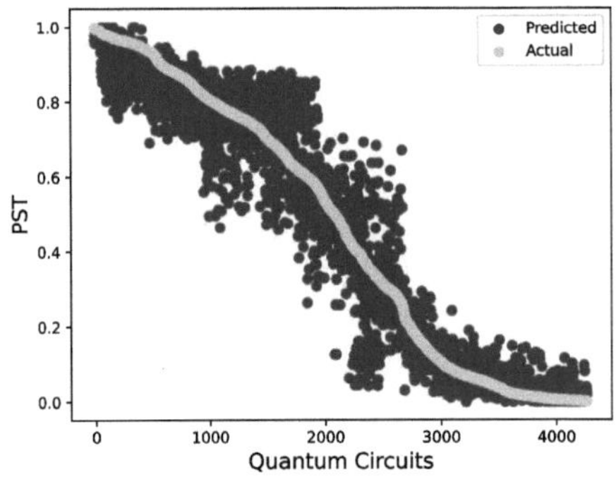

(c) IBM FakeMontreal

Fig. 4. Predicted vs. actual optimal PST values of quantum circuits, sorted in ascending order of PST, for each device.

elu (for the last one, we have considered clamping the function in the interval 0 to 1 in the inference part).

The models are trained using a K-fold [20] approach with number of folds equal to 5. Each model is trained for 100 epochs using the early stopping with patience set to 10. The optimizer used is the Adam [21] with learning rate fixed to 1e-3 and decay rate set to 1e-5, while the loss function considered is the Mean Squared Error [22].

4.3 Process Automation

An end-user can exploit the developed predictor by applying to the input circuit an initial pre-processing step, checking that the circuit involves exclusively a predefined set of gates:

```
['ccx', 'ch', 'cp', 'crx', 'cry',
'crz', 'cswap', 'cu1', 'cu3', 'cx',
'cy', 'cz', 'h', 'measure', 'p',
```

```
'rccx', 'rx', 'rxx', 'ry', 'rz',
'rzz', 's', 'sdg', 'swap', 'sx',
'sxdg', 't', 'tdg', 'u', 'u1', 'u2',
'u3', 'x', 'y', 'z'].
```

These gates, which represent the most common set used in quantum circuit descriptions, are the only supported by the trained predictor. If unsupported gates are present, it is necessary to recompile the circuit employing just the gates allowed.

Then, the previously described pre-processing steps must be applied to the quantum circuit: each node is represented by a 41-dimensional feature vector, with the first 35 features corresponding to the type of quantum gate applied, and the remaining 6 encoding the target and control qubits, as well as any associated gate parameters.

The current predictor was trained using only the IBM FakeBrisbane, IBM FakeGeneva, and IBM FakeMontreal backends. However, the proposed methodology is designed to be adaptable to additional backends and quantum technologies.

5 Results

This section reports the results obtained with the best GNN model in predicting the PST of the quantum circuits on each of the target device (IBM FakeBrisbane, IBM FakeGeneva and IBM FakeMontreal). Specifically, Table 1 reports the hyperparameter setting of the selected model, the final loss function and the RMSE obtained with the three backends as targets, calculated as:

$$RMSE = \sqrt{\frac{1}{N}\sum_{i=0}^{N-1}(y_i - \hat{y_i})^2} \tag{1}$$

where y_i and $\hat{y_i}$ are respectively the actual and the predicted PST values. Moreover, in the table presented, it is reported the coefficient of determination (R^2). This metric allows quantifying the proportion of variance in the dependent variable explained by the independent variables in the regression model. Values approaching 1 indicate that the model accounts for a substantial portion of the variance in the outcome variable, while values near 0 suggest minimal explanatory power. It is defined as

$$R^2 = 1 - \frac{SS_{res}}{SS_{tot}}, \tag{2}$$

where SS_{res} is the residual sum of squares, thus the sum of the squared differences between the observed values and the predicted values. Instead, the term SS_{tot} corresponds to the total sum of squares, defined as the sum of the squared differences between the observed values and their mean. Therefore, SS_{tot} represents the error obtained when using the mean of the observations as the predictor.

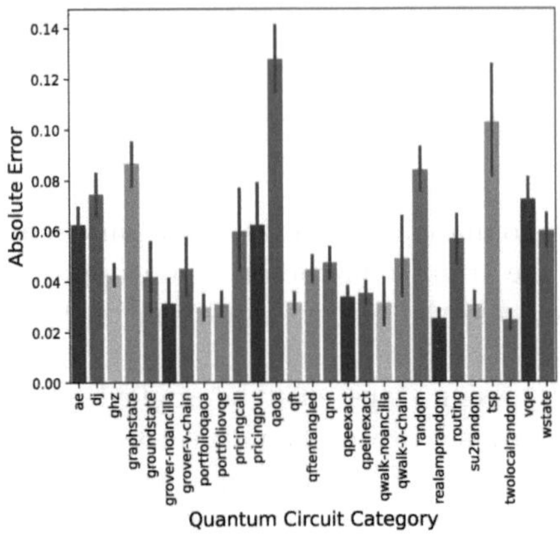

(a) IBM FakeBrisbane

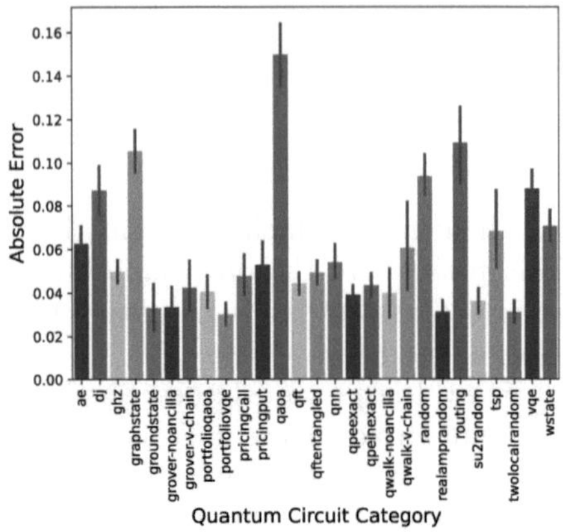

(b) IBM FakeGeneva

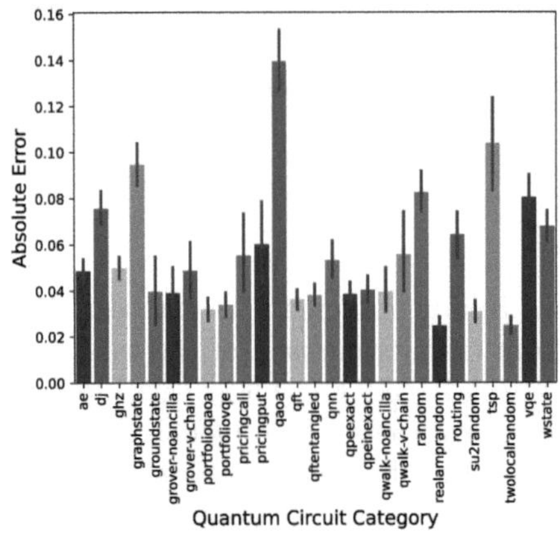

(c) IBM FakeMontreal

Fig. 5. Comparison of the absolute error in PST estimation, grouped by quantum circuit category, for each device.

After selecting the best configuration for each element of the dataset, defined as the model that performed best on average across five-fold cross-validation, we retrained each chosen model on the full data using an 80%/20% train–test split. This final training produces the model we report on, and the test set lets us assess its behavior on unseen data.

Figure 4 compares the predicted and actual PST values for the three considered backends. Overall, the predictor tracks the target PST closely across devices, with particularly good accuracy on Fake Brisbane and Fake Montreal, as also reflected by the metrics reported in Table 1. In these two cases, models trained on circuits compiled for Brisbane and Montreal achieve low test losses (~ 0.007 on average) and strong explanatory power (with R^2 values around 0.95),

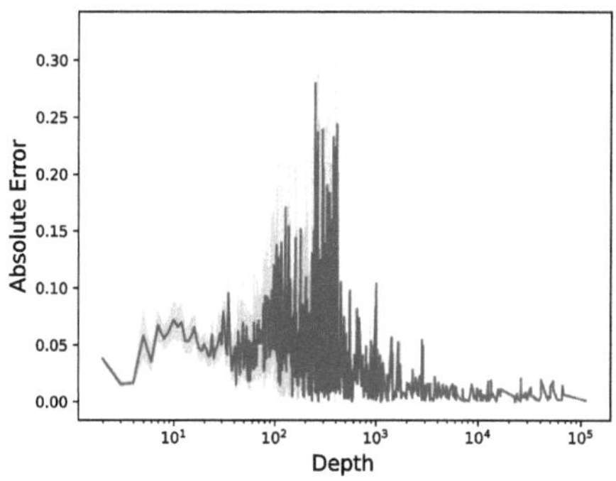

(a) IBM FakeBrisbane

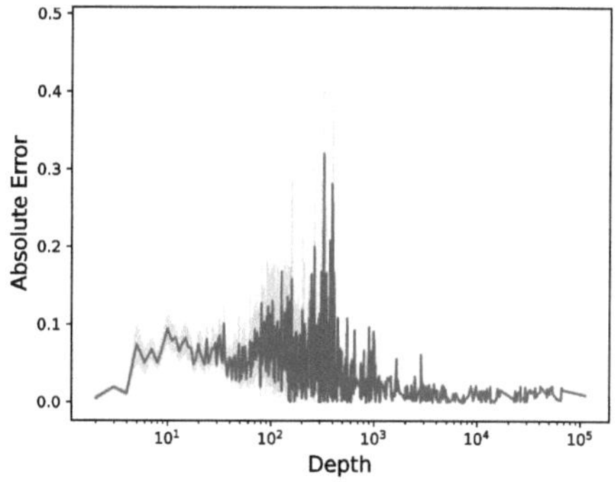

(b) IBM FakeGeneva

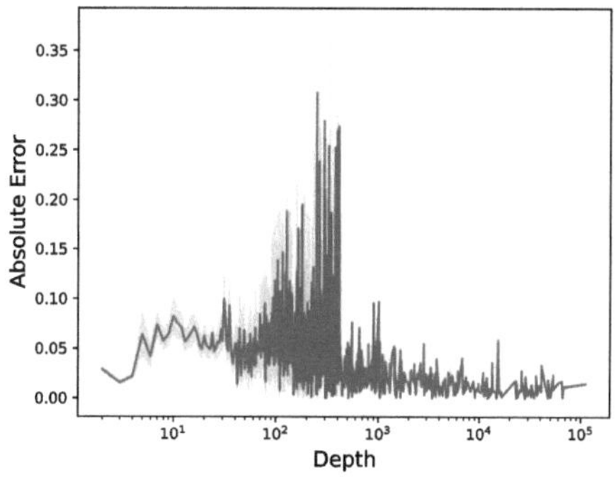

(c) IBM FakeMontreal

Fig. 6. Comparison of the absolute error in PST estimation as a function of quantum circuit depth, for each device.

proving that the model captures the dominant circuit-level factors affecting PST for these devices.

To gain insight beyond aggregate scores, we further analyze the absolute prediction error by grouping results by circuit family (Fig. 5) and by circuit depth (Fig. 6). This plots highlight systematic failure modes that are masked by global averages and helps identify which circuit characteristics are underrepresented or intrinsically harder to model.

Figure 5 shows that QAOA circuits give the highest absolute errors across all target devices. A possible explanation of this behavior is that QAOA instances exhibit higher structural and compilation-induced variability than the other circuit families in the dataset. In particular, QAOA circuits typically involve repeated layers of entangling patterns whose final mapped topology and gate counts can change substantially depending on routing and optimization decisions. This increased sensitivity to compilation can induce a wider PST dispersion even for circuits with similar high-level structure, making the mapping from the input DAG to PST harder to learn. Additionally, if the training set contains fewer QAOA examples or covers a narrower range of QAOA parameters (e.g., depth p, problem graphs, or mixer/cost structures), the model may not generalize well to unseen QAOA variants. In this sense, the observed error pattern suggests not only increasing the number of QAOA circuits, but also diversifying them to better span the space of compilation outcomes.

Figure 6 reports the absolute error as a function of circuit depth and shows a characteristic intermediate-depth regime where errors increase, while shallow and very deep circuits are predicted with near-zero error. This behavior is consistent with a saturation effect of the target metric: for shallow circuits, PST remains close to one on most devices, whereas for deep circuits it is often driven close to zero by accumulated noise and additional routing overhead. In both extremes, the PST distribution is highly concentrated, so even simple predictors can achieve low absolute error. On the other hand, intermediate-depth circuits are in the transition region where PST is neither saturated near one nor collapsed near zero, and small structural or compilation differences (e.g., a few additional two-qubit gates from routing, or different optimization passes) can lead to large relative changes in PST. As a result, this regime is inherently more sensitive to device-specific noise and compilation choices, which explains the larger prediction uncertainty.

These observations suggest two practical directions to reduce error in the most challenging regimes. First, the training dataset can be rebalanced to include more intermediate-depth circuits and a richer set of QAOA instances, potentially improving coverage of the transition region where PST varies most. Second, since a significant portion of the residual error appears to be driven by compilation-induced variability, including auxiliary features that approximate compilation complexity (e.g., estimated two-qubit gate count growth, or topology-aware interaction patterns derived from the input DAG) could further stabilize predictions without requiring full compilation.

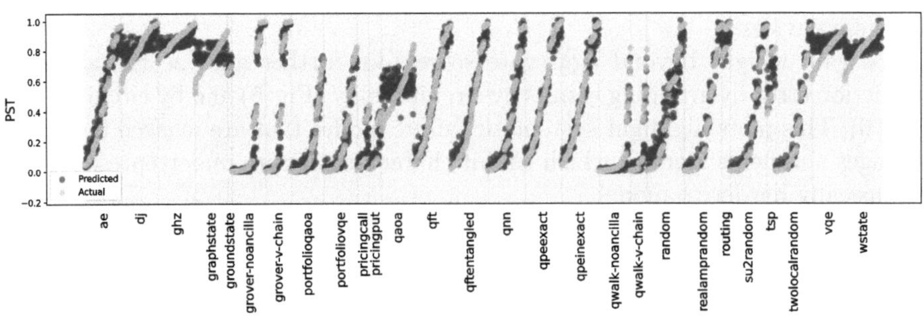

Fig. 7. Predicted vs. actual PST values, grouped by circuit category, from the best-performing model trained on circuits mapped to the FakeBrisbane backend.

Finally, we analyze the predicted and effective PST values for quantum circuits compiled for the Fake Brisbane backend, grouped by circuit category, as shown in Fig. 7. This analysis further confirms that the model exhibits larger prediction errors for QAOA and VQE circuits compared to other algorithmic families.

As mentioned above, a key factor contributing to this effect is the variational nature of QAOA and VQE circuits. These algorithms are largely composed of parametrized single-qubit rotations interleaved with entangling operations, resulting in circuit structures that are highly sensitive to compiler optimizations. In particular, sequences of rotational gates can often be merged, commuted, or eliminated during transpilation, leading to substantial variations in gate count and effective circuit depth after compilation. As a consequence, small changes in circuit structure or compilation strategy can produce disproportionately large changes in PST. This contrasts with algorithms such as Grover's search, whose gate structure is more rigid and less amenable to aggressive gate cancellation or re-synthesis, resulting in more predictable compilation outcomes and, consequently, more stable PST values.

Despite these challenges, the obtained results prove that the proposed GNN-based approach is particularly effective for PST estimation. Across all evaluated circuit families, the average absolute prediction error remains below 0.1, even for more complex circuits where the error can locally increase to approximately 0.2. Moreover, these errors are observed in regimes where PST itself exhibits strong sensitivity to noise and compilation effects, making precise prediction inherently difficult.

From a practical perspective, the proposed method provides a valuable early-stage decision tool for quantum software workflows. By enabling an a priori estimation of PST directly from the high-level circuit description, users can evaluate whether a target backend is likely to deliver acceptable performance before incurring the computational cost of full compilation and execution. This capability is especially relevant in near-term settings, where hardware access is limited and compilation pipelines can be expensive. In this sense, the model supports informed backend selection and compilation strategy choices, helping avoid resource waste on devices that are unlikely to meet application-level performance requirements.

6 Conclusion

This study presents a methodology for developing a predictor for estimating the PST of quantum circuits described in high-level technology-agnostic form executed on specific quantum hardware platforms. The proposed approach exploits GNN models requiring as input the quantum circuit in DAG form. The acquisition from the model of the quantum circuit in the DAG form is the strength of this strategy since permits to avoid the need for manual feature extraction.

The results presented in this article, even through preliminary, prove the potential of the proposed approach for a wide range of applications, providing good accuracy in the PST estimation. However, the model can be further improved. Specifically, we have observed that the model shows reduced performance on certain categories of quantum circuits, particularly those that are underrepresented in the training data. Therefore, future work should focus on augmenting the dataset with additional instances from these categories, as well as including a wider set of randomly generated circuits. Future exploration will extend the approach to additional performance metrics and Figures of Merit, proving the flexibility and applicability of the proposed methodology.

Although the current validation relies on IBM fake backends, the proposed methodology is not inherently tied to simulated environments and can be naturally extended to executions on real quantum hardware. Future work will therefore focus on validating the framework on physical backends and under time-varying noise conditions, further assessing its robustness in realistic operational scenarios.

In conclusion, this work represents a foundational step toward a fully automated tool for pre-compilation analysis of quantum circuits, enabling early hardware selection based on user-defined performance criteria.

References

1. Combarro, E., Gonzalez-Castillo, S., Di Meglio, A.: A practical guide to quantum machine learning and quantum optimization: hands-on approach to modern quantum algorithms (2023)
2. Volpe, D., Orlandi, G., Turvani, G.: Improving the solving of optimization problems: a comprehensive review of quantum approaches. Quant. Reports **7**(1), 3 (2025)
3. Kumar, A., Garhwal, S.: State-of-the-art survey of quantum cryptography. Arch. Comput. Meth. Eng. **28**(5), 3831–3868 (2021)
4. Tychola, K.A., Kalampokas, T., Papakostas, G.A.: Quantum machine learning–an overview. Electronics **12**(11), 2379 (2023)
5. Tannu, S.S., Qureshi, M.K.: Not all qubits are created equal: a case for variability-aware policies for NISQ-era quantum computers. In: Proceedings of the Twenty-Fourth International Conference on Architectural Support for Programming Languages and Operating Systems. Providence RI USA, pp. 987–999. ACM (2019)
6. Quetschlich, N., Burgholzer, L., Wille, R.: MQT bench: benchmarking software and design automation tools for quantum computing. Quantum **7**, 1062 (2023). arXiv:2204.13719 [quant-ph]
7. van de Griend, A.M.: A comparison of quantum compilers using a DAG-based or phase polynomial-based intermediate representation. J. Syst. Softw. **221**(C) (2025)
8. Quetschlich, N., Burgholzer, L., Wille, R.: MQT predictor: automatic device selection with device-specific circuit compilation for quantum computing. ACM Trans. Quant. Comput. **6**(1), 1–26 (2025)
9. xxxxxx. Previous work of the anonymous authors
10. Wang, H., et al.: QuEst: graph transformer for quantum circuit reliability estimation. In: Proceedings of the 41st IEEE/ACM International Conference on Computer-Aided Design, pp. 1–9, arXiv:2210.16724 [quant-ph] (2022)
11. He, Z., Zhang, X., Chen, C., Huang, Z., Zhou, Y., Situ, H.: A GNN-based predictor for quantum architecture search. Quantum Inf. Process. **22**(2), 128 (2023)
12. Vadali, A., Kshirsagar, R., Shyamsundar, P., Perdue, G.N.: Quantum circuit fidelity estimation using machine learning. Quantum Mach. Intell. **6**(1), 1 (2024)

13. Hothem, D., Hines, J., Nataraj, K., Blume-Kohout, R., Proctor, T.: Predictive models from quantum computer benchmarks. In: 2023 IEEE International Conference on Quantum Computing and Engineering (QCE), Bellevue, WA, USA, pp. 709–714. IEEE (2023)
14. FakeBrisbane (latest version). https://docs.quantum.ibm.com/api/qiskit-ibm-runtime/docs.quantum.ibm.com/api/qiskit-ibm-runtime/fake-provider-fake-brisbane
15. FakeGeneva (latest version). https://docs.quantum.ibm.com/api/qiskit-ibm-runtime/docs.quantum.ibm.com/api/qiskit-ibm-runtime/fake-provider-fake-geneva
16. FakeMontrealV2 (latest version). https://quantum.cloud.ibm.com/docs/en/api/qiskit-ibm-runtime/0.27/fake-provider-fake-montreal-v2
17. Veličković, P., Cucurull, G., Casanova, A., Romero, A., Liò, P., Bengio, Y.: Graph Attention Networks (2018). arXiv:1710.10903
18. Kipf, T.N., Welling, M.: Semi-supervised classification with graph convolutional networks. arXiv:1609.02907 [cs] (2017)
19. He, K., Zhang, X., Ren, S., Sun, J.: Deep residual learning for image recognition. arXiv:1512.03385 [cs] (2015)
20. KFold. https://scikit-learn/stable/modules/generated/sklearn.model_selection.KFold.html
21. Kingma, D.P., Ba, J.: Adam: a method for stochastic optimization (2017). arXiv:1412.6980 [cs] (2017)
22. MSELoss — PyTorch 2.7 documentation. https://docs.pytorch.org/docs/stable/generated/torch.nn.MSELoss.html

Reversible Programming Languages

Compiling Roopl++ to HSSA

Lukas Gail, Uwe Meyer(✉), and Tristan Schönhals

Technische Hochschule Mittelhessen, Wiesenstr. 14, 35390 Giessen, Germany
{lukas.gail,uwe.meyer,tristan.schoenhals}@mni.thm.de

Abstract. Whilst compiler techniques are well-known for a wide range of paradigms in conventional programming languages, compilers for reversible languages remain rare and are predominantly limited to the functional and procedural paradigms. In this paper we present our work on a translation from the reversible object-oriented programming language Roopl++ to the hybrid intermediate language HSSA. Our contributions are as follows: This paper provides a translation scheme for all language constructs of Roopl++, as well as a description of the implementation of dynamic memory in HSSA. Runtime error scenarios of Roopl++ are discussed and classified based on whether they need to be explicitly checked at runtime, or whether they manifest naturally as reversibility violations in the generated code. An overview of the techniques used to implement the compiler is given. Finally, we show that HSSA, with its concise kernel and extensible set of primitives, is well-suited as a reversible compilation target, and that introducing HSSA as an intermediate layer enables retargetable compilation, allowing the same Roopl++ frontend to be reused across multiple reversible backends.

Keywords: Reversible computing · Reversible programming languages · Roopl++ · Hybrid static single assignment

1 Introduction

Reversible computing is an alternative computing approach in which programs can be executed both forwards and backwards. Reversible algorithms can be inverted to produce an algorithm that computes the inverse function. This means that reversible programs compute bijective functions.[1]

Reversible computing offers several potential advantages over traditional computing. It can reduce energy consumption by avoiding the Landauer effect [5], and the development of a reversible algorithm automatically yields its corresponding inverse. Applications such as reverse debugging [10] illustrate the practical potential of reversible computation.

[1] Still, even non-bijective functions can be computed by reversible machines since any function can be made into a bijection by adding sufficient auxiliary output data, a technique that goes back to Bennett's work on reversible computation [2].

C. Aubert and L. Roversi (Eds.): RC 2026, LNCS 16626, pp. 167–183, 2026.
https://doi.org/10.1007/978-3-032-30839-9_10

Reversible programming languages provide a formal computational model in which information is preserved rather than destroyed. Most reversible general-purpose languages available today are procedural, such as Janus [16], or functional, such as RFun [15] and Theseus [11]. To our knowledge, Roopl [7,9] and Roopl++ [3] are the only object-oriented reversible languages. We focus on Roopl++ in particular because object-oriented languages are prevalent in today's software development, making Roopl++ a suitable model for studying reversible paradigms in real-world contexts. Object-oriented features are challenging in reversible languages because they typically overwrite state, permit aliasing, rely on dynamic dispatch, and may erase information through heap effects—all of which undermine invertibility unless additional information is explicitly preserved. Consequently, developing efficient compilers and analyses for such languages is difficult, motivating the use of a reversible intermediate representation.

In this work, we adopt Hybrid SSA (HSSA) [6] as the intermediate form. Hybrid SSA combines the benefits of Reversible SSA (RSSA) [13] for reversible computations with the flexibility to explicitly model irreversible operations such as input/output and runtime-error handling. Using HSSA as our intermediate form, we investigate whether a highly compact language—consisting of a minimal kernel and a small set of extensible primitives—is sufficient to implement a substantially larger source language. Moreover, such an intermediate layer improves modularity: optimizations such as constant folding can be implemented once at the intermediate level, enabling retargetable compilation to multiple backends without rewriting the compiler frontend.

Managing dynamic memory is a central challenge in compiling a reversible object-oriented language, because object allocation cannot be uniquely reconstructed during reverse execution unless allocation and deallocation are made explicitly invertible (see Sect. 4.1). In contrast to [3], we do not model the heap as part of the global machine state; instead, we represent dynamic memory as an explicit value type in HSSA. Thus, this approach applies the existing value-based approach of HSSA and leverages HSSA's ability to extend HSSA's kernel with only three new primitives to manage dynamic memory. This work is based on the thesis of T. Schönhals [14].

The remainder of this paper is organized as follows. Section 2 provides a brief overview of Roopl++, followed by a section presenting the main concepts of HSSA. Section 4 describes the translation from Roopl++ to HSSA, including how dynamic memory management is handled in both the compiler and at runtime, as well as the translation of classes and other core language constructs. We then discuss compiler components specific to the Roopl++ translation, including code generation for runtime errors. Lastly, Sect. 6 summarizes the main contributions and presents the results of practical tests.

2 Roopl++

Roopl++ was designed and presented by Cservenka [3] as an extension of the reversible object-oriented programming language (Roopl), which was created by

Haulund [8]. Roopl supports inheritance, subtype-polymorphism, and method overriding. Roopl++ improves program expressiveness by introducing dynamic memory management, object creation and deletion, multiple references to the same object, as well as arrays. The type system of Roopl++ comprises integers, objects, arrays and the nil type. The language combines familiar concepts of object-oriented languages with the reversible paradigm. It is simple yet powerful enough to create complex data structures like doubly linked lists or trees, which makes it well-suited as a compiler's source language.

2.1 Expressions

Expressions in Roopl++ are either literals (numbers or nil), references to variables, or binary operations. The latter may only be performed on integers, unless they are comparing objects and/or nil for equality. Expressions in Roopl++ are free of side effects, even though they do not inherently break reversibility. Conventionally, assignments overwrite a variable with the value of an expression (e.g., i = 5). This breaks reversibility because the previous value of the assignee (i in this example) is lost in this process. Similar to Janus [16], assignments in Roopl++ may only alter the assignee's value through modifying operations (+=, −=, ^=) in order to ensure reversibility. Furthermore, the assignee may not occur on the right side of an assignment, as this quickly leads to irreversible statements such as: i −= i.

2.2 Control Flow

Roopl++ provides control-flow mechanisms in the form of conditionals and loops which, again, resemble their Janus counterparts (cf. Fig. 1).

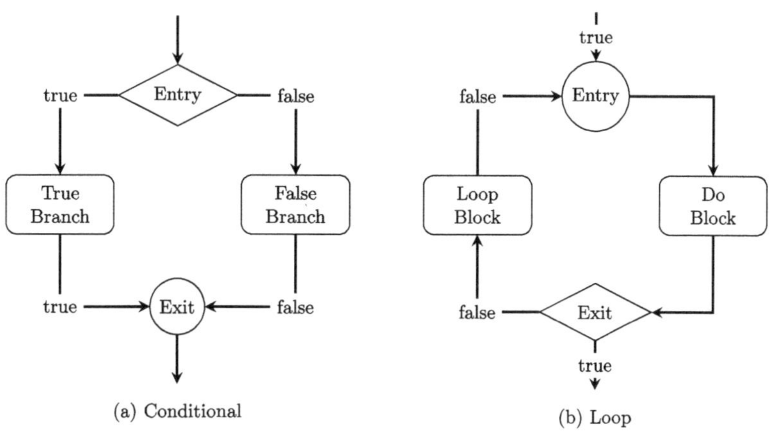

Fig. 1. Roopl++ Control Flow

In addition to the conventional entry condition, which determines the branch in a conditional, conditionals in Roopl++ additionally require an exit condition at the end. This exit expression must evaluate to true if the entry expression evaluates to true and to false otherwise. Thus, the same branch that was chosen in the forward direction would be chosen in the backward direction. Loops operate similarly: they have an entry condition, which must be true in the loop's first iteration, and false in all following iterations. After the evaluation of the entry condition, the loop's do-block is executed, after which the exit condition is tested. If the exit condition is true, the loop ends, and otherwise the loop-block is executed and the loop starts from the beginning.

If any of these conditions evaluates to a value not corresponding to the branch taken, the program terminates with a runtime error.

2.3 Arrays and References

Arrays have fixed sizes and may either contain integers or objects. Both objects and arrays can either be created and destroyed statically (using what Roopl calls local-blocks) or dynamically using the **new** and **delete** keywords. Objects and arrays must be zero-cleared - i.e., brought into the state they were after creation - before deletion, so that programs are reversible.

To create complex data structures (e.g., graphs), multiple references to the same object are required. Roopl++ makes this possible using the **copy** and **uncopy** statements. As with **new** and **delete**, these are the inverse of one another. To prevent dangling references, all copied references to an object must be uncopied before the object may be deleted. Arguments including objects and arrays are passed by reference. Roopl++'s methods do not have return values, therefore results can only be passed back to the caller using reference parameters.

Argument-aliasing describes multiple method arguments being an alias of the same variable or object. This is not allowed as it may lead to statements that violate reversibility. This includes passing a field to a local method, which leads to the same field being in scope using two different names. Aliasing can also occur when an object has a self-reference: method calls on such references appear non-local but are in fact local. This is partially prevented by prohibiting passing an object as a parameter to a method invoked on the same object. Due to copied references, aliasing cannot be fully prevented at compile-time. An array could, for example, contain multiple references to the same object. When iterating over the array and comparing the objects within, reversibility errors might arise.

2.4 Classes and Inheritance

Classes define the types of objects and contain fields and methods, as is common in object-oriented languages. Inheritance is specified using the **inherits** keyword. A subclass may add fields and methods, and override methods. Fields may not be overridden. When overriding a method, both its signature (parameter types) and its body may be overridden. However, overriding the signature is restricted in two ways: Firstly, the number of parameters may not change, otherwise calls to the method, when dispatched to the overriding method, would supply too many or too few arguments. Secondly, the parameter types are contravariant; they may only be generalizations (supertypes) of the overridden types. If they were specializations (subtypes), they could not accept the original types and therefore dispatching would fail. A sample class is shown in Listing 1.

```
class Cat inherits Animal
  int lives
  method eat(Animal prey)
    lives += 1
    delete prey
```

Listing 1. Sample class

3 Hybrid Single Static Assignment

Hybrid Single Static Assignment (HSSA) is a reversible intermediate representation first described in [6]. For this paper, we use a revised, more concise version of HSSA with fewer distinct syntactic constructs, which we briefly describe in the following. Listing 2 shows an example program in HSSA. The grammar of HSSA is given in Fig. 2 and the semantics of the most important primitive operators are given in Fig. 3.

```
ID          = '[A–Za–z_.][A–Za–z0–9._]*' ;
INTEGER     = '–?[0–9]+' ;

SIMPLE_EXP  = ID | INTEGER | "(" [EXP] ")" | "~" SIMPLE_EXP ;
EXP         = SIMPLE_EXP { "," SIMPLE_EXP } ;

LABELS      = ID { "," ID } ;

ENTRY       = EXP ":=" LABELS "←" ;
EXIT        = "→" LABELS "=:" EXP ;
ASSIGNMENT  = EXP ":=" EXP [ EXP ] "=:" EXP ;
BLOCK       = ENTRY { ASSIGNMENT } EXIT ;
PROCEDURE   = "rel" ID [ EXP ] ":" BLOCK { BLOCK } ;
PROGRAM     = { PROCEDURE } ;
```

Fig. 2. HSSA grammar

HSSA programs consist of user-defined procedures that are composed of blocks forming a control flow graph. Each block consists of an entry statement, any number of assignments, and an exit statement. Blocks utilize a linear type system, so that each variable defined within a block must also be finalized within the same block, and variables cannot be used after they have been finalized.

Both primitives and user-defined procedures implement so-called parameterized relations that are instantiated with a parameter value before being applied

$$\begin{array}{ll}
\mathbf{add}_x & = \{(y, x+y) \mid y \in \mathsf{Integers}\} \\
\mathbf{subfrom}_x & = \{(y, x-y) \mid y \in \mathsf{Integers}\} \\
\mathbf{mul}_{(x,y)} & = \{(\mathbf{unit}, x \cdot y)\} \\
\mathbf{div}_{(x,y)} & = \{(\mathbf{unit}, \mathrm{trunc}(\frac{x}{y}))\} \\
\mathbf{mod}_{(x,y)} & = \{(\mathbf{unit}, x - y \cdot \mathrm{trunc}(\frac{x}{y}))\} \\
\mathbf{xor}_x & = \{(y, x\hat{}y) \mid y \in \mathsf{Integers}\} \\
\mathbf{and}_x & = \{(y, x \mathbin{\&} y) \mid y \in \mathsf{Integers}\} \\
\mathbf{or}_x & = \{(y, x \mid y) \mid y \in \mathsf{Integers}\} \\
\mathbf{less}_{(a,b)} & = \begin{cases} \{(\mathbf{unit}, 1)\} & \mathbf{if}\ a < b \\ \{(\mathbf{unit}, 0)\} & \mathbf{otherwise} \end{cases} \\
\mathbf{equal}_{(a,b)} & = \begin{cases} \{(\mathbf{unit}, 1)\} & \mathbf{if}\ a = b \\ \{(\mathbf{unit}, 0)\} & \mathbf{otherwise} \end{cases} \\
\mathbf{dup}_v & = \{(\mathbf{unit}, v)\} \\
\mathbf{discard}_{\mathbf{unit}} & = \{(v, \mathbf{unit}) \mid v \in \mathsf{Values}\} \\
\mathbf{id}_{\mathbf{unit}} & = \{(v, v) \mid v \in \mathsf{Values}\}
\end{array}$$

Fig. 3. HSSA Primitives

to an input value. For example, the statement x.1 := **add** 1 =: x.0 instantiates the primitive **add** with the parameter value 1 and applies it to the input value x.0 to compute the output value x.1[2].x.0 is finalized and x.1 is initialized in this process, so that the information about the previous value of x.0 is preserved in the output value x.1.

Most primitives in HSSA are reversible, i.e., each primitive denotes an injective function (or relation) on program states and therefore admits a well-defined inverse on its image. HSSA is hybrid in the sense that it can also express irreversible computations. This is enabled by the primitive relation discard, which maps any input value to the constant unit value. Since Roopl++ is fully reversible, this hybrid feature is not required for the semantics-preserving translation of well-formed Roopl++ programs. However, we show that using discard to make irreversibility explicit provides a convenient mechanism for handling runtime errors. A semantics-preserving translation of Roopl++ to HSSA without using discard confirms the r-Turing-completeness of the reversible subset of HSSA.

Parameterized relations in HSSA are free of side effects. All data transformation is performed by the left- and right-unique instances of the parameterized relations. Mutable variables and other mutable state have to be explicitly versioned and passed around the program.

Expressions in HSSA are used on both sides of assignment statements and can either be in a finalizing position, an initializing position, or a simple usage position. The three-column layout of the example programs visually distinguishes these three positions: The left-hand side of assignments is the initializing posi-

[2] Note that variable names in HSSA are allowed to contain the dot character. This is useful to distinguish different versions of the same variable, which is necessary because of the single-static assignment property.

tion, the right-hand side is the finalizing position, and expressions in the middle column are simple usages. Expressions simultaneously act as patterns, so that the result of each application of a relation is assigned to a pattern. Patterns act as reversibility assertions, so that if the pattern does not match the actual output of the relation, a reversibility violation occurs and a runtime error is raised. This includes the case of assignments to constants as they are used in RSSA [13].

The control flow graph of an HSSA procedure is defined by the entry and exit statements of its blocks. Labels used in these statements name individual edges of the graph, so that each label must be used exactly once in an entry and once in an exit position. The labels **begin** and **end** form a special case, as they are used to mark the start and end of a procedure, and thus are only used in an entry or exit position respectively. Variables do not implicitly pass between successive blocks, but must always explicitly be passed as part of the data in the entry and exit statements. Entry statements assign a pair consisting of the passed value and the index of the label that was used to reach the block to the pattern on the left-hand side of the entry statement. Likewise, exit statements expect the expression on the right-hand side to evaluate to a pair, where the first element is passed to the next block, and the second element is expected to be an index selecting one of the exit labels. This approach subsumes both the conditional and unconditional cases of the original version of HSSA, while also allowing for n-ary control flow.

```
rel count max:
  (), 0     := begin ←
  a         := id            =: 0
                    → l1     =: a, 0

  a.1, c.1  := l1, l2 ←
  ()        := ~equal a.1, 0 =: c.1
  a.2       := add 1         =: a.1
  c.2       := less a.2, max =: ()
                 → l2, l3    =: a.2, c.2

  a, 0      := l3 ←
                   → end     =: a, 0

rel main ():
  (), 0 := begin ←
  a     := count 10 =: ()
  b     := ~count a =: 10
           → end =: (a, b), 0
```

Listing 2. Example of an HSSA procedure

4 Translating Roopl++ to HSSA

4.1 Dynamic Memory Extension

Roopl++ requires dynamic memory to store objects and arrays at runtime. In languages that support dynamic data structures, the organization of run-time storage typically includes a region called the heap, from which memory for dynamically allocated objects is requested at runtime, when their size and lifetime cannot be determined at compile time [1]. Unfortunately, HSSA per se does not possess the capabilities to manage such dynamic memory elements.

One potential solution would be to split the memory into a static and a dynamic part, but since HSSA does not allow for side effects a different approach is required. With HSSA being a modular language that can easily be extended by plugins, we chose to treat dynamic memory as a new value in HSSA. The dynamic memory value is a fixed-size array holding any HSSA values (e.g., numbers, tuples, relations). Each array element is addressed by its array index and hereafter referred to as a memory slot. Addresses are stored either in HSSA variables or other memory slots (indirection). At runtime, each object is represented in memory by a number of these slots that contain the dispatch table (also called vtable) and the fields of the class. The first slot in memory (address zero) is reserved for the reference to nil.

To manage dynamic memory, we provide three new primitives. Of course, each primitive must implement a reversible operation on the memory, and for each primitive its inverse has to be implemented, too.

- **mmem.new** creates a new, dynamic memory object with a fixed size (currently 1024). **mmem.new** is injective, as it has exactly one valid input (unit) and one valid output (the empty memory object). The inverse operation (~ **mmem.new**) deletes the memory object if all its slots are empty; otherwise, a reversibility violation is thrown in the interpreter. For example, a new dynamic object _m would be created by _m := **mmem.new** =: ().
- **mmem.allocate** <size> allocates a number of consecutive, unallocated memory slots on a memory object and returns the address of the first slot. The number of allocated slots is determined by the parameter size. Allocation of a slot is defined as changing its content from null (no HSSA value) to zero, which represents either the default value of integers in Roopl++ or the nil reference. If the memory object does not contain enough unallocated slots to perform allocation, a runtime error is raised. After allocation, **mmem.allocate** returns the updated memory object and the address (array index) of the first allocated slot. **mmem.allocate** is injective, because size is preserved as a parameter and the rest of memory is preserved and not altered. Using the size, the returned address and the updated memory object, the original state of memory can be computed backwards by unallocation (~**mmem.allocate**). Starting at the given address, a number of slots equal to the size parameter is unallocated by changing their value from zero to null. If any slot is not zero-cleared before unallocation, a reversibility violation occurs.

- **mmem.readwrite** <address> reads and updates the memory's content. The address parameter determines the slot on which the readwrite operation is performed. The primitive requires a memory object and an HSSA value as input. When **mmem.readwrite** is performed, the value that was previously stored at the given address is read, the input value is written, and both the updated memory object and the previously stored value are returned. **mmem.readwrite** is injective, because the previous value is preserved by returning it as an output. The reverse operation ~**mmem.readwrite** does not require explicit implementation, as the operation is self-inverse. Note that a write operation would destroy information, whereas readwrite preserves the information.

The read-only operation mmem.read is useful for translation but not provided as a primitive, because it can be implemented using **mmem.readwrite** (see Listing 3).

```
rel mmem.read _addr:
  _m, 0            := begin ←
  _m.0, _value     := mmem.readwrite _addr =: _m, ()
  _copy            := dup _value           =: ()
  _m.1             := mmem.readwrite _addr =: _m.0, _value
                                  → end    =: (_m.1, _copy), 0
```

Listing 3. mmem.read Implementation

4.2 Using Managed Memory

The compiler uses the following memory layout: each allocated slot contains either a numeric value or a vtable relation. References to objects and arrays are represented as numeric addresses pointing to their first memory slot. An object reference and the object's runtime representation in memory are demonstrated in Fig. 4, left-hand diagram. In addition, the diagram to the right shows indirection and copied references. The indirection is required to handle copying and swapping of references.

4.3 Operations on Arrays and Objects

This section briefly explains the code created by the compiler to handle memory operations for arrays and objects. In the case of arrays, the compiler simply generates a **mmem.allocate** <size> instruction, such that there will be one memory slot for each array element, and the necessary instructions to zero-clear the memory and delete it.

A **mmem.allocate** <size> instruction is generated for the creation of an object, where <size> is the number of fields of the class plus one for the vtable. The vtable is copied and the address of the object is returned. An example is shown in Listing 4.

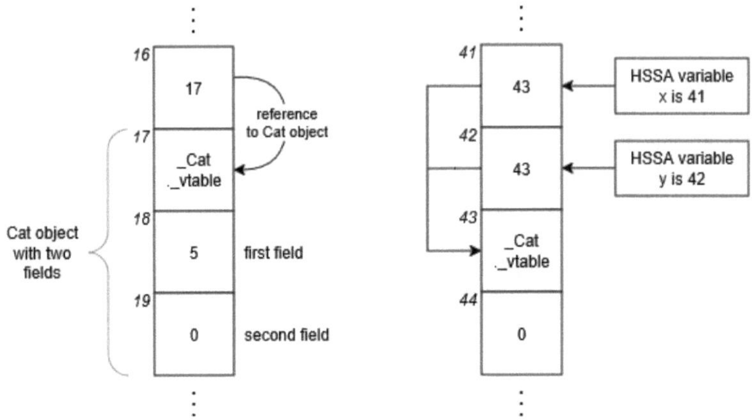

(a) Object in memory (b) Indirection

Fig. 4. Memory layout

```
rel _Animal._new:
    _m.0          := begin ←
    _m.0, _anon   := mmem.allocate 2          =: _m
    _vtable       := dup _Animal._vtable      =: ()
    _m.1, 0       := mmem.readwrite _anon     =: _m.0, _vtable
                                   → end      =: (_m.1, _anon), 0
```

Listing 4. Creation of an object

Using references and the additional layer of indirection, the implementation of the **copy** and **uncopy** statements is trivial: both the source and target addresses are calculated. This is required because copying of references is not exclusive to variables, but may be performed on array elements too. To copy a reference, it is read from the source address and written into the target address. Because copying an object requires the target reference to be zero-cleared, the readwrite operation assumes it previously contained zero. If the target was not zero-cleared, the assignment containing the readwrite causes a runtime error.

4.4 Classes

Classes are the main structural element of Roopl++ and are used to define complex types as well as the methods to manipulate instances of the class. Since HSSA does not have a type system beyond tuples, classes need to be mapped to simpler concepts.

Like many compilers do, our compiler builds a type graph during semantic analysis in order to be able to detect type errors including cyclic inheritance and field overrides. In a second pass, the type graph is transformed into a scope tree, which is an abstract representation of the entire program and includes inheritance and method overrides. (Please note that cyclic dependencies have been eliminated in the previous pass.) The scope tree is used for further semantic analysis and for resolving dynamic dispatching of calls as well as runtime type-checking (please refer to Sect. 5).

A method *m* of class *c* is translated to an HSSA relation _c.m. Within a method call, the receiver object is referenced by _this and passed as an argument to the relation. For example, a method *bar* of class *Foo* with parameters *x,y,z* will be translated into an HSSA relation **rel** _Foo.bar _this, x, y, z : **.**

In the generated HSSA code, all fields are defined in a preamble per method and thereafter accessible by their name (see Listing 5); the compiler generates a postamble that performs the finalization by simply inverting the preamble.

```
rel _Cat.eat _this, prey:
  _m, 0               := begin ←
   _m.0, _this_ref := mmem.read _this =: _m
  age                 := add _this_ref  =: 1
  lives               := add _this_ref  =: 2
```

Listing 5. Preamble of method eat

The code for the method's implementation will be translated into HSSA assignments and entry/exit statements as will be shown in the following subsections.

4.5 Expressions

Besides translating composite expressions into a sequence of simple expressions (i.e., having at most one operator) using temporary variables, variable references read the value directly, while array slots compute the address from the index before reading and storing it in the temporary variable. All temporary expressions will be uncomputed when no longer used. An example can be seen in Listing 6.

```
_t.1           := add 1              =: 0        // index 1
_m.1, _addr.0  := mmem.read x        =: _m.0     // addr. of x
_addr.1        := add _t.1           =: _addr.0  // addr. of x[1]
_m.2, _t.0     := mmem.read _addr.1  =: _m.1     // value of x[1]
```

Listing 6. Translation of expression `x[1]`

4.6 Assignments

Assignments modify the memory and therefore use the **mmem.readwrite** operation. Please note that there is no write operation as this would be inherently irreversible. Thus, **mmem.readwrite** reads the previous value, replaces it temporarily with the unit value, performs the operation and calls **mmem.readwrite** again to store the result. An example is shown in Listing 7.

```
_t.0              := add 1               =: 0
_m.1, _value      := mmem.readwrite x   =: _m.0, ()
_value.0          := add _t.0            =: _value
_m.2, ()          := mmem.readwrite x   =: _m.1, _value.0
```

Listing 7. Translation of Assignment `x += 1`

4.7 Conditionals and Loops

Translating conditionals begins with the translation of the expression. The result of the expression is then checked for equality to zero. This is necessary because in Roopl++, zero is considered false and everything else is considered true. Next, a jump is generated to either the conditional's then or else block. The jump targets else if the expression evaluated to zero and to then otherwise. Now the then and else blocks are generated, each followed by a jump to a third block at the end of the conditional, where the exit expression is translated. Lastly, depending on whether control returns from the then or else branch, the exit expression's result is tested to be non-equal to zero or equal to zero respectively. If this test fails, the conditional is not reversible and a runtime error occurs.

Translation of loops is analogous to the translation of conditionals.

4.8 Method Calls

As described above, each Roopl method is represented as an HSSA procedure. Due to dynamic dispatching, the actual procedure that is called must be determined at runtime by performing a lookup in the virtual method tables (vtables), also known as dispatch tables [4].

Listing 8 shows the code generated for an example method call k.meow(). As explained in Sect. 4.1, the memory layout of objects includes a slot for a reference to the vtable at index zero. The variable k is assumed to contain the address of an object reference.[3] First, this variable is dereferenced to obtain the address of the object, which is stored in _calleeRef. Since the dispatch table is stored at offset zero of the object, _calleeRef can be used to read the dispatch table reference from memory, which is stored in _vtable. Dispatch tables are implemented as a parameterized relation where the parameter is the statically known index of the method in the class's method list. In this example, the index of the meow method is zero, so that the application of the instance _vtable 0 returns the reference to the method's implementation, which is stored in _calleeMethod. Finally, the method is called by instantiating the relation _calleeMethod to the receiver object reference k and applying it to the current state of the global memory object. For **uncall** statements, the inverse of the method (~_calleeMethod) is applied instead.

After the application of the method, the intermediate variables _calleeRef, _vtable, and _calleeMethod are uncomputed after the method call using the inverses of the relations used to compute them.

[3] Mind the double indirection.

```
_m.3, _calleeRef := mmem.read k             =: _m.2
_m.4, _vtable    := mmem.read _calleeRef    =: _m.3
_calleeMethod    := _calleeVtable 0         =: ()

_m.5             := _calleeMethod k         =: _m.4

()               := ~_calleeVtable 0        =: _calleeMethod
_m.6             := ~mmem.read _calleeRef   =: _m.5, _vtable
_m.7             := ~mmem.read k            =: _m.6, _calleeRef
```

Listing 8. Translation of Method Call

4.9 Main

The final step required to translate Roopl++ programs into HSSA is starting the program. Both languages use a main method, or relation respectively as an entry point to execution. However, the Roopl++ main is expected to run inside an implicitly created object of the class defining the main method. Boilerplate code is required to set up this object and call the Roopl++ main afterwards.

The compiler generates code to initialize the managed memory object and allocate a slot for the _main object. Next, the Roopl++ program is started by statically calling the main method on the reference holding the _main object. To finalize the _main variable, it is uncomputed using the ~**dup** relation. This is possible, because the first allocate will always return address 1. _main is not unallocated in order to preserve the state of memory at the end of the program. Afterwards, memory can be examined in the interpreter's output.

5 The Compiler

The Roopl++ to HSSA compiler is fully integrated in the HSSA toolkit[4] and is written in Scala. Similar to the Janus-to-RSSA compiler described in [12], we apply a technique to let the compiler run backwards to generate code for the uncompute statements. This demonstrates that the symmetry inherent in reversible languages is not only preserved at the semantic level, but also in the structure of the translation process itself.

Semantic analysis is performed in three stages:

1. Class graph construction transforms the declared classes into a graph data structure representing inheritance. In this phase, semantic analysis checks that classes, methods and fields are uniquely named, that exactly one main method exists, and that inheritance is not cyclic.

[4] The HSSA toolkit is available at https://github.com/Leridon/hssa and as an archived package at Zenodo (https://doi.org/10.5281/zenodo.20071365).

2. Scope tree construction converts the entire program into a tree structure. The scope tree allows statements to be analyzed in detail. The root node of this tree represents the entire Roopl++ program. Its children represent classes, whose children in turn represent methods. Method nodes contain a composite node type that holds both statements and local blocks. Although local blocks introduce nested scopes, they are syntactically statements and may occur within other statements. Consequently, they are represented at the same structural level as statements. The scope tree structure enables variable lookup in a bottom-up manner. If a variable is referenced but not defined in the current scope (node), the parent node is queried recursively until a class node is reached. If the lookup fails, the referenced variable does not exist, which constitutes a semantic error. Additional error categories detected at this stage include type errors (e.g., using an object where a number is expected), inheritance errors (e.g., invalid method overrides), and invalid method calls (e.g., incorrect number or type of arguments, or argument-aliasing). Several of these checks are specific to reversible computation, since violations such as uncontrolled aliasing would prevent program inversion.
3. Translatable normalization At this point in the compilation process, the compiler guarantees that the input program is well-formed and that code generation will not fail. The scope tree contains meta- information and represents the statements in a form well suited for error detection. To prepare for translation, the scope tree is normalized by converting statement and block nodes into a structure better suited for translation. The result of this final phase of semantic analysis is a translatable intermediate representation of the original Roopl++ source code.

The code generation phase iterates through this intermediate representation to generate the required code for each construct as described in the previous section.

We conclude this section with a note on runtime errors: Some runtime errors are detected naturally through the implementation of reversibility constraints (e.g., finalizing the jump variable at the end of a conditional), while others require explicit detection (e.g., array index out-of-bounds).

An irreversible statement in the source language automatically leads to a runtime error in the target language. For example, an incorrect **fi** condition in Roopl++ would lead in HSSA to a finalization of the variable holding the information about whether the condition evaluates to true or false, which would then fail as well. No special treatment in the compiler is required for these errors.

In general, a reversible handling of errors requiring explicit detection such as array index out-of-bounds is only possible when exceptions including the call stack are treated as values and transported through the entire program.

In Roopl++ such errors are considered undefined behaviour [3][page 70f], whereas the hybrid language HSSA with its irreversible assignments provides the opportunity to raise errors and discard the call stack. Future work could utilize this concept to yield much more specific error messages. This would require inclusion of a source map into the HSSA runtime as well as the generation of

HSSA code to detect runtime errors. Other examples of this type of errors that could be handled this way are dangling pointers, array type-variance, argument-aliasing, parameter type-variance, and deletion type-mismatch.

6 Summary and Conclusion

The compiler was tested using the suite of test programs provided by Cservenka [3]. The generated HSSA code was then manually verified, executed using the HSSA interpreter, and the results were compared. Table 1 shows the results including the lines of code of the Roopl++ program, the generated HSSA code, and the optimized HSSA code (mostly using constant propagation and dead-code elimination).

Table 1. Overview of programs, code size, and optimization results

Program	Lines of Code	HSSA	Optimized	Testing
Program (Cservenka)				
BinaryTree.rplpp	107	715	635	Manually verified
LinkedList.rplpp	79	506	442	Manually verified
DoublyLinkedList.rplpp	86	532	466	Manually verified
RTM.rplpp	252	1717	1452	Manually verified
Program (Own tests)				
Conditional.rplpp	10	89	75	Manually verified
LocalBlock.rplpp	5	65	49	Manually verified
Loop.rplpp	13	100	84	Manually verified
NestedExpression.rplpp	10	78	60	Manually verified

We have shown that the compiler successfully translates non-trivial Roopl++ programs into executable HSSA code. It demonstrates that reversibility can be preserved across the translation from a high-level, object-oriented, reversible language to a lower-level, intermediate representation.

To support dynamic memory management, HSSA was extended with a managed memory module. This extension with only three primitives proves sufficient to realize the full Roopl++ object model in memory, while preserving reversibility constraints.

Roopl++ allows very flexible use of references, leading to a variety of potential runtime errors. This work has discussed the difficulty of handling and preventing such runtime errors, most of which cannot be prevented at compile-time. In conventional languages, runtime errors occur mostly due to incorrect use of features of the language, whereas reversibility constraints require additional logic in a program, and runtime errors are often due to programs not being injective. Future work could investigate whether a reversible object-oriented language with a strong type system and support for comprehensive error handling at runtime might be able to reduce such errors.

Furthermore, HSSA proves to be a viable target language for a compiler, and its hybrid nature can be used to allow for graceful handling of runtime errors. Roopl++ programmers can also benefit from the optimizations that have already been implemented in HSSA, such as constant propagation and folding, as well as dead-code elimination.

Acknowledgments. We would like to thank the anonymous reviewers whose valuable comments were very helpful in improving the paper.

References

1. Aho, A., Sethi, R., Ullman, J.: Compilers: Principles, Techniques and Tools. Addison-Wesley (1986)
2. Bennett, C.H.: Logical reversibility of computation. IBM J. Res. Dev. **17**(6), 525–532 (1973). https://doi.org/10.1147/rd.176.0525
3. Cservenka, M.H.: Design and implementation of dynamic memory management in a reversible object-oriented programming language. arXiv preprint arXiv:1804.05097 (2018)
4. Ellis, M.A., Stroustrup, B.: The Annotated C++ Reference Manual. Addison-Wesley (1990)
5. Frank, M.P.: The future of computing depends on making it reversible. IEEE Spectr. **25**(08) (2017)
6. Gail, L., Meyer, U.: Connecting reversible and classical computing through hybrid SSA. In: Reversible Computation: 16th International Conference, RC 2024, Toruń, Poland, 4–5 July 2024, pp. 161–178. Springer, Heidelberg (2024). https://doi.org/10.1007/978-3-031-62076-8_11
7. Haulund, T.: Design and implementation of a reversible object-oriented programming language. arXiv preprint arXiv:1707.07845 (2017)
8. Haulund, T.: Design and implementation of a reversible object-oriented programming language (2017). https://arxiv.org/abs/1707.07845
9. Haulund, T., Mogensen, T.Æ., Glück, R.: Implementing reversible object-oriented language features on reversible machines. In: Phillips, I., Rahaman, H. (eds.) RC 2017. LNCS, vol. 10301, pp. 66–73. Springer, Cham (2017). https://doi.org/10.1007/978-3-319-59936-6_5
10. Hoey, J., Lanese, I., Nishida, N., Ulidowski, I., Vidal, G.: A case study for reversible computing: reversible debugging of concurrent programs. In: Ulidowski, I., Lanese, I., Schultz, U.P., Ferreira, C. (eds.) RC 2020. LNCS, vol. 12070, pp. 108–127. Springer, Cham (2020). https://doi.org/10.1007/978-3-030-47361-7_5
11. James, R.P., Sabry, A.: Theseus: a high level language for reversible computing. Work-in-progress report presented at RC (2014)
12. Kutrib, M., Meyer, U., Deworetzki, N., Schuster, M.: Compiling Janus to RSSA. In: Yamashita, S., Yokoyama, T. (eds.) RC 2021. LNCS, vol. 12805, pp. 64–78. Springer, Cham (2021). https://doi.org/10.1007/978-3-030-79837-6_4
13. Mogensen, T.Æ.: RSSA: a reversible SSA form. In: Mazzara, M., Voronkov, A. (eds.) PSI 2015. LNCS, vol. 9609, pp. 203–217. Springer, Cham (2016). https://doi.org/10.1007/978-3-319-41579-6_16

14. Schönhals, T.: Design and implementation of a compiler for a reversible object-oriented programming language. Master's thesis, THM (2026). https://doi.org/10.25716/thm-426
15. Thomsen, M.K., Axelsen, H.B.: Interpretation and programming of the reversible functional language RFUN. In: Proceedings of the 27th Symposium on the Implementation and Application of Functional Programming Languages, pp. 1–13 (2015)
16. Yokoyama, T., Axelsen, H.B., Glück, R.: Principles of a reversible programming language. In: Proceedings of the 5th Conference on Computing Frontiers, CF 2008, pp. 43–54. Association for Computing Machinery, New York (2008). https://doi.org/10.1145/1366230.1366239

A Reversible Semantics for Janus

Ivan Lanese[1] and Germán Vidal[2(✉)]

[1] Olas Team, University of Bologna & Inria - Université Côte d'Azur, Bologna, Italy
[2] VRAIN, Universitat Politècnica de València, Valencia, Spain
gvidal@dsic.upv.es

Abstract. Janus is a paradigmatic example of a reversible programming language. Indeed, Janus programs can be executed backwards as well as forwards. However, its current small-step semantics (useful, e.g., for debugging or as a basis for extensions with concurrency primitives) is not reversible, since it discards information while computing forwards. For instance, it does not satisfy the so-called Loop Lemma, stating that any reduction has an inverse, a main property of reversibility in process calculi, where a small-step semantics is commonly used. We present in this paper a novel small-step semantics which is actually reversible (for well-formed Janus programs), while remaining equivalent to the previous one. In particular, this involves the non-trivial challenge of defining a semantics based on a "program counter" for a high-level programming language.

1 Introduction

Reversible computation has emerged as a promising framework for addressing a number of limitations of current computing paradigms [1]. On the one hand, according to Landauer's principle [11], the erasure of one bit of information in an irreversible computation necessarily dissipates a minimum amount of heat. In contrast, Bennett [2] showed that, theoretically, a reversible computation—where no information is discarded—can be performed with less heat dissipation than an irreversible one. Thus, the development of reversible circuits could represent a revolution in reducing the energy consumption of large computing centers.

At the programming level, the Janus language [14] represents one of the first attempts to formalize a *reversible* programming language. Janus performs (deterministic) computations in both forward and backward directions. The development of reversible programming languages like Janus may provide an excellent opportunity to explore the relationship between logical reversibility, energy conservation, and computational expressiveness. A formal semantics for the language was first presented in [23,24,26]. Unfortunately, this semantics follows the so-called *big-step* style, which is less appropriate for some applications, e.g., modeling stepwise execution, program debugging, designing an abstract machine

This work has been partially supported by French ANR project SmartCloud ANR-23-CE25-0012 and by *Generalitat Valenciana* under grant CIPROM/2022/6 (FassLow).

C. Aubert and L. Roversi (Eds.): RC 2026, LNCS 16626, pp. 184–200, 2026.
https://doi.org/10.1007/978-3-032-30839-9_11

for the language, modeling concurrency and interleaving (for a future concurrent extension of Janus), analyzing non-termination, etc.

Recently, [10] has introduced a small-step semantics for Janus that is more appropriate for the applications mentioned above. This semantics employs *contexts* to identify the next statement to be executed. Moreover, the considered configurations include the code to be executed, which is transformed (i.e., reduced) as execution progresses. These features, however, make the semantics irreversible. E.g., a Janus conditional statement of the form "if e_1 then skip else s_2 fi e_2" is reduced to skip when the guard e_2 is true (in [10] the then branch is first reduced to skip when the condition e_1 is true before evaluating the guard). This step, however, is irreversible: we cannot obtain "if e_1 then skip else s_2 fi e_2" from skip. Janus is thus reversible at the level of programs (or statements), in the sense that we can execute any program backwards, recovering input data from results, but not at the level of semantics, since single reduction steps cannot be inverted. This is in striking contrast with the semantics of calculi and languages for concurrency, where the Loop Lemma ensures that single steps have a reverse, e.g., in RCCS [4, Lemma 6], CCSK [16, Proposition 5.1], or reversible Erlang [12, Lemma 11]. This prevents applications such as reversible debugging, the definition of backtracking strategies, etc. Therefore, in this work, we tackle the definition of a *reversible* small-step semantics for Janus.

First, we introduce a simple small-step semantics for Janus that uses a stack to model subcomputations, and which is equivalent to previous semantics for the language. In order to make this semantics reversible, one could add a "history" to the configurations, as it has been done to define a reversible semantics for the concurrent calculi and languages mentioned above. This solution, however, is not very satisfactory, not only because of the cost in memory usage to store the history, but also because it is not strictly necessary when the considered language is reversible (the case of Janus).

Thus, in this paper, we explore an alternative idea. Specifically, our proposal is based on replacing in the configurations the component with the code to be executed with a "program counter" that points to the next statement to be executed. At first glance, one might think that a step could be "undone" simply by moving the program counter back to the previous position. The actual definition of the reversible semantics, however, is far from trivial. In particular, given that Janus is a high-level language, in some cases it is not easy to determine how a program counter should be incremented. On the other hand, backward rules pose certain problems for determining the correct flow when there are several ways to go backwards from a given point in the execution, e.g., when undoing procedure calls. Our small-step semantics is made of a *forward* transition relation, which models normal execution (i.e., which is a conservative extension of the previous small-step semantics), and a *backward* transition relation, which can be used to "undo" the steps of a (forward) computation.

More details and missing proofs can be found in the extended version [13].

$$
\begin{array}{rl}
p ::= & s\ (\textsf{procedure}\ id\ s)^{+} \\
s ::= & x\oplus = e \mid x[e]\oplus = e \mid \textsf{if}\ e\ \textsf{then}\ s\ \textsf{else}\ s\ \textsf{fi}\ e \\
 & \mid\ \textsf{from}\ e\ \textsf{do}\ s\ \textsf{loop}\ s\ \textsf{until}\ e \mid \textsf{call}\ id \mid \textsf{uncall}\ id \mid \textsf{skip} \mid s\ s \\
e ::= & c \mid x \mid x[e] \mid e \odot e \qquad\qquad\qquad\qquad \oplus ::= + \mid - \mid \hat{} \\
c ::= & -2147483648 \mid \cdots \mid 0 \mid \cdots \mid 2147483647 \\
\odot ::= & \oplus \mid * \mid / \mid \% \mid \& \mid \&\& \mid \| \mid '' \mid '' \mid < \mid > \mid = \mid != \mid <= \mid >=
\end{array}
$$

Fig. 1. Language syntax

2 The Reversible Language Janus

In this section, we briefly review the syntax and semantics of Janus [23,24,26], a reversible (imperative) language in which statements can be inverted and executed in both forward and backward directions.

The syntax of Janus is displayed in Fig. 1. Janus is a simple imperative language with assignments, conditionals, loops, and procedure calls. A program consists of a statement (the main body) and a sequence of procedure declarations, introduced by the keyword procedure followed by the procedure name (an identifier) and a statement (the procedure body).

The reversible assignment instruction takes the form "$x\oplus = e$" (or "$x[e_1]\oplus = e_2$" for array element assignments), which is equivalent to $x = x \oplus e$ (resp. $x[e_1] = x[e_1] \oplus e_2$), where $\oplus$ denotes an operator among plus, minus, and bitwise xor. Here, Janus requires that the left-hand side variable, x, does not occur in the expression e (resp. in the expressions e_1 and e_2).

Reversible conditionals take the form "if e_1 then s_1 else s_2 fi e_2." If the test e_1 evaluates to *true*, then s_1 is executed, and the assertion e_2 must also evaluate to *true*. Similarly, if e_1 evaluates to *false*, then s_2 is executed, and the assertion e_2 must also be false.

Reversible loops have the form "from e_1 do s_1 loop s_2 until e_2." Initially, the assertion e_1 must evaluate to *true*. If so, s_1 is executed, followed by the evaluation of the test e_2. If e_2 is true, the loop terminates. Otherwise, s_2 is executed and control returns to e_1, which must evaluate to false in this case; execution then proceeds to execute s_1 and evaluate e_2 again, and so forth (until e_2 is true).

Finally, we assume in this paper that procedures have neither parameters nor local variables. Consequently, a procedure call takes the form "call *id*" and simply executes the procedure body using the values of the program's global variables. Similarly, "uncall *id*" invokes the *inverse* procedure.

For a more detailed explanation of Janus, the reader is referred to [26].

Now, we introduce a *small-step* semantics for Janus (in contrast to the big-step semantics introduced in [23,24,26]). Moving from a big-step semantics to a small-step one typically involves adding a *stack* to the configurations (see, e.g., [17,22]). Alternatively, one can define a small-step semantics using *contexts* to specify where reductions can occur, as done in [10]. In this work, though, we prefer stacks, as they simplify the definition of a reversible version. Furthermore, they may help in clarifying the reason leading to an execution error, which could be useful in a potential extension of the semantics involving error handling.

$$\text{Con}\ \frac{}{\sigma \vdash c \Downarrow [\![c]\!]} \qquad \text{Var}\ \frac{}{\sigma \vdash x \Downarrow \sigma(x)} \qquad \text{Arr}\ \frac{\sigma \vdash e \Downarrow v}{\sigma \vdash x[e] \Downarrow \sigma(x[v])}$$

$$\text{Bop}\ \frac{\sigma \vdash e_1 \Downarrow v_1 \qquad \sigma \vdash e_2 \Downarrow v_2 \qquad [\![\odot]\!](v_1, v_2) = v}{\sigma \vdash e_1 \odot e_2 \Downarrow v}$$

Fig. 2. Semantics of expressions

For the evaluation of expressions, we consider the same rules of the original big-step semantics [26], which are shown in Fig. 2.[1] A judgement of the form $\sigma \vdash e \Downarrow v$ denotes the evaluation of expression e under *store* σ, producing the value v. A *store* σ is a function from variable names and indexed variable names to values. We denote with $\sigma[x \mapsto v]$ the update of σ which assigns value v to variable x. For simplicity we assume that σ is defined (with value zero if not explicitly initialized) for all the variables used in the program, and in writing we omit the bindings of variables whose value is zero. We let ϵ denote an empty store, i.e., an store that maps every variable to zero. Here, $[\![\_]\!]$ denotes an *interpretation* function, e.g., $[\![+]\!](2, 3) = 2 + 3$, where "+" is the standard addition on integers.

A *configuration* in our semantics has the form $\langle \sigma, s, \pi \rangle$, where σ is a global store, s is a statement (the *control* of the configuration), and π is a *stack*, i.e., a list of items of the form $\mathsf{seq}(e_2)$, $\mathsf{if\_true}(e_2)$, $\mathsf{if\_false}(e_2)$, $\mathsf{loop1}(e_1, s_1, e_2, s_2)$, and $\mathsf{loop2}(e_1, s_1, e_2, s_2)$. Given a Janus program $p = (s\ p_1\ \ldots\ p_n)$, an *initial* configuration has the form $\langle \epsilon, s, [\,] \rangle$, where $[\,]$ is an empty list representing the initial, empty stack.

The small-step semantics is defined using a set of transition rules. We split them in two groups: basic statements (Fig. 3) and conditional and loop statements (Fig. 5). A *transition step* with the small-step semantics has the form $\langle \sigma, s, \pi \rangle \rightarrow \langle \sigma', s', \pi' \rangle$. Let us briefly explain the first set of rules (Fig. 3):

- Rules AssVarS and AssArrS define the assignment. AssVarS evaluates the new value of the variable and updates the store, while AssArrS evaluates the index of the array and the new value and updates the value of the array in the store.
- A procedure call (defined by rule CallS) reduces to the body of procedure *id*, retrieved using the mapping Γ. Similarly, a procedure uncall (defined by rule UnCallS) proceeds in much the same way, except that it reduces to the *inversion* $\mathcal{I}[\![\Gamma(id)]\!]$ of the body of procedure *id*. Here, $\mathcal{I}$ is the Janus inverter function defined in Fig. 4, which given a statement computes another statement executing the inverse computation.

[1] Note that this means that the evaluation of expressions is not reversible (but considered a one-step evaluation).

$$\text{AssVarS}\ \frac{\sigma \vdash e \Downarrow v}{\langle \sigma, x \oplus = e, \pi\rangle \rightarrow \langle \sigma[x \mapsto [\![\oplus]\!](\sigma(x), v)], \mathsf{skip}, \pi\rangle}$$

$$\text{AssArrS}\ \frac{\sigma \vdash e_l \Downarrow v_l \qquad \sigma \vdash e \Downarrow v}{\langle \sigma, x[e_l] \oplus = e, \pi\rangle \rightarrow \langle \sigma[x[v_l] \mapsto [\![\oplus]\!](\sigma(x[v_l]), v)], \mathsf{skip}, \pi\rangle}$$

$$\text{CallS}\ \frac{}{\langle \sigma, \mathsf{call}\ id, \pi\rangle \rightarrow \langle \sigma, \Gamma(id), \pi\rangle}$$

$$\text{UnCallS}\ \frac{}{\langle \sigma, \mathsf{uncall}\ id, \pi\rangle \rightarrow \langle \sigma, \mathcal{I}[\![\Gamma(id)]\!], \pi\rangle}$$

$$\text{Seq1}\ \frac{}{\langle \sigma, s_1\ s_2, \pi\rangle \rightarrow \langle \sigma, s_1, \mathsf{seq}(s_2) : \pi\rangle} \qquad \text{Seq2}\ \frac{}{\langle \sigma, \mathsf{skip}, \mathsf{seq}(s_2) : \pi\rangle \rightarrow \langle \sigma, s_2, \pi\rangle}$$

Fig. 3. Small-step semantics: rules for basic constructs

$$\mathcal{I}_{op}[\![+]\!] ::= - \qquad \mathcal{I}_{op}[\![-]\!] ::= + \qquad \mathcal{I}_{op}[\![\hat{}\,]\!] ::= \hat{}$$

$$\begin{aligned}
\mathcal{I}[\![x\oplus = e]\!] &::= x\ \mathcal{I}_{op}[\![\oplus]\!] = e\\
\mathcal{I}[\![x[e_1]\oplus = e_2]\!] &::= x[e_1]\ \mathcal{I}_{op}[\![\oplus]\!] = e_2\\
\mathcal{I}[\![\mathsf{if}\ e_1\ \mathsf{then}\ s_1\ \mathsf{else}\ s_2\ \mathsf{fi}\ e_2]\!] &::= \mathsf{if}\ e_2\ \mathsf{then}\ \mathcal{I}[\![s_1]\!]\ \mathsf{else}\ \mathcal{I}[\![s_2]\!]\ \mathsf{fi}\ e_1\\
\mathcal{I}[\![\mathsf{from}\ e_1\ \mathsf{do}\ s_1\ \mathsf{loop}\ s_2\ \mathsf{until}\ e_2]\!] &::= \mathsf{from}\ e_2\ \mathsf{do}\ \mathcal{I}[\![s_1]\!]\ \mathsf{loop}\ \mathcal{I}[\![s_2]\!]\ \mathsf{until}\ e_1\\
\mathcal{I}[\![\mathsf{call}\ id]\!] &::= \mathsf{uncall}\ id\\
\mathcal{I}[\![\mathsf{uncall}\ id]\!] &::= \mathsf{call}\ id\\
\mathcal{I}[\![\mathsf{skip}]\!] &::= \mathsf{skip}\\
\mathcal{I}[\![s_1\ s_2]\!] &::= \mathcal{I}[\![s_2]\!]\ \mathcal{I}[\![s_1]\!]\\
\mathcal{I}[\![\mathsf{procedure}\ id\ s]\!] &::= \mathsf{procedure}\ id^{-1}\ \mathcal{I}[\![s]\!]
\end{aligned}$$

Fig. 4. Inverter function for Janus statements [26]

- Finally, the execution of a sequence is defined by rules Seq1 and Seq2. For simplicity, we assume that the sequence operator is right-associative so that $s_1\ s_2\ \ldots\ s_n$ is always interpreted as $s_1\ (s_2\ (\ldots(s_{n-1}\ s_n)\ldots))$. Given a sequence $s_1\ s_2$, rule Seq1 moves s_2 to the stack (pushing an element of the form $\mathsf{seq}(s_2)$ onto the stack) and starts the evaluation of s_1. Once s_1 is fully evaluated, rule Seq2 pops $\mathsf{seq}(s_2)$ from the stack and s_2 becomes the current control of the configuration.

The transition rules for conditionals and for loops are shown in Fig. 5. We distinguish the following cases:

- For conditionals, either rule IfTrue1 or IfFalse1 is first applied, depending on whether the condition e_1 evaluates to *true* or *false*, respectively. Rule IfTrue1 (resp. IfFalse1) pushes a new element of the form $\mathsf{if\_true}(e_2)$ (resp. $\mathsf{if\_false}(e_2)$) onto the stack.
- Once the corresponding statement is fully evaluated, rule IfTrue2 (resp. IfFalse2) applies if the assertion evaluates to the same value of the test.

$$\textsc{IfTrue1}\ \frac{\sigma \vdash e_1 \Downarrow v_1 \qquad \mathsf{is\_true?}(v_1)}{\langle \sigma, \mathsf{if}\ e_1\ \mathsf{then}\ s_1\ \mathsf{else}\ s_2\ \mathsf{fi}\ e_2, \pi\rangle \to \langle \sigma, s_1, \mathsf{if\_true}(e_2)\!:\!\pi\rangle}$$

$$\textsc{IfTrue2}\ \frac{\sigma \vdash e_2 \Downarrow v_2 \qquad \mathsf{is\_true?}(v_2)}{\langle \sigma, \mathsf{skip}, \mathsf{if\_true}(e_2)\!:\!\pi\rangle \to \langle \sigma, \mathsf{skip}, \pi\rangle}$$

$$\textsc{IfFalse1}\ \frac{\sigma \vdash e_1 \Downarrow v_1 \qquad \mathsf{is\_false?}(v_1)}{\langle \sigma, \mathsf{if}\ e_1\ \mathsf{then}\ s_1\ \mathsf{else}\ s_2\ \mathsf{fi}\ e_2, \pi\rangle \to \langle \sigma, s_2, \mathsf{if\_false}(e_2)\!:\!\pi\rangle}$$

$$\textsc{IfFalse2}\ \frac{\sigma \vdash e_2 \Downarrow v_2 \qquad \mathsf{is\_false?}(v_2)}{\langle \sigma, \mathsf{skip}, \mathsf{if\_false}(e_2)\!:\!\pi\rangle \to \langle \sigma, \mathsf{skip}, \pi\rangle}$$

$$\textsc{LoopMainS}\ \frac{\sigma \vdash e_1 \Downarrow v_1 \qquad \mathsf{is\_true?}(v_1)}{\langle \sigma, \mathsf{from}\ e_1\ \mathsf{do}\ s_1\ \mathsf{loop}\ s_2\ \mathsf{until}\ e_2, \pi\rangle \to \langle \sigma, s_1, \mathsf{loop1}(e_1, s_1, e_2, s_2)\!:\!\pi\rangle}$$

$$\textsc{LoopBaseS}\ \frac{\sigma \vdash e_2 \Downarrow v_2 \qquad \mathsf{is\_true?}(v_2)}{\langle \sigma, \mathsf{skip}, \mathsf{loop1}(e_1, s_1, e_2, s_2)\!:\!\pi\rangle \to \langle \sigma, \mathsf{skip}, \pi\rangle}$$

$$\textsc{Loop1}\ \frac{\sigma \vdash e_2 \Downarrow v_2 \qquad \mathsf{is\_false?}(v_2)}{\langle \sigma, \mathsf{skip}, \mathsf{loop1}(e_1, s_1, e_2, s_2)\!:\!\pi\rangle \to \langle \sigma, s_2, \mathsf{loop2}(e_1, s_1, e_2, s_2)\!:\!\pi\rangle}$$

$$\textsc{Loop2}\ \frac{\sigma \vdash e_1 \Downarrow v_1 \qquad \mathsf{is\_false?}(v_1)}{\langle \sigma, \mathsf{skip}, \mathsf{loop2}(e_1, s_1, e_2, s_2)\!:\!\pi\rangle \to \langle \sigma, s_1, \mathsf{loop1}(e_1, s_1, e_2, s_2)\!:\!\pi\rangle}$$

Fig. 5. Small-step semantics: rules for if and for loop

- Regarding loops, rule LoopMain enters the loop, requiring the assertion e_1 to be true and starting the execution of statement s_1. Furthermore, an element of the form $\mathsf{loop1}(e_1, s_1, e_2, s_2)$ is pushed onto the stack.
- Each iteration of the loop is formalized using rules Loop1 and Loop2. The first rule, Loop1, applies when s_1 is fully evaluated and the condition e_2 evaluates to *false*. In this case, s_2 becomes the current control of the configuration and $\mathsf{loop1}(e_1, s_1, e_2, s_2)$ is replaced by $\mathsf{loop2}(e_1, s_1, e_2, s_2)$ in the stack. Rule Loop2 is the counterpart to rule Loop1 and is triggered once s_2 is fully evaluated. Here, e_1 must evaluate to *false*. Then, s_1 becomes the current control of the configuration and $\mathsf{loop2}(e_1, s_1, e_2, s_2)$ is reverted to $\mathsf{loop1}(e_1, s_1, e_2, s_2)$ in the stack.
- Finally, rule LoopBaseS applies when s_1 is fully evaluated and, moreover, the test e_2 is true, terminating loop execution.

We denote with $\to^*$ the reflexive and transitive closure of $\to$.

The equivalence of the small-step semantics with the big-step semantics of [23,24,26] (and, thus, the equivalence to the small-step semantics based on contexts of [10]) can be found in the extended version of this paper [13].

$$
\begin{array}{rl}
p ::= & s\ (\textsf{procedure}\ id\ s)^{+} \\
s ::= & [x\oplus = e]^{\ell} \mid [x[e]\oplus = e]^{\ell} \mid \textsf{if}\ [e]^{\ell}\ \textsf{then}\ s\ \textsf{else}\ s\ \textsf{fi}\ [e]^{\ell} \\
\mid & \textsf{from}\ [e]^{\ell}\ \textsf{do}\ s\ \textsf{loop}\ s\ \textsf{until}\ [e]^{\ell} \mid [\textsf{call}\ id]^{\ell} \mid [\textsf{uncall}\ id]^{\ell} \mid [\textsf{skip}]^{\ell} \mid s\ s \\
\mid & [\textsf{start}]^{\ell} \mid [\textsf{stop}]^{\ell}
\end{array}
$$

Fig. 6. Extended language syntax (e and $\oplus$ are as in Fig. 1)

```
[start]1                 procedure sumMul2
[n += 2]2                   [start]5
[call sumMul2]3             [i += 1]6
[stop]4                     from [i == 1]7 do
                              if [(i % 2) == 0]8 then [total += i]9
                                                 else [skip]10
                              fi [(i % 2) == 0]11
                            loop
                              [i += 1]12
                            until [i >= n]13
                            [n += total]14
                            [stop]15
```

Fig. 7. Sum2: a program computing the sum of the multiples of 2 up to `n`

3 A Reversible Semantics for Janus

In this section, we propose a new reversible (small-step) semantics based on the use of a *program counter*. Here, the configurations do not include a piece of code to be executed, as in the small-step semantics of the previous section, but a label that points to the next "block" of the program to be executed. This greatly simplifies the definition of a reversible semantics for the language.

Typically, semantics based on a program counter have been restricted to simple, assembly-like languages, where execution is modeled by simply incrementing a counter or updating it to perform jumps. In contrast, high-level language definitions rarely use an explicit program counter, favoring instead the use of evaluation contexts to manage control flow implicitly. We refer to related work (Sect. 4) for a more detailed discussion on this topic.

In the following, we introduce a control-flow graph (CFG) to manage the evolution of the program counter. To this end, Fig. 6 introduces an extended syntax where *elementary blocks* (i.e., conditions, assignments, call, uncall, and skip) are now labeled. We consider a domain of labels $\mathcal{L}$, where $\ell, \ell_1, \ldots$ range over the set $\mathcal{L}$. All labels are unique in a program. We let $block(\ell) = o$ if $[o]^{\ell}$ belongs to the considered program, where o is an elementary block. Furthermore, we assume all programs (and procedures) have an initial (elementary) statement start and a final (elementary) statement stop that simply mark the beginning and end (and is semantically equivalent to skip). Figure 7 presents a labeled Janus program, Sum2, which serves as our running example.

$$\begin{aligned}
&\mathit{entry}(\mathsf{if}\ [e_1]^{\ell_1}\ \mathsf{then}\ s_1\ \mathsf{else}\ s_2\ \mathsf{fi}\ [e_2]^{\ell_2}) = \ell_1 && \mathit{entry}(s_1\ s_2) = \mathit{entry}(s_1)\\
&\mathit{entry}(\mathsf{from}\ [e_1]^{\ell_1}\ \mathsf{do}\ s_1\ \mathsf{loop}\ s_2\ \mathsf{until}\ [e_2]^{\ell_2}) = \ell_1 && \mathit{entry}([s]^{\ell}) = \ell\ \text{ otherwise}\\
&\mathit{exit}(\mathsf{if}\ [e_1]^{\ell_1}\ \mathsf{then}\ s_1\ \mathsf{else}\ s_2\ \mathsf{fi}\ [e_2]^{\ell_2}) = \ell_2 && \mathit{exit}(s_1\ s_2) = \mathit{exit}(s_2)\\
&\mathit{exit}(\mathsf{from}\ [e_1]^{\ell_1}\ \mathsf{do}\ s_1\ \mathsf{loop}\ s_2\ \mathsf{until}\ [e_2]^{\ell_2}) = \ell_2 && \mathit{exit}([s]^{\ell}) = \ell\ \text{ otherwise}
\end{aligned}$$

Fig. 8. Entry and exit points

Now, Fig. 8 introduces the auxiliary function *entry* (resp. *exit*), which returns the entry (resp. exit) label of a program statement. Note that, in contrast to most (high level) programming languages, *exit* always returns a single label because of Janus conditionals with a single exit point. The definitions are self-explanatory. We also consider the following (partially defined) function, ctx, that identifies the statement where the label of a given expression (a test or assertion) occurs. E.g., if the sentence "if $[e_1]^{\ell_1}$ then s_1 else s_2 fi $[e_2]^{\ell_2}$" occurs in a program, then $\mathsf{ctx}(\ell_1) = \mathsf{ctx}(\ell_2) = (\mathsf{if}\ [e_1]^{\ell_1}\ \mathsf{then}\ s_1\ \mathsf{else}\ s_2\ \mathsf{fi}\ [e_2]^{\ell_2})$. Analogously, if the sentence "from $[e_1]^{\ell_1}$ do s_1 loop s_2 until $[e_2]^{\ell_2}$" occurs in the program, then $\mathsf{ctx}(\ell_1) = \mathsf{ctx}(\ell_2) = (\mathsf{from}\ [e_1]^{\ell_1}\ \mathsf{do}\ s_1\ \mathsf{loop}\ s_2\ \mathsf{until}\ [e_2]^{\ell_2})$.

$$\begin{aligned}
\mathit{flow}(\mathsf{if}\ [e_1]^{\ell_1}\ \mathsf{then}\ s_1\ \mathsf{else}\ s_2\ \mathsf{fi}\ [e_2]^{\ell_2}) &= \{(\ell_1, \mathit{entry}(s_1)), (\mathit{exit}(s_1), \ell_2)\}\\
&\cup \{(\ell_1, \mathit{entry}(s_2), (\mathit{exit}(s_2), \ell_2)\}\\
&\cup \mathit{flow}(s_1) \cup \mathit{flow}(s_2)\\
\mathit{flow}(\mathsf{from}\ [e_1]^{\ell_1}\ \mathsf{do}\ s_1\ \mathsf{loop}\ s_2\ \mathsf{until}\ [e_2]^{\ell_2}) &= \{(\ell_1, \mathit{entry}(s_1)), (\mathit{exit}(s_1), \ell_2)\}\\
&\cup \{(\ell_2, \mathit{entry}(s_2)), (\mathit{exit}(s_2), \ell_1)\}\\
&\cup \mathit{flow}(s_1) \cup \mathit{flow}(s_2)\\
\mathit{flow}(s_1\ s_2) &= \{(\mathit{exit}(s_1), \mathit{entry}(s_2)\} \cup \mathit{flow}(s_1) \cup \mathit{flow}(s_2)\\
\mathit{flow}(s) &= \emptyset \quad \text{otherwise}
\end{aligned}$$

Fig. 9. Control-flow graph of a Janus program

Next, function *flow* (Fig. 9) computes the edges of the CFG of a Janus program. It is worth noting that we do not have edges for call/return (resp. uncall/return) in a CFG. The control flow for these cases will be dealt with dynamically in the corresponding transition rules. We represent an edge (ℓ_1, ℓ_2) graphically as $\ell_1 \longrightarrow \ell_2$. Now, we proceed as follows:

- given a program, for each procedure "procedure *id s*", we introduce an inverse procedure of the form "procedure $id^{-1}\ \mathcal{I}[\![s]\!]$", where the definition of function $\mathcal{I}[\![\ ]\!]$ from Fig. 4 is extended so that $\mathcal{I}[\![\mathsf{start}]\!] ::= \mathsf{stop}$ and $\mathcal{I}[\![\mathsf{stop}]\!] ::= \mathsf{start}$;
- then, we add labels to each elementary block;
- finally, we compute the CFGs of the main program and of each procedure as well as its inverse version.

For example, for program Sum2 (Fig. 7), function *flow* computes the following two CFGs (the graphical representations are shown in Fig. 10):[2]

$$\begin{aligned} CFG_{main} &= \{\ (1,2),(2,3),(3,4)\ \} \\ CFG_{sumMul3} &= \{\ (5,6),(6,7),(7,8),(8,9),(8,10),(9,11),(10,11), \\ &\quad\ (11,13),(13,12),(12,7),(13,14),(14,15)\ \} \end{aligned}$$

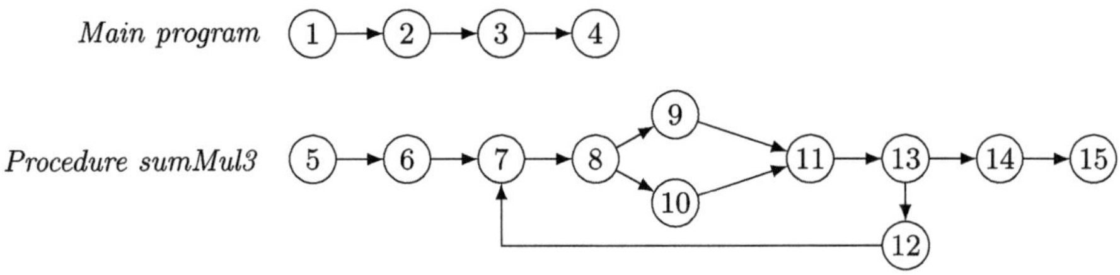

Fig. 10. CFGs for program Sum3

3.1 The Forward Rules

$$\overrightarrow{AssVar}\ \frac{block(\ell') = (x \oplus = e) \qquad \sigma \vdash e \Downarrow v \qquad \ell' \longrightarrow \ell''}{\langle \sigma, \ell, \ell', \pi \rangle \rightharpoonup \langle \sigma[x \mapsto [\![\oplus]\!](\sigma(x), v)], \ell', \ell'', \pi \rangle}$$

$$\overrightarrow{AssArr}\ \frac{block(\ell') = (x[e_l] \oplus = e) \qquad \sigma \vdash e_l \Downarrow v_l \qquad \sigma \vdash e \Downarrow v \qquad \ell' \longrightarrow \ell''}{\langle \sigma, \ell, \ell', \pi \rangle \rightharpoonup \langle \sigma[x[v_l] \mapsto [\![\oplus]\!](\sigma(x[v_l]), v)], \ell', \ell'', \pi \rangle}$$

$$\overrightarrow{Call}\ \frac{block(\ell') = (\mathsf{call}\ id) \qquad entry(\Gamma(id)) \longrightarrow \ell''}{\langle \sigma, \ell, \ell', \pi \rangle \rightharpoonup \langle \sigma, entry(\Gamma(id)), \ell'', \mathsf{call}(\ell') : \pi \rangle}$$

$$\overrightarrow{Return1}\ \frac{block(\ell') = \mathsf{stop} \qquad \ell'' \longrightarrow \ell'''}{\langle \sigma, \ell, \ell', \mathsf{call}(\ell'') : \pi \rangle \rightharpoonup \langle \sigma, \ell'', \ell''', \pi \rangle}$$

$$\overrightarrow{UnCall}\ \frac{block(\ell') = (\mathsf{uncall}\ id) \qquad entry(\Gamma(id^{-1})) \longrightarrow \ell''}{\langle \sigma, \ell, \ell', \pi \rangle \rightharpoonup \langle \sigma, entry(\Gamma(id^{-1})), \ell'', \mathsf{uncall}(\ell') : \pi \rangle}$$

$$\overrightarrow{Return2}\ \frac{block(\ell') = \mathsf{stop} \qquad \ell'' \longrightarrow \ell'''}{\langle \sigma, \ell, \ell', \mathsf{uncall}(\ell'') : \pi \rangle \rightharpoonup \langle \sigma, \ell'', \ell''', \pi \rangle} \qquad \overrightarrow{Skip}\ \frac{block(\ell') = \mathsf{skip} \qquad \ell' \longrightarrow \ell''}{\langle \sigma, \ell, \ell', \pi \rangle \rightharpoonup \langle \sigma, \ell', \ell'', \pi \rangle}$$

Fig. 11. Reversible forward semantics: rules for basic constructs

Now, we introduce the transition relation, $\rightharpoonup$, defining the forward direction of the reversible semantics. Here, configurations have the form $\langle \sigma, \ell, \ell', \pi \rangle$, where the

[2] For simplicity, we do not show the CFG of $sumMul2^{-1}$ since there is no uncall in the program and, thus, it will not be used.

control of the configuration is now determined by a pair of labels representing the *last executed statement* and the *next statement to be executed*, respectively. Note that the transition rules of the forward semantics only use the latter. We include the former in the configurations since it will be used by the transition rules of the backward semantics, and in this way we have a single definition of configuration that works for both directions. The rules defining the basic constructs can be found in Fig. 11. These rules are quite similar to their counterpart in the small-step semantics of Fig. 3. The main differences are the following:

- First, configurations no longer contain the next statement to be executed, but rather a label that identifies it (acting as a *program counter*). Thus, we use the (partially defined) function *block* to identify the block pointed to by that label. Furthermore, in many cases, the rules increment the program counter according to the edges of the CFG.
- Rule $\overrightarrow{\mathit{Call}}$ updates the control of the configuration with the labels from the first two statements of the procedure. Specifically, the first label will point to the statement start (which is not executed), so the second label will point to the actual first statement of the procedure. Rule $\overrightarrow{\mathit{Return1}}$, on the other hand, is triggered when the next statement to be executed is stop. In this case, we update the control of the configuration so that the last executed statement is now the previous call, and the next statement to be executed is the one following it (according to the CFG).
- Rules $\overrightarrow{\mathit{UnCall}}$ and $\overrightarrow{\mathit{Return2}}$ proceed analogously, with the only difference being that, in this case, we consider the inverse procedure.[3]
- Finally, we introduce a new rule, $\overrightarrow{\mathit{Skip}}$, to deal with skip which just increments the program counter (according to the CFG).

The second group of rules, the rules for conditional and loop statements, can be seen in Fig. 12. These rules are perfectly analogous to their counterpart in the small-step semantics of Fig. 5. The only relevant difference lies in the use of a program counter to identify the next block to be executed. Note that the premise $\mathit{block}(\ell) = e$ in a rule acts as a condition: If $\mathit{block}(\ell)$ is undefined or does not return a Boolean expression, then the rule is not applicable. Note also that the use of the (partially defined) function ctx is necessary to determine whether a Boolean expression is part of a conditional statement or of a loop. Moreover, as before, if $\mathsf{ctx}(\ell)$ is undefined or the given equality does not hold, the rule is not applicable.

Let us observe that the stack elements if_true and if_false contain labels for both the test and the assertion of the conditional. In practice, only the second label is required (by either rule $\overrightarrow{\mathit{IfTrue2}}$ and $\overrightarrow{\mathit{IfFalse2}}$). However, the rules of the backward semantics will require the first label (that of the test). Hence, we include both labels in the elements of the stack so that they can be used by both the forward and the backward semantics.

[3] We note that rules $\overrightarrow{\mathit{Return1}}$ and $\overrightarrow{\mathit{Return2}}$ could be merged into a single rule, applicable regardless of whether the top element of the stack is $\mathsf{call}(\ell'')$ or $\mathsf{uncall}(\ell'')$. However, we keep both rules for the sake of clarity.

$$\overrightarrow{\mathit{IfTrue1}}\ \frac{\mathsf{ctx}(\ell_1) = (\mathsf{if}\ [e_1]^{\ell_1}\ \mathsf{then}\ s_1\ \mathsf{else}\ s_2\ \mathsf{fi}\ [e_2]^{\ell_2}) \qquad \sigma \vdash e_1 \Downarrow v_1 \qquad \mathsf{is\_true?}(v_1)}{\langle \sigma, \ell, \ell_1, \pi \rangle \rightharpoonup \langle \sigma, \ell_1, \mathit{entry}(s_1), \mathsf{if\_true}(\ell_1, \ell_2) : \pi \rangle}$$

$$\overrightarrow{\mathit{IfTrue2}}\ \frac{\mathit{block}(\ell_2) = e_2 \qquad \sigma \vdash e_2 \Downarrow v_2 \qquad \mathsf{is\_true?}(v_2) \qquad \ell_2 \longrightarrow \ell_2'}{\langle \sigma, \ell, \ell_2, \mathsf{if\_true}(\ell_1, \ell_2) : \pi \rangle \rightharpoonup \langle \sigma, \ell_2, \ell_2', \pi \rangle}$$

$$\overrightarrow{\mathit{IfFalse1}}\ \frac{\mathsf{ctx}(\ell_1) = (\mathsf{if}\ [e_1]^{\ell_1}\ \mathsf{then}\ s_1\ \mathsf{else}\ s_2\ \mathsf{fi}\ [e_2]^{\ell_2}) \qquad \sigma \vdash e_1 \Downarrow v_1 \qquad \mathsf{is\_false?}(v_1)}{\langle \sigma, \ell, \ell_1, \pi \rangle \rightharpoonup \langle \sigma, \ell_1, \mathit{entry}(s_2), \mathsf{if\_false}(\ell_1, \ell_2) : \pi \rangle}$$

$$\overrightarrow{\mathit{IfFalse2}}\ \frac{\mathit{block}(\ell_2) = e_2 \qquad \sigma \vdash e_2 \Downarrow v_2 \qquad \mathsf{is\_false?}(v_2) \qquad \ell_2 \longrightarrow \ell_2'}{\langle \sigma, \ell, \ell_2, \mathsf{if\_false}(\ell_1, \ell_2) : \pi \rangle \rightharpoonup \langle \sigma, \ell_2, \ell_2', \pi \rangle}$$

$$\overrightarrow{\mathit{LoopMain}}\ \frac{\begin{array}{c}\mathsf{ctx}(\ell_1) = (\mathsf{from}\ [e_1]^{\ell_1}\ \mathsf{do}\ s_1\ \mathsf{loop}\ s_2\ \mathsf{until}\ [e_2]^{\ell_2}) \\ \sigma \vdash e_1 \Downarrow v_1 \qquad \mathsf{is\_true?}(v_1)\end{array}}{\langle \sigma, \ell, \ell_1, \pi \rangle \rightharpoonup \langle \sigma, \ell_1, \mathit{entry}(s_1), \mathsf{loop1}(\ell_1, s_1, \ell_2, s_2) : \pi \rangle}$$

$$\overrightarrow{\mathit{LoopBase}}\ \frac{\begin{array}{c}\mathit{block}(\ell_2) = e_2 \\ \sigma \vdash e_2 \Downarrow v_2 \qquad \mathsf{is\_true?}(v_2) \qquad \ell_2 \longrightarrow \ell_2' \qquad \ell_2' \neq \mathit{entry}(s_1)\end{array}}{\langle \sigma, \ell, \ell_2, \mathsf{loop1}(\ell_1, s_1, \ell_2, s_2) : \pi \rangle \rightharpoonup \langle \sigma, \ell_2, \ell_2', \pi \rangle}$$

$$\overrightarrow{\mathit{Loop1}}\ \frac{\mathit{block}(\ell_2) = e_2 \qquad \sigma \vdash e_2 \Downarrow v_2 \qquad \mathsf{is\_false?}(v_2)}{\langle \sigma, \ell, \ell_2, \mathsf{loop1}(\ell_1, s_1, \ell_2, s_2) : \pi \rangle \rightharpoonup \langle \sigma, \ell_2, \mathit{entry}(s_2), \mathsf{loop2}(\ell_1, s_1, \ell_2, s_2) : \pi \rangle}$$

$$\overrightarrow{\mathit{Loop2}}\ \frac{\mathit{block}(\ell_1) = e_1 \qquad \sigma \vdash e_1 \Downarrow v_1 \qquad \mathsf{is\_false?}(v_1)}{\langle \sigma, \ell, \ell_1, \mathsf{loop2}(\ell_1, s_1, \ell_2, s_2) : \pi \rangle \rightharpoonup \langle \sigma, \ell_1, \mathit{entry}(s_1), \mathsf{loop1}(\ell_1, s_1, \ell_2, s_2) : \pi \rangle}$$

Fig. 12. Reversible forward semantics: rules for if and for loop

On the other hand, when the program counter points to the test of a loop (ℓ_2), we can either terminate the loop and proceed to the next statement or execute s_2 and return to the initial assertion (ℓ_1). Consequently, ℓ_2 has two outgoing edges in the CFG. Therefore, we add the condition $\ell_2' \neq \mathit{entry}(s_1)$ in rule $\overrightarrow{\mathit{LoopBase}}$ in order to ensure that we are considering the right edge.

Finally, the elements of the stack, loop1 and loop2, could in principle contain only four labels, $(\ell_1, \mathit{entry}(s_1), \ell_2, \mathit{entry}(s_2))$. Indeed, this would be enough for the forward semantics. However, in the backward semantics, we will need to access $\mathit{exit}(s_1)$ and $\mathit{exit}(s_2)$. Therefore, we use $(\ell_1, s_1, \ell_2, s_2)$ as arguments of loop1 and loop2, so that they contain enough information for both semantics.

Given a program $p = (s\ p_1\ \dots\ p_n)$, an *initial configuration* has now the form $\langle \epsilon, \mathit{entry}(s), \ell, [\,] \rangle$, where $\mathit{entry}(s) \longrightarrow \ell$ belongs to the CFG of the program.

The equivalence between the small-step semantics of the previous section and the reversible (forward) semantics just introduced is stated as follows:

Lemma 1. *Let s be a statement where $\mathit{entry}(s) \longrightarrow \ell$ belongs to the CFG. Then, $\langle \epsilon, s, [\,] \rangle \rightarrow^* \langle \sigma, \mathsf{skip}, [\,] \rangle$ iff there exist ℓ', ℓ'' such that $\langle \epsilon, \mathit{entry}(s), \ell, [\,] \rangle \rightharpoonup^* \langle \sigma, \ell', \ell'', [\,] \rangle$ with $\mathit{block}(\ell'') = \mathsf{stop}$.*

Example 1. Given the program in Fig. 7 (and the CFG in Fig. 10), we have the forward derivation shown in Fig. 13, where we highlight in red the "active" label in each step (i.e., the label that represents the next statement to be executed by the forward reversible semantics).

$$
\begin{array}{rl}
 & \langle \epsilon, 1, 2, [\,] \rangle \\
\xrightarrow{\mathit{AssVar}} & \langle \{n \mapsto 2\}, 2, 3, [\,] \rangle \\
\xrightarrow{\mathit{Call}} & \langle \{n \mapsto 2\}, 5, 6, \mathsf{call}(3) : [\,] \rangle \\
\xrightarrow{\mathit{AssVar}} & \langle \{n \mapsto 2, i \mapsto 1\}, 6, 7, \mathsf{call}(3) : [\,] \rangle \\
\xrightarrow{\mathit{LoopMain}} & \langle \{n \mapsto 2, i \mapsto 1\}, 7, 8, \mathsf{loop1}(7, s_1, 13, s_2) : \mathsf{call}(3) : [\,] \rangle \\
\xrightarrow{\mathit{IfFalse1}} & \langle \{n \mapsto 2, i \mapsto 1\}, 8, 10, \mathsf{if\_false}(8, 11) : \mathsf{loop1}(7, s_1, 13, s_2) : \mathsf{call}(3) : [\,] \rangle \\
\xrightarrow{\mathit{Skip}} & \langle \{n \mapsto 2, i \mapsto 1\}, 10, 11, \mathsf{if\_false}(8, 11) : \mathsf{loop1}(7, s_1, 13, s_2) : \mathsf{call}(3) : [\,] \rangle \\
\xrightarrow{\mathit{IfFalse2}} & \langle \{n \mapsto 2, i \mapsto 1\}, 11, 13, \mathsf{loop1}(7, s_1, 13, s_2) : \mathsf{call}(3) : [\,] \rangle \\
\xrightarrow{\mathit{Loop1}} & \langle \{n \mapsto 2, i \mapsto 1\}, 13, 12, \mathsf{loop2}(7, s_1, 13, s_2) : \mathsf{call}(3) : [\,] \rangle \\
\xrightarrow{\mathit{AssVar}} & \langle \{n \mapsto 2, i \mapsto 2\}, 12, 7, \mathsf{loop2}(7, s_1, 13, s_2) : \mathsf{call}(3) : [\,] \rangle \\
\xrightarrow{\mathit{Loop2}} & \langle \{n \mapsto 2, i \mapsto 2\}, 7, 8, \mathsf{loop1}(7, s_1, 13, s_2) : \mathsf{call}(3) : [\,] \rangle \\
\xrightarrow{\mathit{IfTrue1}} & \langle \{n \mapsto 2, i \mapsto 2\}, 8, 9, \mathsf{if\_true}(8, 11) : \mathsf{loop1}(7, s_1, 13, s_2) : \mathsf{call}(3) : [\,] \rangle \\
\xrightarrow{\mathit{AssVar}} & \langle \{n \mapsto 2, i \mapsto 2, \mathit{total} \mapsto 2\}, 9, 11, \mathsf{if\_true}(8, 11) : \mathsf{loop1}(7, s_1, 13, s_2) : \mathsf{call}(3) : [\,] \rangle \\
\xrightarrow{\mathit{IfTrue2}} & \langle \{n \mapsto 2, i \mapsto 2, \mathit{total} \mapsto 2\}, 11, 13, \mathsf{loop1}(7, s_1, 13, s_2) : \mathsf{call}(3) : [\,] \rangle \\
\xrightarrow{\mathit{LoopBase}} & \langle \{n \mapsto 2, i \mapsto 2, \mathit{total} \mapsto 2\}, 13, 14, \mathsf{call}(3) : [\,] \rangle \\
\xrightarrow{\mathit{AssVar}} & \langle \{n \mapsto 4, i \mapsto 2, \mathit{total} \mapsto 2\}, 14, 15, \mathsf{call}(3) : [\,] \rangle \\
\xrightarrow{\mathit{Return1}} & \langle \{n \mapsto 4, i \mapsto 2, \mathit{total} \mapsto 2\}, 3, 4, [\,] \rangle
\end{array}
$$

Fig. 13. Forward derivation with the reversible semantics

3.2 The Backward Rules

This section introduces the rules for the *backward* reversible semantics, which are defined via the transition relation $\leftharpoondown$. Intuitively speaking, a backward step $\langle \sigma, \ell_1, \ell_2, \pi \rangle \leftharpoondown \langle \sigma', \ell_1', \ell_2', \pi' \rangle$ proceeds as follows: first, the effects of the execution of $\mathit{block}(\ell_1)$, i.e., the last executed statement, are reverted, thus producing environment σ' and stack π'; then, the control labels ℓ_1, ℓ_2 are updated to ℓ_1', ℓ_2' (mainly traversing the original CFG backwards). Note that the reduction proceeds from left to right, regardless of the direction in which the transition arrow points.

In the following, flow^{-1} denotes the function that computes the *inverse* CFG of a program: $\mathit{flow}^{-1}(s) = \{(\ell', \ell) \mid (\ell, \ell') \in \mathit{flow}(s)\}$. For clarity, in the transition rules of the backward semantics, we denote the edges $(\ell, \ell') \in \mathit{flow}^{-1}(s)$ of the inverse CFG as $\ell \xrightarrow{-1} \ell'$; i.e., $\ell \xrightarrow{-1} \ell'$ is equivalent to $\ell' \longrightarrow \ell$ in the original CFG.

The following result states the equivalence between computing the inverse CFG of a statement and a standard CFG of the corresponding inverse statement:

Lemma 2. *Given a statement s, we have $\mathit{flow}^{-1}(s) = \mathit{flow}(\mathcal{I}[\![s]\!])$.*

$$\overleftarrow{AssVar}\ \frac{block(\ell') = (x \oplus = e) \qquad \sigma \vdash e \Downarrow v \qquad \ell'' \xrightarrow{-1} \ell'}{\langle \sigma, \ell', \ell'', \pi \rangle \leftharpoondown \langle \sigma[x \mapsto \mathcal{I}_{op}[\![\oplus]\!](\sigma(x), v)], \ell, \ell', \pi \rangle}$$

$$\overleftarrow{AssArr}\ \frac{block(\ell') = (x[e_l] \oplus = e) \qquad \sigma \vdash e_l \Downarrow v_l \qquad \sigma \vdash e \Downarrow v \qquad \ell'' \xrightarrow{-1} \ell'}{\langle \sigma, \ell', \ell'', \pi \rangle \leftharpoondown \langle \sigma[x[v_l] \mapsto \mathcal{I}_{op}[\![\oplus]\!](\sigma(x[v_l]), v)], \ell, \ell', \pi \rangle}$$

$$\overleftarrow{Call}\ \frac{block(\ell_s) = \mathsf{start} \qquad \ell' \xrightarrow{-1} \ell}{\langle \sigma, \ell_s, \ell'', \mathsf{call}(\ell') : \pi \rangle \leftharpoondown \langle \sigma, \ell, \ell', \pi \rangle}$$

$$\overleftarrow{Return1}\ \frac{block(\ell'') = (\mathsf{call}\ id) \qquad exit(\Gamma(id)) \xrightarrow{-1} \ell}{\langle \sigma, \ell'', \ell''', \pi \rangle \leftharpoondown \langle \sigma, \ell, exit(\Gamma(id)), \mathsf{call}(\ell'') : \pi \rangle}$$

$$\overleftarrow{UnCall}\ \frac{block(\ell_s) = \mathsf{start} \qquad \ell' \xrightarrow{-1} \ell}{\langle \sigma, \ell_s, \ell'', \mathsf{uncall}(\ell') : \pi \rangle \leftharpoondown \langle \sigma, \ell, \ell', \pi \rangle}$$

$$\overleftarrow{Return2}\ \frac{block(\ell'') = (\mathsf{uncall}\ id) \qquad exit(\Gamma(id^{-1})) \xrightarrow{-1} \ell}{\langle \sigma, \ell'', \ell''', \pi \rangle \leftharpoondown \langle \sigma, \ell, exit(\Gamma(id^{-1})), \mathsf{uncall}(\ell'') : \pi \rangle}$$

$$\overleftarrow{Skip}\ \frac{block(\ell') = \mathsf{skip} \qquad \ell'' \xrightarrow{-1} \ell'}{\langle \sigma, \ell', \ell'', \pi \rangle \leftharpoondown \langle \sigma, \ell, \ell', \pi \rangle}$$

Fig. 14. Reversible backward semantics: rules for basic constructs

The backward rules for basic constructs are shown in Fig. 14. In principle, each rule $\overleftarrow{Rule}$ represents the inverse version of the corresponding forward rule $\overrightarrow{Rule}$ from Fig. 11, executing the inverse of the last executed statement (pointed to by the first label in the control of the configuration) and advancing in the inverse CFG (equivalently, moving backwards in the standard CFG). In particular, note that the rules $\overleftarrow{Call}$ and $\overleftarrow{Uncall}$ are triggered upon reaching the statement start, whereas in the forward rules $\overrightarrow{Return1}$ and $\overrightarrow{Return2}$, the trigger was reaching the stop statement.

The backward rules for conditional and loop statements are shown in Fig. 15. As before, each rule $\overleftarrow{Rule}$ represents the inverse version of the corresponding forward rule $\overrightarrow{Rule}$ from Fig. 12. Let us emphasize only that conditionals and loops are now *undone* from end to start; consequently, the rules $\overleftarrow{IfTrue2}$ and $\overleftarrow{IfFalse2}$ now inspect the context of the label to determine whether it corresponds to a conditional assertion or a loop test, and push a new element onto the stack (while this was done in the forward semantics in rules $\overrightarrow{IfTrue1}$ and $\overrightarrow{IfFalse1}$).

Similarly, for loops, it is rule $\overleftarrow{LoopBase}$ that now inspects the context (and push a new element onto the stack). Conversely, the loop now terminates with the rule $\overleftarrow{LoopMain}$. Here, we verify that $\ell \neq exit(s_2)$, since there are two outgoing edges in the inverse CFG: one that backtracks to the statement preceding the loop (the one of interest), and another one that reverses a further iteration

$$\overleftarrow{\mathit{IfTrue1}}\ \frac{\mathit{block}(\ell_1) = e_1 \qquad \sigma \vdash e_1 \Downarrow v_1 \qquad \mathsf{is\_true?}(v_1) \qquad \ell_1 \xrightarrow{-1} \ell}{\langle \sigma, \ell_1, \ell_1', \mathsf{if\_true}(\ell_1, \ell_2) : \pi \rangle \leftharpoondown \langle \sigma, \ell, \ell_1, \pi \rangle}$$

$$\overleftarrow{\mathit{IfTrue2}}\ \frac{\begin{array}{c}\mathsf{ctx}(\ell_2) = (\mathsf{if}\ [e_1]^{\ell_1}\ \mathsf{then}\ s_1\ \mathsf{else}\ s_2\ \mathsf{fi}\ [e_2]^{\ell_2}) \\ \sigma \vdash e_2 \Downarrow v_2 \qquad \mathsf{is\_true?}(v_2)\end{array}}{\langle \sigma, \ell_2, \ell_2', \pi \rangle \leftharpoondown \langle \sigma, \mathit{exit}(s_1), \ell_2, \mathsf{if\_true}(\ell_1, \ell_2) : \pi \rangle}$$

$$\overleftarrow{\mathit{IfFalse1}}\ \frac{\mathit{block}(\ell_1) = e_1 \qquad \sigma \vdash e_1 \Downarrow v_1 \qquad \mathsf{is\_false?}(v_1) \qquad \ell_1 \xrightarrow{-1} \ell}{\langle \sigma, \ell_1, \ell_1', \mathsf{if\_false}(\ell_1, \ell_2) : \pi \rangle \leftharpoondown \langle \sigma, \ell, \ell_1, \pi \rangle}$$

$$\overleftarrow{\mathit{IfFalse2}}\ \frac{\begin{array}{c}\mathsf{ctx}(\ell_2) = (\mathsf{if}\ [e_1]^{\ell_1}\ \mathsf{then}\ s_1\ \mathsf{else}\ s_2\ \mathsf{fi}\ [e_2]^{\ell_2}) \\ \sigma \vdash e_2 \Downarrow v_2 \qquad \mathsf{is\_false?}(v_2)\end{array}}{\langle \sigma, \ell_2, \ell_2', \pi \rangle \leftharpoondown \langle \sigma, \mathit{exit}(s_2), \ell_2, \mathsf{if\_false}(\ell_1, \ell_2) : \pi \rangle}$$

$$\overleftarrow{\mathit{LoopMain}}\ \frac{\mathit{block}(\ell_1) = e_1 \qquad \sigma \vdash e_1 \Downarrow v_1 \qquad \mathsf{is\_true?}(v_1) \qquad \ell_1 \xrightarrow{-1} \ell \qquad \ell \neq \mathit{exit}(s_2)}{\langle \sigma, \ell_1, \ell', \mathsf{loop1}(\ell_1, s_1, \ell_2, s_2) : \pi \rangle \leftharpoondown \langle \sigma, \ell, \ell_1, \pi \rangle}$$

$$\overleftarrow{\mathit{LoopBase}}\ \frac{\begin{array}{c}\mathsf{ctx}(\ell_2) = (\mathsf{from}\ [e_1]^{\ell_1}\ \mathsf{do}\ s_1\ \mathsf{loop}\ s_2\ \mathsf{until}\ [e_2]^{\ell_2}) \\ \sigma \vdash e_2 \Downarrow v_2 \qquad \mathsf{is\_true?}(v_2)\end{array}}{\langle \sigma, \ell_2, \ell_2', \pi \rangle \leftharpoondown \langle \sigma, \mathit{exit}(s_1), \ell_2, \mathsf{loop1}(\ell_1, s_1, \ell_2, s_2) : \pi \rangle}$$

$$\overleftarrow{\mathit{Loop1}}\ \frac{\mathit{block}(\ell_2) = e_2 \qquad \sigma \vdash e_2 \Downarrow v_2 \qquad \mathsf{is\_false?}(v_2)}{\langle \sigma, \ell_2, \ell', \mathsf{loop2}(\ell_1, s_1, \ell_2, s_2) : \pi \rangle \leftharpoondown \langle \sigma, \mathit{exit}(s_1), \ell_2, \mathsf{loop1}(\ell_1, s_1, \ell_2, s_2) : \pi \rangle}$$

$$\overleftarrow{\mathit{Loop2}}\ \frac{\mathit{block}(\ell_1) = e_1 \qquad \sigma \vdash e_1 \Downarrow v_1 \qquad \mathsf{is\_false?}(v_1)}{\langle \sigma, \ell_1, \ell', \mathsf{loop1}(\ell_1, s_1, \ell_2, s_2) : \pi \rangle \leftharpoondown \langle \sigma, \mathit{exit}(s_2), \ell_1, \mathsf{loop2}(\ell_1, s_1, \ell_2, s_2) : \pi \rangle}$$

Fig. 15. Reversible backward semantics: rules for if and for loop

by jumping to the exit of s_2. This condition ensures that the correct path is followed.

Example 2. Consider the derivation shown in Example 1. Starting from the last configuration, we have the backward derivation shown in Fig. 16. As in the previous example, we highlight in red the "active" label in each step (i.e., the label that represents the last executed statement).

In order to prove the loop lemma below, stating that each forward step can be undone by a backward step and vice versa, we need to restrict our attention to reachable configurations. In the following, we let $\rightleftharpoons$ denote $\rightharpoonup \cup \leftharpoondown$.

Definition 1 (reachable configuration). *A configuration* $\langle \sigma, \ell_1', \ell_2', \pi \rangle$ *is* reachable *if it can be obtained by applying the rules of the semantics starting from an initial configuration, namely* $\langle \epsilon, \ell_1, \ell_2, [\,] \rangle \rightleftharpoons^* \langle \sigma, \ell_1', \ell_2', \pi \rangle$ *for some initial configuration* $\langle \epsilon, \ell_1, \ell_2, [\,] \rangle$.

This rules out, e.g., the case of configurations $\langle \sigma, \ell, \ell', \pi \rangle$ where ℓ and ℓ' are not the two ends of an edge of the CFG.

$$
\begin{array}{rl}
 & \langle \{n \mapsto 4, i \mapsto 2, total \mapsto 2\}, 3, 4, [\,]\rangle \\
\overleftarrow{\text{Return1}} & \langle \{n \mapsto 4, i \mapsto 2, total \mapsto 2\}, 14, 15, \mathsf{call}(3) : [\,]\rangle \\
\overleftarrow{\text{AssVar}} & \langle \{n \mapsto 2, i \mapsto 2, total \mapsto 2\}, 13, 14, \mathsf{call}(3) : [\,]\rangle \\
\overleftarrow{\text{LoopBase}} & \langle \{n \mapsto 2, i \mapsto 2, total \mapsto 2\}, 11, 13, \mathsf{loop1}(7, s_1, 13, s_2) : \mathsf{call}(3) : [\,]\rangle \\
\overleftarrow{\text{IfTrue2}} & \langle \{n \mapsto 2, i \mapsto 2, total \mapsto 2\}, 9, 11, \mathsf{if\_true}(8, 11) : \mathsf{loop1}(7, s_1, 13, s_2) : \mathsf{call}(3) : [\,]\rangle \\
\overleftarrow{\text{AssVar}} & \langle \{n \mapsto 2, i \mapsto 2\}, 8, 9, \mathsf{if\_true}(8, 11) : \mathsf{loop1}(7, s_1, 13, s_2) : \mathsf{call}(3) : [\,]\rangle \\
\overleftarrow{\text{IfTrue1}} & \langle \{n \mapsto 2, i \mapsto 2\}, 7, 8, \mathsf{loop1}(7, s_1, 13, s_2) : \mathsf{call}(3) : [\,]\rangle \\
\overleftarrow{\text{Loop2}} & \langle \{n \mapsto 2, i \mapsto 2\}, 12, 7, \mathsf{loop2}(7, s_1, 13, s_2) : \mathsf{call}(3) : [\,]\rangle \\
\overleftarrow{\text{AssVar}} & \langle \{n \mapsto 2, i \mapsto 1\}, 13, 12, \mathsf{loop2}(7, s_1, 13, s_2) : \mathsf{call}(3) : [\,]\rangle \\
\overleftarrow{\text{Loop1}} & \langle \{n \mapsto 2, i \mapsto 1\}, 11, 13, \mathsf{loop1}(7, s_1, 13, s_2) : \mathsf{call}(3) : [\,]\rangle \\
\overleftarrow{\text{IfFalse2}} & \langle \{n \mapsto 2, i \mapsto 1\}, 10, 11, \mathsf{if\_false}(8, 11) : \mathsf{loop1}(7, s_1, 13, s_2) : \mathsf{call}(3) : [\,]\rangle \\
\overleftarrow{\text{Skip}} & \langle \{n \mapsto 2, i \mapsto 1\}, 8, 10, \mathsf{if\_false}(8, 11) : \mathsf{loop1}(7, s_1, 13, s_2) : \mathsf{call}(3) : [\,]\rangle \\
\overleftarrow{\text{IfFalse1}} & \langle \{n \mapsto 2, i \mapsto 1\}, 7, 8, \mathsf{loop1}(7, s_1, 13, s_2) : \mathsf{call}(3) : [\,]\rangle \\
\overleftarrow{\text{LoopMain}} & \langle \{n \mapsto 2, i \mapsto 1\}, 6, 7, \mathsf{call}(3) : [\,]\rangle \\
\overleftarrow{\text{AssVar}} & \langle \{n \mapsto 2\}, 5, 6, \mathsf{call}(3) : [\,]\rangle \\
\overleftarrow{\text{Call}} & \langle \{n \mapsto 2\}, 2, 3, [\,]\rangle \\
\overleftarrow{\text{AssVar}} & \langle \epsilon, 1, 2, [\,]\rangle
\end{array}
$$

Fig. 16. Backward derivation with the reversible semantics

Lemma 3 (loop lemma). *Let* $\langle \sigma, \ell_1, \ell_2, \pi \rangle$ *be a reachable configuration. Then,* $\langle \sigma, \ell_1, \ell_2, \pi \rangle \rightharpoonup \langle \sigma', \ell_1', \ell_2', \pi' \rangle$ *iff* $\langle \sigma', \ell_1', \ell_2', \pi' \rangle \leftharpoondown \langle \sigma, \ell_1, \ell_2, \pi \rangle$.

The proof is by case distinction on the applied rule. Full details can be found in the extended version [13].

4 Related Work, Conclusion and Future Work

We proposed a small-step semantics for Janus based on a notion of program counter and established its equivalence to a classical small-step semantics based on a notion of stack. They are also equivalent to Janus semantics from the literature [10,23,24,26]. The Janus literature also covers extensions of Janus with other constructs, such as local variables [23,24] and stacks [23,24]. As immediate next step, we will extend our approach to cover such constructs as well. We also plan to apply our approach to define small-step semantics to other pure reversible languages in the literature. These include object-oriented languages such as ROOPL [8,20] and Joule [18], and functional languages such as RFun [25] and CoreFun [9], which are all equipped with big-step semantics.

Notably, at the same time as ours, a reversible semantics for R-CORE [6], a reversible core language has been proposed [15]. The idea is very close to ours, albeit the target language is different and simpler. Technically, they use a • inside the program to represent the current position of the execution, while we use two pointers inside the control flow graph of the program. Their technique allows for a simpler development, hence raising the question of whether it scales to more complex languages like Janus. This is an interesting direction for future work.

The only other small-step reversible semantics we are aware of are for domain-specific languages for specifying assembly sequences in industrial robots [19,21]. However, their semantics is quite different from the one of Janus or functional or object-oriented reversible languages, since it involves the position and actions of the robot in the real world. Hence the relation with our work is quite limited.

As mentioned above, the literature has few semantics of high-level languages based on a program counter. A notable exception is Gurevich and Huggins' semantics of C [7] based on an *Abstract State Machine* (see also [5]). A similar pattern is found in some intermediate representations like the *Static Single Assignment* (SSA), which rely on explicit control-flow graphs—effectively reintroducing a program counter—to facilitate data flow analysis [3].

A promising area for future exploration is the integration of concurrency support into Janus. By enabling the creation of processes and enabling them to exchange messages, such an extension could allow one to write concurrent reversible programs. The definition of the reversible small-step semantics provided in this paper is a relevant first step in this direction.

Acknowledgements. We would like to thank the anonymous reviewers for their suggestions to improve this paper.

References

1. Aman, B., et al.: Foundations of reversible computation. In: Ulidowski, I., Lanese, I., Schultz, U.P., Ferreira, C. (eds.) RC 2020. LNCS, vol. 12070, pp. 1–40. Springer, Cham (2020). https://doi.org/10.1007/978-3-030-47361-7_1
2. Bennett, C.H.: Logical reversibility of computation. IBM J. Res. Dev. **17**(6), 525–532 (1973). https://doi.org/10.1147/rd.176.0525
3. Cytron, R., Ferrante, J., Rosen, B.K., Wegman, M.N., Zadeck, F.K.: Efficiently computing static single assignment form and the control dependence graph. ACM Trans. Program. Lang. Syst. **13**(4), 451–490 (1991). https://doi.org/10.1145/115372.115320
4. Danos, V., Krivine, J.: Reversible communicating systems. In: Gardner, P., Yoshida, N. (eds.) CONCUR 2004. LNCS, vol. 3170, pp. 292–307. Springer, Heidelberg (2004). https://doi.org/10.1007/978-3-540-28644-8_19
5. Dömer, R., Gerstlauer, A., Müller, W.: The formal execution semantics of SpecC. In: Aboulhamid, E.M., Nakamura, Y. (eds.) Proceedings of the 15th International Symposium on System Synthesis (ISSS 2002), pp. 150–155. ACM/IEEE Computer Society (2002). https://doi.org/10.1109/ISSS.2002.1227168
6. Glück, R., Yokoyama, T.: A minimalist's reversible while language. IEICE Trans. Inf. Syst. **100-D**(5), 1026–1034 (2017). https://doi.org/10.1587/TRANSINF.2016EDP7274
7. Gurevich, Y., Huggins, J.K.: The semantics of the C programming language. In: Börger, E., Jäger, G., Kleine Büning, H., Martini, S., Richter, M.M. (eds.) CSL 1992. LNCS, vol. 702, pp. 274–308. Springer, Heidelberg (1993). https://doi.org/10.1007/3-540-56992-8_17
8. Haulund, T.: Design and implementation of a reversible object-oriented programming language (2017). https://doi.org/10.48550/arXiv.1707.07845

9. Jacobsen, P.A.H., Kaarsgaard, R., Thomsen, M.K.: CoreFun: a typed functional reversible core language. In: Kari, J., Ulidowski, I. (eds.) RC 2018. LNCS, vol. 11106, pp. 304–321. Springer, Cham (2018). https://doi.org/10.1007/978-3-319-99498-7_21
10. Lami, P., Lanese, I., Stefani, J.: A small-step semantics for Janus. In: Mogensen, T.Æ., Mikulski, L. (eds.) RC 2024. LNCS, vol. 14680, pp. 105–123. Springer, Cham (2024). https://doi.org/10.1007/978-3-031-62076-8_8
11. Landauer, R.: Irreversibility and heat generation in the computing process. IBM J. Res. Dev. **5**(3), 183–191 (1961). https://doi.org/10.1147/rd.53.0183
12. Lanese, I., Nishida, N., Palacios, A., Vidal, G.: A theory of reversibility for Erlang. J. Log. Algebraic Methods Program. **100**, 71–97 (2018). https://doi.org/10.1016/J.JLAMP.2018.06.004
13. Lanese, I., Vidal, G.: A reversible semantics for Janus. CoRR (2026). https://doi.org/10.48550/arXiv.2602.16913
14. Lutz, C., Derby, H.: Janus: a time-reversible language. Letter to R. Landauer **2** (1986)
15. Makino, T., Yokoyama, T.: Small-step semantics with meta-level reversibility for a reversible core language. In: Aubert, C., Roversi, L. (eds.) RC 2026. LNCS, vol. 16626, pp. xx–yy. Springer, Cham (2026)
16. Phillips, I., Ulidowski, I.: Reversing algebraic process calculi. J. Log. Algebr. Program. **73**(1–2), 70–96 (2007). https://doi.org/10.1016/j.jlap.2006.11.002
17. Sansom, P.M., Peyton Jones, S.L.: Formally based profiling for higher-order functional languages. ACM Trans. Program. Lang. Syst. **19**(2), 334–385 (1997). https://doi.org/10.1145/244795.244802
18. Schultz, U.P.: Reversible object-oriented programming with region-based memory management. In: Kari, J., Ulidowski, I. (eds.) RC 2018. LNCS, vol. 11106, pp. 322–328. Springer, Cham (2018). https://doi.org/10.1007/978-3-319-99498-7_22
19. Schultz, U.P.: Reversible control of robots. In: Ulidowski, I., Lanese, I., Schultz, U.P., Ferreira, C. (eds.) RC 2020. LNCS, vol. 12070, pp. 177–186. Springer, Cham (2020). https://doi.org/10.1007/978-3-030-47361-7_8
20. Schultz, U.P., Axelsen, H.B.: Elements of a reversible object-oriented language. In: Devitt, S., Lanese, I. (eds.) RC 2016. LNCS, vol. 9720, pp. 153–159. Springer, Cham (2016). https://doi.org/10.1007/978-3-319-40578-0_10
21. Schultz, U.P., Laursen, J.S., Ellekilde, L.-P., Axelsen, H.B.: Towards a domain-specific language for reversible assembly sequences. In: Krivine, J., Stefani, J.-B. (eds.) RC 2015. LNCS, vol. 9138, pp. 111–126. Springer, Cham (2015). https://doi.org/10.1007/978-3-319-20860-2_7
22. Sestoft, P.: Deriving a lazy abstract machine. J. Funct. Program. **7**(3), 231–264 (1997). https://doi.org/10.1017/S0956796897002712
23. Yokoyama, T.: Reversible computation and reversible programming languages. Electron. Notes Theor. Comput. Sci. **253**(6), 71–81 (2010). https://doi.org/10.1016/j.entcs.2010.02.007
24. Yokoyama, T., Axelsen, H.B., Glück, R.: Principles of a reversible programming language. In: Proceedings of the 5th Conference on Computing Frontiers, CF 2008, pp. 43–54. ASCM (2008). https://doi.org/10.1145/1366230.1366239
25. Yokoyama, T., Axelsen, H.B., Glück, R.: Towards a reversible functional language. In: De Vos, A., Wille, R. (eds.) RC 2011. LNCS, vol. 7165, pp. 14–29. Springer, Heidelberg (2012). https://doi.org/10.1007/978-3-642-29517-1_2
26. Yokoyama, T., Glück, R.: A reversible programming language and its invertible self-interpreter. In: PEPM, pp. 144–153. ACM Press (2007). https://doi.org/10.1145/1244381.1244404

Small-Step Semantics with Meta-level Reversibility for a Reversible Core Language

Toya Makino and Tetsuo Yokoyama(✉)

Nanzan University, Nagoya 466-8673, Japan
tyokoyama@acm.org

Abstract. This paper investigates reversible operational semantics for R-CORE, a minimal reversible core language that is r-Turing complete. While small-step semantics for reversible languages such as Janus have been previously explored, this work revisits the approach for R-CORE with a specific emphasis on local injectivity of individual inference rules and reversibility at the meta level. Building on the denotational semantics, we define a syntax-based small-step semantics in which control flow is made explicit through the use of a control token. Each inference rule is formulated as a partial injective function, thereby guaranteeing deterministic execution in both the forward and backward directions at the level of individual steps. To bridge structured syntax with reversible control flow, we introduce a finer-grained small-step semantics that decomposes commands into atomic flowchart operations, including steps, tests, and assertions. This formulation follows the reversible flowchart model and clarifies how global reversibility emerges from locally reversible control transfers. It provides a useful semantic perspective for studying reversible execution mechanisms across different reversible languages and systems, including reversible interpreters and reversible debuggers.

Keywords: Reversible programming · Reversible operational semantics · r-Turing completeness · R-CORE

1 Introduction

The study of reversible computation originated from analyses of the physical limits of computation [3,20], particularly the energy cost of information loss [4, 6]. Beyond this physical motivation, reversibility provides a formal means of modeling computation as an information-preserving process. It is a principled framework for reasoning about program execution, inversion, and debugging [19].

Reversible computation can be expressed through reversible programs, which define partial injective transformations on program states (control + stores) and thus enable direct reasoning about both execution and its inverse [11]. To guarantee this property, every computational step must itself be a partial injective

C. Aubert and L. Roversi (Eds.): RC 2026, LNCS 16626, pp. 201–218, 2026.
https://doi.org/10.1007/978-3-032-30839-9_12

function, which motivates the use of small-step operational semantics (ss semantics) in the style of structured operational semantics (SOS) [26]. Prior work on the semantics of high-level reversible programming languages, notably Janus [18] and its extensions such as Concurrent Janus [17], formalized stepwise reversibility using SOS inference rules and established a solid foundation for the formal study of reversible execution and its extension to concurrency.

Although Janus [22,28] has played an important role in establishing structured reversible programming, several issues remain when the language is considered a target for meta-programming or concurrent programming. First, Janus provides a rich set of features whose interactions substantially complicate its formal semantics, in contrast to minimal core models such as the WHILE language [15] and the λ-calculus, which remain foundational in programming language theory for their semantic simplicity and analytical tractability. Second, and more fundamentally, existing semantics of Janus [28], including the recent ss semantics in [18], emphasize reversibility at the program level but do not ensure reversibility at the meta level, i.e., the inference rules themselves are not reversible [9].

For example, consider the standard inference rule

$$\frac{}{(\texttt{skip;}\ \texttt{C}, \sigma) \rightarrow (\texttt{C}, \sigma)} \tag{1}$$

as found in conventional ss semantics (e.g., [27]). Although this inference rule specifies how a configuration $(\texttt{skip;}\ \texttt{C}, \sigma)$ evolves, the resulting configuration $(\texttt{C}, \sigma)$ does not uniquely determine that it was immediately preceded by the command `skip; C`; the information associated with the discarded `skip` is lost, and the transition is therefore irreversible. For simplicity, we use `skip`; however, this kind of structural reduction also occurs in reversible languages including R-CORE, even though R-CORE itself has no skip construct.

Such backward nondeterminism at the meta level becomes a serious obstacle when one seeks to construct reversible interpreters or reversible debuggers that rely on locally deterministic forward and backward execution.

The contribution of this paper is as follows:

- Meta-level reversibility: We define a *reversible* syntax-based ss semantics for the r-Turing-complete core language R-CORE, where each inference rule is a partial injective function of configurations.
- Bridging syntax and topology: We introduce a finer-grained small-step semantics (fss semantics) that exposes the correspondence between structured syntax and language-independent atomic reversible flowchart operations. This abstraction characterizes reversible control flow by topology rather than source-level syntax.
- Equivalence: We show that the ss semantics is equivalent to the existing denotational semantics (ds semantics) [10] and the corresponding fss semantics for terminating computations.

Section 2 reviews the syntax and ds semantics of R-CORE, together with its control flow. Section 3 presents the reversible ss semantics and discusses the underlying design choices. Section 4 bridges the gap between the syntax of R-CORE and the topology of reversible flowcharts by introducing a finer-grained, flowchart-based ss semantics. Section 5 establishes the equivalence of the three semantics and their reversibility at the meta level. Section 6 discusses related work. Section 7 concludes the paper.

```
Variables   ∋ X, Y, Z ::= X0 | X1 | ··· | X9
Expressions ∋    E, F ::= X | nil | hd X | tl X | cons X Y | =? X Y
Commands    ∋    C, D ::= X ^= E | C; D | from X loop C until Y
Programs    ∋       P ::= read X; C; write X
```

Fig. 1. Syntax of the small reversible language R-CORE, adapted from [10].

2 R-CORE: Syntax and Denotational Semantics

R-CORE is a minimal reversible imperative core calculus introduced as a foundational model for reversible computation [10]. It is designed to play a role analogous to that of the WHILE language in (irreversible) programming language theory [15]: small enough to enable precise semantic analysis, yet expressive enough to capture general computation.

Despite its syntactic simplicity, R-CORE is powerful, being r-Turing complete [3,29], meaning that it can simulate any reversible Turing machine without producing garbage [10]. The language imposes restrictions on data and control constructs to their simplest reversible forms, allowing semantic properties to be studied in isolation without the complicated interactions present in richer languages. In contrast to high-level reversible languages such as Janus and ROOPL [12,13], which incorporate a broad range of programming features and abstractions, R-CORE adopts a minimal design that makes it particularly suitable as a semantic core for foundational and meta-theoretical investigations in reversible computation.

Syntax. The syntax is shown in Fig. 1. We assume a fixed finite set of variables. Meta-variables such as `X`, `Y`, and `Z` range over this set. Reversible assignments take the form `X ^= E` and are subject to a syntactic well-formedness condition requiring that the target variable `X` does not occur in the expression `E`. Intuitively, `X ^= E` toggles `X` between `nil` and the value of `E`. If `X` is `nil`, it stores the value of `E`; if `X` already stores that same non-`nil` value, it restores `X` to `nil`.

Semantic Domain. The ds semantics is defined over a simple data domain $\mathbb{D}$ and a store domain. As defined in Fig. 2a, $\mathbb{D}$ contains only the atom `nil` and pairs constructed from it. For readability, we use `f` to denote `nil` and `t` to denote `(nil.nil)`. We regard `f` as false and `t` as true.

A store is defined as a partial function from the set of variables to the data domain, written $\sigma : \texttt{Variables} \rightharpoonup \mathbb{D}$. We write `Stores` to denote the set of such partial functions. A store can be represented as a finite set of bindings of the form $\texttt{X} \mapsto \texttt{d}$, each binding associating a variable with its current value. We sometimes combine stores using the disjoint sum operator $\uplus$. In particular, the notation $\sigma \uplus \{\texttt{X} \mapsto \texttt{d}\}$ indicates that the binding for `X` is added to the store σ.

$$\mathbb{D} \ni \texttt{d} ::= \texttt{nil} \mid (\texttt{d.d})$$

(a) Data values $\mathbb{D}$.

$$\begin{aligned}
\mathcal{E}[\![\texttt{X}]\!]\sigma &= \sigma(\texttt{X})\\
\mathcal{E}[\![\texttt{nil}]\!]\sigma &= \texttt{nil}\\
\mathcal{E}[\![\texttt{hd X}]\!]\sigma &= \texttt{d} \quad \text{if } \sigma(\texttt{X}) = (\texttt{d.e})\\
\mathcal{E}[\![\texttt{tl X}]\!]\sigma &= \texttt{e} \quad \text{if } \sigma(\texttt{X}) = (\texttt{d.e})\\
\mathcal{E}[\![\texttt{cons X Y}]\!]\sigma &= (\sigma(\texttt{X}).\sigma(\texttt{Y}))\\
\mathcal{E}[\![\texttt{=? X Y}]\!]\sigma &= \begin{cases} \texttt{t} & \text{if } \sigma(\texttt{X}) = \sigma(\texttt{Y})\\ \texttt{f} & \text{otherwise}\end{cases}
\end{aligned}$$

(b) Semantic function for expressions $\mathcal{E}$.

$$\begin{aligned}
\mathcal{C}[\![\texttt{X \^{}= E}]\!](\sigma \uplus \{\texttt{X} \mapsto \texttt{d}\}) &= \sigma \uplus \{\texttt{X} \mapsto \texttt{d} \odot \mathcal{E}[\![\texttt{E}]\!]\sigma\} && (\textsc{Asn}_{\text{ds}})\\
&\quad \text{if } \texttt{d} = \texttt{nil} \lor (\texttt{d} = \mathcal{E}[\![\texttt{E}]\!]\sigma \neq \texttt{nil})\\
\mathcal{C}[\![\texttt{C; D}]\!]\sigma &= \mathcal{C}[\![\texttt{D}]\!](\mathcal{C}[\![\texttt{C}]\!]\sigma) && (\textsc{Seq}_{\text{ds}})\\
\mathcal{C}\left[\!\!\left[\begin{array}{l}\texttt{from X}\\ \texttt{loop C}\\ \texttt{until Y}\end{array}\right]\!\!\right]\sigma &= \sigma' \quad \text{if } \mathcal{E}[\![\texttt{X}]\!]\sigma = \texttt{t} \land \sigma' = \mathit{fix}(F)(\sigma) && (\textsc{Loop}_{\text{ds}})
\end{aligned}$$

$$\text{where } F(\varphi) = \{\, (\sigma,\sigma) \mid \sigma(\texttt{Y}) = \texttt{t} \,\} \cup \left\{ (\sigma,\sigma_2) \;\middle|\; \begin{array}{l} \sigma(\texttt{Y}) = \texttt{f}, \sigma_1 = \mathcal{C}[\![\texttt{C}]\!]\sigma,\\ \sigma_1(\texttt{X}) = \texttt{f}, \sigma_2 = \varphi(\sigma_1) \end{array} \right\}$$

(c) Semantic function for commands $\mathcal{C}$.

$$\mathcal{P}_{\text{ds}}[\![\texttt{P}]\!]\texttt{d} = \texttt{d'} \quad \text{if } \mathcal{C}[\![\texttt{C}]\!](\sigma_{\texttt{X}}(\texttt{d})) = \sigma_{\texttt{X}}(\texttt{d'}) \text{ and } \texttt{P} \text{ is } \texttt{read X; C; write X}$$

(d) Semantic function for command programs $\mathcal{P}_{\text{ds}}$.

Fig. 2. Denotational semantics of R-CORE, adapted from [10] with minor notational changes, including an explicit side condition for $\textsc{Asn}_{\text{ds}}$.

Semantics for Expressions. The semantic function for expressions $\mathcal{E}$ is shown in Fig. 2b. Given a store containing the values of the variables appearing in an expression `E`, the semantic function $\mathcal{E}$ maps `E` together with the store σ to the value $\mathcal{E}[\![\texttt{E}]\!]\sigma = \texttt{d}$ ($\in \mathbb{D}$) denoted by `E`. The values of `hd X` and `tl X` are undefined if the value of `X` is `nil`. Formally, $\mathcal{E} : \texttt{Expressions} \to (\texttt{Stores} \rightharpoonup \mathbb{D})$. For a given expression `E`, the partial function $\mathcal{E}[\![\texttt{E}]\!] : \texttt{Stores} \rightharpoonup \mathbb{D}$ is not necessarily injective: different stores can yield the same value. The double brackets $[\![\cdot]\!]$ explicitly indicate that the argument is source code rather than a value. Because it does not appear on the right-hand sides, the function $\mathcal{E}$ is not recursive, as expressions are not recursively defined in Fig. 1.

The store update by an assignment is defined using the update operator:

$$\mathtt{d} \odot \mathtt{e} = \begin{cases} \mathtt{e} & \text{if } \mathtt{d} = \mathtt{nil} \\ \mathtt{nil} & \text{if } \mathtt{d} = \mathtt{e} \neq \mathtt{nil}\,. \end{cases} \tag{2}$$

Note that $(\mathtt{d} \odot \mathtt{e}) \odot \mathtt{e} = \mathtt{d}$ if $\mathtt{d}$ is $\mathtt{nil}$ or $\mathtt{d} = \mathtt{e}$, meaning that applying $(\odot\, \mathtt{e})$ twice results in the original $\mathtt{d}$ in those cases.

For example, when $\sigma = \{\mathtt{X} \mapsto (\mathtt{nil.nil}), \mathtt{Y} \mapsto \mathtt{nil}, \dots\}$, we obtain $\mathcal{E}[\![\mathtt{cons\ X\ Y}]\!]\sigma = ((\mathtt{nil.nil}).\mathtt{nil})$. Since neither $\mathcal{E}$ nor $\mathcal{E}[\![\mathtt{E}]\!]$ is injective, the resulting value `((nil.nil).nil)` does not determine whether it was obtained from the expression `cons X Y` or from the particular store σ.

Semantics for Commands. Whereas expressions compute values, commands introduce control flow and transform the store.

The semantic function for commands $\mathcal{C}$ is shown in Fig. 2c. Given a store σ, the function $\mathcal{C}$ maps `C` together with the store σ to the store $\mathcal{C}[\![\mathtt{C}]\!]\sigma = \sigma'$ ($\in$ `Stores`) that `C` denotes. Formally, $\mathcal{C} : \mathtt{Commands} \to (\mathtt{Stores} \rightharpoonup \mathtt{Stores})$. Because commands may fail to terminate, $\mathcal{C}[\![\mathtt{C}]\!]$ is a partial injective function for all commands `C`.

A reversible loop `from X loop C until Y` uses an assertion `X` and a test `Y` to control the iteration of `C`. At loop entry, `X` must hold the value `t`. If `Y` is `t`, the loop terminates; otherwise, `C` is executed. As long as both `X` and `Y` remain `f`, `C` is repeatedly executed. Thus, the loop behaves as a reversible construct in which `C` may be executed zero or more times. The reversible flowchart [29] corresponding to a reversible loop is shown in Fig. 4b.

Semantics for Programs. For a program to be reversible, the values of all variables must be well defined in both the initial and final stores, that is, before and after the evaluation of the main command `C`. All variables are required to be bound to `nil`, with the exception of the variable `X`, which is used after `read` and `write`. The store $\sigma_{\mathtt{Xi}}(\mathtt{d})$ denotes the mapping that binds the variable `Xi` to the data `d`, while assigning the value `nil` to all other variables:

$$\sigma_{\mathtt{Xi}}(\mathtt{d}) = \{\mathtt{X0} \mapsto \mathtt{nil}, \dots, \mathtt{Xi} \mapsto \mathtt{d}, \dots, \mathtt{X9} \mapsto \mathtt{nil}\}\,. \tag{3}$$

The semantic function for programs $\mathcal{P}_{\text{ds}}$ is shown in Fig. 2d, where the subscript "ds" explicitly indicates that the function is derived from the ds semantics. Given a program `P` and data `d`, the semantic function $\mathcal{P}_{\text{ds}}$ maps `P` together with `d` to the data `d'`. $\mathcal{P}_{\text{ds}}[\![\mathtt{P}]\!]$ is partial and injective.

The ds semantics provides a functional characterization of reversible computation, while leaving the details of step-by-step execution implicit, just as in the irreversible case.

3 Reversible Small-Step Operational Semantics

While the ds semantics presented in Sect. 2 provides a functional characterization of R-CORE programs, it abstracts away intermediate control states and does not describe how execution proceeds in a step-by-step manner. In particular, although commands are interpreted as partial injective functions on stores, the denotational perspective alone does not explain how reversibility is preserved at the level of individual execution steps. This limitation becomes critical when considering reversibility at the meta level, such as the construction of reversible interpreters or debuggers, whose transitions must themselves be invertible.

To tackle this problem, this section introduces a reversible ss semantics. The key idea is to make control explicit by representing execution states as configurations equipped with a control token that indicates the current position within the program. By carefully designing this control-token movement, we define a transition system in which every inference rule is reversible by construction.

Unlike a typical program-counter-based abstract machine, our approach preserves syntactic structure while making control explicit. Because the control token moves within the syntax tree, semantic properties can be proved by structural induction, which simplifies correctness proofs compared to approaches that rely on external control mechanisms.

Reversible Flowcharts. To make control explicit reversibly, we use reversible flowcharts as an intermediate representation of program execution. A reversible flowchart consists of a finite set of nodes connected by directed edges, together with a distinguished entry and exit node. Each node represents an atomic reversible operation, and the direction of edges determines the flow of control. Importantly, the structure of the flowchart is designed so that control flow can be followed uniquely in both the forward and backward directions. This representation is independent of any particular programming language and its implementation.

Figure 3 shows the atomic building blocks used to construct reversible flowcharts. These include steps (corresponding to reversible assignments), tests and assertions (which branch or merge control flow depending on a variable's value), and terminal nodes that delimit the beginning and end of a program.

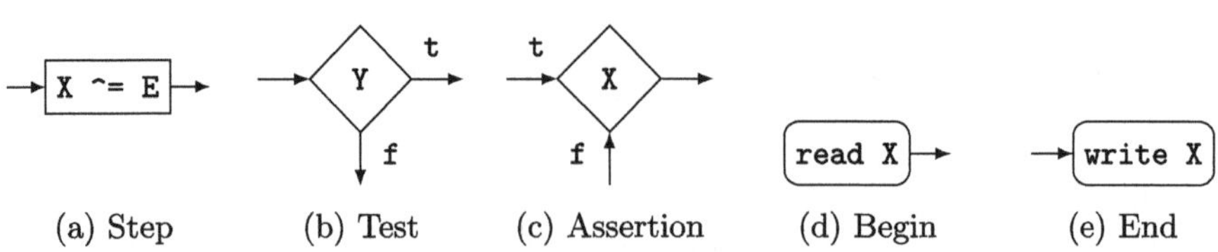

Fig. 3. The three atomic operations of reversible flowcharts (a–c) and the terminal nodes (d–e), based on the definition in [29].

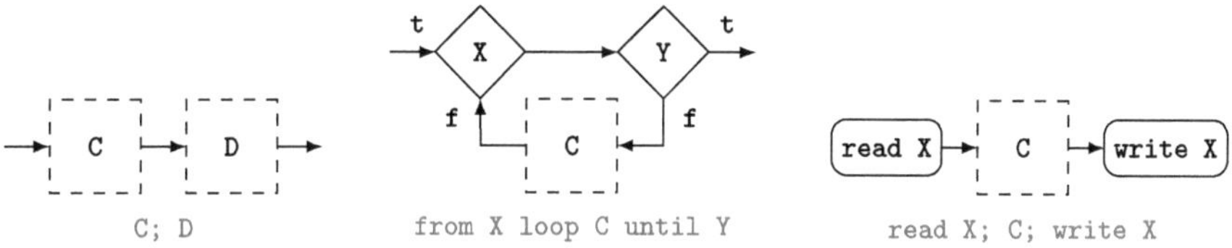

(a) Sequence (b) Reversible loop (c) Structured terminals.

Fig. 4. The two structured reversible control-flow operators of commands (a–b) and structured terminals (c), based on the definition in [29].

A test and an assertion are represented by the same underlying diamond-shaped node. The difference lies solely in the direction and labeling of the incoming and outgoing edges. Flipping all three edge directions exchanges tests and assertions; they are mutually symmetric.

Figure 4 illustrates two reversible structured control-flow operators used to build structured reversible flowcharts, based on the definition presented in [29]. A flowchart constructed only from structured control-flow operators and steps is defined as *structured* if it has exactly one entry point and one exit point.

The gray R-CORE constructs in Fig. 4 correspond to each flowchart operator.

Control in Reversible Flowcharts. To describe stepwise reversible execution, control is made explicit via a control token •, which marks the current position in a reversible flowchart. At any moment, exactly one token is present, and its location determines the next step and the previous step. The movement of the token yields an operational view of control flow. Figures 5, 6 and 7 depict the token movement, where edge labels denote the corresponding inference rules, cited later.

(a) Initialization (b) Finalization

Fig. 5. Control flow on terminals.

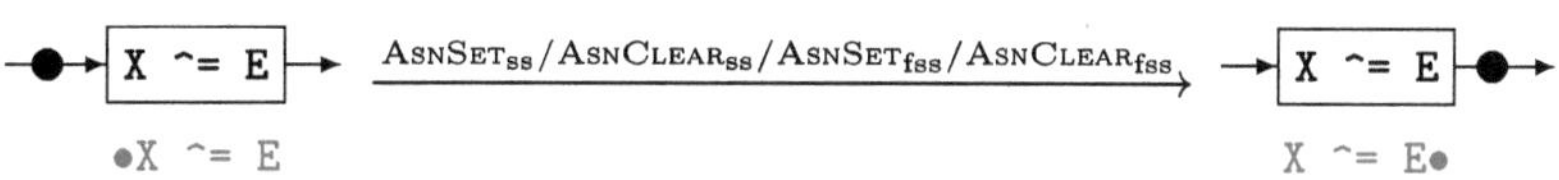

Fig. 6. Control-token flow on steps and their controlled commands.

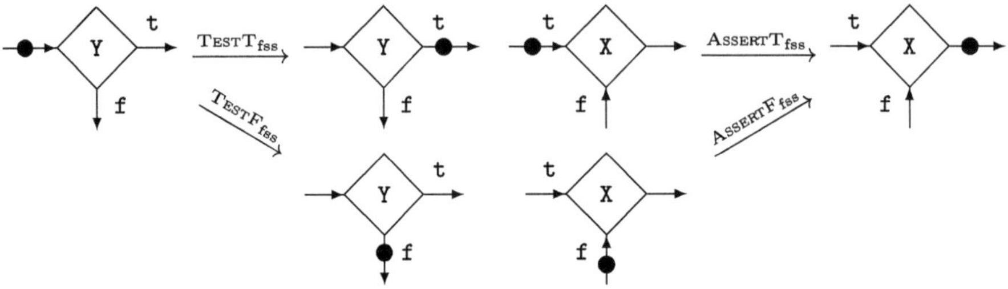

(a) Test (b) Assertion

Fig. 7. Control-token flow on tests and assertions.

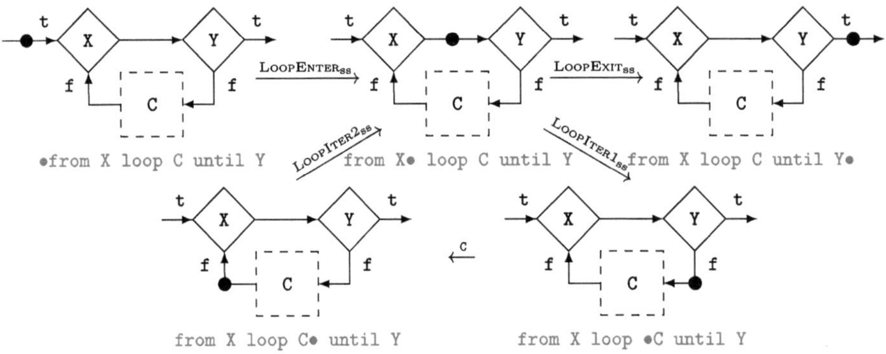

Fig. 8. Control-token flow on reversible loops and their controlled commands.

The initialization transition corresponding to `read X` (Fig. 5a) starts execution by reading an input into `X`, initializing the store as in Eq. 3, and placing the control token immediately after the terminal, while the finalization transition for `write X` (Fig. 5b) outputs the value of `X` and terminates execution by removing the token. An atomic step for a reversible assignment `X ^= E` (Fig. 6) advances the token from the position before the command to the position after it. For conditionals (Fig. 7), a test node directs control flow along the `t` or `f` edge according to the value of the tested variable, whereas an assertion node merges control flow by admitting the token only from an edge consistent with the asserted value. Tests and assertions are structurally dual: flipping all incident edge directions exchanges their roles. This duality guarantees unique traversal in both forward and backward directions. Each atomic transition rule induces a partial injective transition on configurations. Consequently, the overall transition relation is also partial injective.

Figure 8 illustrates the control-token movement for a reversible loop and visualizes how control flows through the loop while preserving reversibility. All transitions in the figure follow the control-token discipline introduced above. Execution enters the loop at the assertion `X`, where `X` is required to hold `t`, and the control token advances along the transition labeled LoopEnter$_{ss}$.

At the test Y, if Y evaluates to t, the control token follows the exit branch labeled $\textsc{LoopExit}_{ss}$ and the loop terminates. Otherwise, it follows $\textsc{LoopIter1}_{ss}$ to the loop body and executes C. After C completes via the transition $\xleftarrow{\mathtt{C}}$, the token returns to the assertion X. At this point, X must evaluate to f, and the token proceeds along the transition $\textsc{LoopIter2}_{ss}$, initiating the next iteration.

Reversible Expression Evaluation. Because standard denotational evaluation is not injective, a conventional small-step rule such as $(\mathtt{X}, \sigma) \rightarrow \sigma(\mathtt{X})$ does not retain sufficient information to recover the input configuration. To guarantee reversibility at the meta level, we therefore make expression evaluation explicitly information-preserving by retaining the original input.

Concretely, an evaluation step records the expression and the store together with the resulting value:

$$(\mathtt{E}, \sigma) \rightarrow (\mathtt{d}, (\mathtt{E}, \sigma))\,. \tag{4}$$

This makes each evaluation step a partial injective function, so its inverse relation $\rightarrow^{-1}$ is also well defined. The resulting inference rules for reversible expression evaluation are shown in Fig. 9a. Since expressions in R-CORE are non-recursive, simply retaining the input alone suffices, without requiring a full compute–copy–uncompute construction.

Reversible Command Evaluation. The store is updated by *command evaluation.* To define a compositional ss semantics while preserving reversibility, we use *evaluation contexts*, commands with exactly one hole [] indicating the next instruction to be evaluated:

$$E ::= [\,] \mid E\texttt{; D} \mid \texttt{D; } E \mid \texttt{from X loop } E \texttt{ until Y}, \tag{5}$$

so that, for any command D, the command $E[\mathtt{D}]$ denotes a well-formed command.

Control flow is made explicit by a control token $\bullet$, marking the current execution position. An *instruction* is a command containing exactly one control token, defined as follows:

$$\begin{aligned} I ::= \; & \bullet\texttt{X ^= E} \mid \texttt{X ^= E}\bullet \\ & \mid \bullet\texttt{from X loop C until Y} \mid \texttt{from X}\bullet\texttt{ loop C until Y} \\ & \mid \texttt{from X loop }\bullet\texttt{C until Y} \mid \texttt{from X loop C}\bullet\texttt{ until Y} \\ & \mid \texttt{from X loop C until Y}\,\bullet \end{aligned} \tag{6}$$

The first two forms correspond to reversible assignments (Fig. 6); the others correspond to reversible loops and match the control-token movements in Fig. 8.

$E[I]$ contains exactly one control token. A command containing exactly one control token in a valid instruction position is called a *controlled command*, written $\underline{\mathtt{C}}$. For all evaluation contexts E and instructions I, $E[I]$ is a controlled command.

Controlled commands are identified up to structural congruences

$$\bullet\,(\texttt{C; D}) \equiv (\bullet\texttt{C})\texttt{; D} \qquad (\texttt{C}\bullet)\texttt{; D} \equiv \texttt{C;}(\bullet\texttt{D}) \qquad (\texttt{C; D})\bullet \equiv \texttt{C;}(\texttt{D}\bullet) \tag{7}$$

These equations are understood up to congruence, i.e., they may be applied to any subcommand. Here, parentheses are meta-level grouping notation and are not part of the syntax of R-CORE. These congruences express that control before, after, or between sequential commands is equivalent. Modulo these congruences, the decomposition of a controlled command $E[I]$ into an evaluation context E and an instruction I is unique whenever the instruction is of the form $I = \bullet\texttt{D}$ or $\texttt{D}\bullet$.

Inference Rules. Figure 9a gives reversible expression-evaluation rules of the form $(\texttt{E}, \sigma) \to (\texttt{d}, (\texttt{E}, \sigma))$, which preserve the original input in the second argument and therefore are invertible, following the convention of Bennett's method [3]. In R-CORE, expression evaluation does not modify the store, although in more general settings the store may also change during reversible evaluation.

Figure 9b defines transitions for controlled commands, where the subscript "ss" denotes the syntax-based ss semantics. Configurations are pairs $(\underline{\texttt{C}}, \sigma)$ of a controlled command and a store (equivalently $(E[I], \sigma)$). By a standard abuse of notation, the same symbol $\to$ is also used for expression-evaluation transitions; the intended relation is always clear from the form of the configurations. The relation $\to$ is taken modulo the structural congruence $\equiv$ on controlled commands. Assignments advance $\bullet$ while toggling `X` between `nil` and a non-`nil` value ($\text{AsnSet}_{\text{ss}}/\text{AsnClear}_{\text{ss}}$), and loop rules move $\bullet$ according to the reversible loop flow (Fig. 8).

Lemma 1 below establishes that $\to$ is a partial injective function on configurations.

Backward execution is obtained by the inverse relation $\leftarrow = \to^{-1}$. Thus, a partially executed program can be run backward by repeatedly applying $\leftarrow$. An explicit set of backward rules could also be given, but it is unnecessary here because each forward rule is partial injective.

Lemma 1 (Reversibility of controlled command evaluation). *For any controlled commands $\underline{\texttt{C}}$, $\underline{\texttt{C}}'$, and $\underline{\texttt{C}}''$, stores σ, σ', and σ'', we have*

$$(\underline{\texttt{C}}, \sigma) \to (\underline{\texttt{C}}', \sigma') \;\wedge\; (\underline{\texttt{C}}, \sigma) \to (\underline{\texttt{C}}'', \sigma'') \;\Rightarrow\; \underline{\texttt{C}}' = \underline{\texttt{C}}'' \wedge \sigma' = \sigma'' \tag{8}$$

$$(\underline{\texttt{C}}, \sigma) \leftarrow (\underline{\texttt{C}}', \sigma') \;\wedge\; (\underline{\texttt{C}}, \sigma) \leftarrow (\underline{\texttt{C}}'', \sigma'') \;\Rightarrow\; \underline{\texttt{C}}' = \underline{\texttt{C}}'' \wedge \sigma' = \sigma'' \tag{9}$$

Equations 8 and 9 express forward and backward determinism, respectively.

Proof. We prove the first implication in Eq. 8. Let $(\underline{\texttt{C}}, \sigma)$ be a configuration. By the unique decomposition modulo congruence discussed above, $\underline{\texttt{C}}$ admits a unique pair (E, I) with $\underline{\texttt{C}} = E[I]$. By definition, $\underline{\texttt{C}}$ contains exactly one control token $\bullet$. Its position determines which inference rules may apply.

We proceed by case analysis on the syntactic form containing the control token. For reversible assignments, suppose the controlled command contains

$$\frac{}{(\mathtt{X},\sigma) \to (\sigma(\mathtt{X}), (\mathtt{X},\sigma))}\ (\text{VAR}_{\text{ss}}) \qquad \frac{}{(\mathtt{nil},\sigma) \to (\mathtt{nil}, (\mathtt{nil},\sigma))}\ (\text{NIL}_{\text{ss}})$$

$$\frac{\sigma(\mathtt{X}) = (\mathtt{d.e})}{(\mathtt{hd\ X},\sigma) \to (\mathtt{d}, (\mathtt{hd\ X},\sigma))}\ (\text{HEAD}_{\text{ss}}) \qquad \frac{\sigma(\mathtt{X}) = (\mathtt{d.e})}{(\mathtt{tl\ X},\sigma) \to (\mathtt{e}, (\mathtt{tl\ X},\sigma))}\ (\text{TAIL}_{\text{ss}})$$

$$\frac{\sigma(\mathtt{X}) = \mathtt{d} \qquad \sigma(\mathtt{Y}) = \mathtt{e}}{(\mathtt{cons\ X\ Y},\sigma) \to ((\mathtt{d.e}), (\mathtt{cons\ X\ Y},\sigma))}\ (\text{CONS}_{\text{ss}})$$

$$\frac{\sigma(\mathtt{X}) = \sigma(\mathtt{Y})}{(\mathtt{=?\ X\ Y},\sigma) \to (\mathtt{t}, (\mathtt{=?\ X\ Y},\sigma))}\ (\text{EQT}_{\text{ss}}) \qquad \frac{\sigma(\mathtt{X}) \neq \sigma(\mathtt{Y})}{(\mathtt{=?\ X\ Y},\sigma) \to (\mathtt{f}, (\mathtt{=?\ X\ Y},\sigma))}\ (\text{EQF}_{\text{ss}})$$

(a) Inference rules for expressions.

$$\frac{(\mathtt{E},\sigma) \to (\mathtt{e}, (\mathtt{E},\sigma)) \qquad \mathtt{e} \neq \mathtt{nil}}{(E[\bullet\mathtt{X\ \hat{}{=}\ E}], \sigma \uplus \{\mathtt{X} \mapsto \mathtt{nil}\}) \to (E[\mathtt{X\ \hat{}{=}\ E}\bullet], \sigma \uplus \{\mathtt{X} \mapsto \mathtt{e}\})}\ (\text{ASNSET}_{\text{ss}})$$

$$\frac{\mathtt{d} \neq \mathtt{nil} \qquad (\mathtt{E},\sigma) \to (\mathtt{d}, (\mathtt{E},\sigma))}{(E[\bullet\mathtt{X\ \hat{}{=}\ E}], \sigma \uplus \{\mathtt{X} \mapsto \mathtt{d}\}) \to (E[\mathtt{X\ \hat{}{=}\ E}\bullet], \sigma \uplus \{\mathtt{X} \mapsto \mathtt{nil}\})}\ (\text{ASNCLEAR}_{\text{ss}})$$

$$\frac{\sigma(\mathtt{X}) = \mathtt{t}}{(E[\bullet\mathtt{from\ X\ loop\ C\ until\ Y}],\sigma) \to (E[\mathtt{from\ X}\bullet\ \mathtt{loop\ C\ until\ Y}],\sigma)}\ (\text{LOOPENTER}_{\text{ss}})$$

$$\frac{\sigma(\mathtt{Y}) = \mathtt{t}}{(E[\mathtt{from\ X}\bullet\ \mathtt{loop\ C\ until\ Y}],\sigma) \to (E[\mathtt{from\ X\ loop\ C\ until\ Y}\bullet],\sigma)}\ (\text{LOOPEXIT}_{\text{ss}})$$

$$\frac{\sigma(\mathtt{Y}) = \mathtt{f}}{(E[\mathtt{from\ X}\bullet\ \mathtt{loop\ C\ until\ Y}],\sigma) \to (E[\mathtt{from\ X\ loop}\ \bullet\mathtt{C\ until\ Y}],\sigma)}\ (\text{LOOPITER1}_{\text{ss}})$$

$$\frac{\sigma(\mathtt{X}) = \mathtt{f}}{(E[\mathtt{from\ X\ loop\ C}\bullet\ \mathtt{until\ Y}],\sigma) \to (E[\mathtt{from\ X}\bullet\ \mathtt{loop\ C\ until\ Y}],\sigma)}\ (\text{LOOPITER2}_{\text{ss}})$$

(b) Inference rules for controlled commands.

$$\mathcal{P}_{\text{ss}}[\![\mathtt{P}]\!](\mathtt{d}) = \mathtt{e} \quad \text{if } (\bullet\mathtt{C}, \sigma_{\mathtt{X}}(\mathtt{d})) \to^{+} (\mathtt{C}\bullet, \sigma_{\mathtt{X}}(\mathtt{e})) \text{ and } \mathtt{P} \text{ is } \mathtt{read\ X;\ C;\ write\ X}$$

(c) Semantic function for programs.

Fig. 9. Small-step reversible operational semantics of R-CORE.

$\bullet\mathtt{X\ \hat{}{=}\ E}$. Since in all loop rules the token is followed by keywords, only the first two assignment rules can match. These rules are distinguished by their premises on the store.

For reversible loops, the applicable inference rule is determined by the keyword immediately following $\bullet$. In the case where the next keyword is `loop`, the premises distinguish the two possibilities by the value of `Y`. Hence, at most one inference rule applies in each case.

The second equation (Eq. 9) follows by the same applied to the inverse relation: each right-hand side (conclusion) of the forward inference rules in Fig. 9b, together with the rule's premises, determines its left-hand side uniquely. □

This result establishes reversibility of command execution at the meta level. Although expressions are evaluated in a single step here, the result is independent of this choice and still holds if expression evaluation requires multiple steps.

The ss semantics of a program P is defined by the *program evaluation* function $\mathcal{P}_{ss}$ shown in Fig. 9c. Here, $\rightarrow^+$ denotes the transitive closure of $\rightarrow$. By Lemma 1, for all P, $\mathcal{P}_{ss}[\![\mathtt{P}]\!]$ is a partial injective function.

```
read X;
from X loop
  Y ^= X; X ^= Y; // move X to Y, assuming Y is nil
  X ^= cons Z Y; // Z=nil
  Y ^= hd X; // zero clear Y
until Z;
write X
```

Fig. 10. A program that terminates abnormally if X is nil, and otherwise loops infinitely, incrementing the unary number stored in X by one in each iteration.

Distinguishing Stuck and Non-terminating States. Our ss semantics makes explicit the distinction between *stuck* and *non-terminating* computations through the position of the control token. Unlike traditional syntax-level semantics [18] where these states are implicitly tied to specific control structures, our approach characterizes them through the movement of the control token •.

A configuration is *stuck* if the control token • does not appear at the end of a command and no inference rule applies. In such a configuration, execution cannot proceed, even though the program has not terminated.

To illustrate this within the context of structured syntax, consider the program in Fig. 10. The following configuration is stuck, since the entry assertion of the loop is violated and no transition is defined in LoopEnter$_{ss}$:

$$(\bullet\mathtt{from\ X\ loop}\cdots\mathtt{until\ Z}, \{\mathtt{X}\mapsto\mathtt{nil},\ldots\})$$

In contrast, a computation is *non-terminating* when an infinite derivation sequence continues. For example, the following program loops infinitely. When the initial value of X is non-nil, the loop body repeatedly increments a unary number stored in X, yielding an infinite sequence of transitions:

$$\begin{aligned}&(\mathtt{from\ X\ loop}\bullet\mathtt{C\ until\ Z}, \{\mathtt{X}\mapsto\mathtt{nil}^2, \mathtt{Y}\mapsto\mathtt{nil}, \mathtt{Z}\mapsto\mathtt{nil},\ldots\})\rightarrow^4\\&(\mathtt{from\ X\ loop\ C}\bullet\mathtt{until\ Z}, \{\mathtt{X}\mapsto\mathtt{nil}^3, \mathtt{Y}\mapsto\mathtt{nil}, \mathtt{Z}\mapsto\mathtt{nil},\ldots\})\rightarrow\\&(\mathtt{from\ X\ loop}\bullet\mathtt{C\ until\ Z}, \{\mathtt{X}\mapsto\mathtt{nil}^4, \mathtt{Y}\mapsto\mathtt{nil}, \mathtt{Z}\mapsto\mathtt{nil},\ldots\})\rightarrow\cdots\end{aligned}$$

Here, $\mathtt{nil}^n$ is the unary numeral for n, defined by nil for $n = 0$ and $(\mathtt{nil.nil}^{n-1})$ for $n \geq 1$. C increments X by one, and $\rightarrow^n$ is the n-step iteration of $\rightarrow$.

In the ss semantics, these properties can be verified using a limited set of syntactic constructs and inference rules, which facilitates formal verification, e.g., in theorem-proving systems.

4 Bridging Syntax and Flowchart Topology

While the ss semantics presented in Sect. 3 captures the behavior of R-CORE as a structured programming language, it abstracts away the topological structure of reversible execution. In the reversible flowchart model [29], computation is defined by movement of a control token through a network of atomic nodes: steps (reversible updates), tests (conditional branches), and assertions (control joins). The atomic nodes underlying R-CORE programs are shown in Fig. 3.

The syntax-based ss semantics in Fig. 9 and the fss semantics in Fig. 11 differ in the granularity of the objects placed in the hole of an evaluation context. In the ss semantics, the hole contains a syntax-level object, such as an assignment or loop with a control. In the fss semantics, the hole contains a flowchart node with a control, namely a step or test/assertion with a control. The two semantics expose control-token movement at different levels of structural detail. The fss semantics therefore refines the syntax-based presentation by describing control-token movement at the level of atomic flowchart nodes. Both semantics describe the same behavior, but the fss semantics observes control flow at the level of the underlying flowchart topology shown in Figs. 5, 6 and 7.

To make this correspondence explicit, we introduce a *finer-grained* small-step semantics, denoted by the subscript "$_{\text{fss}}$". This semantics decomposes each structured command of R-CORE into its flowchart atoms, steps, tests, and assertions, and models execution as movement of the control token • across these atoms. In contrast to the structured small-step semantics, each transition in the fss semantics corresponds to exactly one traversal of a flowchart edge.

We assume suitable *evaluation contexts for flowcharts*, written E_{fss}. A flowchart context is a reversible flowchart with one distinguished hole for an atomic node. Filling the hole with a controlled step, test, or assertion yields a controlled flowchart. These contexts specify the surrounding flowchart topology in which a single atomic node is active and allow the operational semantics to be defined compositionally. One could introduce a textual syntax for such flowcharts, but this would only be another notation for the same flowchart contexts. We therefore present the fss semantics directly over atomic flowchart nodes and flowchart contexts.

This fss semantics serves two purposes. First, it provides a formal verification that the surface syntax of R-CORE corresponds exactly to well-formed reversible flowcharts. Each syntactic control construct induces a unique and admissible movement of the control token, and each movement matches a valid traversal in the underlying flowchart topology.

Second, the finer-grained semantics makes the source of reversibility explicit at the atomic level. Each flowchart atom is defined so that its local transition is a partial injective function. In particular, test and assertion nodes form inverse pairs: a branching decision made by a test node is uniquely recovered by the corresponding assertion node that joins control flow. Consequently, global reversibility follows directly from the local reversibility of these atomic transfers.

This atomic view of reversibility has consequences beyond R-CORE. Because reversibility is enforced locally at individual flowchart nodes and control-token movements, it naturally supports reversible execution at a lower level of computation. As a result, the same principles apply not only to structured languages such as R-CORE but also to unstructured reversible flowcharts and low-level reversible languages. In this sense, the fss semantics is language-independent: it characterizes reversibility as a topological property of control flow rather than a feature tied to surface syntax.

Figure 11 presents the finer-grained small-step reversible operational semantics. Figure 11a defines inference rules for controlled flowcharts, where each rule corresponds to movement of the control token across a single atomic node. Reversible assignments are decomposed into forward and backward steps, while tests and assertions are treated explicitly as branching and joining nodes whose transitions are mutually inverse. Here, $\xrightarrow{\mathrm{X}}$ denotes a subset of the transition relation $\rightarrow$, consisting of those configuration pairs whose transition is given by inference rule X. This makes control flow and information preservation explicit at the level of individual flowchart atoms. Figure 11b defines the semantic function for whole programs in the finer-grained setting. This fss semantics is operationally equivalent to the reversible flowchart semantics of [29].

The ss semantics describes reversible execution using structured syntax, whereas the fss semantics operates directly on reversible flowchart topology. Consequently, the fss semantics can express reversible control structures that are not expressible in R-CORE's syntax, including unstructured reversible control flow.

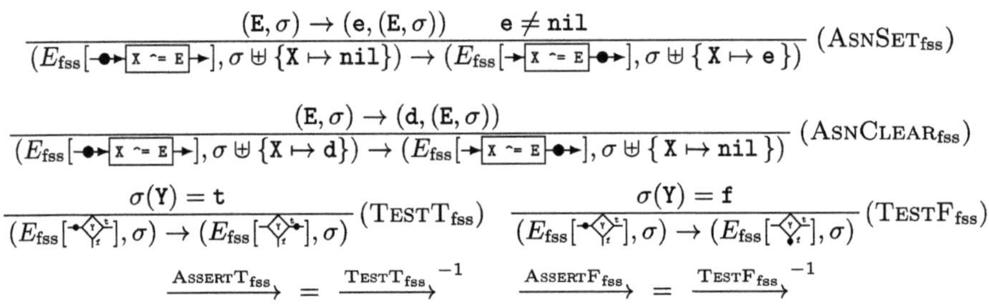

(a) Inference rules for controlled flowcharts.

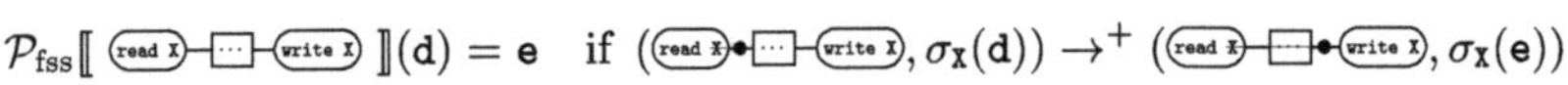

(b) Semantic function for reversible flowcharts with an entry and an exit.

Fig. 11. Finer-grained small-step reversible operational semantics.

5 Semantic Equivalence and Reversibility

We relate the three semantic descriptions of R-CORE introduced here: denotational semantics (ds), syntax-based ss semantics (ss), and topology-based finer-grained semantics (fss). Although defined at different abstraction levels, these semantics coincide on observable program behavior.

More precisely, for any program P and input data d, the ds semantics $\mathcal{P}_{\text{ds}}[\![\texttt{P}]\!](\texttt{d})$ is defined if and only if there exists a finite ss-derivation from the initial configuration to a final configuration producing the same output. Moreover, such an ss-derivation exists if and only if there exists a corresponding fss-derivation in which the control token traverses the underlying reversible flowchart from entry to exit. In all cases, the output data coincide.

Therefore, the three semantics (ds, ss, and fss semantics) define the same partial injective function from inputs to outputs. The three formalisms differ in granularity and presentation: ds abstracts away control flow, ss captures structured control evolution syntactically, and fss makes the underlying flowchart topology explicit.

Theorem 1 (Semantic Equivalence). *For any R-CORE program* P *and input data* d*, the following are equivalent:*

1. *The ds semantics* $\mathcal{P}_{\text{ds}}[\![\texttt{P}]\!](\texttt{d})$ *is defined and yields output* e.
2. *There exists a finite small-step operational derivation (ss):* $(\bullet\texttt{C}, \sigma_{\texttt{X}}(\texttt{d})) \rightarrow^{+} (\texttt{C}\bullet, \sigma_{\texttt{X}}(\texttt{e}))$ *where* P *is of the form* `read X; C; write X`.
3. *There exists a finite finer-grained derivation (fss) in which the control token traverses the underlying reversible flowchart from entry to exit, producing the output* e.

Moreover, when defined, all three semantics yield the same output value e.

The proof proceeds by induction on the structure of commands, together with induction on the length of finite ss and fss derivations.

All semantic descriptions of R-CORE considered here are reversible at the meta level. That is, reversibility holds not only for observable input–output behavior, but also for the semantic definitions themselves.

6 Related Work

Our approach is based on the standard model of reversible flowcharts [11], where traced monoidal categories serve as the theoretical foundation [8]. Our control-token mechanism can be seen as a Geometry of Interaction (GoI) Machine that avoids the overhead of history-keeping by exploiting the structural properties of reversible flowcharts. Reversible GoI machines for Linear Combinatory Logic and Gödel's System T have been investigated [1,23]. R-CORE carefully avoids, through language design, the boundary at which irreversibility arises as identified in [1], while still allowing constants for the binary tree values and conditionals.

Non-destructive state management via tokens is conceptually related to established techniques in reversible concurrent calculi, notably RCCS (Reversible CCS) [5] where each thread carries a stack-like memory of past actions, and CCS with Keys (CCSK) [25] where execution history is tracked by keys while keeping the process structure static. Although these calculi are inherently concurrent, our approach can be understood as a specialization to the sequential case, with the degree of concurrency restricted to one.

From a semantic perspective, structural reductions that discard information correspond to information effects, which explains why conventional inference rules fail to be reversible [14].

Reversible semantics of small granularity have been investigated for various reversible abstractions, such as [1,2,7,16,24], with [18] providing the first small-step semantics for a high-level reversible language. A closely related recent work [21] also gives a reversible small-step semantics for Janus based on a program counter and control-flow graph representation. In contrast, our semantics targets the smaller language R-CORE and uses a control token in the syntax and in the corresponding flowchart topology. We emphasize a clean and simple design at both the object and meta levels, deriving reversibility directly from the injectivity of a small set of atomic transitions in a reversible flowchart.

R-CORE is a restricted fragment of Janus, but our aim here is purification rather than mere restriction. By expressing control reversibility directly through syntactic structure, the semantics facilitates concise and closed proofs of reversibility and semantic equivalence by structural induction, which would be harder to obtain, or at least more involved, in more expressive languages.

7 Conclusion

This paper presented two reversible operational semantics for R-CORE (ss and fss), a core language capturing structured reversible computation. Starting from the ds semantics, we introduced a syntax-based ss semantics that makes control flow explicit via a control token. We then refined this semantics into a finer-grained form that reflects the topology of reversible flowcharts, clarifying the correspondence between structured commands and atomic flowchart operations.

We showed that the ds semantics, the syntax-based ss semantics, and the topology-based fss semantics coincide on observable behavior of R-CORE programs. Although formulated at different abstraction levels, they define the same input–output relation for terminating executions. In addition, each semantics ensures that every evaluation step is partial and injective, guaranteeing reversibility at the meta level, independently of their correspondence.

By making the relationship between syntax and flowchart topology explicit, the fss semantics bridges high-level programs and reversible flowchart execution. The approach is not specific to R-CORE and applies to other reversible languages and intermediate representations. We expect that separating syntax-oriented and topology-oriented semantics will serve as a useful design principle for reversible debuggers, interpreters, and related execution frameworks. Mechanization of the proposed semantics in a proof assistant is left for future work.

Acknowledgments. We thank the anonymous reviewers for their helpful suggestions. This work was supported by JST, CREST Grant Number JPMJCR24I4, Japan.

Disclosure of Interests. The authors have no competing interests to declare that are relevant to the content of this article.

References

1. Abramsky, S.: A structural approach to reversible computation. Theoret. Comput. Sci. **347**(3), 441–464 (2005). https://doi.org/10.1016/j.tcs.2005.07.002
2. Axelsen, H.B., Glück, R., Yokoyama, T.: Reversible machine code and its abstract processor architecture. In: Diekert, V., Volkov, M.V., Voronkov, A. (eds.) CSR 2007. LNCS, vol. 4649, pp. 56–69. Springer, Heidelberg (2007). https://doi.org/10.1007/978-3-540-74510-5_9
3. Bennett, C.H.: Logical reversibility of computation. IBM J. Res. Dev. **17**(6), 525–532 (1973). https://doi.org/10.1147/rd.176.0525
4. Bérut, A., Arakelyan, A., Petrosyan, A., Ciliberto, S., Dillenschneider, R., Lutz, E.: Experimental verification of Landauer's principle linking information and thermodynamics. Nature **483**, 187–189 (2012). https://doi.org/10.1038/nature10872
5. Danos, V., Krivine, J.: Reversible communicating systems. In: Gardner, P., Yoshida, N. (eds.) CONCUR 2004. LNCS, vol. 3170, pp. 292–307. Springer, Heidelberg (2004). https://doi.org/10.1007/978-3-540-28644-8_19
6. De Vos, A.: Endoreversible models for the thermodynamics of computing. Entropy **22**(6), 660 (2020). https://doi.org/10.3390/e22060660
7. Fernández, M., Mackie, I.: A reversible operational semantics for imperative programming languages. In: Lin, S.-W., Hou, Z., Mahony, B. (eds.) ICFEM 2020. LNCS, vol. 12531, pp. 91–106. Springer, Cham (2020). https://doi.org/10.1007/978-3-030-63406-3_6
8. Glück, R., Kaarsgaard, R.: A categorical foundation for structured reversible flowchart languages: soundness and adequacy. Log. Methods Comput. Sci. **14**(3) (2018). https://doi.org/10.23638/LMCS-14(3:16)2018
9. Glück, R., Kaarsgaard, R., Yokoyama, T.: Reversible programs have reversible semantics. In: Sekerinski, E., et al. (eds.) FM 2019. LNCS, vol. 12233, pp. 413–427. Springer, Cham (2020). https://doi.org/10.1007/978-3-030-54997-8_26
10. Glück, R., Yokoyama, T.: A minimalist's reversible while language. IEICE Trans. Inf. Syst. **E100-D**(5), 1026–1034 (2017). https://doi.org/10.1587/transinf.2016EDP7274
11. Glück, R., Yokoyama, T.: Reversible computing from a programming language perspective. Theoret. Comput. Sci. **953**, 113429 (2023). https://doi.org/10.1016/j.tcs.2022.06.010
12. Haulund, T.: Design and implementation of a reversible object-oriented programming language. Master's thesis, University of Copenhagen (2017)
13. Haulund, T., Mogensen, T.Æ., Glück, R.: Implementing reversible object-oriented language features on reversible machines. In: Phillips, I., Rahaman, H. (eds.) RC 2017. LNCS, vol. 10301, pp. 66–73. Springer, Cham (2017). https://doi.org/10.1007/978-3-319-59936-6_5
14. James, R.P., Sabry, A.: Information effects. In: Proceedings of the Principles of Programming Languages, pp. 73–84. ACM (2012). https://doi.org/10.1145/2103656.2103667
15. Jones, N.D.: Computability and Complexity: From a Programming Perspective. MIT Press (1997). https://hjemmesider.diku.dk/~neil/Comp2book.html. Revised version

16. Kluge, W.: A reversible SE(M)CD machine. In: Koopman, P., Clack, C. (eds.) IFL 1999. LNCS, vol. 1868, pp. 95–113. Springer, Heidelberg (2000). https://doi.org/10.1007/10722298_6
17. Kuroda, M., Yuen, S.: A concurrent extension of reversible imperative programming language with runtime. In: Proceedings of the IPSJ SIGPRO (Special Interest Group on Programming), Information Processing Society of Japan, pp. 2025(3)–7:1–22 (2025)
18. Lami, P., Lanese, I., Stefani, J.B.: A small-step semantics for Janus. In: Reversible Computation, pp. 105–123. Springer, Cham (2024). https://doi.org/10.1007/978-3-031-62076-8_8
19. Lami, P., Lanese, I., Stefani, J.B., Sacerdoti Coen, C., Fabbretti, G.: Reversible debugging of concurrent erlang programs: supporting imperative primitives. J. Log. Algebraic Methods Program. **138**, 100944 (2024). https://doi.org/10.1016/j.jlamp.2024.100944
20. Landauer, R.: Irreversibility and heat generation in the computing process. IBM J. Res. Dev. **5**(3), 183–191 (1961). https://doi.org/10.1147/rd.53.0183
21. Lanese, I., Vidal, G.: A reversible semantics for Janus. In: Aubert, C., Roversi, L. (eds.) RC 2026. LNCS, vol. 16626, pp. xx–yy. Springer, Cham (2026)
22. Lutz, C.: Janus: a time-reversible language (1986). Letter to R. Landauer
23. Mackie, I.: A geometry of interaction machine for Gödel's system T. In: Kennedy, J., de Queiroz, R.J.G.B. (eds.) WoLLIC 2017. LNCS, vol. 10388, pp. 229–241. Springer, Heidelberg (2017). https://doi.org/10.1007/978-3-662-55386-2_16
24. Morita, K.: Theory of Reversible Computing. Monographs in Theoretical Computer Science. Springer, Cham (2017). https://doi.org/10.1007/978-4-431-56606-9
25. Phillips, I., Ulidowski, I.: Reversing algebraic process calculi. J. Logic Algebraic Program. **73**(1–2), 70–96 (2007). https://doi.org/10.1016/j.jlap.2006.11.002
26. Plotkin, G.D.: The origins of structural operational semantics. J. Logic Algebraic Program. **60–61**, 3–15 (2004). https://doi.org/10.1016/j.jlap.2004.03.009
27. Winskel, G.: The Formal Semantics of Programming Languages: An Introduction. MIT Press (1993)
28. Yokoyama, T., Axelsen, H.B., Glück, R.: Principles of a reversible programming language. In: Proceedings of the Computing Frontiers, pp. 43–54. ACM Press (2008). https://doi.org/10.1145/1366230.1366239
29. Yokoyama, T., Axelsen, H.B., Glück, R.: Fundamentals of reversible flowchart languages. Theoret. Comput. Sci. **611**, 87–115 (2016). https://doi.org/10.1016/j.tcs.2015.07.046

PisoLang: a User-Friendly Reversible Programming Language with Inductive Types

Kosuke Onodera[1](✉), Keisuke Nakano[2], Kazuyuki Asada[2], and Kentaro Kikuchi[2]

[1] Graduate School of Information Sciences, Tohoku University, Sendai, Japan
onodera.kosuke.s5@dc.tohoku.ac.jp

[2] Research Institute of Electrical Communication, Tohoku University, Sendai, Japan
{ksk,asada,kentaro.kikuchi}@riec.tohoku.ac.jp

Abstract. Reversible programming languages aim to guarantee that every user-defined function can be inverted automatically, typically by imposing syntactic or typing restrictions. Existing high-level languages often trade usability for reversibility: for example, they may lack algebraic data types, provide nonstandard pattern matching, or require explicit type annotations. We present PisoLang, a user-oriented reversible functional language that extends the reversible core calculus of Chardonnet et al. [2] with a surface syntax with fewer restrictions, algebraic data types with constructors, and Hindley–Milner style type inference. PisoLang supports inductive types and higher-order functions, and permits controlled non-linear use of variables (including repeated variables in patterns) while preserving injectivity of pattern matching. We describe the core language with typing and evaluation rules, develop a type inference algorithm for it, and present a desugaring procedure that elaborates nested applications into an invertible let-normal form. We show expressiveness via case studies including arithmetic, polymorphic list processing, and run-length compression.

Keywords: reversible computation · functional programming · programming languages

1 Introduction

Reversible programming has been studied in a range of formalisms and language paradigms, including imperative [3,12], functional [4,7,11], and object-oriented languages [5], as well as reversible Turing machines [1] and term rewriting systems [9]. Among high-level reversible programming languages, Janus [6] and Theseus [4] are notable examples; they enable programmers to take advantage of

The full version of this paper is available at the following:
https://www.riec.tohoku.ac.jp/~ksk/pub/Onodera26rc-full.pdf.

C. Aubert and L. Roversi (Eds.): RC 2026, LNCS 16626, pp. 219–235, 2026.
https://doi.org/10.1007/978-3-032-30839-9_13

built-in abstractions: stacks with reversible push/pop in Janus and algebraic data types in Theseus. However, each language has its own shortcomings and lacks some features typically expected in high-level languages. For instance, Janus does not offer algebraic data types (ADTs), while Theseus lacks a conventional grammar for pattern matching. More specifically, a let-expression cannot appear in a branch of pattern matching, requiring users to write *labels*, which is not common among programming languages in general. Moreover, neither language supports polymorphism or type inference.

Chardonnet et al. [2] propose a Theseus-based reversible language with inductive types and pattern matching, where the body of each pattern-matching branch is expressed as a sequence of let-bindings on the right-hand side. Their focus is on expressivity and denotational semantics under reversibility constraints; accordingly, the language adopts a strict, syntactically disciplined form of pattern matching and leaves polymorphism and type inference out of scope.

Our proposed language PisoLang is based on the language of Chardonnet et al. [2], and adds several features aimed at making practical programming more convenient. PisoLang supports algebraic data types and allows programmers to use them without explicit type annotations. Thanks to type inference, functions are polymorphic by default. Moreover, PisoLang offers OCaml-style pattern matching, while requiring patterns to be non-overlapping. Finally, PisoLang is expressive enough to simulate any reversible Turing machine, and it can also encode programs written in the original language.

PisoLang is named after *p*artial *iso*morphism, and we note that it allows partial injections in addition to total bijections.

The following PisoLang program computes Fibonacci numbers. The program defines two functions `add` and `fib`. The auxiliary function `add` takes two natural numbers m and n and returns a pair $(m+n, n)$ in order to make the function injective. For example, `add (3, 4)` evaluates to `(7, 4)`. The function `fib` takes a natural number n and returns a pair of the $(n+1)$-th and the $(n+2)$-th Fibonacci numbers. The whole program evaluates to `((55, 89), 5)`: the first component is computed by `fib 9`, while the second is obtained by running `fib` backward on `(8, 13)` using `inv fib`. The operator `inv` denotes the inverse of a function; although it is primitive syntax, it can also be used in a functional style by eta-expanding it, for example as `fun f -> inv f`.

```
type nat = Z | S of nat

iso rec add = case
| (m, Z)   <-> (m, Z)
| (m, S n) <-> let (m', n') = add (S m, n) in
               (m', S n')
in

iso rec fib = case
| Z   <-> (S Z, S Z)
| S n <-> let (S (S m), n) = add (fib n) in
          (n, S (S m))
in

(fib 9, inv fib (8, 13))
```

The type `nat` of natural numbers is defined as an inductive type in a user-friendly manner. The function `add` is defined recursively by pattern matching.

Note that the case-expression represents a function with an argument. The argument is matched against the pattern on the left-hand side of one branch. Patterns in a case-expression must be pairwise non-overlapping so that the semantics does not depend on branch order. Users can use let-bindings with patterns even inside the right-hand side of a branch (`let (m', n') = add (S m, n)`) and use the bound variables for the output expression (`(m', S n')`). During backward computation, each output expression is seen as a pattern; thus, output expressions must not overlap with each other either. The function `fib` is defined in a similar manner. Notable features include nested patterns and function applications. One may use nested patterns in the left-hand side of a let-binding (`let (S (S m), n) = ...`). One may use nested function applications (`add (fib n)`), which are not available in the original language [2].

Main differences from the original language [2] are as follows:

- First-order type constructors (e.g., polymorphic lists) are supported, whereas in the original language one must define a separate list type for each element type *and* reimplement the associated operations (e.g., `map`) for each such type.
- User-defined data constructors are supported, rather than relying on generic coproduct constructors $\mathtt{inj}_l$ and $\mathtt{inj}_r$.
- Nested patterns are permitted not only in case-expressions but also in let-bindings.
- Nested function applications are also allowed in the right-hand side of a pattern-matching branch, whereas in the original language the same effect typically requires introducing a sequence of let-bindings.
- An expression may contain multiple occurrences of the same variable, which enables one to duplicate values; in the original language, duplication is expressed via a recursive macro.
- A pattern may contain multiple occurrences of the same variable, enabling equality tests that enforce equality constraints; in the original language, this is hard to express, despite being the inverse of duplication, since duplication is defined only through *recursive macros.*

$$
\begin{array}{rrl}
\text{(Variables)} & x, y, \phi ::= & [\mathtt{a}-\mathtt{z}][\mathtt{a}-\mathtt{z}0-9\_']* \\
\text{(Constructors)} & c ::= & [\mathtt{A}-\mathtt{Z}][\mathtt{a}-\mathtt{z}\mathtt{A}-\mathtt{Z}0-9]* \\
\text{(Patterns)} & p ::= & () \mid x \mid c \mid c\ p \mid (p_1, ..., p_n) \\
\text{(Values)} & v ::= & () \mid c \mid c\ v \mid (v_1, ..., v_n) \\
\text{(Expressions)} & e ::= & p \mid \mathtt{let}\ p_1 = \omega\ p_2\ \mathtt{in}\ e \\
\text{(Isos)} & \omega ::= & \phi \mid \mathtt{fix}\ \phi \to \omega \mid \mathtt{fun}\ \phi \to \omega \mid \omega_1\ \omega_2 \mid \\
 & & \mathtt{inv}\ \omega \mid (\mathtt{case}\ p_1 \leftrightarrow e_1 \mid ... \mid p_n \leftrightarrow e_n) \\
\text{(Terms)} & t ::= & () \mid x \mid c \mid c\ t \mid (t_1, ..., t_n) \mid \omega\ t \mid \\
 & & \mathtt{let}\ p = t_1\ \mathtt{in}\ t_2 \mid \mathtt{iso}\ \phi = \omega\ \mathtt{in}\ t
\end{array}
$$

Fig. 1. Grammar for terms

(Type identifiers)	$X ::= [\mathtt{a}-\mathtt{z}][\mathtt{a}-\mathtt{z0}-\mathtt{9\_'}]*$
(Type variables)	$V ::= '[\mathtt{a}-\mathtt{z}][\mathtt{a}-\mathtt{z0}-\mathtt{9\_}]*$
(Base types)	$A, B ::= \mathtt{unit} \mid X \mid V \mid A_1 \otimes ... \otimes A_n \mid (A_1, ..., A_n)\ X$
(Iso types)	$T ::= A \leftrightarrow B \mid T_1 \to T_2$

Fig. 2. Grammar for types

Outline. We design PisoLang, a reversible functional language with an OCaml-like surface syntax and ADTs, intended for programming via injective pattern matching (Sect. 2). We extend the core language of Chardonnet et al. with constructors, constructor patterns, nested applications in case branches via an elaboration to an invertible let-normal form, and controlled non-linear variable usage (Sect. 3). We give a brief overview of a Hindley–Milner style type inference algorithm for PisoLang programs (Sect. 4). We present example programs that exercise key language features and illustrate the practical expressiveness of the language (Sect. 5).

This work also has potential applications to our other project of defining a programming language that simulates involutory Turing machines [8]. A full implementation can be found here: https://github.com/42067/reversible_lang.

2 Core Language

We shall first define the core language of PisoLang. Although it is not intended to be used directly by users, its grammar and rules can be defined somewhat easily thanks to its simplicity. Note that the language allows partial functions, which implies pattern matching and the left-hand side of let-bindings are not required to be exhaustive. Furthermore, every function is guaranteed to be injective due to its restrictions.

The grammar is presented in Figs. 1 and 2. Isos consist of variables, the fixpoint combinator, function abstraction, function applications, inversion, and case-expression. The parentheses around a case-expression may be omitted; they are included in the grammar only to avoid confusion between meta-level and object-level vertical bars. Terms consist of the unit value, variables, constructors c and $c\ t$, tuples, applications $\omega\ t$, and two binding forms. As shown in the evaluation rules below, the iso ω in an application $\omega\ t$ is evaluated until it becomes a case-expression; therefore, we call this application a *case application*. Regarding the two binding forms, `iso` binding is ordinary let-binding for isos, whereas `let` binding performs pattern matching against a pattern p.

Note that $(A_1, ..., A_n)\ X$ in Fig. 2 represents a first-order type constructor application that is analogous to OCaml's postfix style (e.g., `int list` or `('a, 'b) result`). Higher-order type constructors do not exist by design.

PisoLang features *isos*, which are mostly inherited from the original language. Isos represent reversible functions of type $A \leftrightarrow B$ or $T_1 \to T_2$. Isos and terms are separated grammatically because they use different notions of substitution.

Expressions are used only in the right-hand side of pattern matching as terms with more restrictions.

In order to define typing rules in a concise manner, we provide definitions for orthogonality, type inversion, substitution, and inversion of isos. Type inversion and inversion of isos correspond to each other. Given an iso $\omega : A \leftrightarrow B$, the inverse of ω, denoted by ω^{-1}, is of type $B \leftrightarrow A$ for instance. Orthogonality indicates the non-overlap of two patterns, which determines whether a pattern matching is valid (i.e., injective) or not.

Definition 1 (Type inversion). *T^{-1}, the* inverse type *of an iso type T, is defined as $(A \leftrightarrow B)^{-1} := B \leftrightarrow A$; $(T_1 \rightarrow T_2)^{-1} := T_1^{-1} \rightarrow T_2^{-1}$.*

Definition 2 (Substitution on terms). *Let v and x be a value and a variable, respectively. A substitution on a term t, denoted by $t\langle v/x\rangle$, is defined as*

$$
\begin{aligned}
()\langle v/x\rangle &:= () & x\langle v/x\rangle &:= v & y\langle v/x\rangle &:= y \quad \text{if } y \neq x \\
c\langle v/x\rangle &:= c & (c\ t)\langle v/x\rangle &:= c\ t\langle v/x\rangle & (\omega\ t)\langle v/x\rangle &:= \omega\ t\langle v/x\rangle
\end{aligned}
$$

$$
\begin{aligned}
(t_1, ..., t_n)\langle v/x\rangle &:= (t_1\langle v/x\rangle, ..., t_n\langle v/x\rangle) \\
(\texttt{let}\ p = t_1\ \texttt{in}\ t_2)\langle v/x\rangle &:= \texttt{let}\ p = t_1\langle v/x\rangle\ \texttt{in}\ t_2\langle v/x\rangle \\
(\texttt{iso}\ \phi = \omega\ \texttt{in}\ t)\langle v/x\rangle &:= \texttt{iso}\ \phi = \omega\ \texttt{in}\ t\langle v/x\rangle.
\end{aligned}
$$

Furthermore, we write $\sigma(t)$ for $t\langle v_1/x_1\rangle...\langle v_n/x_n\rangle$ where $\sigma = \{(x_1 \mapsto v_1), ..., (x_n \mapsto v_n)\}$.

Note that capture-avoiding substitutions are not required due to the variable-free definition of values. Additionally, substitutions on terms do not substitute variables in isos. On the other hand, substitutions on isos are defined in an ordinary manner as in Definition 3.

Definition 3 (Substitution on isos). *Let ω' and ϕ be an iso and a variable, respectively. A substitution on an iso ω, denoted by $\omega[\omega'/\phi]$, is defined as*

$$
\begin{aligned}
\phi[\omega'/\phi] &:= \omega' \\
\psi[\omega'/\phi] &:= \psi && \text{if } \psi \neq \phi \\
(\texttt{fix}\ \psi \rightarrow \omega)[\omega'/\phi] &:= \texttt{fix}\ \psi \rightarrow \omega[\omega'/\phi] && \text{if } \psi \neq \phi \text{ and } \psi \notin \mathrm{FV}(\omega') \\
(\texttt{fun}\ \psi \rightarrow \omega)[\omega'/\phi] &:= \texttt{fun}\ \psi \rightarrow \omega[\omega'/\phi] && \text{if } \psi \neq \phi \text{ and } \psi \notin \mathrm{FV}(\omega') \\
(\omega_1\ \omega_2)[\omega'/\phi] &:= \omega_1[\omega'/\phi]\ \omega_2[\omega'/\phi] \\
(\texttt{inv}\ \omega)[\omega'/\phi] &:= \texttt{inv}\ \omega[\omega'/\phi]
\end{aligned}
$$

$$
\begin{aligned}
&(\texttt{case}\ p_1 \leftrightarrow e_1 \mid ... \mid p_n \leftrightarrow e_n)[\omega'/\phi] := \\
&\qquad \texttt{case}\ p_1 \leftrightarrow e_1[\omega'/\phi] \mid ... \mid p_n \leftrightarrow e_n[\omega'/\phi]
\end{aligned}
$$

where, for expression e, we define $e[\omega'/\phi]$ inductively as follows: $p[\omega'/\phi] := p$ and $(\texttt{let}\ p = \omega\ p'\ \texttt{in}\ e)[\omega'/\phi] := \texttt{let}\ p = \omega[\omega'/\phi]\ p'\ \texttt{in}\ e[\omega'/\phi]$.

Definition 4 (Orthogonality). Orthogonality, *denoted by* $\perp$, *is a binary relation on patterns such that* $p_1 \perp p_2 \overset{\text{def}}{\Leftrightarrow} \sigma(p_1) \neq \sigma(p_2)$ *for any substitution on term* σ. *We extend this definition for expressions as well:* $e_1 \perp e_2 \overset{\text{def}}{\Leftrightarrow} f(e_1) \perp f(e_2)$ *where* $f(p) = p$ *and* $f(\texttt{let}\ p_1 = \omega\ p_2\ \texttt{in}\ e) = f(e)$.

Definition 5 (Inversion of isos). ω^{-1}, *the inverse of an iso* ω, *is defined as*

$$\phi^{-1} := \phi \qquad (\omega_1\ \omega_2)^{-1} := \omega_1^{-1}\ \omega_2^{-1} \qquad (\texttt{inv}\ \omega)^{-1} := \texttt{inv}\ \omega^{-1}$$

$$(\texttt{fix}\ \phi \rightarrow \omega)^{-1} := \texttt{fix}\ \phi \rightarrow \omega^{-1} \qquad (\texttt{fun}\ \phi \rightarrow \omega)^{-1} := \texttt{fun}\ \phi \rightarrow \omega^{-1}$$

$$(\texttt{case}\ p_1 \leftrightarrow e_1 \mid \ldots \mid p_n \leftrightarrow e_n)^{-1} := \texttt{case}\ (p_1 \leftrightarrow e_1)^{-1} \mid \ldots \mid (p_n \leftrightarrow e_n)^{-1}$$

$$\text{where} \begin{pmatrix} p \leftrightarrow \texttt{let}\ p_1 = \omega_1\ p'_1\ \texttt{in} \\ \quad \ldots \\ \quad \texttt{let}\ p_n = \omega_n\ p'_n\ \texttt{in} \\ \quad p' \end{pmatrix}^{-1} := \begin{array}{l} p' \leftrightarrow \texttt{let}\ p'_n = {\omega_n}^{-1}\ p_n\ \texttt{in} \\ \quad \ldots \\ \quad \texttt{let}\ p'_1 = {\omega_1}^{-1}\ p_1\ \texttt{in} \\ \quad p \end{array}$$

Typing judgments are defined for terms, isos, and expressions in Fig. 3, 4, and 5, respectively. In the definitions, Ψ represents a context of isos while Δ denotes that of terms. Note that the rule X-Let treats Δ as a linear context, and that isos are typed without Δ; these aspects contribute to the reversibility of isos. In the pattern-typing premises of rules T-Let, I-Case, and X-Let, we use the empty iso context rather than the surrounding iso context Ψ. This is only a presentational choice. Since patterns contain no isos and since patterns contain neither `let` nor `case`, the choice of iso context in such premises does not affect the derivability of any typing judgment.

The evaluation relations are defined in Fig. 6. Our definition follows that of Chardonnet et al. [2]. For an evaluation context $I_{\Rightarrow}$, we write $I_{\Rightarrow}[\omega]^{\text{i}}$ for the iso obtained by substituting an iso ω for the iso hole $[]^{\text{i}}$. Similarly, for an evaluation context $T_{\Rightarrow}$, we write $T_{\Rightarrow}[t]^{\text{t}}$ and $T_{\Rightarrow}[\omega]^{\text{i}}$ for the terms obtained by substituting a term t for the term hole $[]^{\text{t}}$ and an iso ω for the iso hole $[]^{\text{i}}$, respectively. We usually omit these superscripts t and i, since the classes of terms and isos are disjoint and the intended hole is therefore clear.

As specified by rules E-AppFun and E-Iso, function application $\omega\ \omega'$ and let-like binding $\texttt{iso}\ \phi = \omega\ \texttt{in}\ t$ are evaluated lazily. In contrast, as specified by rules E-AppCase and E-Let, case application $\omega\ t$ and pattern-matching binding $\texttt{let}\ p = t_1\ \texttt{in}\ t_2$ are evaluated strictly: the terms to be matched are fully evaluated to values. More specifically, in the case application, the iso part ω is first reduced to a case-expression, and the argument t is then evaluated to a value before a branch is selected; similarly, in the `let` binding, t_1 is evaluated to a value before it is matched against p. In these two rules, the condition $\text{dom}(\sigma) = \text{FV}(p_i)$ (or $\text{FV}(p)$) represents that σ is a *minimal* substitution on terms: it consists of only substitutions required for pattern matching. If no branch admits such a substitution, evaluation is stuck, as illustrated by Example 6 below.

$$\frac{}{\Psi; \Delta \vdash () : \texttt{unit}}\ (\text{T-Unit}) \qquad \frac{}{\Psi; \Delta, x : A \vdash x : A}\ (\text{T-Var})$$

$$\frac{c : A}{\Psi; \Delta \vdash c : A}\ (\text{T-Ctor0}) \qquad \frac{c : A \leftrightarrow B \qquad \Psi; \Delta \vdash t : A}{\Psi; \Delta \vdash c\ t : B}\ (\text{T-Ctor1})$$

$$\frac{\Psi; \Delta \vdash t_1 : A_1 \qquad ... \qquad \Psi; \Delta \vdash t_n : A_n}{\Psi; \Delta \vdash (t_1, ..., t_n) : A_1 \otimes ... \otimes A_n}\ (\text{T-Tuple})$$

$$\frac{\Psi \vdash_\omega \omega : A \leftrightarrow B \qquad \Psi; \Delta \vdash t : A}{\Psi; \Delta \vdash \omega\ t : B}\ (\text{T-App})$$

$$\frac{\Psi \vdash_\omega \omega : T \qquad \Psi, \phi : T; \Delta \vdash t : A}{\Psi; \Delta \vdash \texttt{iso}\ \phi = \omega\ \texttt{in}\ t : A}\ (\text{T-Iso})$$

$$\frac{\begin{array}{c}\{x_1, ..., x_n\} = \text{FV}(p) \quad \emptyset; x_1 : A_1, ..., x_n : A_n \vdash p : A \\ \Psi; \Delta \vdash t_1 : A \quad \Psi; \Delta, x_1 : A_1, ..., x_n : A_n \vdash t_2 : B\end{array}}{\Psi; \Delta \vdash \texttt{let}\ p = t_1\ \texttt{in}\ t_2 : B}\ (\text{T-Let})$$

Fig. 3. Typing rules for terms

$$\frac{}{\Psi, \phi : T \vdash_\omega \phi : T}\ (\text{I-Var}) \qquad \frac{\Psi, \phi : T \vdash_\omega \omega : T}{\Psi \vdash_\omega \texttt{fix}\ \phi \to \omega : T}\ (\text{I-Fix})$$

$$\frac{\Psi \vdash_\omega \omega^{-1} : T}{\Psi \vdash_\omega \texttt{inv}\ \omega : T}\ (\text{I-Inv}) \qquad \frac{\Psi, \phi : T_1 \vdash_\omega \omega : T_2}{\Psi \vdash_\omega \texttt{fun}\ \phi \to \omega : T_1 \to T_2}\ (\text{I-Fun})$$

$$\frac{\Psi \vdash_\omega \omega_1 : T_2 \to T_1 \qquad \Psi \vdash_\omega \omega_2 : T_2}{\Psi \vdash_\omega \omega_1\ \omega_2 : T_1}\ (\text{I-App})$$

$$\frac{\begin{array}{c}\emptyset; \Delta_1 \vdash p_1 : A \quad ... \quad \emptyset; \Delta_n \vdash p_n : A \quad \forall i \neq j, p_i \perp p_j \\ \Psi; \Delta_1 \vdash_e e_1 : B \quad ... \quad \Psi; \Delta_n \vdash_e e_n : B \quad \forall i \neq j, e_i \perp e_j\end{array}}{\Psi \vdash_\omega \texttt{case}\ p_1 \leftrightarrow e_1 \mid ... \mid p_n \leftrightarrow e_n : A \leftrightarrow B}\ (\text{I-Case})$$

Fig. 4. Typing rules for isos

$$\frac{}{\Psi; \emptyset \vdash_e () : \texttt{unit}}\ (\text{X-Unit}) \qquad \frac{}{\Psi; x : A \vdash_e x : A}\ (\text{X-Var})$$

$$\frac{c : A}{\Psi; \emptyset \vdash_e c : A}\ (\text{X-Ctor0}) \qquad \frac{c : A \leftrightarrow B \qquad \emptyset; \Delta \vdash_e p : A}{\Psi; \Delta \vdash_e c\ p : B}\ (\text{X-Ctor1})$$

$$\frac{\emptyset; \Delta \vdash_e p_1 : A_1 \quad ... \quad \emptyset; \Delta \vdash_e p_n : A_n}{\Psi; \Delta \vdash_e (p_1, ..., p_n) : A_1 \otimes ... \otimes A_n}\ (\text{X-Tuple})$$

$$\frac{\begin{array}{c}x_1, ..., x_n = \text{FV}(p_1) \quad \emptyset; x_1 : A_1, ..., x_n : A_n \vdash_e p_1 : B \\ \Psi \vdash_\omega \omega : A \leftrightarrow B \quad \emptyset; \Delta' \vdash_e p_2 : A \quad \Psi; \Delta, x_1 : A_1, ..., x_n : A_n \vdash_e e : C\end{array}}{\Psi; \Delta, \Delta' \vdash_e \texttt{let}\ p_1 = \omega\ p_2\ \texttt{in}\ e : C}\ (\text{X-Let})$$

Fig. 5. Typing rules for expressions

$$\frac{}{(\texttt{fix}\ \phi \to \omega) \rightsquigarrow \omega[(\texttt{fix}\ \phi \to \omega)/\phi]}\ \text{(E-Fix)}$$

$$\frac{}{(\texttt{fun}\ \phi \to \omega_1)\ \omega_2 \rightsquigarrow \omega_1[\omega_2/\phi]}\ \text{(E-AppFun)} \qquad \frac{}{\texttt{inv}\ \omega \rightsquigarrow \omega^{-1}}\ \text{(E-Inv)}$$

$$\frac{\sigma(p_i) = v \qquad \mathrm{dom}(\sigma) = \mathrm{FV}(p_i)}{(\texttt{case}\ p_1 \leftrightarrow e_1 \mid \dots \mid p_n \leftrightarrow e_n)\ v \rightsquigarrow \sigma(e_i)}\ \text{(E-AppCase)}$$

$$\frac{\sigma(p) = v \qquad \mathrm{dom}(\sigma) = \mathrm{FV}(p)}{\texttt{let}\ p = v\ \texttt{in}\ t \rightsquigarrow \sigma(t)}\ \text{(E-Let)} \qquad \frac{}{\texttt{iso}\ \phi = \omega\ \texttt{in}\ t \rightsquigarrow t[\omega/\phi]}\ \text{(E-Iso)}$$

$$\frac{t \rightsquigarrow t'}{T_{\Rightarrow}[t] \Rightarrow T_{\Rightarrow}[t']}\ \text{(E-CtxTerm)} \qquad \frac{\omega \rightsquigarrow \omega'}{T_{\Rightarrow}[\omega] \Rightarrow T_{\Rightarrow}[\omega']}\ \text{(E-CtxIsoTerm)}$$

$$\frac{\omega \rightsquigarrow \omega'}{I_{\Rightarrow}[\omega] \Rightarrow I_{\Rightarrow}[\omega']}\ \text{(E-CtxIso)}$$

where
$$\begin{aligned} T_{\Rightarrow} &::= []^{\mathrm{t}} \mid c\ T_{\Rightarrow} \mid (T_{\Rightarrow}, t_2, \dots, t_n) \mid \dots \mid (v_1, \dots, v_{n-1}, T_{\Rightarrow}) \mid \\ &\quad I_{\Rightarrow}\ t \mid (\texttt{case}\ p_1 \leftrightarrow e_1 \mid \dots \mid p_n \leftrightarrow e_n)\ T_{\Rightarrow} \mid \texttt{let}\ p = T_{\Rightarrow}\ \texttt{in}\ t \\ I_{\Rightarrow} &::= []^{\mathrm{i}} \mid I_{\Rightarrow}\ \omega \end{aligned}$$

Fig. 6. Evaluation relations

Example 6 (Failure of progress). Assuming the usual Boolean constructors, the well-typed term

$$(\texttt{case True} \leftrightarrow ())\ \texttt{False}$$

is not a value, but no evaluation rule applies to it.

The adequacy of the language is shown by Theorem 8, Corollary 9 and Theorem 10. Omitted proofs are available in the full version.

Lemma 7 (Inversion is an involution). *For any well-typed iso ω, we have $(\omega^{-1})^{-1} = \omega$.*

Proof. By straightforward induction on ω. □

Theorem 8 (Semantics of isos and their inversions). *For all well-typed isos $\emptyset \vdash_\omega \omega : A \leftrightarrow B$ and for all well-typed values $\emptyset; \emptyset \vdash v : A$, if $\omega\ v \Rightarrow^* v'$, then $\omega^{-1}\ v' \Rightarrow^* v$.*

Corollary 9 (Iso is partial isomorphism). *For all well-typed isos $\emptyset \vdash_\omega \omega : A \leftrightarrow B$ and for all well-typed values $\emptyset; \emptyset \vdash v : A$, $\omega\ v \Rightarrow^* v'$ if and only if $\omega^{-1}\ v' \Rightarrow^* v$.*

Proof. Immediate from Lemma 7 and Theorem 8. □

Theorem 10 (Preservation of types of terms). *If $\Psi; \Delta \vdash t : A$ and $t \Rightarrow t'$, then $\Psi; \Delta \vdash t' : A$.*

Type inference can be realized as in Fig. 7, 8, and 9. The inference rules are of the form $\Psi; \Delta \vdash t : A \mid_\chi \mathcal{E}$, where $\mathcal{E}$ is a set of constraints. A constraint is a simple equation of types that must hold. χ represents a set of type variables used in each subderivation, allowing us to have a fresh type variable whenever it is required. Note that we may elide χ in some arguments.

Definition 11 defines substitutions on types, which lets us state Theorem 12 concisely.

$$\frac{}{\Psi; \Delta \vdash () : \texttt{unit} \mid_\emptyset \emptyset}\ (\text{CT-Unit}) \qquad \frac{}{\Psi; \Delta, x : A \vdash x : A \mid_\emptyset \emptyset}\ (\text{CT-Var})$$

$$\frac{c : A}{\Psi; \Delta \vdash c : A \mid_\emptyset \emptyset}\ (\text{CT-Ctor0}) \qquad \frac{c : A \leftrightarrow B \qquad \Psi; \Delta \vdash t : A' \mid_\chi \mathcal{E}}{\Psi; \Delta \vdash c\ t : B \mid_\chi \mathcal{E} \cup \{A = A'\}}\ (\text{CT-Ctor1})$$

$$\frac{\Psi; \Delta \vdash t_1 : A_1 \mid_{\chi_1} \mathcal{E}_1 \quad \dots \quad \Psi; \Delta \vdash t_n : A_n \mid_{\chi_n} \mathcal{E}_n}{\Psi; \Delta \vdash (t_1, \dots, t_n) : A_1 \otimes \dots \otimes A_n \mid_{\chi_1, \dots, \chi_n} \cup_{i \in [n]} \mathcal{E}_i}\ (\text{CT-Tuple})$$

$$\frac{\begin{array}{c}\Psi \vdash_\omega \omega : T \mid_{\chi_1} \mathcal{E}_1 \quad \Psi; \Delta \vdash t : A \mid_{\chi_2} \mathcal{E}_2 \\ V \notin T, A, \mathcal{E}_1, \mathcal{E}_2, \Psi \text{ or } \Delta \qquad \chi_1 \cap \mathrm{FV}(A) = \chi_2 \cap \mathrm{FV}(T) = \emptyset\end{array}}{\Psi; \Delta \vdash \omega\ t : V \mid_{\chi_1, \chi_2, V} \mathcal{E}_1 \cup \mathcal{E}_2 \cup \{T = A \leftrightarrow V\}}\ (\text{CT-App})$$

$$\frac{\Psi \vdash_\omega \omega : T \mid_{\chi_1} \mathcal{E}_1 \qquad \Psi, \phi : T; \Delta \vdash t : A \mid_{\chi_2} \mathcal{E}_2}{\Psi; \Delta \vdash \texttt{iso}\ \phi = \omega\ \texttt{in}\ t : A \mid_{\chi_1, \chi_2} \mathcal{E}_1 \cup \mathcal{E}_2}\ (\text{CT-Iso})$$

$$\frac{\begin{array}{c}\{x_1, \dots, x_n\} = \mathrm{FV}(p) \quad \emptyset; x_1 : A_1, \dots, x_n : A_n \vdash p : A \mid_\emptyset \emptyset \\ \Psi; \Delta \vdash t_1 : A' \mid_{\chi_1} \mathcal{E}_1 \quad \Psi; \Delta, x_1 : A_1, \dots, x_n : A_n \vdash t_2 : B \mid_{\chi_2} \mathcal{E}_2\end{array}}{\Psi; \Delta \vdash \texttt{let}\ p = t_1\ \texttt{in}\ t_2 : B \mid_{\chi_1, \chi_2} \mathcal{E}_1 \cup \mathcal{E}_2 \cup \{A = A'\}}\ (\text{CT-Let})$$

Fig. 7. Constraint-based typing rules for terms

Definition 11 (Substitution on types). *A* type substitution *is a finite mapping from type variables to types. Application of a substitution to a type is defined in a straightforward way:*

$$\sigma(\texttt{unit}) := \texttt{unit} \qquad \sigma(X) := X \qquad \sigma(V) := \begin{cases} \tau & \text{if } (V \mapsto \tau) \in \sigma \\ V & \text{otherwise} \end{cases}$$

$$\sigma(A_1 \otimes \dots \otimes A_n) := \sigma(A_1) \otimes \dots \otimes \sigma(A_n)$$

$$\sigma((A_1, \dots, A_n)\ X) := (\sigma(A_1), \dots, \sigma(A_n))\ X$$

$$\sigma(A \leftrightarrow B) := \sigma(A) \leftrightarrow \sigma(B) \qquad \sigma(T_1 \to T_2) := \sigma(T_1) \to \sigma(T_2).$$

The definition is extended naturally for contexts as follows: $\sigma(x_1 : \tau_1, \dots, x_n : \tau_n) := x_1 : \sigma(\tau_1), \dots, x_n : \sigma(\tau_n)$.

Theorem 12 shows that the constraint-based typing rules are sound, that is, whenever a substitution satisfies the constraints produced by these rules, the corresponding ordinary typing judgment is derivable.

$$\frac{}{\Psi, \phi : T \vdash_\omega \phi : T \mid_\emptyset \emptyset}\ \text{(CI-Var)} \qquad \frac{\Psi, \phi : T \vdash_\omega \omega : T \mid_\chi \mathcal{E}}{\Psi \vdash_\omega \texttt{fix}\ \phi \to \omega : T \mid_\chi \mathcal{E}}\ \text{(CI-Fix)}$$

$$\frac{\Psi, \phi : T_1 \vdash_\omega \omega : T_2 \mid_\chi \mathcal{E}}{\Psi \vdash_\omega \texttt{fun}\ \phi \to \omega : T_1 \to T_2 \mid_\chi \mathcal{E}}\ \text{(CI-Fun)} \qquad \frac{\Psi \vdash_\omega \omega^{-1} : T \mid_\chi \mathcal{E}}{\Psi \vdash_\omega \texttt{inv}\ \omega : T \mid_\chi \mathcal{E}}\ \text{(CI-Inv)}$$

$$\frac{\begin{array}{c}\Psi \vdash_\omega \omega_1 : T_1 \mid_{\chi_1} \mathcal{E}_1 \quad \Psi \vdash_\omega \omega_2 : T_2 \mid_{\chi_2} \mathcal{E}_2 \\ V \notin T_1, T_2, \mathcal{E}_1, \mathcal{E}_2 \text{ or } \Psi \quad \chi_1 \cap \mathrm{FV}(T_2) = \chi_2 \cap \mathrm{FV}(T_1) = \emptyset\end{array}}{\Psi \vdash_\omega \omega_1\ \omega_2 : V \mid_{\chi_1, \chi_2, V} \mathcal{E}_1 \cup \mathcal{E}_2 \cup \{T_1 = T_2 \to V\}}\ \text{(CI-App)}$$

$$\frac{\begin{array}{c}\emptyset; \Delta_1 \vdash p_1 : A_1 \mid_\emptyset \emptyset \quad \dots \quad \emptyset; \Delta_n \vdash p_n : A_n \mid_\emptyset \emptyset \qquad \forall i \neq j, p_i \perp p_j \\ \Psi; \Delta_1 \vdash_e e_1 : B_1 \mid_{\chi_1} \mathcal{E}_1 \quad \dots \quad \Psi; \Delta_n \vdash_e e_n : B_n \mid_{\chi_n} \mathcal{E}_n \qquad \forall i \neq j, e_i \perp e_j \\ \mathcal{E} = \cup_{i \in [n]} \mathcal{E}_i \cup \{A_1 = A_i \mid i \in \{2, \dots, n\}\} \cup \{B_1 = B_i \mid i \in \{2, \dots, n\}\}\end{array}}{\Psi \vdash_\omega \texttt{case}\ p_1 \leftrightarrow e_1 \mid \dots \mid p_n \leftrightarrow e_n : A_1 \leftrightarrow B_1 \mid_{\chi_1, \dots, \chi_n} \mathcal{E}}\ \text{(CI-Case)}$$

Fig. 8. Constraint-based typing rules for isos

$$\frac{}{\Psi; \emptyset \vdash_e () : \texttt{unit} \mid_\emptyset \emptyset}\ \text{(CX-Unit)} \qquad \frac{}{\Psi; x : A \vdash_e x : A \mid_\emptyset \emptyset}\ \text{(CX-Var)}$$

$$\frac{c : A}{\Psi; \emptyset \vdash_e c : A \mid_\emptyset \emptyset}\ \text{(CX-Ctor0)} \qquad \frac{c : A \leftrightarrow B \qquad \emptyset; \Delta \vdash_e p : A \mid_\emptyset \emptyset}{\Psi; \Delta \vdash_e c\ p : B \mid_\emptyset \emptyset}\ \text{(CX-Ctor1)}$$

$$\frac{\emptyset; \Delta \vdash_e p_1 : A_1 \mid_\emptyset \emptyset \quad \dots \quad \emptyset; \Delta \vdash_e p_n : A_n \mid_\emptyset \emptyset}{\Psi; \Delta \vdash_e (p_1, \dots, p_n) : A_1 \otimes \dots \otimes A_n \mid_\emptyset \emptyset}\ \text{(CX-Tuple)}$$

$$\frac{\begin{array}{c}\emptyset; x_1 : A_1, \dots, x_n : A_n \vdash_e p_1 : A \mid_\emptyset \emptyset \\ \{x_1, \dots, x_n\} = \mathrm{FV}(p_1) \qquad \Psi \vdash_\omega \omega : T \mid_{\chi_1} \mathcal{E}_1 \\ \emptyset; \Delta' \vdash_e p_2 : B \mid_\emptyset \emptyset \qquad \Psi; \Delta, x_1 : A_1, \dots, x_n : A_n \vdash_e e : C \mid_{\chi_2} \mathcal{E}_2\end{array}}{\Psi; \Delta, \Delta' \vdash_e \texttt{let}\ p_1 = \omega\ p_2\ \texttt{in}\ e : C \mid_{\chi_1, \chi_2} \mathcal{E}_1 \cup \mathcal{E}_2 \cup \{T = B \leftrightarrow A\}}\ \text{(CX-Let)}$$

Fig. 9. Constraint-based typing rules for expressions

Theorem 12 (Soundness of constraint-based typing). *The following three statements hold.*

1. *Suppose that* $\Psi; \Delta \vdash t : A \mid \mathcal{E}$. *If* σ *satisfies* $\mathcal{E}$, *then* $\sigma(\Psi); \sigma(\Delta) \vdash t : \sigma(A)$.
2. *Suppose that* $\Psi \vdash_\omega \omega : T \mid \mathcal{E}$. *If* σ *satisfies* $\mathcal{E}$, *then* $\sigma(\Psi) \vdash_\omega \omega : \sigma(T)$.
3. *Suppose that* $\Psi; \Delta \vdash_e e : A \mid \mathcal{E}$. *If* σ *satisfies* $\mathcal{E}$, *then* $\sigma(\Psi); \sigma(\Delta) \vdash_e e : \sigma(A)$.

3 Language

The grammar of expressions in Fig. 1 has a specific form so that they can be inverted. However, it does not allow us to write an expression such as $f\ (g\ x)$, which is equivalent to $\texttt{let}\ a = g\ x\ \texttt{in}\ \texttt{let}\ b = f\ a\ \texttt{in}\ b$ for some fresh variables

a and b. To solve this problem, we define *intermediate* expressions as:

$$\begin{aligned} &\text{(Non-let terms)} && \hat{t} ::= () \mid x \mid c \mid c\ \hat{t} \mid (\hat{t}_1, ..., \hat{t}_n) \mid \omega\ \hat{t} \\ &\text{(Intermediate expressions)} && \hat{e} ::= \hat{t} \mid \texttt{let}\ p = \hat{t}\ \texttt{in}\ \hat{e} \end{aligned}$$

which are less restrictive and can be expanded into the expressions we have already defined in Fig. 1. Intermediate expressions comprise *non-let* terms and let-expressions.

The functions *pump* and *expand* are defined in Fig. 10. The pump function collects all function applications in a non-let term so that they can be converted into let-expressions later using the expand function.

$$\begin{aligned} \text{pump}(()) &:= (\emptyset, ()) \\ \text{pump}(x) &:= (\emptyset, x) \\ \text{pump}(c) &:= (\emptyset, c) \\ \text{pump}(c\ \hat{t}) &:= (s, c\ p) \quad \text{where } (s, p) = \text{pump}(\hat{t}) \\ \text{pump}((\hat{t}_1, ..., \hat{t}_n)) &:= (s_1 ... s_n, (p_1, ..., p_n)) \quad \text{where } (s_i, p_i) = \text{pump}(\hat{t}_i) \text{ for all } i \in [n] \\ \text{pump}(\omega\ \hat{t}) &:= ((x, \omega, p) \cdot s, x) \quad \text{where } (s, p) = \text{pump}(\hat{t}) \text{ and } x \text{ is a fresh variable} \end{aligned}$$

$$\begin{aligned} \text{expand}(\hat{t}) &:= \texttt{let}\ x_n = \omega_n\ p_n\ \texttt{in}\ ...\ \texttt{let}\ x_1 = \omega_1\ p_1\ \texttt{in}\ p \\ &\quad\ \text{where } ((x_1, \omega_1, p_1) \cdot ... \cdot (x_n, \omega_n, p_n), p) = \text{pump}(\hat{t}) \\ \text{expand}(\texttt{let}\ p = \hat{t}\ \texttt{in}\ \hat{e}) &:= \texttt{let}\ x_n = \omega_n\ p_n\ \texttt{in}\ ...\ \texttt{let}\ x_1 = \omega_1\ p_1\ \texttt{in} \\ &\quad\ \texttt{let}\ p = (\texttt{case}\ x \leftrightarrow x)\ p'\ \texttt{in}\ \text{expand}(\hat{e}) \\ &\quad\ \text{where } ((x_1, \omega_1, p_1) \cdot ... \cdot (x_n, \omega_n, p_n), p') = \text{pump}(\hat{t}) \end{aligned}$$

Fig. 10. The pump and expand functions

Finally, we introduce the grammar for programs along with syntactic sugar. As shown in Fig. 11, a program begins with zero or more type definitions, followed by a single term. Thus, the minimal valid program would be `()`. A type may be defined with type variables, allowing one to define types such as `type 'a option = None | Some of 'a`.

The syntactic sugar defined in Fig. 11 introduces more concise ways to write programs.

4 Implementation

We implemented an algorithm for type inference to eliminate type annotations. It is based on algorithm W, which is used for inferring types in the Hindley–Milner type system. The function used for unification (`unify_type` shown below) is the only function that is heavily modified due to the existence of inverted types and two kinds of arrows ($\leftrightarrow$ and $\rightarrow$).

$$
\begin{aligned}
&\text{(Programs)} && \pi ::= \tau^* \; t \\
&\text{(Type definitions)} && \tau ::= \textbf{type}\ (V, ..., V)\ X = \gamma \mid ... \mid \gamma \\
&\text{(Constructors)} && \gamma ::= c \mid c\ \textbf{of}\ A
\end{aligned}
$$

$$
\begin{aligned}
\begin{pmatrix}\texttt{match}\ t\ \texttt{with} \\ p_1 \leftrightarrow \hat{e}_1 \mid ... \mid p_n \leftrightarrow \hat{e}_n\end{pmatrix} &:= (\texttt{case}\ p_1 \leftrightarrow \hat{e}_1 \mid ... \mid p_n \leftrightarrow \hat{e}_n)\ t \\
\hat{e} &:= \text{expand}(\hat{e}) \\
\texttt{iso}\ \phi\ \phi_1\ ...\ \phi_n = \omega\ \texttt{in}\ t &:= \texttt{iso}\ \phi = \texttt{fun}\ \phi_1 \to ...\ \texttt{fun}\ \phi_n \to \omega\ \texttt{in}\ t \\
\texttt{iso rec}\ \phi\ \phi_1\ ...\ \phi_n = \omega\ \texttt{in}\ t &:= \texttt{iso}\ \phi = \texttt{fix}\ \phi \to \texttt{fun}\ \phi_1 \to ...\ \texttt{fun}\ \phi_n \to \omega\ \texttt{in}\ t
\end{aligned}
$$

Fig. 11. Grammar for programs and syntactic sugar

Type Unification. This algorithm tries to solve a set of equations of types by eliminating inversions, arrows, and type constructors, and by substituting type variables. More specifically, the function `unify_type` takes a list of equations, and then returns either a solution represented by a list of substitutions, or an error if no solution is found.

First, if the list of equations is empty, so is the resulting substitution. Otherwise, the first equation is inspected. If either side of the equation is a type variable and it does not appear in the other side, then the equation is added to the resulting substitutions. The rest of the equations are handled recursively after eliminating the type variable by substitution. As for the other cases, the algorithm simply destructs the types as in the code below. The time complexity is quadratic in the size of equations.

```
type equation = typ * typ
type subst = { what : int; into : typ }
let ( let** ) = Result.bind
let ( let++ ) x f = Result.map f x
let rec unify_type : equation list -> (subst list, string) Result.t
  = function [] -> Ok []
    | e :: e' -> begin match e with
    (* ignore trivial cases *) | a, b when a = b -> unify_type e'
    (* eliminate inversions *)
    | Inverted a, Inverted b -> (a, b) :: e' |> unify_type
    | Inverted i, BiArrow { a; b } ->
        (i, BiArrow { a = b; b = a }) :: e' |> unify_type
    | BiArrow { a; b }, Inverted i ->
        (i, BiArrow { a = b; b = a }) :: e' |> unify_type
    | Inverted i, Arrow { a; b } ->
        let** a = invert_iso_type a in
        let** b = invert_iso_type b in
        (i, Arrow { a; b }) :: e' |> unify_type
    | Arrow { a; b }, Inverted i ->
        let** a = invert_iso_type a in
        let** b = invert_iso_type b in
        (i, Arrow { a; b }) :: e' |> unify_type
    (* substitute with rhs *)
    | Var x, b when occurs x b |> not ->
        let s = { what = x; into = b } in let++ unified =
        subst_in_equations s e' |> unify_type in s :: unified
    (* substitute with lhs *)
    | a, Var x when occurs x a |> not ->
        let s = { what = x; into = a } in let++ unified =
        subst_in_equations s e' |> unify_type in s :: unified
    (* products *)
    | Product l, Product r when List.compare_lengths l r = 0 ->
        List.combine l r @ e' |> unify_type
```

```
(* eliminate arrows *)
| BiArrow { a = a_1; b = b_1 }, BiArrow { a = a_2; b = b_2 } ->
    (a_1, a_2) :: (b_1, b_2) :: e' |> unify_type
| Arrow { a = a_1; b = b_1 }, Arrow { a = a_2; b = b_2 } ->
    (a_1, a_2) :: (b_1, b_2) :: e' |> unify_type
(* eliminate constructors *)
| Ctor (l_1, x_1), Ctor (l_2, x_2)
  when x_1 = x_2 && List.compare_lengths l_1 l_2 = 0 ->
    List.combine l_1 l_2 @ e' |> unify_type
(* fail *) | a, b -> Error ("unification failed") end
```

Orthogonality Checker. This unification-based algorithm checks the orthogonality of two patterns. The function `unify` is quite similar to `unify_type` in the sense that it takes a list of equations, and then returns either a solution represented by a list of substitutions, or an error if no solution is found. $p_1 \perp p_2$ if `unify` $[(p_1, p_2)]$ evaluates to `Error` () and $p_1 \not\perp p_2$ if `unify` $[(p_1, p_2)]$ evaluates to `Ok` e, in which case e is a solution for $p_1 = p_2$. The time complexity is quadratic in the size of patterns.

```
type equation = pattern * pattern
type subst = { what : int; into : pattern }
let ( let+ ) x f = Result.map f x
let rec unify : equation list -> (subst list, unit) result
  = function [] -> Ok [] | e :: e' -> begin match e with
    (* ignore trivial cases *) | a, b when a = b -> unify e'
    (* substitute with rhs *) | Var x, b when occurs x b |> not ->
      let  s  = { what = x; into = b } in
      let+ e' = subst_in_equations s e' |> unify in s :: e'
    (* substitute with lhs *) | a, Var x when occurs x a |> not ->
      let  s  = { what = x; into = a } in
      let+ e' = subst_in_equations s e' |> unify in s :: e'
    (* constructor applications *)
    | Ctor { c = c_1; p = p_1 }, Ctor { c = c_2; p = p_2 }
      when c_1 = c_2 -> (p_1, p_2) :: e' |> unify
    (* tuples *) | Tuple a, Tuple b when List.compare_lengths
      a b = 0 -> List.combine a b @ e' |> unify
    (* fail *) | _ -> Error () end
```

Inversion. This algorithm inverts isos with linear time complexity. The function `invert_expr` inverts an expression in a tail-recursive manner, which is analogous to list reversal except that the patterns on both sides are swapped and the function in between is also inverted for each let-expression. The implementation of `invert` closely follows the definition of inversion, though it returns ω for `invert` (`inv` ω) as an optimization whose correctness is based on Lemma 7 combined with E-Inv.

```
let rec invert_expr (e : expr) (acc : expr) = match e with
  | Value v -> (v, acc) | Let { p_1; omega; p_2; e } ->
    Let { p_1 = p_2; omega = invert omega;
          p_2 = p_1; e = acc } |> invert_expr e
and invert (omega : iso) : iso = match omega with
  | Cases c -> let invert_case (v, e) = invert_expr e (Value v) in
    Cases (List.map invert_case c)
  | Fix { phi; omega } -> Fix { phi; omega = invert omega }
  | Lambda { psi; omega } -> Lambda { psi; omega = invert omega }
  | Var _ -> omega | App { omega_1; omega_2 } ->
    App { omega_1 = invert omega_1; omega_2 = invert omega_2 }
  | Invert omega -> omega
```

5 Examples

Example 13 (Operations on natural numbers). The function `add` m n computes $(m+n, n)$ and `fib` n computes the $(n+1)$-th and $(n+2)$-th numbers of the Fibonacci sequence. The following program produces an output `((55, 89), 5)`. Numerical literals are converted by the mapping $f : \mathbb{N} \to$ `nat` defined as $f(0) :=$ `Z` and $f(n) :=$ `S` $(f(n-1))$ if $n > 0$. In the second branch of `fib`, `S (S m)` contributes to the non-overlap of the pattern matching. The type inference system derives the following:

- `add : nat * nat <-> nat * nat`
- `fib : nat <-> nat * nat`.

```
type nat = Z | S of nat
iso rec add = case
| (m, 0)   <-> (m, 0)
| (m, S n) <-> let (m', n') = add (S m, n) in
               (m', S n')
in
iso rec fib = case
| 0   <-> (1, 1)
| S n <-> let (S (S m), n) = add (fib n) in
          (n, S (S m))
in
(fib 9, inv fib (8, 13))
```

Example 14 (Operations on lists). The following program produces an output `([2; 0; 1], [[True; False]; []; [False]])`. In the function `map`, `f x :: map f xs` is automatically expanded into `let _0 = f x in let _1 = map f xs in _0 :: _1` . The type inference system derives the following:

- `len : 'a list <-> nat * 'a list`
- `map : ('a <-> 'b) -> ('a list <-> 'b list)`
- `split : ('a * 'b) list <-> 'a list * 'b list`.

```
type    bool = False | True
type 'a list = Nil | Cons of 'a * 'a list
iso rec len = case
| []      <-> (0, [])
| x :: xs <-> let (n, xs) = len xs in
              (S n, x :: xs)
in
iso rec map f = case
| []      <-> []
| x :: xs <-> f x :: map f xs
in
iso rec split = case
| []           <-> ([], [])
| (x, y) :: t <-> let (xs, ys) = split t in
                  (x :: xs, y :: ys)
in
split (map len [[True; False]; []; [False]])
```

Example 15 (Polymorphic run-length compression). In the term `run_length eq xs`, `xs` is compressed by representing each consecutive run of equal values (e.g., x, x, x, x) as a pair (e.g., $(x, 3)$) of the value and the number of values following the first occurrence of the value. The iso `eq` is expected to have type `'a * 'a <-> bool * ('a * 'a)` as it is inferred below. Semantically, `eq x y` should return `(e, (x, y))` where `e` indicates the equality of `x` and `y`. The type inference system derives the following:

- run_length : ('a * 'a <-> bool * ('a * 'a)) -> ('a list <-> ('a * nat) list)
- nat_eq : nat * nat <-> bool * (nat * nat).

```
type ('l, 'r) either = Left of 'l | Right of 'r
iso rec run_length eq = case
| []       <-> []
| x :: xs <-> let lr = match (x, run_length eq xs) with
    | (x, [])            <-> Left x
    | (x, (y, n) :: ys) <-> Right (
        match (eq (x, y), n, ys) with
        | ((True, (x, x)), n, ys)  <-> (x, S n) :: ys
        | ((False, (x, y)), n, ys) <-> (x, 0) :: (y, n) :: ys
      )
  in let x :: xs = match lr with
    | Left x                     <-> [(x, 0)]
    | Right ((x, S n) :: ys)     <-> (x, S n) :: ys
    | Right ((x, 0) :: y :: ys) <-> (x, 0) :: y :: ys
  in x :: xs
in
iso rec nat_eq = case
| (0, 0)     <-> (True, (0, 0))
| (S m, 0)   <-> (False, (S m, 0))
| (0, S n)   <-> (False, (0, S n))
| (S m, S n) <-> let (b, (m, n)) = nat_eq (m, n) in
                 (b, (S m, S n))
in
run_length nat_eq [1; 1; 1; 5; 3; 3]
```

6 Related Work

Reversible programming has been explored in multiple paradigms, including imperative and functional languages as well as machine models. Janus is a classic high-level reversible language [6,12], and subsequent work developed structured imperative cores and implementations, e.g., reversible While-style languages [3] and reversible languages equipped with invertible self-interpreters [12]. These lines of research demonstrate that practical programming constructs can be made reversible, but they typically require design constraints that are nonstandard from the viewpoint of mainstream declarative ML-style programming.

On the functional side, Theseus [4] advocates a high-level reversible functional style in which reversibility is enforced by (injective) pattern matching. However, the grammar for pattern matching in Theseus is not conventional; in particular, *iteration labels* and their types are required to handle patterns of recursive types. This line of work has recently been put on a firmer semantic and expressiveness foundation by Chardonnet et al. [2], who study a Theseus-based higher-order reversible core language with inductive types and recursion, establish strong expressiveness results (including an encoding of reversible Turing machines), and give a sound and adequate categorical semantics. PisoLang takes its core calculus as its semantic basis and focuses on usability: we provide an OCaml-like surface syntax with algebraic data types and constructor patterns, together with Hindley–Milner style type inference and an elaboration strategy that preserves the injective pattern-matching discipline inherited from the Theseus-based core.

PisoLang and the second version of a language named RFUN [10], which we shall refer to as RFUN v2, share a number of similarities in terms of their design. However, we are not aware of a formal specification of RFUN v2 despite the original RFUN being defined formally. This makes it difficult to clarify the differences between PisoLang and RFUN v2, especially those related to their type systems, since the original RFUN is an untyped language. Still, based on the implementation (https://github.com/kirkedal/rfun-interp), we observe that:

- PisoLang infers types, while RFUN v2 does not.
- PisoLang performs static unification-based checks, while RFUN v2 employs a run-time check called *first match policy* to guarantee the injectivity of pattern matching.
- PisoLang checks the equality of two values via patterns, while RFUN v2 requires the use of a predefined function.

From a more foundational perspective, Mu et al. present *Inv*, an injective language for reversible computation formulated in a point-free, combinator-style functional setting with a relational semantics [7]. In Inv, the design discipline is "injectivity by construction": only injective transformations are directly definable, and non-injective computations can be accommodated via standard history-carrying encodings. While this point-free style is quite different from ML-like variable-binding languages with pattern matching, it provides a clean semantic account of reversibility through injectivity. PisoLang supports a more user-friendly programming style, though users may write reversible programs in the point-free style even in PisoLang if desired.

7 Conclusion

We extended the language defined by Chardonnet et al. [2] to specify the new reversible programming language PisoLang and to demonstrate how injective functions can be expressed in it by utilizing its abstractions and features.

Several directions remain for future work. For instance, we should be able to replace `iso` $\phi = \omega$ `in` t with `let` $p = t_1$ `in` t_2 by determining the type of ω and t_1. Formal verification of the type-inference algorithm also remains future work. Another possible direction is a feature similar to polymorphic variants, with which the type system would be able to describe the possible structures of values returned from a function. This could reduce verbosity, for example in `let (S (S m), n) = ...` in the `fib` function in Example 13.

References

1. Axelsen, H.B., Glück, R.: On reversible Turing machines and their function universality. Acta Inform. **53**, 509–543 (2016). https://doi.org/10.1007/s00236-015-0253-y

2. Chardonnet, K., Lemonnier, L., Valiron, B.: Semantics for a turing-complete reversible programming language with inductive types. In: Rehof, J. (ed.) 9th International Conference on Formal Structures for Computation and Deduction (FSCD 2024). Leibniz International Proceedings in Informatics (LIPIcs), vol. 299, pp. 19:1–19:19. Schloss Dagstuhl – Leibniz-Zentrum für Informatik, Dagstuhl (2024). https://doi.org/10.4230/LIPIcs.FSCD.2024.19
3. Glück, R., Yokoyama, T.: A minimalist's reversible while language. IEICE Trans. Inf. Syst. **E100-D**(5), 1026–1034 (2017). https://doi.org/10.1587/transinf.2016EDP7274
4. James, R.P., Sabry, A.: Theseus: a high level language for reversible computing (2014). https://api.semanticscholar.org/CorpusID:10756936
5. Li, T.: A rule-based and object-oriented AI programming language. SIGPLAN Not. **30**(12), 17–24 (1995). https://doi.org/10.1145/219726.219736
6. Lutz, C.: Janus: a time-reversible language (1986). Letter to R. Landauer
7. Mu, S.-C., Hu, Z., Takeichi, M.: An injective language for reversible computation. In: Kozen, D. (ed.) MPC 2004. LNCS, vol. 3125, pp. 289–313. Springer, Heidelberg (2004). https://doi.org/10.1007/978-3-540-27764-4_16
8. Nakano, K.: Time-symmetric Turing machines for computable involutions. Sci. Comput. Program. **215**, 102748 (2022). https://doi.org/10.1016/j.scico.2021.102748
9. Nishida, N., Palacios, A., Vidal, G.: Reversible computation in term rewriting. J. Log. Algebraic Methods Program. **94**, 128–149 (2018). https://doi.org/10.1016/j.jlamp.2017.10.003
10. Thomsen, M.K., Axelsen, H.B.: Interpretation and programming of the reversible functional language RFUN. In: Proceedings of the 27th Symposium on the Implementation and Application of Functional Programming Languages, IFL 2015, pp. 8:1–8:13. Association for Computing Machinery, New York (2015). https://doi.org/10.1145/2897336.2897345
11. Yokoyama, T., Axelsen, H.B., Glück, R.: Towards a reversible functional language. In: De Vos, A., Wille, R. (eds.) RC 2011. LNCS, vol. 7165, pp. 14–29. Springer, Heidelberg (2012). https://doi.org/10.1007/978-3-642-29517-1_2
12. Yokoyama, T., Glück, R.: A reversible programming language and its invertible self-interpreter. In: Proceedings of the 2007 ACM SIGPLAN Symposium on Partial Evaluation and Semantics-Based Program Manipulation, PEPM 2007, pp. 144–153. Association for Computing Machinery, New York (2007). https://doi.org/10.1145/1244381.1244404

Support for Reversible Programming

A Graph Rewriting-Based Semantics and Implementation for $\rho\pi$

Julie Cailler(✉) and Martin Vassor(✉)

Université de Lorraine, CNRS, Inria, LORIA, 54000 Nancy, France
{julie.cailler,martin.vassor}@univ-lorraine.fr

Abstract. Reversibility in the higher-order process calculus $\rho\pi$ relies on tracking causal dependencies between processes and their (causal) ancestors. This bookkeeping introduces extra complexity to the calculus both syntactically—through the use of tags—and semantically, via additional structural congruence rules to manage them. Although this additional complexity is not a problem for the familiar reader, it creates a steep learning curve for newcomers. To soften this learning curve, we present a graph rewriting-based semantics for $\rho\pi$. We also present an implementation of this graph-based approach with a step-by-step interface, allowing one to familiarize quickly with concepts and intuitions of $\rho\pi$ in a graphical and user-friendly way.

Keywords: Reversible Process Calculus · Graph Rewriting · Causal Consistent Reversibility

1 Introduction

Motivation. The reversible higher-order π calculus $\rho\pi$ [17,18] is a simple, yet expressive, causally-consistent reversible process calculus. Its simplicity lies in its semantics, which consists in only two rules: one for forward computation that performs a communication, and one for backward computation that undoes one of the *last* communications[1]. This minimal semantic core served as the foundation for numerous variants proposed in recent years [15,16,28].

The counterpart of this simplicity comes with the complexity of the structural congruence rules and the heavy syntax. Processes are annotated with *keys*, which act as references to track causal dependencies. Upon communication, the sender and the receiver are frozen in a memory, and the continuation is created with a fresh key, which is included in the memory. However, due to name restriction and parallel composition, the structural congruence has to accommodate splitting keys and moving key binders.

In this paper, we introduce an alternative semantics for $\rho\pi$ based on graph rewriting [9], as well as a $\rho\pi$ interpreter using this graph rewriting-based

[1] Due to concurrency, we consider the order of events with respect to causal order (see Lamport's *happen-before* relation [14]), which is a partial order; not with respect to temporal order. As such, there might be multiple *last* events at once.

C. Aubert and L. Roversi (Eds.): RC 2026, LNCS 16626, pp. 239–257, 2026.
https://doi.org/10.1007/978-3-032-30839-9_14

semantics. Our goal, with this semantics and this tool, is to provide a more visual approach to this reversible process calculus, helping readers unfamiliar with the domain as well as students to develop intuitions of what happens under the hood.

On the calculus side, using graphs to track causal dependencies allows us to drop keys (which are replaced with edges), which in turn allows us to drop key binders and the need for configurations. Memories still exist, but are shown as vertices with outgoing edges. On the interpreter side, we provide a Python implementation of our semantics. It supports both *interactive* executions—where the user explicitly selects a graph node and a rule—and an automatic mode.

Contributions. Our contributions are (i) a new semantics for $\rho\pi$, based on graph rewriting instead of structured operational semantics rules; and (ii) $\mathsf{G}\rho\pi\mathsf{F}^2$, a publicly available implementation of graph rewriting-based $\rho\pi$ in Python [5].

Outline. In Sect. 2, we informally introduce the $\rho\pi$ calculus and graph rewriting, the formalism used to specify the semantics of $\rho\pi$. The graph structures employed to encode $\rho\pi$, together with the encoding of rewrite rules, are described in Sect. 3. In this paper, we do not aim to prove the correctness of our encoding, but we nonetheless state the conjecture that one would need to prove to formally establish the correspondence between $\rho\pi$ and the graph-based approach. We then present the interpreter in Sect. 4. Finally, in Sect. 5, we discuss the benefits of graphical approaches, showing how improvements of $\rho\pi$ can easily be expressed in terms of graph rewriting, and we discuss related works.

2 Preliminaries

2.1 The $\rho\pi$ Calculus

In this section, we briefly introduce $\rho\pi$, a reversible higher-order process calculus. In the rest of this paper, we are mostly interested in (i) the syntax of processes; (ii) the recording of memories; and (iii) the tracking of causal dependencies.

The syntax of $\rho\pi$ is given in Fig. 1. Processes (noted P, Q...) are processes of the asynchronous higher-order π calculus. In $\rho\pi$, processes do not execute directly. Instead, they are embedded in *configurations*, which contain as well memories of past actions and track causal dependencies between different parts of a term, thanks to tags.

$$
\begin{array}{llll}
\mathcal{P},\mathcal{Q} & ::= 0 \mid X \mid \nu c.\,(\mathcal{P}) \mid \mathcal{P} \,||\, \mathcal{Q} \mid c\langle\mathcal{P}\rangle \mid c(X) \triangleright (\mathcal{P}) & & \textit{Processes} \\
\mathcal{M},\mathcal{N} & ::= 0 \mid \nu u.\,(\mathcal{M}) \mid \mathcal{M} \,||\, \mathcal{N} \mid \kappa : P \mid [\mu; k] & & \textit{Configurations} \\
\kappa & ::= k \mid \langle h, \tilde{h}\rangle \cdot k & & \textit{Tags} \\
\mu & ::= \kappa_1 : c\langle\mathcal{P}\rangle \,||\, \kappa_2 : a(X) \triangleright (\mathcal{Q}) & & \textit{Memory content}
\end{array}
$$

Fig. 1. Syntax of $\rho\pi$ ($c \in \mathbb{N}$: channel names; $k \in \mathbb{K}$: keys; $X \in \mathbb{V}_p$: process variables; $u \in \mathbb{N} \cup \mathbb{K}$: identifiers).

[2] Which stands for *Graph-based $\rho\pi$ Framework*.

The two communication primitives of $\rho\pi$ are those of **HO**π: either a message P is sent on a channel c: $c\langle P\rangle$; or a message is received on that channel (called a *trigger*): $c(X) \triangleright (Q)$. A trigger binds variable X in Q. Upon reception of P, X is substituted by P in Q. Channel names used for communication can be restricted to some processes only: $\nu c.\,(P)$ binds c in P, thus preventing communications on that name between P and its surrounding environment. Other forms of processes include parallel composition ($P \mid\mid Q$); terminated process (0); and process variables, to be substituted upon communication (X).

In order to record memories and to track causal dependencies, processes are embedded into *configurations*: upon communication, e.g. $c\langle P\rangle \mid\mid c(X) \triangleright (Q)$ not only the communication happens, but a memory is created to record previous processes. The communication above reduces to $Q\{^P/_X\} \mid\mid [c\langle P\rangle \mid\mid c(X) \triangleright (Q)]$ where $Q\{^P/_X\}$ denotes the process Q where free occurrences of variable X are substituted with P[3]. The memory is the part of the resulting configuration denoted with squared brackets. In order to keep track of the causal dependency between the memory and the continuation, $\rho\pi$ uses *tags*: for instance, upon communication, a fresh tag k is generated, which annotates both the memory and the continuation:

$$\nu k.\,(k:\ Q\{^P/_X\} \mid\mid [c\langle P\rangle \mid\mid c(X) \triangleright (Q); k])$$

Notice the head restriction, which works as channel name restriction, to ensure tag freshness[4].

Formally, the forward semantics of $\rho\pi$ consists of the least evaluation-closed relation on terms that includes the following rule[5,6]:

$$\text{(R.Fw)}\ \frac{}{\kappa_1:\ P \mid\mid \kappa_2:\ Q \twoheadrightarrow \nu k.\,(k:\ Q\{^P/_X\} \mid\mid [\kappa_1:\ P \mid\mid \kappa_2:\ Q; k])}$$

Conversely, reversible behavior consists of removing a live process (i.e. not contained in a memory), and restoring the memory that created that process. Tags are used to find which memory to restore:

$$\text{(R.Bw)}\ \frac{}{\nu k.\,(k:\ Q\{^P/_X\} \mid\mid [\kappa_1:\ P \mid\mid \kappa_2:\ Q; k]) \rightsquigarrow \kappa_1:\ P \mid\mid \kappa_2:\ Q}$$

As shown above, the continuation $P' = Q\{^P/_X\}$ of a communication is tagged with a fresh k. When P' is a parallel composition $k:\ P' = k:\ L \mid\mid R$, we have to find a way to tag L and R independently. To do so, $\rho\pi$'s structural

[3] In the following, we also use this notation for substituting channel names.

[4] Formally, processes before the communication are also tagged, and thus also processes occurring in the memory. Tags not shown for the sake of simplicity.

[5] See [17] for more details on structural congruence and evaluation-closed contexts.

[6] We prefix the names of the reduction rules with R, to distinguish them from (Fw) and (Bw) below.

congruence allows splitting tags: e.g. $\langle h_1, \{h_1, h_2\}\rangle \cdot k$ is a split tag, which indicates that tag k has been split into two tags (h_1 and h_2), and the shown tag is the first of those two tags. Thus, structural congruence allows splitting $k: L \parallel R$ as $\langle h_1, \{h_1, h_2\}\rangle \cdot k: L \parallel \langle h_2, \{h_1, h_2\}\rangle \cdot k: R$.

Splitting tags allows treating both sides of a parallel composition independently, while keeping track of causal links: a single memory can causally precede multiple processes, which have been split around.

Example 1. Consider the following configuration:

$$\nu a. (k: a\langle P\rangle \parallel l: a(X) \triangleright (X \parallel Q))$$

In this process a sender emits a message P on channel a and a receiver waits for a message X on the same channel before running $X \parallel Q$. Thus a communication can occur, resulting in $P \parallel Q\{^P/_X\}$. When that communication occurs, a memory is created in order to store the state of the sender and receiver. A new tag, m, is created to record the causal dependence between the memory and continuation:

$$\nu a. \left(\nu m. \left(m: P \parallel Q\{^P/_X\} \parallel [k: a\langle P\rangle \parallel l: a(X) \triangleright (X \parallel Q); m]\right)\right)$$

2.2 Graph Rewriting

Using graphs to represent dynamic systems has a long history, dating at least from the early 1970s [8], with applications in a wide range of domains [7,8]. In this paper, a graph $G = (V, E)$ consists of a finite set V of vertices and a set $E \subseteq V \times V$ of edges. Intuitively, graph rewriting operates by applying a set of *rewriting rules*, each of which specifies how to transform a graph L (the left-hand side) into a graph R (the right-hand side). These rules are applied to graphs G, for example transforming G in Fig. 3a into H in Fig. 3c. Formally, applying a rule $L \longrightarrow R$ to G involves finding a subgraph of G that matches L and replacing it with R to obtain a new graph H. Different approaches exist for implementing this substitution, which leads to different semantics of graph rewriting. In this work, we adopt the *Double Pushout* (DPO) approach [3,9,10].

The main difference with other approaches lies in how L is matched in G. The idea behind the DPO approach is to distinguish a subset of nodes and edges that should appear both in L and R. These nodes form the *interface* with the surrounding graph: they are the only nodes and edges allowed to maintain connections to the rest of G during the application of the rule (as explained below and illustrated in Example 2). In DPO, a rule is a triplet $\langle L, K, R\rangle$ where the graph K is the interface mentioned above. Applying the rule to a graph G proceeds in three steps: (i) find a mapping m from nodes and edges of L to G; (ii) remove nodes and edges of L not in K to obtain an intermediate graph $D = G \setminus m(L \setminus K)$; and (iii) add nodes and edges of R not in K to produce the final graph $H = D \cup (R \setminus K)$. In short, $L \setminus K$ identifies elements to be removed, while $R \setminus K$ identifies elements to be added.

The important point, w.r.t. other approaches, is that the intermediate graph *D has to be a graph*, without dangling edges. In particular, this means that nodes to be removed *must not have* other edges than the one specified in the rule.

Example 2 (Double pushout rule). Consider the rule $r = \langle L, K, R \rangle$ in Fig. 2. We can apply this rule to the graph G, as shown in Fig. 3. First, we have to find a candidate mapping: consider $m = \{A \mapsto 1, B \mapsto 2, C \mapsto 3\}$ (for the sake of clarity, we do not detail the mapping of edges as it is trivial). In the rule, A and C belong to K, so they are not removed. B does not appear in K, so it is removed: we obtain graph $D = G \setminus m(L \setminus K)$. Then, in R, two nodes D_1 and D_2 do not exist in K and have to be created, which gives us graph H.

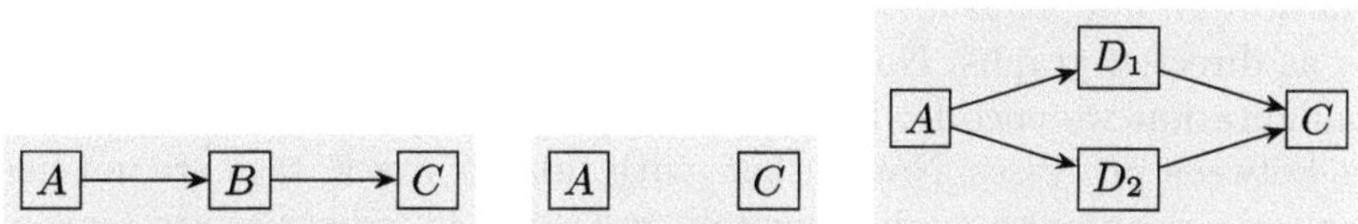

(a) Graph L (b) Graph K (c) Graph R

Fig. 2. A graph rewriting rule consisting of a triplet $\langle L, K, R \rangle$ of graphs.

Conversely, consider the rule in Figure 2 and G' shown in Figure 4. If we try to apply the rule with the same mapping, then D, obtained after removing one node and two edges, would be as shown in Figure 4b. Notice the dangling edge. D being ill-formed, the rule does not apply. Other approaches, such as *single pushout* [20], allow the existence of temporary dangling edges, as illustrated in this example. In our case, we will exploit the fact that all edges must be explicitly shown, which can prevent rule application in certain situations.

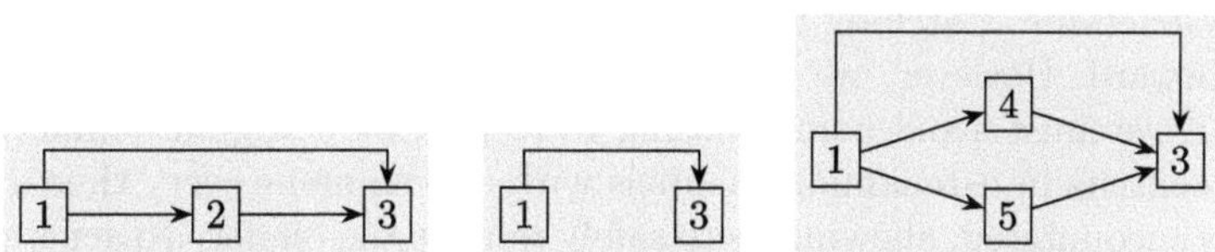

(a) Graph G (b) Graph D (c) Graph H

Fig. 3. Application of the rule in Fig. 2 to a graph G.

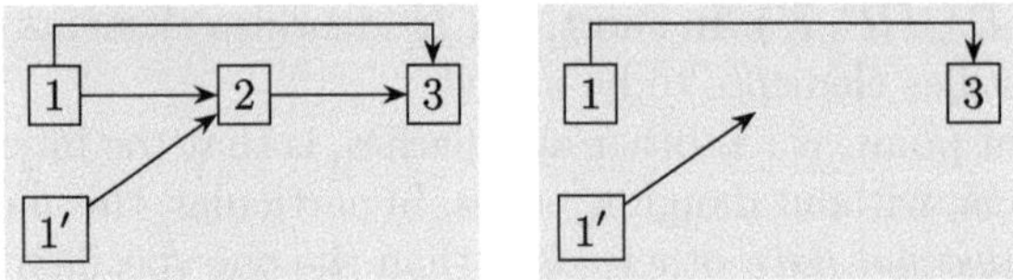

(a) Graph G' (b) H', which is not a graph

Fig. 4. Trying to apply rule r (Fig. 2) when it creates a dangling edge.

3 Encoding $\rho\pi$ as a Graph Rewriting System

3.1 Informal Presentation

Communication and Causal Dependencies. Our goal is to represent $\rho\pi$ configurations as directed graphs. Nodes of graphs represent processes that appear in the configuration we encode. Edges in the graphs represent the causal dependencies between processes. Notice that, with this approach, tags are not needed, and memories require no explicit syntax: processes in memories are represented by nodes with outgoing edges.

Example 3. We encode $\nu k. ([\kappa_1 : a\langle 0\rangle \mid\mid \kappa_2 : a(X) \triangleright (0); k] \mid\mid k : 0)$ as:

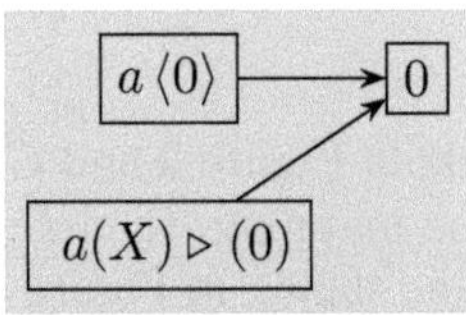

The two nodes on the left have outgoing arrows: there is a process (0 here) that causally depends on them, and they occur in a memory in $\rho\pi$. In this case, we have only one causal link: the interaction between the sender and the receiver creates the continuation. The tag k is used to track this causal link in the $\rho\pi$ configuration, and the two edges are used in the graph.

Name Restrictions. Catching the structure of the causal dependence relations is straightforward. However, we also need to deal with names and ν binders. In particular, we must avoid name aliasing to respect $\rho\pi$'s original semantics. Our strategy consists in α-renaming channels with a fresh name every time a leading $\nu a. (...)$ is encountered, allowing us to safely remove the binder. To generate fresh names, we use the unique special node $\texttt{gen}(a_i)$ as a name generator, creating channel names a_i, with increasing indices. Throughout this paper, we assume that no such channel a_i is present in the initial process.

Example 4 (Managing name restrictions). Consider the following $\rho\pi$ term:

$$T = \kappa : \nu b. (\nu c. (b\langle 0\rangle \mid\mid c\langle 0\rangle))$$

Initially, the graph encoding of that term has a single process node, and the generator node (see Fig. 5, left). Since the term contains a head restriction[7], a fresh name a_1 is generated (using the $\texttt{gen}(a_1)$ node as memory), and free occurrences of b in the continuation are replaced by a_1. We therefore only keep the continuation without the head restriction (i.e. $\nu c.\,(a_1\langle 0\rangle \mid\mid c\langle 0\rangle)$) in a new node. The generator is updated with the next fresh name available (here $\texttt{gen}(a_2)$). This leads to Fig. 5, middle. Proceeding similarly with the next restriction ($\nu c.\,(...)$), we replace free occurrences of c with a_2, and we update the generator, leading to Fig. 5, right.

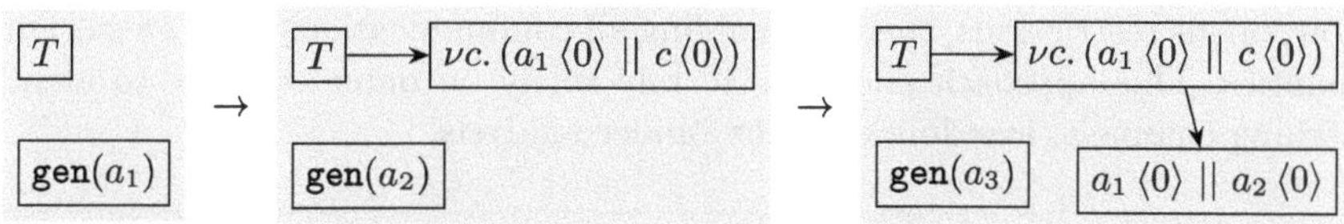

Fig. 5. Renaming channels and removing restrictions. Notice how the $\texttt{gen}(a_i)$ node always contains the next available name.

3.2 Graph Structure

Our graphs are composed of labeled vertices and unlabeled edges. Vertex labels are terms of $\mathbf{HO}\pi$ or $\texttt{gen}(a_i)$ for any i. Only a single vertex has a label $\texttt{gen}(a_i)$ for some i (thus ensuring freshness of names), others are labeled with $\mathbf{HO}\pi$ terms. The initial graph of a computation contains only two nodes: one labeled with the initial process, and one labeled with $\texttt{gen}(a_1)$.

3.3 Graph Rewriting Rules

We now focus on the graph rewriting rules required to implement the semantics of $\rho\pi$. We begin with two core rules, (Fw) and (Bw), which correspond to the forward and backward reductions of $\rho\pi$, respectively. Contrary to $\rho\pi$, we deal with ν binders by substituting bound occurrences of the name with a fresh name and removing the binder. This enables the communication rule to operate simply by checking name equality, ignoring binders. To achieve this result, we introduce in Sect. 3.3 a (NuFresh) rule, which performs this substitution. Finally, although our graph-based approach removes the need for most structural equivalence rules, we must still address parallel composition: a parallel composition must be splittable into its sub-processes. In this section, we introduce the rules for splitting and merging nodes.

[7] We say a term has a head restriction when it is of the form $\nu a.\,(...)$ for some a.

Forward Computation. The only forward computation that $\rho\pi$ processes can perform is communication. For that, we match two vertices—a sender and a receiver—using the same channel name. When a match is found, we create a new node whose label corresponds to the continuation of the communication. As in $\rho\pi$, if a trigger (a.k.a. a receive) binds X in Q, upon receiving a message P, the process continues with $Q\{^P/_X\}$. We then add causal dependency edges from the original processes to this continuation. To prevent a communication from occurring multiple times, the rule is restricted: it can only be applied if both the sender and the receiver have no outgoing causal edges.

Notice that, formally, this rule allows communication on open channel names: the a in the rule is not bound nor restricted. The (NuFresh) rule, introduced below, opens restrictions, thereby enabling all communications as in $\rho\pi$'s original semantics. This approach allows us to rely solely on name equality to identify matching channels, avoiding complex binder analysis.

Rule: (Fw)

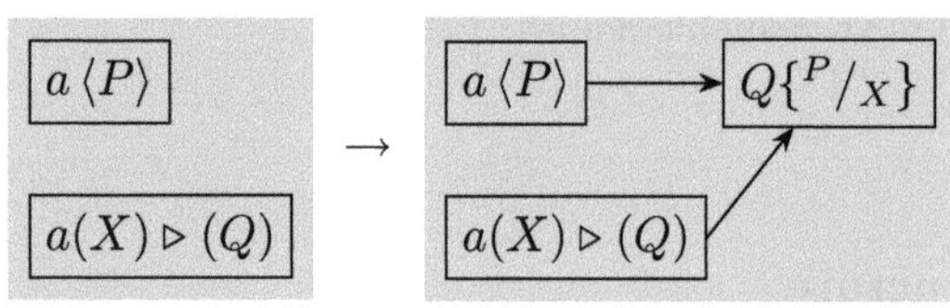

If there is no outgoing edge from the nodes in the left-hand side.

Backward Computation. In $\rho\pi$, backward computation is performed by removing processes and restoring the memory that generated them. The causal dependencies are tracked by using keys. In our approach, these causal dependencies are represented by graph edges.

Two points require special attention. First, the process to be removed has to be *live*, i.e. it must not have any consequences. This is checked by ensuring it has no outgoing edge[8]. Second, all consequences of the restored communication must be removed simultaneously. This is ensured by forbidding the existence of other outgoing edges from the restored process. In order to trigger the rule, all sub-processes of the continuation have to be merged together in a single vertex.

[8] Notice that the DPO approach prevents removed vertices to have edges except those that are explicitly shown in the left-hand side of the rule. We explicitly add the (spurious) condition in the rule for the sake of clarity.

Rule: (Bw)

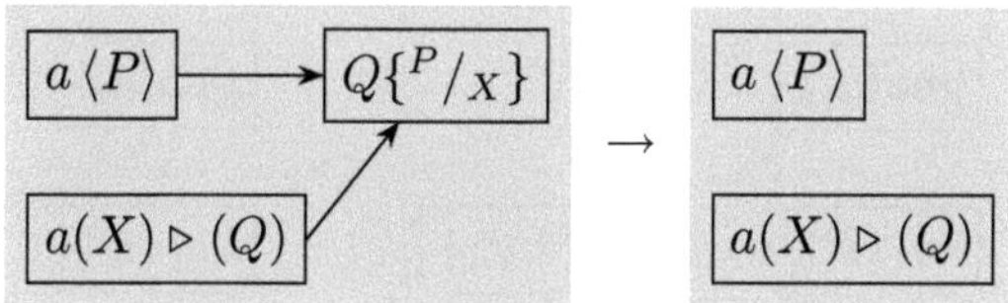

If there is no other outgoing edge from the three vertices of the left-hand side.

Name Binding Rules. As explained above, to identify matching channels for communication, we rely on channel name equality, disregarding binders. To this end, we introduce the rule (NuFresh), which *opens* restrictions. This rule transforms a term of the form $\nu a.\,(P)$ into $P\{^{a_i}/_a\}$, where a_i is a fresh name. Freshness is ensured by using the unique generator node of the graph, which is incremented simultaneously with the application of the rule.

Notice that, since a_i is fresh, all surrounding open channel names are distinct from a_i. Moreover, bound names cannot participate in communications with (Fw) before being open themselves, i.e. freshly renamed. The correctness of this approach relies on the observation that, for all P, Q, a: $P \mid\mid \nu a.\,(Q) \equiv \nu a_i.\,(P \mid\mid Q\{^{a_i}/_a\})$, provided that a_i does not occur free in P, which is guaranteed when it is fresh. This term behaves similarly to $P \mid\mid Q\{^{a_i}/_a\}$[9].

Rule: (NuFresh)

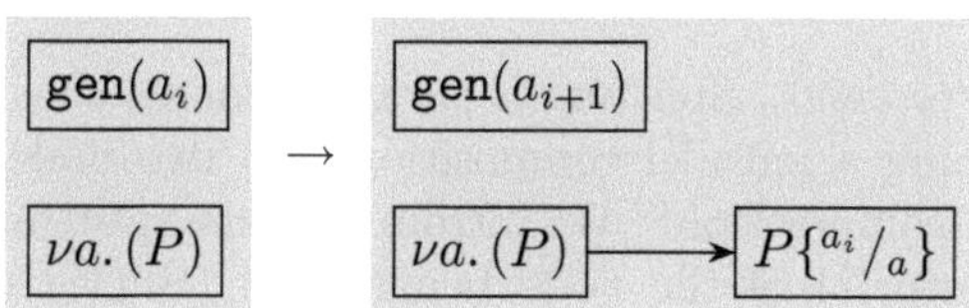

If there is no outgoing edge from $\nu a.\,(P)$.

[9] Note, however, that this approach breaks barbed similarity of processes. In our graph approach: we cannot freely merge two graphs.

Rule: (NuRestrict)

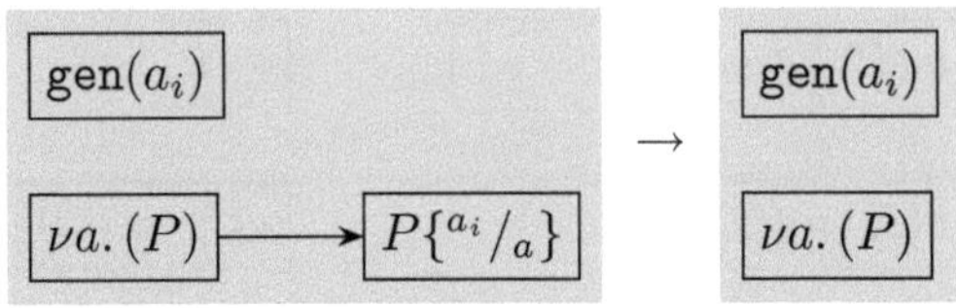

If there is no outgoing edge from $P\{^{a_i}/_a\}$.

Structural Equivalence Rules. As mentioned in the introduction of the section, using a graph approach simplifies most structural equivalence rules (e.g. commutativity and associativity of the parallel composition are ensured by the very structure of the graph). Nonetheless, one point must still be addressed: when a single vertex contains a parallel composition of processes, we have to be able to split it into two vertices, each containing one side of the composition. Conversely, this implies having the ability to merge such split vertices in order to reassemble them into a single vertex before backward computation. This mechanism is essentially the counterpart of tag splitting and merging in $\rho\pi$.

In this graph rewriting-based approach, the split operation is performed by replacing a vertex by two new vertices (and conversely for merging). The only point of attention is the preservation of incoming edges: they have to be replicated in the newly generated nodes. Since incoming edges can originate from different kind of ancestors (either from a communication or from a restriction opening), we actually have a *family* of split (resp. merge) rules. In the following, we first introduce the splitting rules, and then their merging counterparts.

Splitting Parallel Processes. Splitting a parallel process consists in replacing a single node containing a parallel composition into two nodes containing both sides of the parallel composition[10].We introduce three splitting rules, depending on the causal ancestor(s) of the node being split: (SplitCom) applies when the process originates from a communication, (SplitNu) when it results from opening a restriction, and (SplitInit) when it corresponds to the initial process.

Moreover, no rule introduces outgoing edges from parallel processes. This enforces the invariant that parallel processes have no causal descendants, ensuring that the nodes being split do not belong to memories.

[10] Note that, contrary to $\rho\pi$'s structural congruence, which allows (and requires) a tag to be split into all subprocesses at once, our approach must rely on binary composition. This is because graph rewriting rules are defined over (finite and fixed) graphs: allowing an arbitrary number of parallel components to be split simultaneously would require an infinite family of rules.

Rule: (SplitCom)

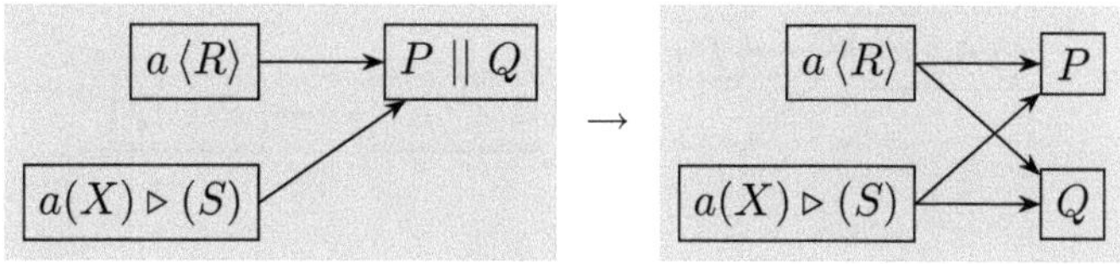

Rule: (SplitNu)

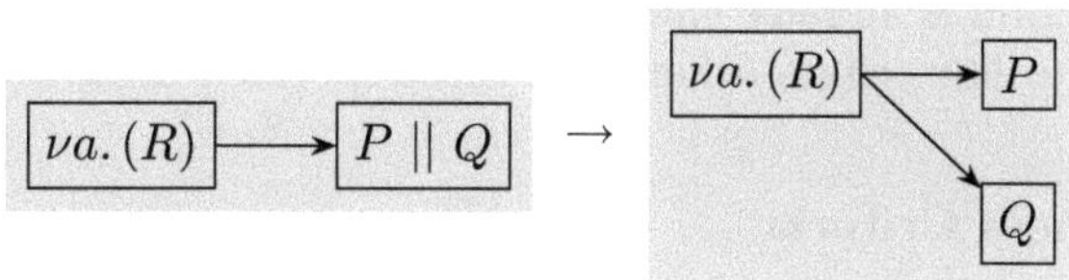

In the case of (SplitInit), we explicitly require that the initial $P \parallel Q$ node has no incoming edges, to indicate that it corresponds to the initial process. This restriction is, however, redundant: under the DPO semantics, any rule must explicitly specify all edges incident to removed nodes, which already prevents the rule from applying when incoming edges are present.

Merging Parallel Vertices. The (Bw) rule requires the vertex to be removed to be the only successor of the memory being restored. Consequently, if the continuation of a communication has been split in order to continue the forward computation, the corresponding sub-processes must first be merged back into a single vertex to perform backward computation. For that, we introduce a family of merge rules. Similar to split rules, we have to accommodate three different cases, depending on the origin of the vertices to be merged: continuations created by a communication (MergeCom), by opening a restriction (MergeNu), or belonging to the initial process (MergeInit).

Rule: (MergeCom)

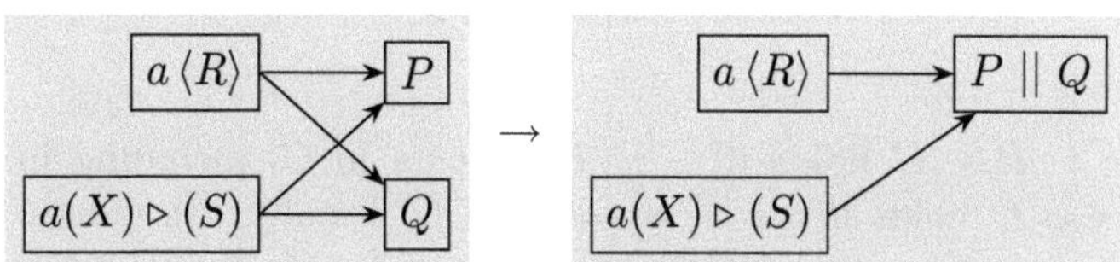

If there is no edges from or to P and Q in the left-hand side.

Rule: (MergeNu)

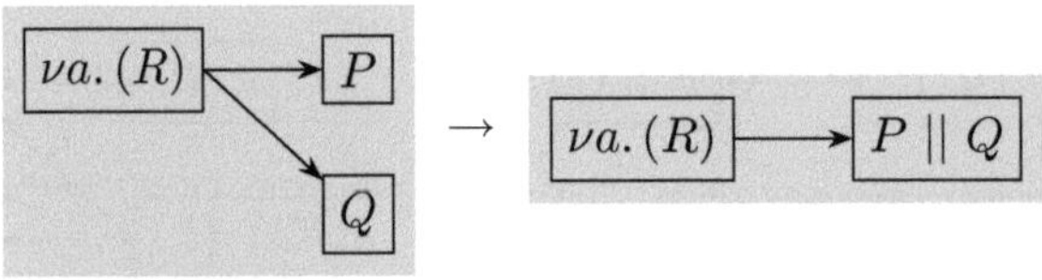

If there is no outgoing edges from P and Q in the left-hand side.

Notice that in the three rules, we explicitly add the condition that the vertices containing P and Q must have no outgoing edges. However, and as in the split rule, this restriction is already enforced by the DPO semantics, which prevents removed nodes to have edges other than those specified in the rule.

3.4 Correctness Criteria

In this section, we present the relationship between $\mathsf{G}\rho\pi\mathsf{F}$ and $\rho\pi$. A formal proof of the correspondence between the two systems lies beyond the scope of this work and is left for future research. First, we present how to convert a graph into a $\rho\pi$ configuration; and then we state the correctness conjecture.

Encoding $\rho\pi$ Terms as Graphs. Our goal is to encode any $\rho\pi$ configuration as a graph. To this end, we define a encoding function $[\![\cdot]\!]$ that maps a configuration to a graph. We assume this function is constant for structurally equivalent configurations. Therefore, for the sake of simplicity, we restrict its definition to configurations in thread-normal form.

The encoding proceeds as follows. First, it ignores leading channel restrictions, since these are replaced with fresh names in $\mathsf{G}\rho\pi\mathsf{F}$ and, in thread-normal form, names are not aliased. It then creates a node for each tagged process or memory. Edges are introduced to represent causal dependencies, which are tracked via tags. Formally, we define two functions $\mathrm{nodes} : C \mapsto V$ and $\mathrm{edges} : C \mapsto E$, which return the set of nodes and edges, respectively, of the graph corresponding to the configuration to encode:

$$\mathrm{nodes}(C) = \{\kappa : P \mid \kappa : P \in C\}$$

$$\mathrm{edges}(C) = \{(\kappa_1 : P, \kappa_2 : Q) \mid \exists\, [\mu; k]^{\circ} \in_M C \cdot k >_C \kappa_2 \wedge \kappa_1 : P \in \mu\}$$

where $\kappa : P \in C$ holds iff $\kappa : P$ appears in C, including in memories; and $[\mu; k]^{\circ} \in_M C$ holds iff $[\mu; k]^{\circ}$ appears in C. Finally, we assume a function rmvTags which removes tags from processes in nodes of a graph, while preserving edges. Thus, our encoding function is $[\![C]\!] = \mathrm{rmvTags}(\langle \mathrm{nodes}(C), \mathrm{edges}(C)\rangle)$.

In future works, our goal would be to prove a form of behavioural correspondence between $\rho\pi$ configurations and their encodings in $\mathsf{G}\rho\pi\mathsf{F}$. We conjecture the relation $\{\langle C, [\![C]\!]\rangle\}$ is a weak bisimulation. Reduction rules of $\rho\pi$ are matched by

(Fw) and (Bw), but additional steps are needed in G$\rho\pi$F to mimic structural equivalence reshaping. Having such bisimulation is sufficient to prove that our semantics preserves $\rho\pi$'s causal consistency.

3.5 Example

Figure 6 illustrate the derivation of the *replication* construct by adapting the **HO**π replicator introduced in [2]:

$$\nu c.\, (c(X) \triangleright (X \mid\mid c\langle X\rangle \mid\mid P) \mid\mid c\langle c(X) \triangleright (X \mid\mid c\langle X\rangle \mid\mid P)\rangle).$$

Intuitively, the left process $c(X) \triangleright (X \mid\mid c\langle X\rangle \mid\mid P)$ acts as a replication core: upon receiving a process X, it executes X, re-sends it along the same channel, and generates an occurrence of a process P. By sending this replication core to itself, we obtain an infinite behaviour generating a new process P each time a communication on c occurs. We illustrate the semantics of G$\rho\pi$F using this example. For the sake of simplicity, throughout the example, the generator node is omitted whenever it plays no role in the transition. For the sake of conciseness, unless a communication rule occurs, we note $\mathbf{R}_c$ for the replication core $c(X) \triangleright (X \mid\mid c\langle X\rangle \mid\mid P)$, where the index denotes the channel used for replication, in nodes that do not take part in the transition.

The derivation starts with a (NuFresh) step, which introduces a fresh channel (namely c_1) to ensure locality and avoid name capture. The (SplitNu) rule then splits the body of the restriction, generating two nodes communicating through c_1.

Successive applications of (Fw) and (SplitCom) develops the communication structure, exhibiting a sender-receiver couple and making them interact.

Then, the subsequent backward steps ((Bw), (MergeCom), (MergeNu), (NuRestrict)) shows that the transformation is reversible and preserves the global structure of the system, without loss of information. Finally, an additional (NuFresh) step (e.g. producing c_2) highlights the α-renaming mechanism of channel management.

4 Implementation

G$\rho\pi$F is the Python implementation accompanying this paper, designed to provide both a faithful realization of the graph-based semantics of $\rho\pi$ and an accessible interface for experimentation. The interpreter, together with instructions for running it, are available at [5].

Overview. ??

Since $\rho\pi$ is uncontrolled and π-calculi are inherently nondeterministic, G$\rho\pi$F is designed to be interactive. Its main goal is to let users, including those unfamiliar with the calculus, experiment with processes by explicitly trying possible (and

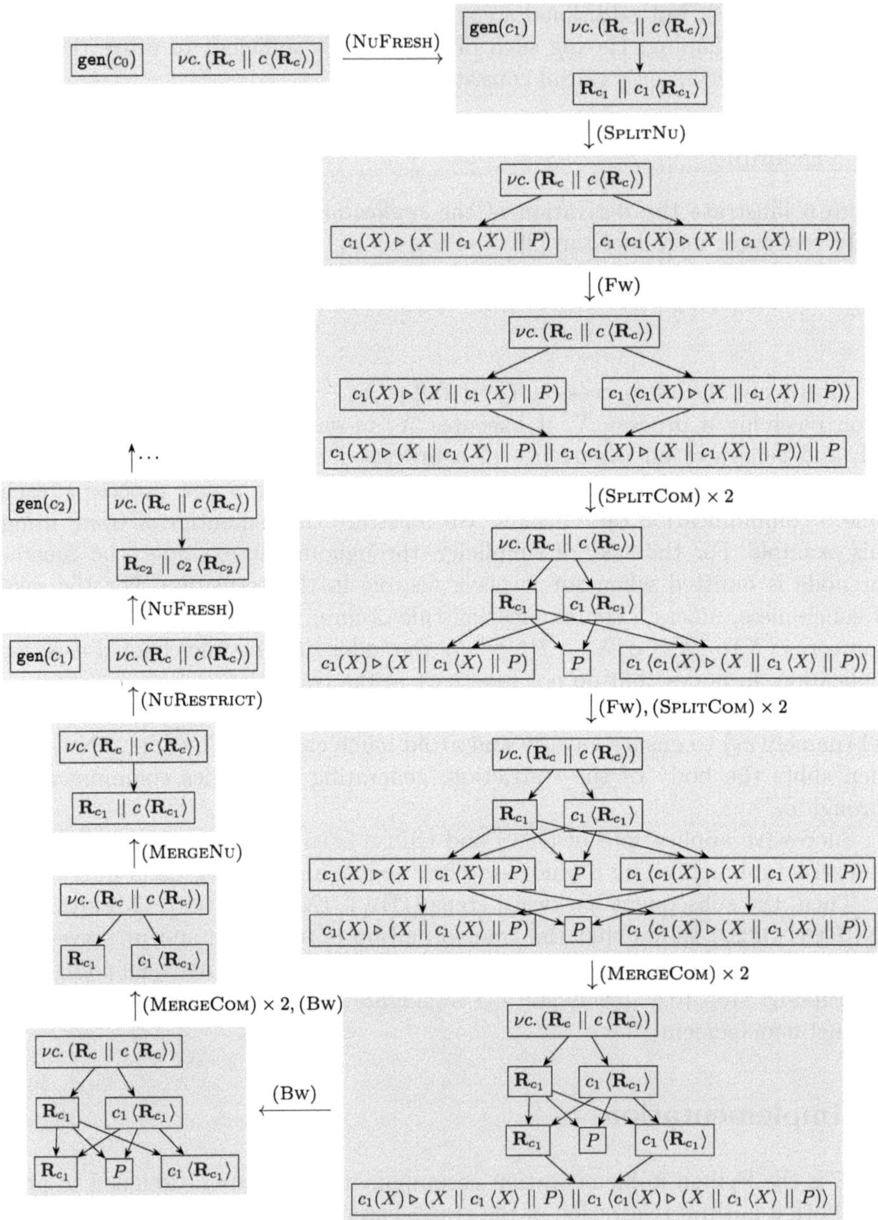

Fig. 6. Example of derivation starting from the process $\nu c.\,(\mathbf{R}_c \parallel c\,\langle \mathbf{R}_c \rangle)$ on the top-left corner.

impossible) applications of rewriting rules. Users interact through a web interface (see Fig. 7), where buttons at the top allow applying rules to nodes previously selected in the graph. This enables step-by-step exploration of process reductions and causal dependencies. For the sake of clarity, split (resp. merge) rules have a single button instead of three separate ones. Depending on the selected node, the adequate rule is inferred.

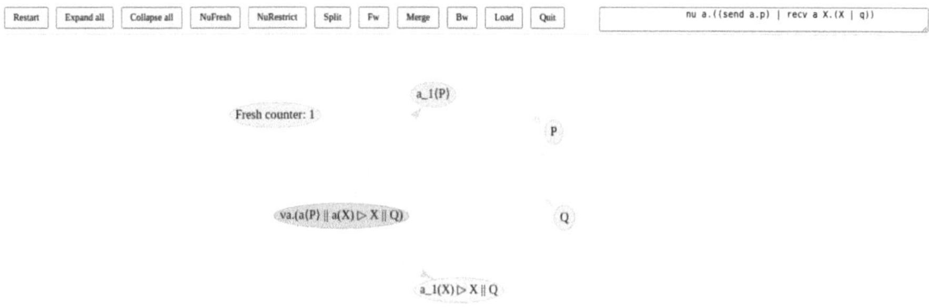

Fig. 7. Overview of the web interface of G$\rho\pi$F.

Automated Mode. In addition to the interactive mode, G$\rho\pi$F provides an automated execution mode. The *Expand all* button repeatedly applies all enabled forward-oriented rules, namely (NuFresh) and the family of splitting rules ((SplitInit), (SplitNu), (SplitCom)), until no further application is possible. Conversely, the *Collapse all* button repeatedly applies merge rules ((MergeInit), (MergeNu), (MergeCom)) together with (Bw), rolling back the configuration as far as possible. These automated operations allow users to quickly explore maximal forward computations or revert configurations without manually selecting individual nodes[11]. Combined with the interactive mode, they provide a user-friendly way to explore the global behavior of $\rho\pi$ processes.

Parser. On the top-right corner of the page, the user can write a $\rho\pi$ term, which is then parsed and loaded as the initial term of the computation using the `Load` button. The interpreter parses $\rho\pi$ terms using a dedicated grammar that closely mirrors the formal syntax. Parallel composition is left-associative, and parentheses can be used to group processes. When writing terms, only variables can be capitalized, while channel and process names must be lowercase. Parallel composition is denoted with `|`, and the termination process is written as `0`.

Example 5 (G$\rho\pi$F input terms). The following entry corresponds to the communication example shown in Example 1.

```
nu a.((send a.p) | recv a X.(X | q))
```

[11] Note that, in order to avoid skipping steps, rules must be applied in a specific order (i.e. by performing merge rules before (Bw)).

The following entry corresponds to the replicator example shown in Sect. 3.5.

```
nu c.(recv c X.((X | send c.X) | p)) | send c.(recv c X.((X | send c.X) | p))
```

5 Conclusion

5.1 Related Work

Multiple works use graph-based descriptions of reversible process calculi (at least informally). In this subsection, we review some of these contributions to highlight how our formalization can bridge the gap between intuitive graphical ideas and formal descriptions.

First, Petri Nets enjoy intuitive graph-based representations. Extensive work has been propose in recent years to study reversibility in Petri Nets [21,24,25].

Regarding process calculi, in [11], Fabbretti et al. informally present a mechanism for rollback when some causal dependencies are lost. While the authors did not focus on providing a formal framework to introduce their idea, it can easily be expressed in ours: they examine what happens when some vertices or edges in the graph are arbitrarily removed, and how to recover from such removal. From this description, we can close the gap and express their work in $\rho\pi$: they study what happens when some memories or tags (or even live processes) are erased in $\rho\pi$'s configurations.

On the other hand, graph-based approaches help with pattern identification. In [19], Lanese et al. develop a variant of **roll** $-\, \pi$ [16] (itself a variant of $\rho\pi$ with controlled reversibility) where some communications can be committed. Thanks to a graph-based approach, they realized a form of duality between rollbacks and commits: each operation removes extrema of the *happens-before* relation. Reverting communication consists in removing vertices without outgoing edges, while committing consists in removing vertices without incoming edges. This illustrates how graphical approaches could be useful, even for accustomed researchers.

On the practical side, graph transformation has led to the development of various tools and environments. General-purpose systems such as `AGG` [26] support algebraic graph transformation based on the DPO approach, together with features such as critical pair analysis and consistency checking. Similarly, `GROOVE` [13] provides a modelling and verification environment for graph transformation systems, with automated state-space generation, exploration, and model checking. More generally, the `Maude` [6] is a rewriting logic framework that offers a general infrastructure for specifying and analyzing rewrite systems.

Graph rewriting has also been applied in more specialized domains. In systems biology, rule-based languages such as `Kappa` [4] and `BioNetGen` [12] rely on graph rewriting to model molecular interactions and their causal dependencies. In model-driven engineering, `Henshin` [1] and `VIATRA` [27] support rule-based model transformations over the Eclipse Modeling Framework, where transformation rules are expressed as graph patterns and executed directly on model instances.

Although our system could in principle be implemented using existing tools, we developed a dedicated interpreter in order to better control the semantics and adapt design choices to the specific needs of reversible process calculi.

5.2 Future Work

We introduced a graph-based semantics for $\rho\pi$. While the rules are close to $\rho\pi$'s original semantics, in this work, we focused on the presentation and the implementation of the framework, without formally proving the correspondence with the original semantics. Therefore, in the current state, the framework ought to be understood as a supporting tool for intuitively introducing readers to $\rho\pi$, or to develop intuition on reversible process calculi. In the future, we hope to formally prove the correspondence with $\rho\pi$, thus allowing researchers to develop variants (such as the one mentioned in the related works above) in a graphical way, while keeping a formal relation to well established $\rho\pi$.

An example of such variants would be to merge memories to have coarsed grained memories. Such variant would be difficult to formalize in $\rho\pi$, due to the accumulation of tags, but would be very intuitive in our graph approach: one simply needs to allow merging vertices while preserving incoming and outgoing edges.

Finally, while $\mathsf{G}\rho\pi\mathsf{F}$ currently supports both interactive exploration and automated forward/backward rule application, future work will focus on improving automation features. One possibility is to allow the tool to automatically apply sequences of rules, exploring the different ways a process can evolve or searching for paths between two states, inspired by e-graph search techniques [22,23]. This would help users experiment with process behaviors more efficiently and observe possible computations without manually selecting each step. Such automation could also serve as a first step toward checking simple properties, such as whether a particular state can be reached, while keeping the tool easy to use.

References

1. Arendt, T., Biermann, E., Jurack, S., Krause, C., Taentzer, G.: Henshin: advanced concepts and tools for in-place EMF model transformations. In: Petriu, D.C., Rouquette, N., Haugen, Ø. (eds.) MODELS 2010. LNCS, vol. 6394, pp. 121–135. Springer, Heidelberg (2010). https://doi.org/10.1007/978-3-642-16145-2_9
2. Barwell, A.D., Hou, P., Vassor, M., Yoshida, N.: Encoding choice and replication in roll-π. In: Glück, R., Kaarsgaard, R. (eds.) Reversible Computation, pp. 27–36. Springer Nature Switzerland, Cham (2025). https://doi.org/10.1007/978-3-031-97063-4_3
3. Bonchi, F., Gadducci, F., Kissinger, A., Sobocinski, P., Zanasi, F.: String diagram rewrite theory I: rewriting with Frobenius structure. J. ACM **69**(2) (2022). https://doi.org/10.1145/3502719
4. Boutillier, P., et al.: The kappa platform for rule-based modeling. Bioinformatics **34**(13), i583–i592 (2018)

5. Cailler, J., Vassor, M.: G$\rho\pi$F: graphical $\rho\pi$ framework (2026). https://doi.org/10.5281/zenodo.18662588
6. Clavel, M., et al.: All About Maude-a High-Performance Logical Framework: How to Ppecify, Program, and Verify Systems in Rewriting Logic, vol. 4350. Springer (2007)
7. Ehrig, H., Engels, G., Kreowski, H.J., Rozenberg, G. (eds.): Handbook of Graph Grammars and Computing by Graph Transformation: vol. 2: Applications, Languages, and Tools. World Scientific Publishing Co., Inc., USA (1999)
8. Ehrig, H., Kreowski, H.J., Montanari, U., Rozenberg, G. (eds.): Handbook of Graph Grammars and Computing by Graph Transformation: vol. 3: Concurrency, Parallelism, and Distribution. World Scientific Publishing Co., Inc., USA (1999)
9. Ehrig, H., Ehrig, K., Prange, U., Taentzer, G.: Fundamentals of Algebraic Graph Transformation. Monographs in Theoretical Computer Science. An EATCS Series. Springer-Verlag, Heidelberg (2006). https://doi.org/10.1007/3-540-31188-2
10. Ehrig, H., Pfender, M., Schneider, H.J.: Graph-grammars: an algebraic approach. In: 14th Annual Symposium on Switching and Automata Theory (SWAT 1973), pp. 167–180. IEEE (1973)
11. Fabbretti, G., Lanese, I., Stefani, J.B.: Reversibility with holes. In: Mogensen, T.Æ., Mikulski, Ł. (eds.) Reversible Computation, pp. 69–74. Springer Nature Switzerland, Cham (2024). https://doi.org/10.1007/978-3-031-62076-8_5
12. Faeder, J.R., Blinov, M.L., Hlavacek, W.S.: Rule-based modeling of biochemical systems with BioNetGen. In: Systems Biology, pp. 113–167. Springer (2009)
13. Ghamarian, A.H., de Mol, M., Rensink, A., Zambon, E., Zimakova, M.: Modelling and analysis using groove. Int. J. Softw. Tools Technol. Transfer **14**(1), 15–40 (2012)
14. Lamport, L.: Time, clocks and the ordering of events in a distributed system. Commun. ACM **21**(7), 558–565 (1978). Reprinted in several collections, including Distributed Computing: Concepts and Implementations, McEntire et al. (ed.), pp. 558–565. IEEE Press, 1984 (1978). https://www.microsoft.com/en-us/research/publication/time-clocks-ordering-events-distributed-system/
15. Lanese, I., Lienhardt, M., Mezzina, C.A., Schmitt, A., Stefani, J.-B.: Concurrent flexible reversibility. In: Felleisen, M., Gardner, P. (eds.) ESOP 2013. LNCS, vol. 7792, pp. 370–390. Springer, Heidelberg (2013). https://doi.org/10.1007/978-3-642-37036-6_21
16. Lanese, I., Mezzina, C.A., Schmitt, A., Stefani, J.-B.: Controlling reversibility in higher-order Pi. In: Katoen, J.-P., König, B. (eds.) CONCUR 2011. LNCS, vol. 6901, pp. 297–311. Springer, Heidelberg (2011). https://doi.org/10.1007/978-3-642-23217-6_20
17. Lanese, I., Mezzina, C.A., Stefani, J.-B.: Reversing higher-order Pi. In: Gastin, P., Laroussinie, F. (eds.) CONCUR 2010. LNCS, vol. 6269, pp. 478–493. Springer, Heidelberg (2010). https://doi.org/10.1007/978-3-642-15375-4_33
18. Lanese, I., Mezzina, C.A., Stefani, J.B.: Reversibility in the higher-order π-calculus. Theor. Comput. Sci. **625**, 25–84 (2016). https://doi.org/10.1016/j.tcs.2016.02.019
19. Lanese, I., Mezzina, C.A., Vassor, M.: Bounded reversibility in HOπ. In: Mezzina, C.A., Schmitt, A. (eds.) Components Operationally: Reversibility and System Engineering: Essays Dedicated to Jean-Bernard Stefani on the Occasion of His 65th Birthday, pp. 24–45. Springer Nature Switzerland, Cham (2025). https://doi.org/10.1007/978-3-031-99717-4_2
20. Löwe, M.: Algebraic approach to single-pushout graph transformation. Theoret. Comput. Sci. **109**(1–2), 181–224 (1993)

21. Melgratti, H., Mezzina, C.A., Ulidowski, I.: Reversing P/T Nets. In: Riis Nielson, H., Tuosto, E. (eds.) Coordination Models and Languages, pp. 19–36. Springer International Publishing, Cham (2019). https://doi.org/10.1007/978-3-030-22397-7_2
22. Nelson, G., Oppen, D.C.: Fast decision procedures based on congruence closure. J. ACM (JACM) **27**(2), 356–364 (1980)
23. Nieuwenhuis, R., Oliveras, A.: Proof-producing congruence closure. In: International Conference on Rewriting Techniques and Applications, pp. 453–468. Springer (2005)
24. Philippou, A., Psara, K.: Reversible computation in petri nets. In: Kari, J., Ulidowski, I. (eds.) RC 2018. LNCS, vol. 11106, pp. 84–101. Springer, Cham (2018). https://doi.org/10.1007/978-3-319-99498-7_6
25. Philippou, A., Psara, K., Siljak, H.: Controlling reversibility in reversing petri nets with application to wireless communications. In: Thomsen, M.K., Soeken, M. (eds.) RC 2019. LNCS, vol. 11497, pp. 238–245. Springer, Cham (2019). https://doi.org/10.1007/978-3-030-21500-2_15
26. Taentzer, G.: AGG: a graph transformation environment for modeling and validation of software. In: International Workshop on Applications of Graph Transformations with Industrial Relevance, pp. 446–453. Springer (2003)
27. Varró, D., Bergmann, G., Hegedüs, Á., Horváth, Á., Ráth, I., Ujhelyi, Z.: Road to a reactive and incremental model transformation platform: three generations of the VIATRA framework. Softw. Syst. Model. **15**(3), 609–629 (2016)
28. Vassor, M.: Reversibility and predictions. In: Yamashita, S., Yokoyama, T. (eds.) RC 2021. LNCS, vol. 12805, pp. 163–181. Springer, Cham (2021). https://doi.org/10.1007/978-3-030-79837-6_10

Automatic Generation of Generators for Property-Based Testing with Inverse Interpretation

Joachim Tilsted Kristensen[1], Triera Gashi[2], and Michael Kirkedal Thomsen[1,3(✉)]

[1] Department of Informatics, University of Oslo, Oslo, Norway
{joachkr,michakt}@ifi.uio.no
[2] Statens Pensjonskasse, Oslo, Norway
triera.gashi@spk.no
[3] Department of Computer Science, University of Copenhagen, Copenhagen, Denmark

Abstract. Property-based testing offers program validation by generating random inputs to validate behavioural program properties. However, manually writing test-input generators remains a high barrier to adoption in industrial settings.

This paper introduces pun, a proof-of-concept programming language that supports property-based testing natively. pun aims to generate inputs automatically based on inverse interpretation of its typing judgement rules. This approach significantly lowers the barrier of entry, but our evaluation shows that it unfortunately can also lower the quality of the generated inputs.

The main reason for this quality decrease, is that arbitrarily chosen inputs rarely satisfy any pre-conditions that properties may require. However, the inputs do not need to be completely arbitrary and the quality of the generated inputs can be improved by applying non-deterministic inverse interpretation of the property that the test is trying to falsify. We outline in this paper how this approach can be a first step to make manually writing input-generators unnecessary in property-based testing.

Keywords: Property-based Testing · Program Inversion · Inverse Interpretation · Input-generation · QuickCheck

1 Introduction

It is expected that future software developers will rely more and more on generative methods for many of their programming tasks. In order for such co-piloted programming approaches to scale from websites to applications like traffic lights and rocket ship systems, these developers will need effective validation methods, particularly to ensure the reliability of the generated code.

C. Aubert and L. Roversi (Eds.): RC 2026, LNCS 16626, pp. 258–276, 2026.
https://doi.org/10.1007/978-3-032-30839-9_15

Unit testing can be counter-productive in this setting, as LLMs might implement programs to fulfil just these cases, and, furthermore, it is not a very popular activity among developers [10,30]. Besides, developers cannot trust co-piloted unit tests any more than they can trust the co-piloted code itself. On the other hand, property-based testing may justify great confidence in program correctness by generating a large number of random inputs for a set of predicates about the program's behaviour. Libraries for property-based testing, such as QuickCheck [3] for Haskell, are well-known testing tools, especially in the academic environment, but are also used in industry settings [8]. Besides providing the desired properties to test, the user of such tools must also provide *generators* for all non-standard datatypes used in the properties. However, writing generators is not always easy, and has proven to be a significant hindrance to their adoption in industry [18].

The obvious alternative is to aid the programmer by creating the generators for them and this idea is not novel [19]. However, this is easier said than done. We need the generators to be specific to the individual constructs and programs, and not just any generator that makes an arbitrary guess of the correct type. Creating an arbitrary random generator will most likely result in many uninteresting test cases that validate obviously correct parts of the program and, thus, testing of low quality. However, approaches to generating well-typed terms will make this easier [2,6].

High quality testing, on the other hand, should be likely to expose bugs in erroneous programs. More specifically, for a predicate `p`, our goal is to generate a witness `i` such that the proposition `p(i) = False` holds. This suggests an inverse interpretation of testing, where faulty inputs are derived from a fixed undesirable output, namely `False`. In an idealised setting, one could imagine a procedure computing an inverse image `inv(p, False) :: Maybe i`, which is `Nothing` exactly when no counterexample exists. Such a procedure would effectively amount to an automated theorem prover capable of deciding the validity of the predicate. This, however, is not the setting we target: rather than proving the absence of counterexamples, testing aims to efficiently discover likely violating inputs.

An obvious approach to solve this is to apply program inversion [1]. Especially relevant is following the approach of Glück and Kawabe [7], which builds on methods of Korf [14] and Eppstein [4], where inversion is defined over a set of programs. This would allow test generators to be included in addition to the property when deriving the inverse program; but it would still require an enumeration of the (at least faulty) inputs to have full inversion. Alternatively, semi-inversion [13,23] holds the promise to define the inverted property as a relational program (e.g. Prolog), thus potentially giving us all possible faulty inputs. But if one is not careful and limit backtracking, execution of relational programs is likely to diverge.

We note, that this inverse interpretation of testing is quite close to a one-to-many understanding of McCarthy's *generate-and-test* algorithm [22]. Whereas the generate-and-test algorithm is designed to search for inputs to an injective function, property based testing is inherently a search for inputs to a non-injective function. However, we know that generate-and-test is an extremely inefficient algorithm. So how can we then efficiently generate these inputs? If we were working within a fully reversible programming model (such as RFUN or its typed variant [12,28,32]), it would be easy to call the inverse of the property with false: `i = (inv p)(False)`, given that the execution of the reversible program is efficient [16].

However, this does still not account for the test generators and the potential numerous faulty inputs. Furthermore, predicates are particularly trivial functions in the reversible setting, and most interesting testing properties are about conventional deterministic non-injective programs. This forces us to take a relaxed approach that is closer to invertible programming languages (like Jeopardy [15,17] and SPARCL [21]).

Thus, we note that any efficient way of computing a partial inverse relation, `q`, of a property, `p`, will also be an efficient solution to generating inputs, since then

```
p (q False) = False.
```

But finding exact solutions to the above is generally not possible. Therefore, the goal should be to implement generators automatically by means of property-driven inverse methods. Though this builds on the understanding of property-based testing as inverse interpretation semantics, it differs in that only the test generators are derived with inverse program inversion. Tests are still run forward as normal deterministic computations. But with automatic access to test generators, we can expect this to result in higher-quality testing.

In this paper, we present the functional programming language pun, which is designed to support property-based testing natively. Properties written in pun do not rely on a handwritten generator, but the interpreter for pun will instead *automatically generate* test inputs following the random judgements approach presented in Fetscher et al. [5]. However, whereas [5] generate well-typed expressions from standard judgement rules, we derive the inverse interpretation over the typing judgements of pun properties and use these for the test generators. The goal of this inverse approach is to make the generated test more specific to the intended outcomes. Thus, our resulting generator-generator can be viewed as the non-deterministic inverse of the usual inference algorithms generated from the inverse judgements of the properties.

In order to specify a property in pun, the programmer must use the `property` keyword, followed by a name for the property, any arguments that the property may take, and a boolean-typed term to be checked by the system. Consider, for instance, the following property:

```
property plus0-id f n . (f (n) + 0) == (f (n + 0)).
```

This is a well-formed property since the term (after the first ".") is typeable by the built-in type `boolean`, where `f` has type `integer -> integer` and `n` has type `integer`. Running the property checker with this property generates a number of choices for `f` and `n` by randomly choosing judgements from the pun typing rules (Fig. 2), resulting in the output:

```
$ pun --check examples/rc1.pun
testing:plus0-id> ............................ ok
```

On the other hand, consider the following property, which is well-formed for similar reasons.

```
property plus1-id f n . (f (n) + 1) == (f (n + 1)).
```

This property does not hold and the output from pun looks like this:

```
pun --check examples/rc2.pun
testing:plus1-id> .x failed:
shrinking> (((\x -> x + x)(17)) + 1) ==
            ((\x -> x + x)(17 + 1))
after 1 tests.
```

Here pun has chosen f and n arbitrarily, in such a way that the term evaluates to False.

The experiments will show that generating test inputs with pun is feasible; we can find the same errors as state-of-the-art QuickCheck, but have to increase the number of test cases. To remedy this, we will exemplify how it is possible to use inverse interpretation in search of an input that make it yield the output False.

To evaluate this approach to generating test generators, we conduct a comparison to the benchmark of [11]. Specifically, we have implemented the same benchmark in pun and compare the coverage of the two tests.

Structure: Sect. 2 will give a larger example that details our approach. Section 3 formalises the syntax and type system of pun, while Sect. 4 describes how to generate generators from pun programs. Section 5 evaluates the generator generation in pun with a comparison to QuickCheck. Section 6 discusses how to limit the generators for cases where inputs quickly diverge and the relation to other work. Finally, in Sect. 7 we conclude the work.

The implementation of pun, and the benchmarks can be found at https://github.com/jtkristensen/pun-lang. Instructions on how to reproduce the examples shown in the introduction can be found in the file README.md.

2 Do We Need to Write Input Generators Manually at All?

Although writing an input generator for each property in a test-suite is quite a laborious task, doing so is usually superior to using automatic input generators. This section outlines the process of handcrafting generators using QuickCheck in Haskell, which we consider state-of-the-art. This serves to highlight the considerations that must be made when implementing pun. Each example is accompanied by a corresponding pun program and an outline of the differences for further discussion. We start with the example from Sect. 1, which looks like this in Haskell:

```
plus0_id :: Fun Int Int -> Int -> Bool
plus0_id (Fun _ f) n = f n + 0 == f (n + 0)
```

The most notable difference is that the Haskell property is not defined on a function and an integer, but instead on something of type `Fun Int Int` and an integer. The reason is that QuickCheck needs an instance for the type class `Arbitrary`[1] in order to produce inputs for `plus0_id`. `Int` is already an instance of `Arbitrary` as provided by the QuickCheck library, but Haskell's function type is not (and cannot be) an instance of this class. Instead, there is an `Arbitrary` instance for the datatype `Fun` which comes with the following constraints:

```
instance (Function a, CoArbitrary a, Arbitrary b)
   => Arbitrary (Fun a b)
```

For intuition, `b` needs to be an instance of `Arbitrary` because we need to be able to generate the outputs of our arbitrarily generated functions. Furthermore, we must ensure that we generate equal outputs on equal inputs. QuickCheck guarantees the latter by choosing the seed based on its input (and hence it will choose equal seeds for equal inputs).

This first example serves to show that the example from the introduction is indeed achievable using QuickCheck. The Glasgow Haskell Compiler is, in many cases, capable of deriving an instance of a type class called `Generic` from which `CoArbitrary` can be instantiated with very little (and trivial) boilerplate.

The hard part is still implementing `Arbitrary`. One choice for doing so automatically, is to inverse-interpret a collection of typing judgements such as [5], which allows us to produce syntax tree for terms of any type. However, doing so is not always as desirable as one would think.

To make this point, we outline a couple of properties from [11], in which Hughes describes techniques for writing properties of pure functions. The common example is a library for dealing with binary search trees. We have implemented said library in pun, in order to be comparable, and will use this as a benchmark for comparing the Haskell and pun implementations in Sect. 5. In the pun implementation, the first properties look like this:

```
property insert-valid k v t .
  if   valid t
  then valid (insert k v t)
  else true .

property find-post-present k v t .
  if   valid t
  then (find k (insert k v t)) == (Just [v])
  else true .
```

The property `insert-valid` says that `insert` preserves the binary search tree property; `valid` checks that all keys in the left sub-tree are smaller than the key

[1] In essence, the class of things which can be generated based on an integer seed.

in any node, and that the sub-trees are also valid. `find-post-present` checks that you can always find an element that has just been inserted. In Haskell, an equivalent implementation may look like this:

```
data BST = Leaf | Node BST Int Int BST

instance Arbitrary BST where
    arbitrary =
      oneof [ return Leaf
            , insert <$> arbitrary <*> arbitrary <*> arbitrary
            ]

prop_InsertValid :: Int -> Int -> BST -> Bool
prop_InsertValid k v t = valid (insert k v t)

prop_FindPostPresent :: Int -> Int -> BST -> Property
prop_FindPostPresent k v t = find k (insert k v t) === Just v
```

There are several differences between the Haskell and the pun implementations. Most notably, the pun implementation checks a pre-condition in each test (namely that the tree is valid to begin with), whereas the Haskell implementation does not. On the other hand, the Haskell implementation contains an instance of the `Arbitrary` type class. This particular instance is more involved than what meets the eye, because it uses `insert` to generate arbitrary binary search trees. Doing so requires a guarantee that `insert` preserves the binary search tree property, but this is exactly what the first property is testing. In subsequent tests, the Haskell implementation can assume that binary search trees are always valid, but for the benchmark the pun program can only rely on the probability that completely arbitrary binary search trees are sometimes valid.

In the case of binary search trees, this is a fair assumption if the generator sticks to generating small terms. For instance, the valid permutation of a 5-element binary search tree will occur with probability $\frac{1}{5!}$, which is significant. However, any more involved data structure or precondition is generally too unlikely to occur at random to rely entirely on randomness.

3 The pun Programming Language

We present here the syntax and semantics of pun. The language pun is a higher-order functional language that uses call-by-value parameter passing. It is a straightforward extension over simple textbook functional programming languages [26,31] and, thus, we omit details of the operational semantics in the interest of saving space for discussing term generation.

The pun syntax can be found in Fig. 1. A program Δ is a sequence of definitions, each terminated by a dot. An algebraic data type definition is denoted by the keyword `data`, a property by the keyword `property`. Function definitions are denoted by equations as usual, and the syntax $f : \tau$ declares that the program contains a function named f of the type τ; see Fig. 2. The subscript

$$\begin{aligned}
\Delta &::= \texttt{data}\ x = (\mathcal{C}[\tau_i])_j\ .\ \Delta \mid \texttt{property}\ x\ x_i\ .\ t\ .\ \Delta \mid f : \tau\ .\ \Delta \mid f x_i = t\ .\ \Delta \mid \epsilon \\
t &::= x \mid \overline{n} \mid \textbf{true} \mid \textbf{false} \mid \mathcal{C}[t_i] \mid t_0 + t_1 \mid t_0 \leq t_1 \mid \lambda x.t_0 \mid t_1\ t_2 \\
&\quad \mid \textbf{case}\ t\ \textbf{of}\ ;\ p_i \to t_i \mid \textbf{let}\ x = t_1\ \textbf{in}\ t_2 \mid \textbf{rec}\ x.t \\
p &::= x \mid \overline{n} \mid \textbf{true} \mid \textbf{false} \mid \mathcal{C}\ [p_i] \\
c &::= \overline{n} \mid \textbf{true} \mid \textbf{false} \mid \mathcal{C}[c_i] \mid \lambda x.t_0 \\
\tau &::= x \mid \texttt{int} \mid \texttt{bool} \mid \tau_1 \to \tau_2 \mid (\tau_1 \times \tau_2)
\end{aligned}$$

Fig. 1. The syntax of pun, consists of programs Δ, canonical terms c, patterns p and terms t, as well as the grammar of types τ.

notation generally denotes zero or more things, indexed by a (possibly empty) set of integers. For instance, a datatype declaration may look like:

```
data T = C1 [T1, T2] | C2 [ ] | C3 [T1, T2]
```

A property definition consists of a name x, the parameters x_i of the property, and a term t about the x_i that must implicitly be of the built-in type `bool`.

Finally, a term can be a variable x, an integer literal $\overline{n}$, a binary operation (+, ==, $\leq$) on terms. pun also features standard lambda abstraction and application, case expressions, let-expressions and recursive terms. Additionally, a term can be a constructor $\mathcal{C}$ applied to zero or more terms t_i of the appropriate type(s), as dictated by the definition of the datatype.

The typing system for pun can be found in Fig. 2. The typing judgement $\Delta\Gamma \vdash t : \tau$ denotes that a term t has type τ in the typing environment Γ, given a pun program Δ. Γ maps variables to their types. The denotion $\Gamma[x \mapsto \tau]$ means that the typing environment Γ contains the variable x with the type τ. A similar denotion is used to look up defined data declarations in the pun program Δ.

The typing system is fairly standard. A type is either the name of a datatype, one of the built-in types `int` or `bool`, or it is the function type $\tau_1 \to \tau_2$, denoting functions from τ_1 to τ_2.

4 Arbitrary Generator Generation

The ultimate goal of this work is to enable property-based testing *without* requiring the programmer to implement generators alongside their properties. The current implementation of pun adopts a relatively naive approach to this problem by inverse-interpreting the typing rules in Fig. 2, following the method of Fetscher et al. [5]. In essence, the type system is treated not only as a verifier of terms, but also as a constructive specification from which well-typed terms may be generated. We discuss this approach here, although subsequent sections argue that such generators may not be necessary in the first place. Rather than generating inputs directly from the typing relation, we will see that one may instead inverse-interpret the property itself. Alternatively, certain classes of properties might be translated into logical formulas suitable for SMT solving. Another possibility is to analyse the property semantically, searching for an inverse execution path that begins at `False` and terminates with a concrete counterexample.

$$\boxed{\Delta\Gamma \vdash t : \tau}$$

$$\text{Lookup} : \frac{}{\Delta\Gamma \vdash x : \tau}(\Gamma(x) = \tau) \qquad \text{Number} : \frac{}{\Delta\Gamma \vdash \overline{n} : \mathtt{int}}$$

$$\text{True} : \frac{}{\Delta\Gamma \vdash \mathbf{true} : \mathtt{bool}} \qquad \text{False} : \frac{}{\Delta\Gamma \vdash \mathbf{false} : \mathtt{bool}}$$

$$\tau\text{-Constructor} : \frac{\Delta\Gamma \vdash t_i : \tau_i}{\Delta[\mathbf{data}\ \tau = (\mathcal{C}\ [\tau_i])_j]\Gamma \vdash \mathcal{C}\ [t_i]\ : \tau}$$

$$\text{LessThanOrEqual} : \frac{\Delta\Gamma \vdash t_0 : \mathtt{int} \quad \Delta\Gamma \vdash t_1 : \mathtt{int}}{\Delta\Gamma \vdash t_0 \leq t_1 : \mathtt{bool}}$$

$$\text{Addition} : \frac{\Delta\Gamma \vdash t_0 : \mathtt{int} \quad \Delta\Gamma \vdash t_1 : \mathtt{int}}{\Delta\Gamma \vdash t_0 + t_1 : \mathtt{int}}$$

$$\text{Abstraction} : \frac{\Delta\Gamma[x \mapsto \tau_1] \vdash t_0 : \tau_2}{\Delta\Gamma \vdash \lambda x.t_0 : \tau_1 \to \tau_2} \qquad \text{Application} : \frac{\Delta\Gamma \vdash t_1 : \tau_1 \to \tau_2 \quad \Delta\Gamma \vdash t_2 : \tau_1}{\Delta\Gamma \vdash t_1\ t_2 : \tau_2}$$

$$\text{Let} : \frac{\Delta\Gamma \vdash t_1 : \tau_1 \quad \Delta\Gamma[x \mapsto \tau_1] \vdash t_1 : \tau_2}{\Delta\Gamma \vdash \mathbf{let}\ x = t_1\ \mathbf{in}\ t_2 : \tau_2} \qquad \text{Recursion} : \frac{\Delta\Gamma[x \mapsto \tau] \vdash t_0 : \tau}{\Delta\Gamma \vdash \mathbf{rec}\ x.t_0 : \tau}$$

$$\text{Case} : \frac{\Delta\Gamma \vdash t_0 : \tau_1 \quad \Delta\Gamma[x_i \mapsto \tau_i] \vdash p_i : \tau_1 \quad \Delta\Gamma[x_i \mapsto \tau_i] \vdash t_i : \tau_2}{\Delta\Gamma \vdash \mathbf{case}\ t_0\ \mathbf{of}\ ;\ p_i \to t_i\ : \tau_2}(x_i \in \text{free}(p))$$

Fig. 2. The typing rules for pun, given a pun program Δ and a typing environment Γ.

At a high level, generation is formulated as a search procedure for proofs of type inhabitation. Given a specific target type, the generator recursively applies typing rules backwards, reducing the goal to the subgoals induced by the premises of the rule. A successful derivation corresponds directly to a well-typed term inhabiting the target type. Whereas Fetscher et al. target arbitrary user-defined type system, pun has a fixed language definition. This removes several sources of generality required in the original formulation. Consequently, our implementation is significantly smaller and more direct than a general-purpose derivation engine, while preserving the central idea of generating terms through typing derivations.

For instance, consider again the introductory property

```
property plus0-id f n . (f (n) + 0) == (f (n + 0)).
```

where one `f` must inhabit the type[2] $\mathtt{int} \to \mathtt{int}$, and the goal derivation has the form:

$$? : \frac{\begin{matrix} ? \\ \vdots \end{matrix}}{\Delta\Gamma \vdash \mathtt{f} : \mathtt{int} \to \mathtt{int}}$$

The only rule which matches this form is the Abstraction rule (since the conclusion contains an arrow), so the only immediate subgoal must look like:

[2] In this example, we write `int` rather than `integer` in the interest of staying within the page margin.

$$\text{Abstraction}: \frac{?: \dfrac{\begin{matrix}?\\ \vdots\end{matrix}}{\Delta\Gamma[x \mapsto \texttt{int}] \vdash t_0 : \texttt{int}}}{\Delta\Gamma \vdash \texttt{f} : \texttt{int} \rightarrow \texttt{int}} \ (\texttt{f} = \lambda x.t_0)$$

From here, the search for a derivation has several options as the Lookup, Number, Addition, Application, Let, Recursion and Case rules all could possibly conclude a derivation where the type is `int` . For this example, let us pick the Lookup rule which applies because Γ contains the binding $[x \mapsto \texttt{int}]$

$$\text{Abstraction}: \frac{\text{Lookup}: \dfrac{}{\Delta\Gamma[x \mapsto \texttt{int}] \vdash x : \texttt{int}} (\Gamma[x \mapsto \texttt{int}](x) = \texttt{int})}{\Delta\Gamma \vdash \texttt{f} : \texttt{int} \rightarrow \texttt{int}} \ (\texttt{f} = \lambda x.x)$$

Since the derivation is now closed, the generator can safely choose $\lambda x.x$ to instantiate `f`. □

Because the underlying derivation strategy follows directly from Fetscher et al., we do not reproduce the full algorithmic development here. We note, however, that to ensure termination, the generation is parameterized by a size budget that decreases when choosing a rule. When the budget becomes small, the generator preferably chooses canonical terms (in our example above the canonical terms for `int` can only use the Number rule). Additionally, we impose conservative restrictions on the Recursion rule to avoid generating non-terminating terms. For readers interested in additional implementation details, the core derivation procedure is implemented by the function `generateGenerator` in `/src/GeneratorGenerator.hs`. Notably, its return type:

```
Type -> Gen (Term Type)
```

can be viewed as the non-deterministic inverse of the usual type associated with type inference algorithms, which more commonly have types such as:

```
Term () -> Maybe Type
```

5 Evaluating pun

This section evaluates pun by implementing a benchmark based on the binary search tree library presented in *How to Specify it!* [11]. Hughes gives a solid assessment of property-based testing in general (and QuickCheck specifically), which therefore is chosen to be the basis for our benchmark. It is also used to compare the amount of work saved by writing properties in pun.

The goal of this benchmark is *not* to provide a direct comparison to [11] or QuickCheck, which is used by Hughes, but instead to give a reasonable assessment of pun. It gives an indication of how well the automatic generation of generators in pun compares to hand-made generators.

In [11], Hughes presents eight buggy implementations of a library and checks which properties are able to find them, all of which are used here. The bugs that will be searched for are shown in Table 1 and have been re-implemented in pun. The result of the benchmark is shown in Table 2.

Table 1. Bugs that are searched for in the benchmark. This is identical to the bugs that can be found in [11].

Bug #	Description
#1	`insert` discards the existing tree, returning a single-node tree just containing the newly inserted value.
#2	`insert` fails to recognize and update an existing key, inserting a duplicate entry instead.
#3	`insert` fails to update an existing key, leaving the tree unchanged instead.
#4	`delete` fails to rebuild the tree above the key being deleted, returning only the remainder of the tree from that point on.
#5	Key comparisons reversed in `delete`; only works correctly at the root of the tree.
#6	`union` wrongly assumes that all the keys in the first argument precede those in the second.
#7	`union` wrongly assumes that if the key at the root of `t` is smaller than the key at the root of `t'`, then all the keys in `t` will be smaller than the key at the root of `t'`.
#8	`union` works correctly, except that when both trees contain the same key, the left argument does not always take priority.

5.1 The Effect of Test-Case Generation

The automatic test generation always makes a trade-off, between programmer time and test case execution time, where each test case takes a couple of seconds to run, but the programmer saves the work of writing a generator. pun is no exception here, and tests generated with it are expected to run many more test cases than a comparable QuickCheck test in order to find the same bugs. However, with the outlined optimisations, the generator is quite fast and can easily run 100,000 test cases per property within a reasonable time of about 2 s on the mobile edition of an AMD Ryzen 7 PRO 5850U. This should be contrasted with QuickCheck's default 100 test cases, which only give a reasonable test coverage due to specialised hand-written generators.

In Hughes' implementation, he creates a generator for generating valid binary search trees. This is exactly what should not be done in pun since it generates the generator for you. This generator does however not always generate valid binary search trees and, thus, requires us to add a pre-condition in each property to filter out any invalid binary search tree. Generating a valid binary search tree is unfortunately not very likely. However, since both generation and validation of binary trees are relatively fast, we have chosen to run 100,000 tests per property to ensure that we have enough valid trees for our properties.

5.2 Benchmark Implementation

To make a true comparison, the Haskell implementation is used as benchmark for pun. The properties tested when providing a generator, should yield similar results when written in pun as they do for Hughes' QuickCheck implementation. This means that, if we introduce an error in the Haskell implementation that provides an error, then the equivalent error in pun should provide an error message as well. The benchmark suite therefore includes several faulty properties, which Hughes describes in [11], to check that pun does in fact find the same errors as QuickCheck does for the Haskell implementation. Using Hughes' examples exposes pun to several kinds of properties, such as validity, metamorphic, inductive, model-based, post-conditions and preservation of equivalence. This way we can verify that pun finds the same errors as QuickCheck regardless of the kind of property that is being checked.

Part of the result is checking whether pun finds a bug that has been planted intentionally; another part is measuring how much work is saved by not having to provide a generator. The amount of work saved is measured in lines of code.

For metamorphic properties, Hughes checks whether two trees have the same content by first converting them to lists and then comparing them. Because pun does not have built-in lists, we use a particular binary search tree as a way of representing lists when defining our properties in pun.

Let us have a look at the following tree.

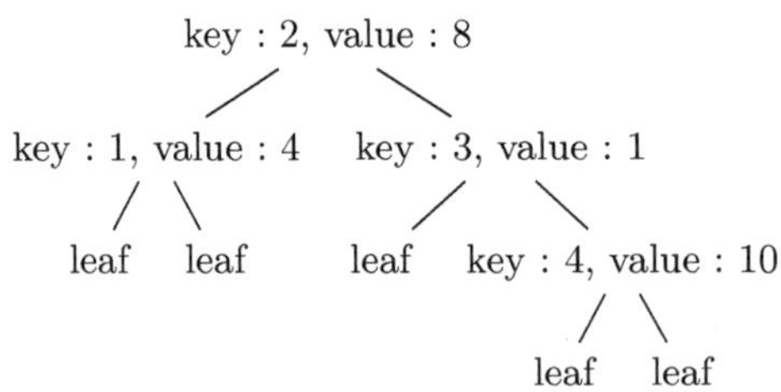

The list representation of this tree in Haskell would be `(1, 4), (2, 8), (3, 1), (4, 10)`. It contains tuples of the nodes' keys and values, sorted in an ascending key-order. Our list representation also expresses these two properties.

Our pun function `model` takes the tree above as input and gives us the following one.

Table 2. Result of benchmark comparing pun to QuickCheck as found in [11]. The description of the bug numbers can be found in Table 1. Bugs found by pun are annotated with ✓, while bugs from [11] are annotated with ✗.

	Insert bugs			Delete bugs		Union bugs		
Validity properties	#1	#2	#3	#4	#5	#6	#7	#8
insert-valid		✓✗						
nil-valid								
delete-valid		✗						
union-valid		✓✗				✓✗	✓✗	
Post-conditions	#1	#2	#3	#4	#5	#6	#7	#8
insert-post	✓✗	✓✗	✓✗					
delete-post		✗		✓✗	✓✗		✓	
find-post-present		✓✗	✓✗					
find-post-absent		✗		✓	✓✗			
insert-delete-complete	✓	✓✗		✓✗				
union-post	✓	✓	✓			✓✗	✓✗	✓✗
Metamorphic properties	#1	#2	#3	#4	#5	#6	#7	#8
insert-insert-weak	✓✗							
insert-insert	✓✗	✓✗	✓✗					
insert-delete-weak				✓✗			✓	
insert-delete		✓✗	✓✗	✓✗			✓	
insert-union	✗	✗	✗			✓✗	✓✗	✓✗
delete-nil							✓	
delete-insert-weak			✓	✓✗			✓	
delete-insert	✓✗	✓✗	✓	✓✗	✓✗		✓	
delete-delete			✓	✓✗	✓✗			
delete-union	✓	✓✗	✓	✓✗	✓✗	✓✗	✓✗	✗
union-nil-1								
union-nil-2	✓						✓	
union-delete-insert	✓✗	✓✗	✓✗	✓✗	✓✗	✓✗	✓✗	✗
union-union-idem	✓	✓				✓✗		
union-union-assoc						✗	✓✗	✗
find-nil								
find-insert	✓✗	✓✗	✓✗					
find-delete	✓	✗		✓✗	✓✗		✓	
find-union	✓	✓	✓			✓✗	✓✗	✓✗
Preservation of equivalence	#1	#2	#3	#4	#5	#6	#7	#8
insert-preserves-equiv								
delete-preserves-equiv	✓✗			✓✗	✓✗	✓	✓	
union-preserves-equiv	✓✗					✓	✓✗	✗
find-preserves-equiv	✓✗							
Completeness of insertions	#1	#2	#3	#4	#5	#6	#7	#8
insert-complete	✓							
insert-complete-for-delete	✓							
insert-complete-for-union	✓✗					✓✗	✓✗	
Model-based properties	#1	#2	#3	#4	#5	#6	#7	#8
nil-model								
insert-model	✓✗	✓✗	✓✗					
delete-model	✓	✗		✓✗	✓✗		✓	
union-model		✗				✗	✗	✗
find-model								
Total failure (pun/[11])	21/12	15/17	13/8	13/12	9/9	10/10	19/10	3/8

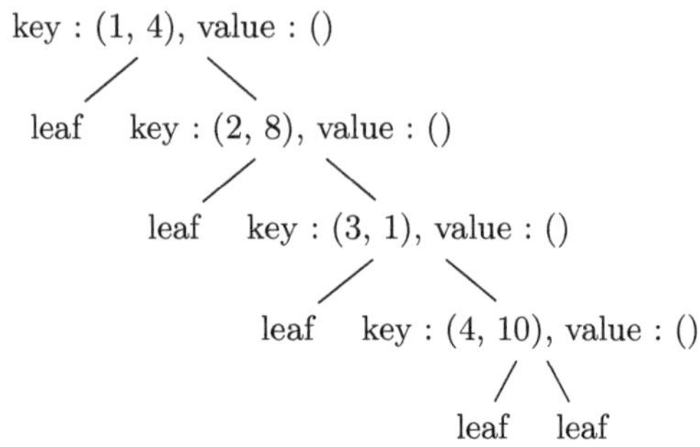

The regular trees contain a key and a value as separate information about the tree, whereas the modified tree contains both the key and value as a tuple where only the key would originally have been stored. The value is replaced by unit, which is used as a way of representing that there is no extra information there. All the left subtrees are replaced with a *leaf* which does not add any new information. The tree is built from left to right, so any new node appears as a right subtree. This construction lets us traverse the tree by following the right subtrees to get the next greater key. By following the parent nodes you get the previous lesser key.

Hughes also uses lists as a model for the model-based properties, in which case we also use the same function that turns a regular binary search tree to one that is isomorphic to lists. The reason this structure is isomorphic is that there are equally many elements in the tree as there would have been in a list. Each key that contains a tuple of the form *(key, value)* counts as an element. There are also mappings in both directions, such that you can have a list and represent it as this specific binary tree structure, and also go from that tree back to its original list form.

5.3 Take-Away from the Benchmark

The result of the benchmark is shown in Table 2. In general, the benchmark results shows that at least blatant errors are easily detected by `pun`, though it may run more tests before finding a counterexample. For instance, when changing the implementation of `insert` from Sect. 2 to

```
insert k1 v1 t = [node leaf k1 v1 leaf].
```

The property `find-post-present` usually fails within 50 tests in both implementations.

However, the benchmark cannot completely imitate the tests from [11]. For certain bugs, such as Bug #1, there are several more properties that fail. The bug is implemented in the `insert` function, and because we have used `insert` in our implementation of `delete` and `union` some of the properties that test those functions fail too. This indicates that Hughes' implementation of `insert` is probably more isolated and has less coverage in the library. The cases where the bugs yield several failed properties do not include all the properties that failed for QuickCheck. < Most of the properties that fail for Hughes, but do not fail in our benchmark, are those that test `delete`. It is therefore likely that his implementation is different from ours.

The validity properties perform poorly and are missing many bugs, but this is similar to Hughes' benchmark. However, post-conditions and metamorphic properties find all the bugs! One difference is that Hughes also mentions that the model-based properties find all the bugs, which is not the case in our benchmark. Our implementation of the missing property 'union-model' in our benchmark did not catch all errors, otherwise it might have failed for bug eight and we would have gotten the same result.

5.4 Work Reduction

Besides comparing what bugs our implementation is able to find compared to Haskell's QuickCheck, part of the result is also showing that our implementation potentially saves several lines of code. Let us have a look at the property `prop_DeleteValid` from Hughes' [11] and the generator it requires.

```
instance (Ord k, Arbitrary k, Arbitrary v) => Arbitrary (BST k v) where
  arbitrary = do
    kvs <- arbitrary
    return $ foldr (uncurry insert) nil (kvs::[(k, v)])
  shrink = filter valid . genericShrink

prop_DeleteValid k t = valid t ==> valid (delete k t)
```

Writing the same property in `pun` lets the programmer write the property without the prerequisite of writing the generator.

```
property insert-valid k v t . if valid t then valid (insert k v t) else true .
```

The difference between the two implementations at first glance is four lines of code, but you have also saved the complexity of figuring out how to write the generator and even writing tests for the generator itself.

Of course, writing properties that do not require a generator does not save you any lines of code in `pun`, but it is not worse, the properties are rather similar except for the syntax. We can have a look at the property `prop_plus0-id` from the introduction written in Haskell,

```
prop_Plus0Id f n = f n . (f (n) + 0) == (f (n + 0))
```

versus the `pun` implementation of the same property.

```
property plus0-id f n . (f (n) + 0) == (f (n + 0)).
```

We could also argue that writing properties in `pun` is easier in the sense that the programmer does not have to write a generator, but that would be an objective matter. It would require us to have programmers write properties in both `pun` and using Haskell's QuickCheck and compare them. That would be an entire paper on its own. However, we can subjectively and with certainty say that if one were to write a generator in Haskell then the work would be reduced in `pun` even if the difference is as little as a single line of code.

6 Improved Searching for Counterexamples

Given a set of typing rules and an interpreter, it is surprisingly easy to write a function that checks a property. Essentially, each free variable in the body of the property can be substituted by a term of the correct type, and polymorphic variables can be substituted by terms of type `int` without loss of generality [9]. However, the terms that provoke an error are usually subtle corner cases for some algorithms. Consider, for instance, the interpreter for a small arithmetic language in pun[3], and a (very) simple optimiser.

```
data Exp = Const [integer] | Plus [Exp, Exp] | Times [Exp, Exp] .

eval : Exp -> integer.
eval (Const [n])       = n.
eval (Plus  [e1, e2]) = eval e1 + eval e2.
eval (Times [e1, e2]) = eval e1 + eval e2. // <-- copy paste bug

simplify : Exp -> Exp.
simplify (Plus  [e1, Const[0]]) = simplify e1.
simplify (Times [e1, Const[1]]) = simplify e1.
simplify e                      = e.

property semantics-preserving e . eval e == (eval (simplify e)) .
```

There is a copy-and-paste error in the code, where the programmer has implemented `Times` using the binary operator +. Additionally, there is a property that states that the optimiser preserves the semantics of the evaluator. Further, if we check this program using pun, it runs significantly more tests to find the error than the examples from Sect. 1:

```
$ pun --check examples/rc3.pun
testing:semantics-preserving> .x failed:
shrinking> eval (Times [Plus [Const [1], Const [-24]], Const [1]])
    == eval (simplify (Times [Plus [Const [1], Const [-24]], Const [1]]))
after 1017 tests.
```

The cause of this increased number of tests, is that it does not always occur that the outermost connective is `Times` and that its left argument is `Const`, and it happens equally rarely that the constant is 1. As such, most possible inputs are uninteresting, because they do not invoke the case in `simplify` that reveals the bug. The probability of getting such "boring" results increases rapidly with the simplest of extensions to the datatype `Exp`.

However, non-deterministic inverse interpretation of the property `semantics-preserving` does not require the same kind of guessing. For instance, in the same manner as we did for computing random judgements, we can analyse the different reasons why this property might evaluate to `False`. Since pun is a pure language, `eval e` is always equal to `eval e`, so there are two possible answers to this question. Either

[3] `examples/rc3.pun` in the repository.

```
(invert simplify) e = Plus[e, Const[0]] .
```

or

```
(invert simplify) e = Times[e, Const[1]] .
```

Checking those two cases will find the above case (in at most two tests), but, in general, we may have to search through inverted function calls recursively.

6.1 Related Work

We compare pun to other programming languages that also include some form of first-class properties.

Liquid Haskell [29] extends Haskell with refinement types that allow functions to be annotated with logical expressions that express behavioural constraints. Refinement types are similar to pun's properties, and Liquid Haskell can sometimes automatically prove for certain that the property holds, but the properties are limited. The syntax of the constraints is limited to expressions that an SMT solver can understand.

Automated theorem provers like Dafny [20] are similar to Liquid Haskell. Programmers can write automatically-checked properties as pre- and post-conditions on functions, provided those properties fit into a restricted language.

Interactive theorem provers like Rocq [27] and Lean [24] are the closest to pun syntactically. Like pun, interactive theorem provers allow programmers to write arbitrary logical properties about their code as a first-class feature in the language. Rocq even allows programmers to test those properties, via a library called QuickChick [25]. The main difference between Rocq/QuickChick and pun is the way data is generated: QuickChick generates values directly, whereas pun generates pun programs that evaluate to values. This meta-level generation allows pun to more easily generate higher-order functions.

7 Conclusion

In this paper, we have presented initial work on a programming language pun, which enables property-based testing without asking the programmer to provide a generator. We have shown that the path of automatic generator generation based on inverse interpretation of typing judgements is feasible in simple cases, such as the binary search tree example, but will not scale to software projects where the properties have many pre-conditions. To this end, we have proposed a way towards input-generator-free property-based testing, which is based on making arbitrary *evaluation* judgements, in the inverse interpretation introduced in the Jeopardy programming language [17].

The experiments with automatic generator generation were based on the proposed programming language pun, a higher order functional language, extended with properties. This can find the same bugs of the comparable properties to what Hughes did in the paper *How to Specify it!* [11], by trading an increased number of tests for programmer hours. Rather than trading with computation, the property checker could trade in non-determinism, by introducing probabilistic program inversion.

The limitations of generating terms as "trying to make a good guess" arbitrarily are obvious, but arbitrarily making evaluation judgements as a template for an execution path provides a much better guess although it is still non-deterministic. However, any property-based method has to be non-deterministic, since there is no counterexample to be found, in the cases where the property holds (cannot evaluate to `False`). This could be determined by program analysis in some cases.

In future work, we would like to extend inverse interpretation further, as a search strategy for property-based testing property counter examples.

Acknowledgements. The authors thank Sophie Adeline Solheim Bosio for inputs to this work.

References

1. Abramov, S., Robert, G.: The universal resolving algorithm and its correctness: inverse computation in a functional language. Sci. Comput. Program. Math. Program Constr. (MPC 2000) **43**(23), 193–229 (2002). https://doi.org/10.1016/S0167-6423(02)00023-0
2. Claessen, K., Duregård, J., Pałka, M.H.: Generating constrained random data with uniform distribution. In: Codish, M., Sumii, E. (eds.) FLOPS 2014. LNCS, vol. 8475, pp. 18–34. Springer, Cham (2014). https://doi.org/10.1007/978-3-319-07151-0_2
3. Claessen, K., Hughes, J.: Quickcheck: a lightweight tool for random testing of Haskell programs. In: Proceedings of the Fifth ACM SIGPLAN International Conference on Functional Programming, pp. 268–279. ICFP '00, Association for Computing Machinery (2000). https://doi.org/10.1145/351240.351266
4. Eppstein, D.: A heuristic approach to program inversion. IJCAI **85**, 219–221 (1985)
5. Fetscher, B., Claessen, K., Pałka, M., Hughes, J., Findler, R.B.: Making random judgments: automatically generating well-typed terms from the definition of a type-system. In: Vitek, J. (ed.) ESOP 2015. LNCS, vol. 9032, pp. 383–405. Springer, Heidelberg (2015). https://doi.org/10.1007/978-3-662-46669-8_16
6. Frank, J., Quiring, B., Lampropoulos, L.: Generating well-typed terms that are not "useless". Proc. ACM Program. Lang. **8**(POPL) (2024). https://doi.org/10.1145/3632919
7. Glück, R., Kawabe, M.: Revisiting an automatic program inverter for lisp. SIGPLAN Not. **40**(5), 8–17 (2005). https://doi.org/10.1145/1071221.1071222
8. Goldstein, H., Cutler, J.W., Dickstein, D., Pierce, B.C., Head, A.: Property-based testing in practice. In: Proceedings of the IEEE/ACM 46th International Conference on Software Engineering. ICSE '24, Association for Computing Machinery (2024). https://doi.org/10.1145/3597503.3639581
9. Hou (Favonia), K.B., Wang, Z.: Logarithm and program testing. Proc. ACM Program. Lang. **6**(POPL) (2022). https://doi.org/10.1145/3498726

10. Hughes, J.: Experiences with quickcheck: testing the hard stuff and staying sane. In: Lindley, S., McBride, C., Trinder, P., Sannella, D. (eds.) A List of Successes That Can Change the World. LNCS, vol. 9600, pp. 169–186. Springer, Cham (2016). https://doi.org/10.1007/978-3-319-30936-1_9
11. Hughes, J.: How to Specify It! In: Bowman, W.J., Garcia, R. (eds.) TFP 2019. LNCS, vol. 12053, pp. 58–83. Springer, Cham (2020). https://doi.org/10.1007/978-3-030-47147-7_4
12. Jacobsen, P.A.H., Kaarsgaard, R., Thomsen, M.K.: CoreFun: a typed functional reversible core language. In: Kari, J., Ulidowski, I., (eds.) RC 2018. LNCS, vol. 11106, pp. 304–321. Springer, Cham (2018). https://doi.org/10.1007/978-3-319-99498-7_21
13. Kirkeby, M.H., Glück, R.: Semi-inversion of conditional constructor term rewriting systems. In: Gabbrielli, M. (ed.) LOPSTR 2019. LNCS, vol. 12042, pp. 243–259. Springer, Cham (2020). https://doi.org/10.1007/978-3-030-45260-5_15
14. Korf, R.E.: Inversion of applicative programs. In: Proceedings of the IJCAI, pp. 1007–1009 (1981)
15. Kristensen, J.T., Kaarsgaard, R., Thomsen, M.K.: Branching execution symmetry in Jeopardy by available implicit arguments analysis. In: Rutle, A. (ed.) Proceedings of 34th Norwegian ICT Conference for Research and Education, NIKT 2022, no. 1 (2022)
16. Kristensen, J.T., Kaarsgaard, R., Thomsen, M.K.: Tail recursion transformation for invertible functions. In: Kutrib, M., Meyer, U., (eds.) Reversible Computation, pp. 73–88. Springer (2023). ISBN:978-3-031-38100-3
17. Kristensen, J.T., Kaarsgaard, R., Thomsen, M.K.: Jeopardy: an invertible functional programming language. In: Mogensen, T.Æ., Mikulski, Ł., (eds.) Reversible Computation, pp. 124–141. Springer (2024). ISBN:978-3-031-62076-8
18. Lampropoulos, L., et al.: Beginner's luck: a language for property-based generators. In: Proceedings of the 44th ACM SIGPLAN Symposium on Principles of Programming Languages, pp. 114–129. POPL '17, Association for Computing Machinery (2017). https://doi.org/10.1145/3009837.3009868
19. Lampropoulos, L., Paraskevopoulou, Z., Pierce, B.C.: Generating good generators for inductive relations. Proc. ACM Program. Lang. **2**(POPL), 1–30 (2017). https://doi.org/10.1145/3158133
20. Leino, K.R.M.: Dafny: an automatic program verifier for functional correctness. In: Clarke, E.M., Voronkov, A. (eds.) LPAR 2010. LNCS (LNAI), vol. 6355, pp. 348–370. Springer, Heidelberg (2010). https://doi.org/10.1007/978-3-642-17511-4_20
21. Matsuda, K., Wang, M.: Sparcl: a language for partially-invertible computation. Proc. ACM Program. Lang. **4**(ICFP) (2020). https://doi.org/10.1145/3409000
22. McCarthy, J.: The inversion of functions defined by Turing machines. In: Shannon, C.E., McCarthy, J., (eds.) Automata Studies. Annals of Mathematics Studies, Princeton University Press (1956). https://doi.org/10.1515/9781400882618-009
23. Mogensen, T.Æ.: Semi-inversion of functional parameters. In: Proceedings of the 2008 ACM SIGPLAN symposium on Partial evaluation and semantics-based program manipulation, pp. 21–29. PEPM '08, Association for Computing Machinery (2008). https://doi.org/10.1145/1328408.1328413
24. Moura, L., Ullrich, S.: The lean 4 theorem prover and programming language. In: Platzer, A., Sutcliffe, G. (eds.) CADE 2021. LNCS (LNAI), vol. 12699, pp. 625–635. Springer, Cham (2021). https://doi.org/10.1007/978-3-030-79876-5_37

25. Paraskevopoulou, Z., Hriţcu, C., Dénès, M., Lampropoulos, L., Pierce, B.C.: Foundational property-based testing. In: Urban, C., Zhang, X. (eds.) ITP 2015. LNCS, vol. 9236, pp. 325–343. Springer, Cham (2015). https://doi.org/10.1007/978-3-319-22102-1_22
26. Pierce, B.C.: Types and Programming Languages. The MIT Press (2002)
27. Team, R.: Welcome to a World of Rocq (2025). https://rocq-prover.org
28. Thomsen, M.K., Axelsen, H.B.: Interpretation and programming of the reversible functional language. In: Proceedings of the 27th Symposium on the Implementation and Application of Functional Programming Languages, pp. 8:1–8:13. IFL '15, Association for Computing Machinery (2016). https://doi.org/10.1145/2897336.2897345
29. Vazou, N., Seidel, E.L., Jhala, R., Vytiniotis, D., Peyton-Jones, S.: Refinement types for Haskell. In: Proceedings of the 19th ACM SIGPLAN International Conference on Functional Programming, pp. 269–282. ICFP '14, Association for Computing Machinery (2014). https://doi.org/10.1145/2628136.2628161
30. Whittaker, J.: What is software testing? And why is it so hard? IEEE Softw. **17**(1), 70–79 (2000). https://doi.org/10.1109/52.819971
31. Winskel, G.: The Formal Semantics of Programming Languages: An Introduction. The MIT Press (1993)
32. Yokoyama, T., Axelsen, H.B., Glück, R.: Towards a reversible functional language. In: De Vos, A., Wille, R. (eds.) RC 2011. LNCS, vol. 7165, pp. 14–29. Springer, Heidelberg (2012). https://doi.org/10.1007/978-3-642-29517-1_2

PEARL: A Partial Evaluation Toolbox for a Reversible Language

Louis Marott Normann(✉) and Robert Glück

DIKU, Department of Computer Science, University of Copenhagen, Copenhagen, Denmark
Louis.Normann@simcorp.com, glueck@acm.org

Abstract. This tool demonstration presents PEARL, a partial evaluator for the reversible programming language ARL, along with its associated tools. Partial evaluation is a program optimization technique that specializes a program with respect to known inputs, typically producing more efficient programs. ARL is a reversible flowchart language based on pattern matching and dynamic data structures, making it well suited for symbolic manipulation.

The demonstration shows how PEARL translates a reversible combinational circuit into an executable ARL simulation by specializing an interpreter for the circuit description language. The example is presented in full and illustrates how reversible languages can be prototyped using reversible interpreters. Currently, PEARL is the only freely available partial evaluator for a reversible programming language. It has also served as a foundation for novel experiments with inversion and partial evaluation.

Keywords: Specialization · Reversible flowcharts · Reversible circuits · Interpreters · Translation · Futamura projection

1 Introduction

Partial evaluation is a program optimization technique that specializes a program with respect to known inputs [14]. The resulting residual program is generally faster and more power-efficient, as a result of optimizing away all control flow and calculations dependent on the known inputs. Partial evaluation synergizes with reversible programs, since both approaches improve power consumption [3,16] compared to unspecialized, irreversible programs. Reversible languages enable efficient program inversion [12], opening up new possibilities for combining different program transformations, such as specialization and inversion. However, applying partial evaluation in reversible languages presents many unique challenges [18,19].

This tool demonstration presents *PEARL*, an offline *partial evaluator* for the reversible programming language *ARL* and its associated tools [19]. We will cover PEARL, the reversible flowchart language ARL, and give a non-trivial example of their use by prototyping a reversible hardware description language. This partial evaluation example utilizes the first Futamura projection [6]. The same approach can be used to prototype other reversible languages.

C. Aubert and L. Roversi (Eds.): RC 2026, LNCS 16626, pp. 277–284, 2026.
https://doi.org/10.1007/978-3-032-30839-9_16

(a)

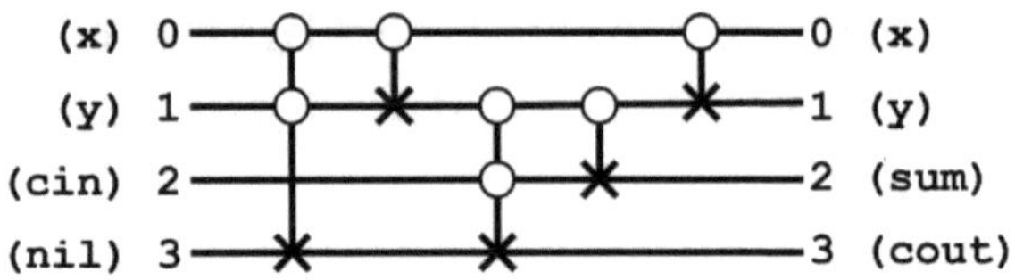

(b)

```
[CCNOT 0 1 3, CNOT 0 1, CCNOT 1 2 3, CNOT 1 2, CNOT 0 1]
```

(c)

```
(lines) -> (lines) with (v1 v2 v3)
init: entry
      v1 <- lines['0]
      v2 <- lines['1]
      v3 <- lines['3]
      v3 ^= v1 && v2
      lines['3] <- v3
      lines['1] <- v2
      lines['0] <- v1
      v1 <- lines['0]
      v2 <- lines['1]
      v2 ^= v1
      lines['1] <- v2
      lines['0] <- v1
      v1 <- lines['1]
      v2 <- lines['2]
      v3 <- lines['3]
      v3 ^= v1 && v2
      lines['3] <- v3
      lines['2] <- v2
      lines['1] <- v1
      v1 <- lines['1]
      v2 <- lines['2]
      v2 ^= v1
      lines['2] <- v2
      lines['1] <- v1
      v1 <- lines['0]
      v2 <- lines['1]
      v2 ^= v1
      lines['1] <- v2
      lines['0] <- v1
      exit
```

Fig. 1. Tool demo: (a) diagram of Feynman's reversible full adder [5], (b) reversible circuit description, and (c) residual program generated by the ARL partial evaluator.

Demonstration. We demonstrate how a reversible hardware description can be translated into an executable ARL program that reversibly simulates the circuit.

(a) For this purpose, we use Feynman's well-known reversible full adder [5, Fig. 5], whose circuit diagram is shown in Fig. 1. The 4-bit reversible circuit consists of two CCNOT (Toffoli) gates and three CNOT (Feynman) gates. The input bits (left) are the operands x and y, together with the carry-in *cin*. The output bits (right) are the *sum*, the carry-out *cout*, and the unchanged operands x and y. For the reversible adder to function correctly, line *nil* must be set to 0.The circuit is evaluated from left to right. A 2-bit CNOT gate negates the target bit (marked $\times$) if the control bit (marked $\circ$) is 1; a 3-bit CCNOT gate does so iff both control bits are 1.

(b) The circuit description language is deliberately kept simple to allow the complete example to be presented in full. The description of the combinational circuit (Fig. 1(a)) consists of a list of reversible logic gates (Fig. 1(b)), read from left to right, where the line connections are defined for each gate. For example, the first CCNOT gate is connected to control lines `0` and `1` and acts on target line `3`; this is written as `CCNOT 0 1 3`. The operational semantics of the description language is defined by the reversible interpreter in Fig. 2. The interpreter will be explained later in more detail to illustrate ARL.

(c) Fig. 1(c) shows PEARL's translation of the circuit description into an ARL program that simulates the full adder. This translation is achieved by specializing the interpreter for the description language with respect to the circuit description (first Futamura projection). The generated program is reversible, allowing the ARL program inverter to transform it into a program that simulates a subtractor. That all programs remain accessible to reversible-specific transformations and optimizations is a distinctive feature of PEARL.

```
(gates lines) -> (gates lines)
with (gate gatesRev ls l1 l2 l3 v1 v2 v3)
init: entry
      goto act1
act1: fi gatesRev from act2 else init
      ((gate . ls) . gates) <- gates
      if gate = 'CCNOT goto toff else cnot
toff: from act1
      [l1, l2, l3] <- ls
      v1 <- lines[l1]
      v2 <- lines[l2]
      v3 <- lines[l3]
      v3 ^= v1 && v2
      lines[l3] <- v3
      lines[l2] <- v2
      lines[l1] <- v1
      ls <- [l1, l2, l3]
      goto act2
cnot: from act1
      [l1, l2] <- ls
      v1 <- lines[l1]
      v2 <- lines[l2]
      v2 ^= v1
      lines[l2] <- v2
      lines[l1] <- v1
      ls <- [l1, l2]
      goto act2
act2: fi gate = 'CCNOT from toff else cnot
      gatesRev <- ((gate . ls) . gatesRev)
      if gates goto act1 else act3
act3: fi gates from act3 else act2
      (gate . gatesRev) <- gatesRev
      gates <- (gate . gates)
      if gatesRev goto act3 else stop
stop: from act3
      exit
```

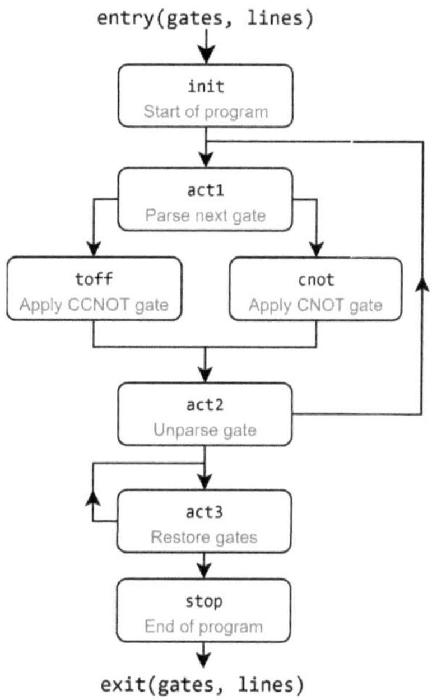

Fig. 2. Interpreter for reversible circuits as ARL program and control-flow diagram

2 Toolbox

The PEARL toolbox contains three core tools for developing and experimenting with ARL: an interpreter, an inverter, and a partial evaluator. The interpreter takes a program and all its inputs and produces its output. The inverter takes a program and produces its inverse. The partial evaluator takes a program and a part of its input and produces a residual program which, when run with the remaining input, produces the same result as the original program.

PEARL was originally developed as a proof-of-concept implementation for research on partial evaluation of reversible programs [19]. Since then, it has also served as a basis for novel experiments in its own right [10], particularly

```
# Specialize circuit interpreter
> PEARL interpret int.rl fulladder.in          # Bits in: [one, nil, one, nil]
gates: ...                                     # Circuit description; see Fig. 1(b)
lines: [one, nil, nil, one]                    # Bits out
> PEARL spec int.rl res.rl fulladder.spec      # Translate circuit to res.rl
gates: ...                                     # Static out; res.rl is in Fig. 1(c)
> PEARL interpret res.rl lines.in              # Bits in: [one, nil, one, nil]
lines: [one, nil, nil, one]                    # Bits out

# Invert circuit interpreter
> PEARL invert int.rl invint.rl                # Invert int.rl into invint.rl
> PEARL interpret invint.rl fulladder.out      # Bits in: [one, nil, nil, one]
gates: ...                                     # Circuit description; see Fig. 1(b)
lines: [one, nil, one, nil]                    # Bits out
```

Fig. 3. Command line interface (`int.rl` is the interpreter in Fig. 2; all `fulladder` files include the circuit from Fig. 1(b), with `fulladder.in` and `fulladder.out` also including an initial list of bits; `lines.in` contains the same bit list as `fulladder.in`)

in investigating the algebra of the program transformations mentioned above, including the specialization of inverted programs and the inversion of residual programs (e.g., [1,12]).

The toolbox enables the prototyping of a reversible language by implementing its operational semantics in ARL and translating programs written in the defined language into ARL utilizing the first Futamura projection. Because ARL is a reversible language this guarantees the reversibility of the defined language by construction [9]. Moreover, during prototyping, implementing and modifying an interpreter is typically easier than developing a translator or other tools.

2.1 ARL – A Reversible Language

ARL is a *reversible flowchart language* that supports symbolic values, dynamic data structures[1], and pattern matching [19]. The language is inspired by the reversible languages RL and R-WHILE [11,23]. It includes traditional conditional and unconditional jumps (`if`, `goto`) as well as their inverse counterparts, the come-from statements (`fi`, `from`). Each block is uniquely labeled and consists of a come-from statement, followed by any number of reversible updates, and ends with a jump. Each program has a single `entry` and a single `exit`. Input, output, and temporary variables are declared at the beginning of the program.

Figure 2 shows the interpreter for reversible circuits written in ARL, both as a program and as a control-flow diagram. It iterates over all gates in `gates`, branches according to the gate type, and updates the values in `lines` accordingly (blocks `act1` to `act2`). For brevity, only the `CCNOT` and `CNOT` gates are implemented (in `toff` and `cnot`, respectively), but other gates can easily be added. (Since `CCNOT` is universal for reversible combinational circuits [3,21], any such

[1] Similar to cons cells in LISP [17], but with support for indexing list structures.

circuit can be simulated.) After all gates have been applied, the original gate list is restored (block `act3`), and the unchanged `gates` and final `lines` are returned.

Unlike a conventional interpreter, the reversible interpreter returns the simulated `gates` to preserve reversibility (cf., [11, Sect. 2]). The list `lines` contains the symbols `nil` and `one`, representing the bits 0 and 1, respectively. For simplicity, the interpreter assumes well-formed inputs and performs no error checking.

2.2 Running PEARL

The source-code for PEARL can be found online[2] with additional information on how to compile and run it. PEARL is meant to be used in the terminal, as it is a programming-oriented toolbox that primarily works with files and can be used in shell scripts. The repository also includes example ARL programs.

Figure 3 shows how to run the circuit interpreter with the full-adder circuit description, how to specialize the interpreter with respect to the adder, and finally how to run the residual program that simulates the adder. In terms of partial evaluation, this corresponds to the first Futamura projection [6].

Another way to use the tools, shown in the lower part of Fig. 3, is to invert the circuit interpreter and then run the inverted interpreter with the full-adder description, thereby simulating the circuit in reverse. Since the inverted interpreter is itself an interpreter, it can also be specialized with respect to the circuit description (analogously to the upper part of Fig. 3), yielding an ARL implementation of the circuit's inverse. A similar experiment was conducted with a reversible Turing machine interpreter written in ARL [10]. This showcases the power of interpreter inversion and non-standard interpretation [1,2,15].

2.3 Architecture

The PEARL toolbox consists of over 4.000 lines of Haskell code, with each tool providing its own functionality while sharing a common parser [19]. Figure 4 shows the overall structure of the partial evaluator. It includes both the steps of a traditional offline partial evaluator (BTA, annotation, and specialization) and the additional steps required for reversible programs (normalization, explication, and post-processing).

In the tool demonstration, the interpreter (Fig. 2) is the ARL source program (top left). The initial division Δ_{init} separates the program parameters into static (`gates`) and dynamic (`lines`). The static environment σ_{init} assigns the description from Fig. 1(b) to `gates`. With these inputs, PEARL generates the ARL residual program shown in Fig. 1(c). Partial evaluation translates the circuit description into a linear program. The two loops and the syntax parsing in the interpreter are eliminated, and the gate implementations are instantiated. In general, however, a residual program may still contain loops and conditionals. Even though not relevant for this small circuit description, it is clear that the residual program simulates the circuit faster than the interpreter.

2 https://github.com/Yakokse/PEARL.

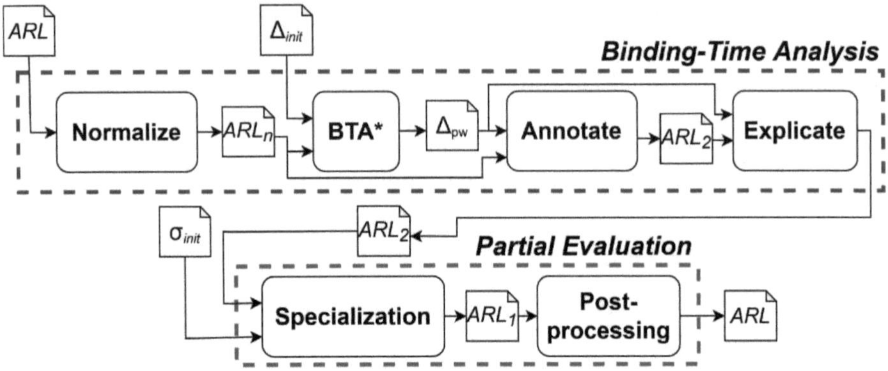

Fig. 4. Architecture of the ARL partial evaluator

We now summarize the phases of the partial evaluator in Fig. 4. For additional details, see PEARL [19] and the introductions to partial evaluation [13,14].

- **Normalize:** The ARL source program is normalized to enable more precise analysis, with each block containing exactly one statement. This step is required only when the subsequent BTA is pointwise.
- **BTA:** The normalized program is analyzed using an initial division Δ_{init} of its parameters into static and dynamic [14]. The BTA can be uniform or pointwise [13]: the uniform BTA requires static variables to remain static throughout the program, while the pointwise BTA (default) allows variables to change between static and dynamic at different points in the program.
- **Annotate:** The results of the BTA are encoded in the program, producing a two-level program [13]. The first level (static) is evaluated at specialization time, and the second level (dynamic) forms the residual program.
- **Explicate:** After the pointwise BTA, special explicator blocks [4] are inserted when static variables become dynamic. They ensure the well-formedness of the final reversible program.
- **Specialization:** The annotated program is partially evaluated with respect to the static values in the initial environment σ_{init}.
- **Post-processing:** After specialization, additional transformations are applied to guarantee that the residual program is well-formed and reversible. This phase generates the final ARL residual program.

3 Conclusions

We introduced PEARL, a partial evaluator for the reversible programming language ARL, together with a collection of tools. This shows that in the field of reversible computing, not only translators and inverters, but also partial evaluators are available as tools for program development, thereby expanding the possibilities for building reversible software systems. The example program also illustrates how the reversible flowchart language ARL supports symbolic processing through its dynamic data structures and pattern-matching replacements.

We showed how PEARL can be used for prototyping reversible languages. A complete example demonstrated how the circuit description of Feynman's full adder can be translated into an executable simulation by partially evaluating a circuit interpreter written in ARL. It is clear that this small reversible hardware description language can be extended by modifying the interpreter, e.g., to support symbolic line names and parameterized circuit modules [20,22]. The same approach can also be used to prototype other reversible languages. Writing interpreters for reversible languages in ARL reflects our view that reversible languages can and should be defined using reversible metalanguages [9], since this captures their distinct properties at the meta-level.

A distinctive feature compared to existing partial evaluators (e.g., [7,8,13, 14]) is that PEARL preserves the source program's reversibility in the residual program. This means that all programs remain accessible to reversible-specific optimizations and analyses. For example, both the circuit interpreter and the residual program can be inverted. This new combination of transformations has led to a new result [10]: the classic Futamura projections and the inversion projections can generate programs of comparable quality.

Possible directions for extending the toolbox include quality-of-life improvements, such as adding a web interface and a debugger, and language extensions.

References

1. Abramov, S.M., Glück, R.: Combining semantics with non-standard interpreter hierarchies. In: Kapoor, S., et al., (eds.) FST TCS. LNCS, vol. 1974, pp. 201–213. Springer (2000). https://doi.org/10.1007/3-540-44450-5_16
2. Abramov, S.M., Glück, R.: The universal resolving algorithm: inverse computation in a functional language. In: Backhouse, R., Oliveira, J.N., (eds.) Mathematics of Program Construction. Proceedings. LNCS, vol. 1837, pp. 187–212. Springer (2000). https://doi.org/10.1007/10722010_13
3. De Vos, A.: Reversible computing: fundamentals, quantum computing, and applications. Wiley-VCH, Weinheim (2010). https://doi.org/10.1002/9783527633999
4. Ershov, A.P., Ostrovski, B.N.: Controlled mixed computation and its application to systematic development of language-oriented parsers. In: Meertens, L.G.L.T., (ed.) Program Specification and Transformation, pp. 31–48. North-Holland (1987)
5. Feynman, R.P.: Quantum mechanical computers. Found. Phys. **16**(6), 507–531 (1986). https://doi.org/10.1007/BF01886518
6. Futamura, Y.: Partial evaluation of computing process - an approach to a compiler-compiler. Syst. Comput. Controls **2**(5), 45–50 (1971)
7. Futamura, Y., Konishi, Z., Glück, R.: Program transformation system based on generalized partial computation. N. Gener. Comput. **20**(1), 75–99 (2002). https://doi.org/10.1007/BF03037260

8. Glück, R., Jørgensen, J.: Fast binding-time analysis for multi-level specialization. In: Bjørner, D., et al., (eds.) PSI. LNCS, vol. 1181, pp. 261–272. Springer (1996). https://doi.org/10.1007/3-540-62064-8_22
9. Glück, R., Kaarsgaard, R., Yokoyama, T.: Reversible programs have reversible semantics. In: Sekerinski, E., et al., (eds.) Formal Methods. FM 2019 International Workshops. Part II. Proceedings, pp. 413–427. LNCS 12233, Springer-Verlag (2020). https://doi.org/10.1007/978-3-030-54997-8_26
10. Glück, R., Normann, L.M.: Inversion by partial evaluation: a reversible interpreter experiment. In: Bieniusa, A., et al., (eds.) A Second Soul: Celebrating the Many Languages of Programming. Electronic Proceedings in Theoretical Computer Science, vol. 413, pp. 1–14 (2024). https://doi.org/10.4204/EPTCS.413.1
11. Glück, R., Yokoyama, T.: A linear-time self-interpreter of a reversible imperative language. Comput. Softw. **33**(3), 108–128 (2016). https://doi.org/10.11309/jssst.33.3_108
12. Glück, R., Yokoyama, T.: Reversible computing from a programming language perspective. Theor. Comput. Sci. **953**, Article 113429 (2023). https://doi.org/10.1016/j.tcs.2022.06.010
13. Hatcliff, J.: An introduction to online and offline partial evaluation using a simple flowchart language. In: Hatcliff, J., et al., (eds.) Partial Evaluation. Practice and Theory. LNCS, vol. 1706, pp. 20–82. Springer (1999). https://doi.org/10.1007/3-540-47018-2_2
14. Jones, N.D.: An introduction to partial evaluation. Comput. Surv. **28**(3), 480–503 (1996). https://doi.org/10.1145/243439.243447
15. Kawabe, M., Glück, R.: The program inverter LRinv and its structure. In: Hermenegildo, M., et al., (eds.) PADL. LNCS, vol. 3350, pp. 219–234. Springer (2005). https://doi.org/10.1007/978-3-540-30557-6_17
16. Krakovsky, M.: Taking the heat. Commun. ACM **64**(6), 18–20 (2021). https://doi.org/10.1145/3460214
17. McCarthy, J.: Recursive functions of symbolic expressions and their computation by machine, part I. Commun. ACM **3**(4), 184–195 (1960). https://doi.org/10.1145/367177.367199
18. Mogensen, T.Æ.: Partial evaluation of the reversible language Janus. In: Proceedings of the 20th ACM SIGPLAN Workshop on Partial Evaluation and Program Manipulation, pp. 23–32. ACM Press (2011). https://doi.org/10.1145/1929501.1929506
19. Normann, L.M., Glück, R.: Partial evaluation of reversible flowchart programs. In: Proceedings of the 2024 ACM SIGPLAN International Workshop on Partial Evaluation and Program Manipulation, pp. 119–133. ACM (2024). https://doi.org/10.1145/3635800.3636967
20. Thomsen, M.K., Axelsen, H.B., Glück, R.: Cleaning up: garbage-free reversible circuits by design languages. In: Proceedings of the International Symposium on Electronic System Design, pp. 6–10. IEEE (2012). https://doi.org/10.1109/ISED.2012.20
21. Toffoli, T.: Reversible computing. In: de Bakker, J.W., van Leeuwen, J., (eds.) Automata, Languages and Programming. Proceedings, pp. 632–644. LNCS 85, Springer-Verlag (1980). https://doi.org/10.1007/3-540-10003-2_104
22. Wille, R., Drechsler, R.: Towards a design flow for reversible logic. Springer (2010). https://doi.org/10.1007/978-90-481-9579-4
23. Yokoyama, T., Axelsen, H.B., Glück, R.: Fundamentals of reversible flowchart languages. Theoret. Comput. Sci. **611**, 87–115 (2016). https://doi.org/10.1016/j.tcs.2015.07.046

Introducing Time Passage to the Reversible Semantics for Erlang

Yuna Sadamoto[1], Shoji Yuen[1(✉)], and Claudio Antares Mezzina[2]

[1] Nagoya University, Nagoya, Japan
{yunas30211,yuen}@sqlab.jp
[2] University of Bari, Bari, Italy
cmezzina@gmail.com

Abstract. Processes in Erlang interact asynchronously through message passing via a mailbox. Specifying the timing of message receipt helps ensure the system's correct behaviour, which depends on message delivery. A process may alter its behaviour if no message is received in the mailbox within a specified time interval. CauDEr is a reversible debugger grounded in Erlang's reversible semantics. CauDEr supports causal-consistent reversible debugging for concurrent Erlang programs. However, CauDEr does not account for the causal nature of time passage; instead, it treats time solely as a value. This work introduces discrete time passage into the reversible semantics of Erlang, enabling timeout operations in receive actions as expected. A formal description of the time tick is incorporated into the reversible semantics of CauDEr. Finally, an implementation of our time passage in CauDEr is presented under the maximal progress assumption.

1 Introduction

Executing distributed and concurrent programs in reverse order facilitates the analysis of nondeterministic behaviour. In such programs, causality depends on runtime conditions and varies across executions. Concurrency bugs [10] are unexpected malfunctions that occur nondeterministically due to uncertain causality introduced by the runtime environment, including process scheduling and interactions among processes. Debugging concurrency bugs is challenging because runtime nondeterminism changes causality across executions, and the bugs may not be reproducible while debugging. Reversible debugging addresses this by enabling backward execution. After suspending forward execution at a breakpoint, the debugger executes the program backwards to identify the cause, thereby preserving the causality of the erroneous execution.

CauDEr [8,9] is a causally consistent reversible debugger for the Erlang programming language [4]. Erlang is a distributed, concurrent programming language that employs actor-based communication. Processes execute concurrently, sending and receiving messages through a mailbox. A process sends a message to the mailbox by specifying the recipient process and receives a message from the

C. Aubert and L. Roversi (Eds.): RC 2026, LNCS 16626, pp. 285–292, 2026.
https://doi.org/10.1007/978-3-032-30839-9_17

mailbox if it is available for that process. Although Erlang's operational semantics do not specify timing for message sending and receiving, it is reasonable to assume that processes perform these actions as promptly as possible, since communication is non-blocking. To avoid process blocking due to the absence of messages, a receive action may time out after a predetermined interval. This mechanism is important for both fault tolerance and time-aware behaviour.

In the example shown in Fig. 1, the root process `main` concurrently invokes three processes. Two of these, `p1` and `p2`, send messages to process `p0` via the mailbox. When a process evaluates `timer:sleep(`n`)`, it suspends execution for n milliseconds. Since `p1` suspends for 2 milliseconds and `p2` for 1 millisecond, assuming all processes execute sufficiently quickly, the message with value 1 for `p0` becomes available after the message with value 2. Therefore, `p0` is expected to receive the message with 2 from `p2` first.

The existing CauDEr interpreter evaluates `timer:sleep(`n`)` as a function call that returns n. Therefore, no precedence exists between messages from `p1` and `p2` in Fig. 1. In Erlang [4], `timer:sleep(`n`)` is defined as the expression that receives no message for n milliseconds without performing any action to be evaluated to n. A receive expression with `after` is not included in CauDEr [8]. Hence, time-dependent behaviour is inaccurately implemented in CauDEr.

```
main() ->
          Pid = spawn(?MODULE,p0,[]),
          spawn(?MODULE,p1,[Pid]),
          spawn(?MODULE,p2,[Pid]).

p0() -> receive {N}
          -> io:format("Rec: ~p~n",[N])
          end.
p1(Pid) -> timer:sleep(2), Pid!{1}.
p2(Pid) -> timer:sleep(1), Pid!{2}.
```

Fig. 1. Time-dependent program.

This paper introduces discrete-time passage into the reversible semantics of Erlang, ensuring that timeout behaviour in receive actions accurately reflects time passage during execution. Timeticks and timeout events are recorded in histories. A forward time passage occurs only when all processes are waiting to receive messages or are terminated. The timed-reversible semantics is incorporated into the CauDEr interpreter.

2 Reversible Erlang

We follow the syntax in CauDEr, except for receive expressions, which are shown below. The imperative primitives [8] are omitted for simplicity in this paper.

2.1 Receive Expression with Timeout

In this paper, a receive expression is assumed to include a description for timeout. The syntax for receiving messages with a timeout is defined as follows:

`receive` *cr_clause* `after` *tout_clause* `end`

where *cr_clause* denotes a sequence of pattern-expression pairs. When a message to the process matches a pattern, the corresponding expression is evaluated.

tout_clause represents a pair consisting of a timeout constraint and an expression. A timeout constraint is defined as an integer-typed expression, or the atom `infinity`. When the timeout constraint is `infinity`, it is never satisfied. In CauDEr, timeout constraints are always set to `infinity`. Otherwise, the constraint evaluates to an integer value n when the receive expression is evaluated. If the *cr_clause* does not match any message in the mailbox within n milliseconds, the expression evaluates to the body of *tout_clause*.

If *cr_clause* is empty, the expression suspends execution for the duration of the timeout. The `timer` module defines `timer:sleep(e)` as follows.

```
sleep(T)->receive after T->T end.
```

2.2 Reversible Semantics for Untimed Behaviour

A process is defined as a triple (θ, e, S), where θ represents the local environment, e denotes the expression under evaluation, and S is a stack of expressions storing the continuation. The sequential semantics for each process is given by $(\theta, e.S) \xrightarrow{\ell} (\theta', e', S')$, where ℓ is either the internal action τ or an observable action. Actions include $\mathsf{send}(p, v)$, $\mathsf{rec}(\kappa, \overline{cl}, v^T \rightarrow exprs)$, $\mathsf{spawn}(\kappa, exprs)$, and $\mathsf{self}(\kappa)$. The symbol κ is substituted in the system semantics as described in [5,8]. The receive action is extended with a timeout clause $v^T \rightarrow exprs$, where the timeout constraint v^T is evaluated as an integer.

A system configuration of a program is represented as a pair $\Gamma; \Pi$, where Γ denotes a mailbox consisting of a set of messages, and Π is a collection of processes. Each message has the form $(p_s, p_d, \{\lambda, v\})$, where p_s is the sender's process identifier (pid), p_d is the receiver's pid, and λ, v is a pair comprising a unique key and the message value. Define Γ_p as the subset of messages in Γ directed to process p, i.e., $\{(p_s, p_r, \{\lambda, v\}) \in \Gamma \mid p_r = p\}$.

Each process in the system is represented as a 6-tuple $\langle p, h, \theta, e, S, t\rangle$, where p is a unique process identifier, h is the sequence of action history, and (θ, e, S) defines the process state. A process pool is denoted by $P_1 \mid \cdots \mid P_n$, where each P_i is a process and $\mid$ represents parallel composition, which is both commutative and associative. The variable t is a timer that accumulates the elapsed time since the process initiated the receive action; it determines when to evaluate the timeout behaviour. For untimed behaviour, t is set to zero.

Untimed forward transitions $\Gamma; \Pi \rightharpoonup \Gamma'; \Pi'$ and untimed backward transitions $\Gamma; \Pi \leftharpoondown \Gamma'; \Pi'$ are those in [8]. These rules extend the label to include the timeout clause:

$$(\theta, C[\mathsf{receive}\, \overline{cl}\, \mathsf{after}\, v^T \rightarrow exprs\, \mathsf{end}], S) \xrightarrow{\mathsf{rec}(\kappa, \overline{cl}, v^T \rightarrow exprs)} (\theta, \kappa, C[\_] : S)$$

When a process evaluates a receive expression, it searches for a message sent to the process in the mailbox, whose value matches a pattern in $\overline{cl}$. The patterns are instantiated by the process environment θ. If there exists a valuation θ_i such that $v = \theta_i(\theta(pat_i))$ for some $pat_i \rightarrow e_i$ in $\overline{cl}$, then $\mathsf{matchrec}(\overline{cl}\theta, v)$ returns the corresponding θ_i and e_i. The receive expression is then evaluated as e_i, with θ_i applied to the environment, and the value is bound to κ.

3 Reversible Timed Semantics

For a process (θ, e, S), the following predicates are defined as follows:

- $\delta(\theta, e, S)$ holds if $(\theta, e, S) \xrightarrow{\ell}$ implies $\ell = \mathsf{rec}(\kappa, \overline{cl}, v^T \rightarrow exprs)$.
- $\mathsf{Alive}(\theta, e, S)$ holds if $(\theta, e, S) \xrightarrow{\ell} (\theta', e', S')$ for some (θ', e', S') and ℓ.

Let $e \xrightarrow{\kappa, \overline{cl}, v^T \rightarrow exprs}$ in process $\langle p_r, h, \theta, e, S, t\rangle$. $\mathsf{matchmes}(\overline{cl}\theta, \Gamma_{p_r})$ is defined by $\{(p_s, p_r, \{\lambda, v\}) \in \Gamma_p \,|\, \mathsf{matchrec}(\overline{cl}\theta, v) = (\theta_i, e_i)\}$. We call a process $\langle p, h, \theta, e, S, t\rangle$ *active* when $\mathsf{Alive}(\theta, e, S)$ holds, and *inactive* otherwise.

3.1 Forward Timed Semantics

The passage of time influences behaviour in forward execution through a *timeout* that occurs after a specified amount of time.

Timeout: When a process evaluates a receive expression and no message is available in the mailbox, the timeout value specified in the timeout clause is checked. If the elapsed time since the start of the receive reaches this value, the body of the timeout clause is executed.

Delay: An active process advances time when evaluating a receive expression and no message is available in the mailbox. Otherwise, the process executes actions instantaneously if possible. Time passage should occur synchronously across all active processes.

The rules in Fig. 2 define the timed behaviour. $|_{i \le n}\langle p_i, h_i, \theta_i, e_i, S_i, t_i\rangle$ is written for the compositions of $\langle p_1, h_i, \theta_1, e_1, S_1, t_1\rangle | \cdots | \langle p_n, h_n, \theta_n, e_n, S_n, t_n\rangle$.

[Receive]: The receive rule is redefined to record the timer at message reception. This value is necessary to recover the timer for the receiving action.

[Timeout]: When a process evaluates a receive action with no message available and the delay timer t reaches v_T, the process evaluates the body of the timeout clause $exprs$, and '$\mathsf{tout}(\theta, e, S, v^T)$' is pushed to h. The timer t is then reset to zero.

[Delay]: When all active processes evaluate receive actions and receive no message, and all timeout values exceed timers by at least d, the system allows d units of time to pass, increasing all timers by d. The symbol '$\delta(d)$' is pushed to h in all processes. If $v_i^T = \texttt{infinity}$, then $v_i^T - t_i \ge d$ always holds.

Since $\delta(\theta_i, e_i, S_i)$ holds for all active processes in the premise of [Delay], the environment Γ remains unchanged until a process times out. The property of time additivity holds for the system: $\Gamma; \Pi \overset{\delta(d_1)\delta(d_2)}{\rightharpoondown} \Gamma'; \Pi'$ if and only if $\Gamma; \Pi \overset{\delta(d)}{\rightharpoondown} \Gamma'\Pi'$ with $d = d_1 + d_2$.

$$[\textsc{Receive}]\ \frac{\theta, e, S \xrightarrow{\mathsf{rec}(\kappa,\overline{cl},v^T \to exprs)} \theta', e', S' \qquad \mathsf{matchrec}(\overline{cl}\theta, v) = (\theta_i, e_i)}{\begin{array}{l}\Gamma \cup \{(p_s, p_r, \{v, \lambda\})\}; \langle p_r, h, \theta, e, S, t\rangle \mid \Pi \rightharpoonup \\ \quad \Gamma; \langle p_r, \mathsf{rec}(\theta, e, S, p_s, \{v, \lambda\}, t) : h, \theta'\theta_i, e'[\kappa \mapsto e_i], S', 0\rangle \mid \Pi\end{array}}$$

$$[\textsc{Timeout}]\ \frac{\begin{array}{c}\delta(\theta, e, S) \ \wedge \theta, e, S \xrightarrow{\mathsf{rec}(\kappa,\overline{cl},v^T \to exprs)} \theta', e', S' \\ \wedge\ \mathsf{matchmes}(\overline{cl}\theta, \Gamma_p) = \varnothing\end{array}}{\Gamma; \langle p, h, \theta, e, S, v^T\rangle \mid \Pi \rightharpoonup \Gamma; \langle p, \mathsf{tout}(\theta, e, S, v^T) : h, \theta', e'[\kappa \mapsto exprs], S', 0\rangle \mid \Pi}$$

$$[\textsc{Delay}]\ \frac{\begin{array}{l}\forall\, i \leq n. \left[\begin{array}{l}\mathsf{Alive}(\theta_i, e_i, S_i) \Rightarrow (\mathsf{matchmes}(\overline{cl_i}\theta_i, \Gamma_{p_i}) = \varnothing \ \wedge\ \delta(\theta_i, e_i, S_i) \\ \quad \wedge\ (\theta_i, e_i, S_i \xrightarrow{\mathsf{rec}(\kappa_i,\overline{cl_i},v_i^T \to exprs_i)} \theta_i', e_i', S_i') \ \wedge\ v_i^T - t_i \geq d)\end{array}\right] \\ \wedge\ d > 0 \ \wedge\ \exists j \leq n. \mathsf{Alive}(\theta_j, e_j, S_j)\end{array}}{\begin{array}{l}\Gamma; |_{i \leq n} \langle p_i, h_i, \theta_i, e_i, S_i, t_i\rangle \xrightarrow{\delta(d)} \\ \quad \Gamma; |_{i \leq n} \langle p_i, \delta(d) : h_i, \theta_i', e_i'[\kappa_i \mapsto \mathsf{receive}\ \overline{cl_i}\ \mathsf{after}\ v_i^T \to exprs_i\ \mathsf{end}], S_i, t_i + d\rangle\end{array}}$$

Fig. 2. Forward Timed Semantics of Erlang.

3.2 Backward Timed Semantics

Figure 3 presents the rules defining backward timed behaviour.

[<u>TIMEOUT</u>]: When '$\mathsf{tout}(\theta, e, S, v_T)$' appears at the top of h, the process restores the state and timer to the value recorded in the history.
[<u>DELAY</u>]: When '$\delta(d)$' is on the top of h, all processes have '$\delta(d)$' on the top of h. d-unit time is reversed by popping $\delta(d)$'s from all h's in Π.

Note that $\delta(d)$'s are uniformly pushed by [DELAY] in forward execution.

4 Integration to CauDEr

The timed semantics has been integrated into the CauDEr interpreter[1]. The interpreter exhibits the following differences compared to the definition presented in the previous section. The interpreter implements the rules presented in the previous section in addition to the existing interpreter. The debugger needs the following two features to work properly.

Maximal time advance: The delay rule applies to the minimum timeout values among all active processes. Since systems are time-additive, checking the earliest timeout of $(v^T - t)$ for timer t suffices.

No unbounded delay: If the minimum timeout is `infinity` for all active processes, the system cannot perform any transition. According to [DELAY], when no finite timeout exists, the system may undergo an unlimited number of delays. However, the implementation prohibits this delay transition.

[1] https://github.com/yuna943/Time-extended-CauDEr.

$$[\underline{\text{REVERSE}}] \quad \Gamma; \langle p_r, \mathsf{rec}(\theta, e, S, p_s, \{v, \lambda\}, v_T) : h, \theta', e', S', 0\rangle \mid \Pi \\ \leftharpoondown \Gamma \cup (p_s, p_r, \{v, \lambda\}); \langle p_r, h, \theta, e, S, v_T\rangle \mid \Pi$$

$$[\underline{\text{TIMEOUT}}] \quad \Gamma; \langle p, \mathsf{tout}(\theta, e, S, v_T) : h, \theta', e', S', 0\rangle \mid \Pi \leftharpoondown \Gamma; \langle p, h, \theta, e, S, v_T\rangle \mid \Pi$$

$$[\underline{\text{DELAY}}] \quad \Gamma; |_{i \leq n} \langle p_i, \delta(d) : h_i, \theta_i, e_i, S_i, v_i\rangle \overset{\delta(d)}{\leftharpoondown} \Gamma; |_{i \leq n} \langle p_i, h_i, \theta_i, e_i, S_i, v_i - d\rangle$$

Fig. 3. Backward Timed Semantics of Erlang.

We introduce two additional icons to indicate the timing status of a process with waiting "🕔" and timeout "!". 🕔 means a process is active and lets time pass with no capability for other actions forward. In backward, a process needs to rewind time passage since it has $\delta(n)$ at the top of its history. ! means a process just reached the timeout point and is capable of doing some action in the forward direction. In the backward, all actions are rewound, and the process is ready to rewind time.

We briefly illustrate the extended CauDEr for the example shown in Fig. 1.

First, the program is loaded into CauDEr and starts running. Figure 4 shows that after several forward steps, process `main` has spawned all subprocesses, and they are all active and capable of some actions.

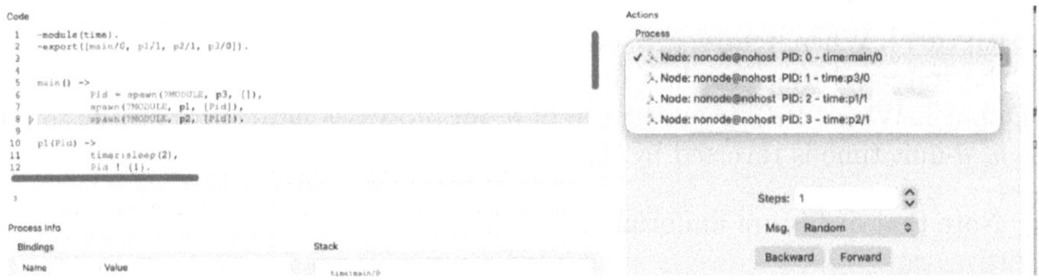

Fig. 4. CauDEr screenshot for the example in Fig. 1.

We proceed forward further until `p0`, `p1`, and `p2` are all waiting to receive messages, where `main` is inactive, as shown in Fig. 5(a). By advancing one process, time advances until at least one of the processes timeout following the maximal time advance. Then, `p2` first reaches timeout as shown in Fig. 5(b).

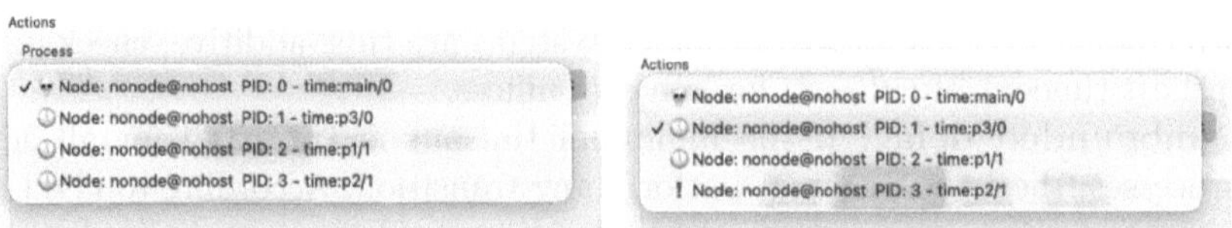

(a) (b)

Fig. 5. Process status of the example in Fig. 1.

Fig. 6 shows a backward step of receiving a message p3. From (a) p3 steps backwards to (b) by putting the message back in the mailbox. And p3 becomes incapable of doing any action and ready to rewind time passage.

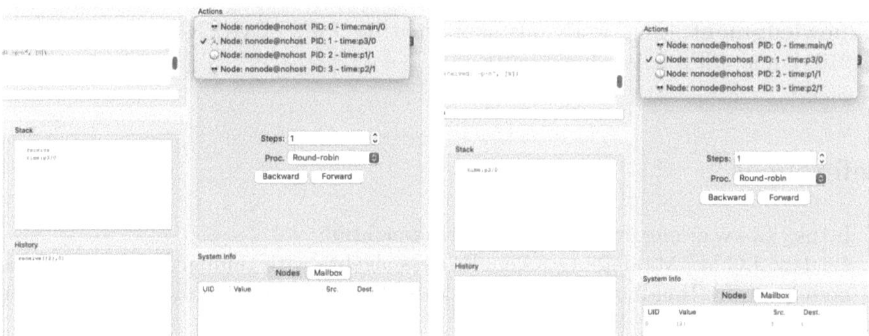

(a) (b)

Fig. 6. A backward step of receiving a message for the example in Fig. 1.

5 Concluding Remarks

This work presents a reversible semantics for Erlang, extended with discrete-time passage. The semantics specifies causality derived from time passage and reverses timeouts while preserving causal consistency. It is assumed that processes perform actions and communications sufficiently fast relative to a time tick. The behaviour aligns with assumptions in the reference implementation of OTP [1].

Timed behaviour has been formally studied in models such as communicating timed automata [7] and process calculi [2,6,14]. Key characteristics of time passage include synchronous occurrence across all running processes and the lowest priority among all actions [12,13]. Additionally, time determinacy and maximal progress are essential for accurate modelling of timed behaviour [13]. The revTPL framework [3] extends TPL [6] with reversible semantics, investigating semantic correspondence to the untimed reversible process calculus CCSK [11]. In revTPL, a time tick σ is assigned a unique key. The timed extension presented here uses a timer within a process, combined with uniform $\delta(d)$ values in the history information, to implement a similarly rigorous correspondence for time passage.

The aforementioned assumption may not hold for larger systems, particularly regarding immediate message reception. Future work includes introducing an uncertainty parameter that represents an interval during debugging to infer correct and incorrect behaviours in Erlang. Additionally, improving the CauDEr interface to support timed behaviour is planned. For simplicity, we excluded the imperative primitives in the syntax. In theory, those primitives happen instantaneously and can be introduced as other actions. However, a more complex mechanism would introduce more uncertainty in timed behaviour. This is also future work to debug timing uncertainty in practice.

Acknowledgment. This work was supported by JSPS KAKENHI Grant Number 23K21654, and JSPS fellowship S25016.

References

1. https://www.erlang.org/doc/system/readme.html
2. Baeten, J.C.M., Middelburg, C.A.: Process algebra with timing: real time and discrete time. In: Handbook of Process Algebra, pp. 627–684. North-Holland/Elsevier (2001)
3. Bocchi, L., Lanese, I., Mezzina, C.A., Yuen, S.: revTPL: the reversible temporal process language. Log. Methods Comput. Sci. **20**(1) (2024)
4. Cesarini, F., Thompson, S.: Erlang Programming - A Concurrent Approach to Software Development. O'Reilly (2009)
5. González-Abril, J.J., Vidal, G.: Causal-consistent reversible debugging: improving CauDEr. In: Morales, J.F., Orchard, D. (eds.) PADL 2021. LNCS, vol. 12548, pp. 145–160. Springer, Cham (2021). https://doi.org/10.1007/978-3-030-67438-0_9
6. Hennessy, M., Regan, T.: A process algebra for timed systems. Inf. Comput. **117**(2), 221–239 (1995). https://doi.org/10.1006/inco.1995.1041
7. Krcal, P., Yi, W.: Communicating timed automata: the more synchronous, the more difficult to verify. In: Ball, T., Jones, R.B. (eds.) CAV 2006. LNCS, vol. 4144, pp. 249–262. Springer, Heidelberg (2006). https://doi.org/10.1007/11817963_24
8. Lami, P., Lanese, I., Stefani, J., Coen, C.S., Fabbretti, G.: Reversible debugging of concurrent erlang programs: Supporting imperative primitives. J. Log. Algebraic Methods Program. **138**, 100944 (2024)
9. Lanese, I., Nishida, N., Palacios, A., Vidal, G.: CauDEr: a causal-consistent reversible debugger for erlang. In: Gallagher, J.P., Sulzmann, M. (eds.) FLOPS 2018. LNCS, vol. 10818, pp. 247–263. Springer, Cham (2018). https://doi.org/10.1007/978-3-319-90686-7_16
10. Torres Lopez, C., Marr, S., Gonzalez Boix, E., Mössenböck, H.: A study of concurrency bugs and advanced development support for actor-based programs. In: Ricci, A., Haller, P. (eds.) Programming with Actors. LNCS, vol. 10789, pp. 155–185. Springer, Cham (2018). https://doi.org/10.1007/978-3-030-00302-9_6
11. Phillips, I., Ulidowski, I.: Reversing algebraic process calculi. J. Log. Algebraic Methods Program. **73**(1–2), 70–96 (2007)
12. Reed, G.M., Roscoe, A.W.: A timed model for communicating sequential processes. Theor. Comput. Sci. **58**, 249–261 (1988)
13. Ulidowski, I., Yuen, S.: Process languages with discrete relative time based on the ordered SOS format and rooted eager bisimulation. J. Log. Algebraic Methods Program. **60–61**, 401–460 (2004)
14. Yi, W.: CCS + time = an interleaving model for real time systems. In: Albert, J.L., Monien, B., Artalejo, M.R. (eds.) ICALP 1991. LNCS, vol. 510, pp. 217–228. Springer, Heidelberg (1991). https://doi.org/10.1007/3-540-54233-7_136

Author Index

C. Aubert and L. Roversi (Eds.): RC 2026, LNCS 16626, p. 293, 2026.
https://doi.org/10.1007/978-3-032-30839-9

MIX
Papier aus verantwortungsvollen Quellen
Paper from responsible sources
FSC® C105338

If you have any concerns about our products,
you can contact us on
ProductSafety@springernature.com

In case Publisher is established outside the EU,
the EU authorized representative is:
Springer Nature Customer Service Center GmbH
Europaplatz 3, 69115 Heidelberg, Germany

Printed by Libri Plureos GmbH
in Hamburg, Germany